COLLEGE OF MARIN LIBRARY
KENTFIELD, CALIFORNIA

P9-EDK-578

Neighborhood
and Ghetto

ISSUES AND TRENDS
IN SOCIOLOGY

a series of

The American Sociological Association

INTERGROUP RELATIONS
Edited by Pierre van den Berghe

THE FORMAL ORGANIZATION
Edited by Richard H. Hall

NEIGHBORHOOD AND GHETTO
Edited by Scott Greer and Ann Lennarson Greer

SOCIOLOGICAL OBSERVATION
Edited by Matilda White Riley and Edward E. Nelson

Neighborhood and Ghetto

The Local Area in Large-Scale Society

EDITED BY

Scott Greer AND Ann Lennarson Greer

HT
123
.G724

Basic Books, Inc., Publishers

NEW YORK

© 1974 by Basic Books, Inc.
Library of Congress Catalog Card Number: 73–75307
SBN 465–04929–x
Manufactured in the United States of America
74 75 76 77   10 9 8 7 6 5 4 3 2 1

Contributors

Harry V. Ball is Professor of Sociology, University of Hawaii, Honolulu

Richard A. Ball is Professor of Sociology, University of West Virginia, Morgantown

Wendell Bell is Professor of Sociology, Yale University

Robert Bierstedt is Professor of Sociology, University of Virginia, Charlottesville

Leonard Broom is Professor of Sociology, Australian National University, Canberra

Theodore Caplow is Professor of Sociology, University of Virginia, Charlottesville

James Cowhig is Research Advisor to the Federal Government in Washington, D.C.

Walter Firey is Professor of Sociology, University of Texas, Austin

Maryanne T. Force is Associate in Urban Studies, The Bishop Museum, Honolulu, Hawaii

William H. Form is Professor of Sociology, University of Illinois, Urbana

Robert Forman is Professor of Sociology, University of Toledo, Ohio

H. W. Gilmore, deceased

Ann Lennarson Greer is Assistant Professor of Urban Affairs and Sociology, University of Wisconsin, Milwaukee

Scott Greer is Professor of Sociology and Urban Affairs, University of Wisconsin, Milwaukee

Paul Hatt, deceased

Guy B. Johnson, emeritus, University of North Carolina, Chapel Hill

Christen T. Jonassen is Professor of Sociology, The Ohio State University, Columbus

Harvey Molotch is Professor of Sociology, University of California, Santa Barbara

Peter A. Munch is Professor of Sociology, Southern Illinois University, Carbondale

Peter Orleans is a Lecturer in Sociology, University of Denver

H. Laurence Ross is Professor of Sociology in the College of Law, University of Denver

Julian Samora is Professor of Sociology, Notre Dame University, Indiana

Leo F. Schnore is Professor of Sociology, University of Wisconsin, Madison

Eshref Shevky, deceased

Joel Smith is Professor of Sociology, Duke University, Durham, North Carolina

Gregory P. Stone is Professor of Sociology, University of Minnesota, Minneapolis

Melvin Tumin is Professor of Sociology, Princeton University

James B. Watson is Professor of Sociology, University of Washington, Seattle

William Foote Whyte is Professor of Industrial Relations, Cornell University

Douglas S. Yamamura is Professor of Sociology, University of Hawaii, Honolulu

Preface

This volume is one of a series on Issues and Trends in Sociology sponsored by the American Sociological Association. Each is the product of a distinguished editor's work. His task has been to assemble from past numbers of the Association's periodical publications the accumulated thought on a selected topic, supplementing those contributions with materials from other sources as needed, and to examine and interpret the state of knowledge represented in the collected papers with reference to its implications for current intellectual and social trends. By this means the Association has sought to foster both the advance of scholarship and the understanding of an important issue of the day. We take pleasure in presenting this volume on behalf of the American Sociological Association.

THE EDITORIAL BOARD

Theodore R. Anderson
Arnold Feldman
E. William Noland
W. Richard Scott
Pierre van den Berghe
Amos H. Hawley, CHAIRMAN

Contents

PART III

The Neighborhood in the Larger Setting

Figures and Tables

Figures and Tables

Neighborhood
and Ghetto

Introduction

Editing this collection of articles from the *American Sociological Review* has been a pleasure and a challenge. It has been a pleasure to survey the materials on neighborhoods and ghettos that have appeared in the *Review*, and it has been a challenge to create a meaningful volume from them. Since in choosing twenty-two articles we had to reject several times as many, the reader may be interested in our criteria for selection.

We insisted on three things: a spatial component in the problem treated, relevance as social fact, and lasting value.

That a volume on neighborhoods should insist on a spatial dimension is obvious enough; what is not so obvious is the relative scarcity of work with such an emphasis. The sample survey loses the smaller spatial unit in totals for a metropolis or nation. Much of the work reported since the *Review* was first published in 1936 deals with social attitudes without respect to community context; thus, work on ethnic enclaves and ghettos is sparse, and articles on the black ghettos are rare. The range of sociological attention (or at least editorial interest) has, at least until recently, veered considerably from that of the early Chicago school.

To collect a volume of articles treating the neighborhood or ghetto as social fact, we looked for essays that showed concern for the social causes of neighborhoods and that showed social consequences flowing from the nature of those causes. We sought scholars who had translated geography into sociology by showing that proximity had affected sociation of the subjects. We saw the local area as a site for social action rather than as a result of the market in land and the activities of the building trades.

As for the lasting value of the articles selected, that is always open to question. At a minimum, we tried to avoid period pieces, dead issues,

3

material whose value was descriptive and highly time-bound, polemics whose sociological value lay in their use as objects to analyze rather than works of analysis. We tried to choose work of intellectually respectable structure, which might, in at least some cases, be readable and useful long after its empirical subject matter had disappeared.

Our first task in the preparation of this collection was to examine all potentially relevant articles in all thirty-six volumes (1936–1971) of the *American Sociological Review*. Although we planned no chronological presentation of our selections, we found in the course of our reading several interesting general trends that merit some mention here.

American sociology showed an early interest in neighborhood. The second issue of the *Review* carried an article by R. E. Park on "Succession: An Ecological Concept." Patterns of movement, specifically the movement of ethnic groups, underline a more general concern of Park and the field of sociology: the differentiation of urban neighborhoods. For those sociologists the focus was upon the diversity of ethnic neighborhoods and social class to be found in cities such as Chicago. For a later group, it was the new variations in life style emerging from the affluence that followed World War II. Their interest was the diversity of the city, the multiple social worlds constituting the whole.

Over the years there was a concern with the nature of the neighborhood as a social group. Recurring questions were: what was the internal order of that group, and how much difference did the internal order of that group make for other aspects of social life? Theories of mass society tend to assume the deterioration and even withering away of the neighborhood, yet many authors noted the presence of a considerable social order at the local level, even in the slum.

A related theme is that of interethnic relationships at the local level, and much good work was carried out in the general framework of "race relations." These were generally studies of ethnic discrimination whose approach usually included a vague commitment, stated or not, to the value of assimilation—or at least integration. Thus the ghetto was usually seen from the standpoint of the majority.

A note is in order on the changing technologies in the field and their effects upon research. Early investigators tended to rely upon nonquantitative methods, from careful observation and analysis of the thing itself to casual reportage. With the growing facility in the use of punch cards and calculators, mass data analysis became popular. Since it was usually based upon data from the Bureau of the Census, that bureau's collecting and summarizing units became sociological units. Thus the census tract became of increasing importance, allowing for a wider generality over space and time.

Equally important was the development and dissemination of sample survey techniques. These had been used earlier, but their exploitation by the U.S. Army in World War II not only produced a major research series but also acquainted a large number of sociologists, later to be very influential, with the nature and power of this new tool. Thus it became possible to sample a metropolitan population, to generalize to the whole, or to study the variety of census tracts and use them to sample kinds of neighborhoods that could again be generalized to the population as a whole.

Accompanying these technological gains was a steady critical dialogue over methods. The referents of indices, the nature of units, the statistical significance of findings are all matters of increasing interest as one follows the urban sociology reported in the *Review* over the past thirty-six years. This has resulted in an increasingly sophisticated research, sometimes clearly superior to earlier work and almost always more aware of the complexity of both theories of social behavior and methods for studying it.

Besides our three main criteria for selection—a spatial component, relevance as social fact, and lasting value—we hoped to find articles with adequate prose styles, clear tabular materials, and data relevant to the argument. Our hope was often fulfilled. The articles reprinted in this volume represent, of course, a variety of prose styles and methods of presenting data; similarly, they manifest a variety of copy editing styles used by the *Review* in the course of the years. With the exception of renumbering tables and figures to conform to the chapter numbers of this collection, no attempt has been made to impose an overall editorial consistency.

As we planned, we have followed no chronological pattern in arranging the articles we selected. It seemed useful to group separately those articles dealing with neighborhood as such, those focused upon ethnic differences, and those dealing with systems for classifying neighborhoods. It is in these terms that we will survey the remainder of the volume.

Neighborhoods: The Local Area as Social Fact

Part I deals with the social consequences of spatial contiguity. Through most of our history as sedentary animals living by agriculture, fishing, and forestry, most people have inhabited a very small world. Their village and, later, their neighborhood in the city, enclosed most of the world they would ever see. Work, play, kin, religion, death all occurred in the same small space, among the same people. Under such circumstances there developed a rich and complex set of relationships among people, as well as a generalized identification with the village or neighborhood.

It is often assumed that in modern, large-scale society this picture is radically changed. Mobility, or change of residence, and fluidity, or change in the site of activities during the day, have been assumed to be powerful corrosives, destroying attachment to place within the metropolis. Yet efforts to create metropolitan government perennially run into a strong emotional identification with local "autonomy," particularly among suburbanites. The neighborhoods of the city also retain some social and emotional values, from the lively streets of Greenwich Village to the "turf" of the street-corner gang. This first section deals with some of the reasons for these survivals, indicating under what conditions and in what degree the local area is also a social fact.

In their article "Neighborhood Interaction in a Homogeneous Community" (Chapter 1), Caplow and Forman may appear to "stack the deck" in favor of a strong neighborhood interaction system, but their discussion of what occurs when nigh-dwellers share a common fate gives real clues to what must be if a neighborhood is to be a social group. Further, their use of sociogramatic techniques allows us to see the structure of relationships, the nature of "star clusters," and perhaps most important, makes it clear that the extensity of social relationships does not necessarily depress the intensity of these relationships among neighbors. Under what conditions, and to what degree, neighboring occurs is clarified by this study.

Whyte's "Social Organization in the Slums" (Chapter 2), is concerned with dispelling certain myths. Life in a slum neighborhood is not necessarily life in a human jungle; the slum has its own forms of *social* organization. Most importantly, Whyte adduces first the continuing institutions of the ethnic group and, second, the possibilities of social order inherent in those social groups indigenous to slums—the gangs. He emphasizes the order that is possible in an area that approaches the polar opposite to Caplow's neighborhood of middle-class college students.

In "The Local Community: A Survey Approach" (Chapter 3), H. Laurence Ross deals in considerable detail with differentiation in the city as it appears to ordinary citizens. He shows how clearly demarcated are the various local areas in the "internal maps" his samples of urban residents carry. He also demonstrates the overwhelming importance of ethnicity and social rank as attributes of living areas, from the point of view of the ordinary man.

Caplow, then, states some of the conditions conducive to intense and rather uniformly distributed social bonds in a neighborhood. If his neighborhood seems very special, seems indeed a variety of the "total institution" comparable to the prison or the military base, it nevertheless approximates that *gemeinschaftlich* community for which many seem to yearn these days. Whyte's description of Cornerville, the Boston "slum" neighborhood where *Street Corner Society* takes place, indicates how ubiquitous such community is. One may note that this was an *ethnic* neighborhood, a concentration of Italian *paisani*; it may be that most of the intense community bonds found in the metropolis are based upon common origin, culture, and language.

In "Urbanism Reconsidered: A Comparative Study of Local Areas in a Metropolis" (Chapter 4), Scott Greer takes a skeptical view of the usual stereotypes of urban life. Looking at variations in life style not conditioned by either social rank or ethnicity, he describes the social networks in two Los Angeles census tracts in which the differences that remain are consequent to choice of life style. His two areas, by most statistical criteria, appear identical, but they turn out to be very different indeed. One is a semireplication of the small town of America's childhood; the other approaches the ideal type of "urbanism as a way of life." Neither fits its stereotype.

Wendell Bell and Maryanne T. Force carry this kind of inquiry further, varying both life style and social rank. "Urban Neighborhood Types and Participation in Formal Associations" (Chapter 5) is based on the study of four census tracts in the San Francisco Bay Region that lie at the polar extremes. They ask the question: "What is the effect of life style independent of social rank, and vice versa?" They investigate a wide range of associational ties, with an emphasis upon formal but voluntary groups. They also test the independent effects of individual characteristics and neighborhood characteristics; their findings suggest that each has an impact and that the neighborhood cannot be reduced to the sum of individual characteristics. It is a social context.

In "Uptown and Downtown: A Study of Middle-class Residential Areas" (Chapter 6), H. Laurence Ross controls all three variables to test the importance of distance from the center of the metropolis for social behavior. Comparing apartment-house dwellers of the same social rank, ethnicity, and family status in downtown Manhattan and a peripheral neighborhood in the Bronx, he concludes that distance from the center produces very little difference. However, *within* the downtown Manhattan sample there are striking differences associated with marital status. Singles enjoy a more varied leisure life in an urbane milieu.

Enclaves and Ghettos: The Concentrated and the Segregated

Part II deals more specifically with ethnicity as it affects human settlement. By *ethnicity* we mean those biologically or culturally inherited patterns that characterize a population and set it off from the social environment. Such differentiation may be horizontal or vertical; if horizontal, it simply indicates a variation, but if vertical, it denotes a difference in power.

Horizontal differentiation leads to voluntary concentration of a population. Common culture, common language, and the belief in a common (and distinctive) origin lead to folk institutions, economic organizations, and intramarriage. Political alliances are often a consequence.

Vertical differentiation includes not only differences in culture and descent but a common position in a rank order of groups. At an extreme, the ethnic population is forced by law to concentrate its residence in a given area; this is what is meant by *ghetto*. Regardless of desire, the population is segregated from the larger society. This political concentration of a people need not be governmental; in the United States today it works through a complex of governmental, political, and market forces.

In "The Sociology of Majorities" (Chapter 7), Robert Bierstedt emphasizes the critical role of the quantitatively dominant population as an integrative force. In most cases the control is backed by political power emanating from the sheer advantage of numbers. However, it is frequently even more powerful by virtue of culture, for the majority tends to define the situation—the roles of minority groups and their proper place in the hierarchy of honor vis-à-vis each other and the majority. We do find cases, however, where the majority is subordinate to the minority, and here Bierstedt's argument ceases to deal with *direct* control and emphasizes, instead, the degree to which the majority conditions what can be done by any minority. Thus French-speaking Canadians are a majority in Quebec, while Quebec is a minority within the nation; this has resulted in a "special status" for Quebec within Canada, despite the fact that her economy is controlled by English Canadians and U. S. citizens. Majorities, then, are almost always present and theoretically presumed in any study of ethnic enclaves. As Bierstedt notes, they have not had the attention from sociologists that they deserve, perhaps because they *are* so obvious.

Richard A. Ball in Chapter 8 discusses a population that is a majority in its region, the hill country of the South, but a minority in the United States as a whole. "A Poverty Case: The Analgesic Subculture of the Southern Appalachians" might almost be taken as a theory of ghetto culture, despite the fact that he is talking about rural Anglo-Saxon Protestants whose presence extends backward for centuries. Their isolation and poverty, however, have produced a syndrome of norms and beliefs that very nearly guarantee failure, even as it is a result of failure in the past. Their "nonpurposive behavior" does serve the purpose of holding the individual together, even as it handicaps him in solving his objective problems. This approach illuminates some of the complex of actions labeled "the culture of poverty."

It has become fashionable lately to speak of the "culture of poverty." Perhaps Ball's descriptive analysis can clarify some exceedingly muddy water. Without adducing ethnicity or the plight of the slum dweller in large-scale urban society, he presents a plausible picture of a culture developed to protect one from the shock of failure, but having the consequence that its members "can't win for losing."

James B. Watson and Julian Samora in Chapter 9 analyze another aspect of the cultural-structural system by which a population may remain poor and powerless to control its fate. "Subordinate Leadership in a Bicultural Community: An Analysis" deals with a ghettoized majority, the Spanish-speaking in a small southwestern town. The complex system that maintains and reinforces castelike relations between them and the dominant "Anglos" is viewed as both a cultural pattern and an organizational structure. The great discrepancy in resources and rewards between the two populations is perpetuated by differential treatment of the Spanish by the major holders of social powers. The treatment is then justified by Anglo stereotypes of the Spanish as lazy, ignorant, and untrustworthy. Noting the quiet submission of the Spanish to the situation, Watson and Samora attempt to explain it by suggesting that lack of leaders is a key reason, although they conclude that the handful of persons with the prerequisites for leadership do not want to lead. The Spanish, they point out, are unwilling to be led by anyone who has succeeded, for he has obviously "sold out" to the Anglos. The Anglos, in turn, reinforce this state of affairs by discriminating between those Spanish who succeed ("the real Spanish") and the great majority who do not. These are agricultural proletarians and are "Mexicans"—a pejorative term.

In "Social Adjustment among Wisconsin Norwegians" (Chapter 10), Peter A. Munch compared the distinctive situations of two nearby settlements of Norwegian-Americans. In one the Norwegians are the overwhelming majority, practicing large-scale agriculture, while in the other they are a minority. In both communities they have been acculturated to American norms and values, but in the first their Norwegian social identity is preserved through isolation, while in the second it shifts to an identity created *contra* their ethnic stereotype. The first community may be seen as a case of "separatism" in which isolation allows for solidarity and acculturation to such American norms as egalitarianism; the second is a case of "integration" in which solidarity is created by relations with the majority. These self-consciously Norwegian people have defined themselves as the "elect," thereby reversing the value hierarchy of the surrounding population, with a consequent emphasis upon Norwegian culture, religion, and lineage. Both groups are, of course, very different from contemporary Norwegians in the homeland; they demonstrate variant responses to the situation of being a minority and the process of "ethnicization."

"Personality in a White-Indian-Negro Community" (Chapter 11) is Guy B. Johnson's fascinating study of a triethnic community that ghettoizes the races. The ghetto is rural, but it ghettoizes nevertheless. The Croatan Indians play a tight defensive game, trying to avoid classification as Negro but failing to achieve reception as white. Further, they are determined to maintain this triracial system to avoid "downgrading," thus a Croatan is not allowed to mingle with Negroes, as the whites are prohibited from mingling with the Croatans. Again, the entire system is a function of the nature of the majority and its norms.

In Melvin Tumin's study of caste in Guatemala, "Reciprocity and Stability of Caste in Guatemala" (Chapter 12), we have another case of vertical differentiation. Again, as in the Watson and Samora study of the Spanish in the Southwest, we see that it is the minority that dominates the majority. In Guatemala, the Ladinos dominate the Indians. Their techniques in doing so are analyzed at length; perhaps the godparental complex is the most ingenious, for the reciprocity it builds into the system. Yet even so, as Tumin underlines, it is made possible only by the ignorance and traditionalism of the Indians. In a society very different from that of the United States, the Indians simply do not *mind* the caste structure. Tumin demonstrates the great variety of adjustments possible in relations between dominant and dominated in human society.

The Norwegian community in metropolitan New York has had a history quite different from the stereotyped "ethnic minority." Christen T. Jonassen, in "Cultural Variables in the Ecology of an Ethnic Group" (Chapter 13), describes in detail the history of an immigrant population that did not use the common "port of entry," the slums; that did not suffer poverty, segregation, and degradation. On the contrary, because of the "fit" between their cultural values and the opportunities they found in New York, they became prosperous, home-owning citizens with very little difficulty. Their ecological movements, over a hundred years, were due to those same cultural values, for they disliked density, noise, and the bustle of the center; in short, they disliked cities. Here is an instance of a concentration of an ethnic group that is not vertical at all; it is purely horizontal —concentration, not segregation.

Paul Hatt, in "The Relation of Ecological Location to Status Position and Housing of Ethnic Minorities" (Chapter 14), provides another clue to the spatial organization of ethnic minorities. His study indicates that "status relations between minority and majority ethnic categories are such that invasion can take place in a majority area only when the minority population has achieved a definitely higher economic status than is characteristic of the resident majority type." This suggests that the major advantage of the Norwegians in New York was economic viability. The groups Hatt reports on were generally of quite low social rank. (In light of their rapid upward mobility since the study was done with 1940 data, it is interesting to note the low status of Japanese and Jews.)

In his analysis of black interaction with whites on the Chicago South Shore, "Racial Integration in a Transitional Community" (Chapter 15), Harvey Molotch is interested in the degree of integration resulting from contiguity. Using a "head count" technique, i.e., observation of people in public places, he finds interaction common only in public places where private relationships are unnecessary. The pattern is very similar to the one Tumin describes for the Indians and Ladinos, with no such reciprocity as the godparental relationship at hand. However, he does identify a few face-to-face groups manifesting transracial solidarity, and in his analysis of their attributes sets forth conditions he feels are necessary for genuine integration, rather than propinquity, of ethnic populations. In such transitional areas as this, one might say that neighborhood and ghetto are interspersed; the vertical discrepancy of the ethnic populations prevents the creation of multiethnic neighborhoods.

In terms of the subject of this collection, Honolulu is one of the richest research sites in the world, teeming as it is with a wide variety of ethnic populations. Harry V. Ball and Douglas S. Yamamura, in their chapter on "Ethnic Discrimination and the Marketplace: A Study of Landlords' Preferences in a Polyethnic Community" (Chapter 16), unearth and explain, through careful analyses of data on housing and landlords' preferences, a seeming paradox. In brief, although a majority of landlords express a preference for tenants of their own ethnicity, and a large minority exclude other ethnics, from the viewpoint of residents there is no effective discrimination. This they explain through the nature of the market. "The presence of a variety of ethnic groups in fairly large numbers seems to provide considerable fluidity for landlords with separatist orientation." At the same time, they argue that this fortunate situation (for tenants) is reinforced by a widespread adherence to nondiscrimination and assimilation among a large minority of landlords. The housing market described is, effectively, an "equal opportunity" market.

The term *ghetto* originated in Eastern Europe, where it referred to those urban areas, usually walled, in which Jewish residence and enterprise were largely impounded. Leonard Broom and Eshref Shevky, in their study of "The Differentiation of an Ethnic Group" (Chapter 17), indicate how far the Jews of Los Angeles are from such conditions. Over half of them live in neighborhoods where they comprise less than 5 percent of the population; only 37 percent live in areas of a higher concentration. Using the Shevky-Bell typology of neighborhoods, Broom and Shevky are able to specify the very real differentiations within the more "Jewish" neighborhoods by both status and urbanization of life style. Their analysis continues with an investigation of ex-Jewish "name changers," underlining the importance of the typology in predicting differences in behavior. Name-changers are preponderantly from census tracts at the high levels of status and urbanization. The assimilationist argument is strengthened by locating the home residences of members in high- and low-ranking Jewish fraternities at U.C.L.A. in social-attribute space. The lesson is again clear. As Russian Jews rise in social rank and urbanity, they become assimilated to the point of changing the name, the label of ethnic identity, leaving the vestiges of the pseudo-ghetto presumably for good.

The Neighborhood in the Larger Setting

Part III of this volume deals with the city or metropolis as the unit, the neighborhood as a sub-unit. Within the overall structure of the city, given spatial areas are differentiated by the structures and activities located within them. We are here primarily interested in residential structures and the kinds of people and quality of life they bear. We are also concerned with the processes by which they develop a given quality, maintain it, or replace it with others.

New Orleans is a city in which "sentiment and symbolism" have had a basic effect upon land use and the creation of neighborhoods. H. W. Gilmore, in "The Old New Orleans and the New: A Case for Ecology" (Chapter 18), details the intricate interactions of political control, ethnicity, and topography in creating and maintaining the city. Particularly interesting are the mechanisms involved in holding the French Quarter and the Garden District, two famous neighborhoods, viable and intact. Because of scarcity of land, houses in these areas were cherished and maintained—there was no suburban competition. Thus they became antiques and were, in Gilmore's word, "museumized," with statutory protection of the French Quarter and the same kind of piety that prevails on Beacon Hill upholding the Garden District. Meanwhile, the ancient hostility of the "Creole" population, dating back to the period when it was a conquered majority, affects land use and land values. As in the next study, the sociologist is cautioned to resist a simple economic determinism; much vacant land became a "quicksand for real estate speculators who knew land, but did not know New Orleans."

In his parallel study of Boston, "Sentiment and Symbolism as Ecological Variables" (Chapter 19), Walter Firey first presents in synoptic form the "classic" ecological explanation for land use, one that is essentially economic determinism. He then demonstrates that in Boston there are at least three different kinds of symbolic values that prevent the predicted land use, in the interest of various forms of piety. The wealthy cling to Beacon Hill as the site of the ancestral hearths (frequently including their own) of famous Bostonians. Some undetermined but large number of Bostonians believe in the maintenance of large colonial burying grounds and the Boston Common in the center of the city as symbols of a collective past and therefore identity. And the working class Italians of the North End regard their neighborhood as a symbol of their ethnic identity as well as the location of their kin, *paisani*, and folk organizations. (These Italians are, interestingly, the people described by Whyte in Chapter 2.) In short, Firey concludes that we cannot explain the use of land in our cities by "profane" reasons alone; there remains the "sacred."

In the last century, and particularly since the 1920s, the basic map of American cities has been changing rapidly; the dense inner-city residential areas once seen as characteristic are now overshadowed by the more spacious neighborhoods of suburbia. The nature of this change and the nature of suburbs are investigated by Leo F. Schnore in "The Growth of Metropolitan Suburbs" (Chapter 20). In his words, "increasing territorial differentiation has been made possible by the increasing flexibility of movement within the total community." This has in turn allowed cheaper housing with larger lots, and the development of a new variant on "urbanism as a way of life," as Greer puts it in Chapter 4.

Our penultimate chapter deals with methodological and theoretical problems in the study of urban sub-areas, neighborhood or ghetto. William H. Form, Joel Smith, Gregory P. Stone, and James Cowhig, in their article on "The Compatibility of Alternative Approaches to the Delimitation of Urban Sub-Areas" (Chapter 21), apply sophisticated reasoning and techniques to the problem of establishing meaningful census tracts for the city of Lansing, Michigan. Using conventional ecological boundaries (topography, major streets, and nonresidential land use) they develop one set of sub-units. This, however, does not coincide in any regular and meaningful way with boundaries based upon demographic units, and neither set is related to social intimacy and commitment to the local area. In short, it was found impossible to develop a census tract grid that combined the three dimensions of local community postulated by the three approaches. There was, however, some evidence of a strong relationship between those demographic characteristics that Scott Greer and Peter Orleans in Chapter 22 refer to as "familism" and a high degree of local intimacy and identification. This study not only raises serious questions about the delimitation of urban sub-units; it suggests caution in the interpretation of research based upon such units as census tracts.

The word *suburbs* today refers to much more than governmental boundaries, as Schnore's interest in their socioeconomic status indicates. They have been seen as sites for a particular kind of life style. Greer and Orleans, in "The Mass Society and the Parapolitical Structure" (Chapter 22), approach the St. Louis, Missouri metropolitan area with a major concern for "style of life." They examine one dimension, "urbanism-familism," without respect to where it is on the geopolitical map of the city. They find it highly related to the participation of the population in voluntary associations (the "parapolitical") and this is, in turn, related to overt political action and competence. Separating central city and suburbia, however, they find that even with the same life style, there is a substantial difference in political behavior, which they speculate may be due to the structure and scale of suburban municipal government. In any event, they do not find strong evidence for the "massified" society, atomistic and unorganized.

Some Continuing Policy Issues

Sociology as an enterprise now lies somewhere between lore and primitive science. Much of the work we do is good and useful, standing on its own feet as knowledge that increases our intellectual control, at least, of our society. However, the field tends to be defined, not by its theoretical structures, but by the widely publicized issues of the day. With this in mind, let us look at some current controversies with respect to the three foci of this collection: the neighborhood as social fact, the enclave and ghetto, and the neighborhood in the larger setting.

The neighborhood, or local area, is frequently described as though it were a continuation of small town America. In Robert Wood's classic phrase, it is considered a "Republic in miniature." In the small suburb or big city ward, so the argument goes, lies true community. Such smaller units allow government to be closer to the people, and should therefore be allowed governmental power. Decentralization of control, such as that proposed and in some degree tried in the New York City school system, is one manifestation of this policy. The continued proliferation of suburban municipalities and independent school systems is another. The thrust of the argument is that those who share a common fate should have both the power to choose and the responsibility for the results, and that this applies particularly to residential areas which are also administrative districts.

It is also argued that the smaller area is critical for many social amenities. It can generate strong neighborly relationships, mutual aid through voluntary organizations, and a lively political process accessible to women and children as well as professional politicians and (occasionally) interested male citizens. It can be, in short, the basis for a *community* as against a segment of *society*.

Finally, it is argued that the neighborhood has intrinsic value because it is a concentration of people with similar backgrounds—ethnicity, life style, and social rank. A revitalized system of local areas controlling many of their own public policies should allow for the strengthening of that cultural diversity which has given this nation its unique strength in variation and innovation. *E Pluribus Unum*, then, with the accent on *pluribus*, is the motto of the neighborhood pluralist.

The arguments against neighborhood autonomy are equally strong. This is a complex, specialized society—one in which the average person is a specialist and, as such, must rely on other specialists for his confidence in almost any course of action. The average set of parents in a school district are not competent to judge educational policy and will, sooner or later, be coopted by the superintendent, the Parent-Teachers Association, the teachers' union, or the demagogues railing against higher taxes or racial discrimination. Thus the teaching of skills becomes inextricably involved with a wide variety of deep-rooted historically inherited problems, many of them totally irrelevant to the issues.

Furthermore, it is argued, many local areas in the metropolis are in no sense communities of concerned citizens who know and like one another. To devolve public decision making to such non-communities would be a hollow gesture, but one which would make the local public budget prey to incompetent administrators, controlled if at all by a part time, amateur government. And indeed, Greer and Orleans in Chapter 22 indicate a wide variety in associational patterns, from a fairly luxuriant network in middle-class suburbs to anonymity in the high-rise urban areas. But even in the most "community oriented" suburbs one out of five citizens is a complete isolate from his local community.

Finally, opponents of local self-government within the metropolis emphasize the divisive results of such an arrangement. Since local areas do coincide with basic social differences, local autonomy would have the effect of exacerbating frictions between different ethnic groups, social classes, and lifestyles. Inside the community the pressure would be for conformity, while between communities the competition for scarce public resources would result in a recreation of the highly segregated, race conscious society of seventy years ago.

As for the ghetto, as we learn more about its many uses, from newly articulate spokesmen in various positions, its value becomes ambiguous. Not long ago, very few would have argued for maintaining it, at least outside the South. In principle most of those interested supported integration. Whether they believed in assimilationism to white Protestant values, or saw the melting pot as creating a new alloy, they saw little value and much danger in the situation in which race, class, and geographical boundaries were coterminous. Recently, however, black militants have spoken out vociferously for "separatism," which can only mean self-segregation, while some scholars, despairing of creating equal opportunity through integration, have advocated "enriching the ghetto." Similarities of life style, speech patterns, and in some degree, common fate, are adduced for this policy; there is also a degree of rationalization involved, for it is dubious if the black ghetto—or any other—maintains a distinct sub-culture adequate for existing in large-scale society. Instead we have variants of a national, polyglot and hybrid culture appropriate, in many respects, to the world we live in. Many yearn to rewrite history, but at the rate of change we now experience it hardly seems worthwhile to divert our energies to such a task. No ethnic group in the United States has the cultural and material resources to exist independently of the larger society. At most, some might create parallel societies, not in any significant fashion much different from the one we now inhabit.

As for the neighborhood in the larger setting, there have been some arguments for the expanding galaxy of suburban developments around the old central city. Some argue that the autonomy of the suburbs politically, their variety in social attributes, allows the consumer to choose what amenities he wants at what cost. Whether a society in which children

rarely remain where they were educated can afford a system which would allow a suburb to choose a fifth-rate educational system for its children is a profound issue. If the children are the future, all share in a proper concern that they become viable people, productive citizens.

The overall social costs of rampant local autonomy are difficult to sum up. The benefits are equally hard to assay. Perhaps the reader will gain, at least, a better evidential ground for making such judgments from the empirical data and the theories set forth in this volume.

This collection does not represent the entire literature dealing with neighborhood and ghetto in sociology. Yet these articles, taken from the official journal of the American Sociological Association are, in their way, indicative of the treatment of these matters in "mainline" sociology. It is clear that they represent rich, cumulative, somewhat confused, and very promising approaches to the study of human communities. Needless to say, we do not agree with all of their conclusions; to do so would reduce us to nervous wrecks. We *are* grateful to those whose struggles with recalcitrant data and tenuous theory have brought us this far. For those who have little sympathy with some of the research (and these there always will and should be, to the health of the discipline), we can only say: Go you and do likewise—after *your* fashion.

PART I

Neighborhoods: The Local Area as Social Fact

1

THEODORE CAPLOW AND ROBERT FORMAN

NEIGHBORHOOD INTERACTION IN A HOMOGENEOUS COMMUNITY

The studies reported here arose out of a previous attempt by one of the writers to demonstrate the absence of secure empirical evidence for two propositions which are rather generally accepted in the discussion of urbanism: (1) that residential mobility is a progressive function of community growth; and (2) that residential mobility is in some sense a cause of family disorganization.[1]

In the consideration of these problems, it soon became evident that answers must be sought on the level of the face-to-face neighborhood, which may be considered either as the smallest of locality groups,[2] or as the largest of the primary groups.[3]

The few available studies on urban neighborhoods and neighboring focussed attention either upon the neighborhood as a locality group[4] or upon neighboring as an interpersonal process.[5] It appears to us, however, that the importance of the neighborhood as a unit of investigation lies precisely in its double aspect; and that the ecological and interpersonal elements of neighboring need to be considered simultaneously.

To do this, it was necessary to study the correlates of neighborliness, together with the patterns of inter-family relationship in the residential area. The pilot study, undertaken in the Winter of 1948, was based upon a non-selected sample of 134 neighborhoods in the Minneapolis–St. Paul metropolitan district. Its major instrument was a Neighborhood Interaction Scale designed to measure the amount of informal interaction between the responding family and each of its neighbor families.

The findings of the pilot study tended to support our expectations that little direct association would be found between mobility and isolation on the neighborhood level. At the same time, it raised questions which

Reprinted with permission from *American Sociological Review* 15 (1950): 357–366.

appeared to us to be of considerably greater significance than the initial hypotheses, and which seem to involve the basic mechanisms of group formation.

In this original study, it was not found practicable to verify the respondent family's report on its neighboring relationships by interviewing each of the other families with whom it reported association. A supplementary difficulty arose from the impossibility of evaluating the sampling, since we know virtually nothing about the universe of neighborhoods within a given metropolitan community. Moreover, our working definition of a neighborhood as "a family dwelling unit and the ten family dwelling units most accessible to it" was far too crude for general application. It appeared to us that these inadequacies could be overcome only by research directed to the clarification of the neighboring process itself. What was needed, therefore, was a relatively homogeneous and clearly defined residential area in which the entire population could be interviewed.

Such an area was found in University Village, a student housing project owned and operated by the University of Minnesota. A block of 50 family dwelling units, occupied by married veterans with children, was selected, and each of the 50 families interviewed in a four-week period in the Spring of 1949. The basic instrument used was the Neighborhood Interaction Scale. Each respondent family was asked to describe its relationship to every one of the other families in the block, as well as to families in other blocks of University Village. While the intervals between the scale-points are unknown, the rank order is believed to be correct. The scale is shown as Table 1–1.

In addition to the scale, the interview included information on the number and age of children; the age, academic status, and outside employment of the husband; the activities of the wife; the family's length of residence in the Village and in its present dwelling unit; a level of living scale based on the possession of furniture and appliances; a count of relatives' households in the metropolitan district; the Chapin Formal Social Participation Scale; and a number of open-ended questions on adjustment.

This material provides some insight into a considerable variety of related problems:

1. The first category is what may be roughly described as *micro-ecology*. Within this block of 50 dwelling units, we have a reasonably reliable measure of the relationship between each pair of families, as described independently by each of them. The data may be combined with the length of residence of each family, the exact position of each dwelling unit (see Figure 1-1) and the

TABLE 1-1

Neighborhood Interaction Scale

SCALE VALUE	DESCRIPTION
0	Do not know their names or faces.
1	Recognize them on the street, but have only a greeting acquaintance.
2	Stop and talk with them outside regularly. (Only one adult from each family involved)
3	Stop and talk with them outside regularly. (All adults involved)
4	Mutual aid and/or common activities. (Involving one adult from each family)
5	Mutual aid and/or common activities. (Involving all adults)
6	Mutual visiting and entertaining in each other's houses, including drinking or dining.[6]

functional significance of "lanes" and "rows" to give us a rather minute description of basic distributional factors.

2. *Community structure.* It became apparent as the interviewing proceeded that the block itself must be regarded as a community since it was so identified by its residents and possessed a definite internal structure. It was thus possible to study stratification, clique formation, formal leadership, group integration, and the influence of mobility in some detail.

3. The data could be made to yield a number of attributes for each family, which seemed to be related to such diffuse traits as popularity, leadership, seclusiveness, and selectivity. A typical index of this kind was one which reported the ratio of the family's close relationships with "outsiders" to the total of its close relationships with families in the block. A somewhat more complex measure, tentatively described as social expansiveness, was derived by comparing the ratings given and the ratings received for each family.

Much to our surprise, the comparison of these family attributes with such background factors as age, length of residence, level of living, outside employment, and formal participation, gave results which were quite inconclusive. A study designed to get at "individual differences" in social expansiveness is now under way, but the summary which follows is concerned only with "micro-ecology" and community structure.

Before turning to the detailed findings, it is necessary to note a number of parallel developments which enabled us to envisage the possibilities of neighborhood research more clearly.

In October, 1949, several months after the completion of the University

Village study, there was made available to us, through the kindness of Dr. Stanley Schachter, the unpublished manuscript of the Westgate study undertaken at Massachusetts Institute of Technology in 1946.[7] Although we had no conscious knowledge of the earlier Westgate study, the fields are remarkably similar, and the methods parallel. Westgate—a student housing project of M.I.T.—contains an equally homogeneous population (except that some families are childless) and was designed and occupied under nearly identical conditions. Data similar to ours were derived from all families by use of the sociometric question, "What three people in Westgate or Westgate West do you see most of socially?"

The curious parallelism of the two studies is further illustrated by the independent invention of a number of concepts. Among these are the distinction between physical distance (linear measurement) and functional distance (accessibility); the concept of social expansiveness; the development of the same definition of a clique; the concept of passive or unavoidable contact; and the concept of chain-distance. In collaboration with Messrs. Albert Perry and Duncan Luce, the M.I.T. investigators developed a method for the application of matrix multiplications to the analysis of sociometric patterns which provides the number of two-step, three-step, or n-step connections between items in a given sociometric pattern. This information, which is crucial in the analysis of intra-group communication, was secured in crude form by graphic inspection of the University Village data.

A second study whose results are of crucial importance for neighborhood research was that of rumor undertaken by Stuart Dodd and his associates at the Duwamish Housing Project in Seattle.[8] This study converges with both the Westgate and the University Village study at two points: (a) the emphasis upon micro-ecology, particularly upon the effects of accessibility, and (b) the function of channels of communication in the spread of rumor.

Another set of possibilities was suggested by the work of students in a seminar on urban sociology conducted by Caplow in the Spring of 1949. The seminar, searching for some quantitative expression for the sociopsy-chological differences between urban and rural environments and among communities having different degrees of "urbanism," developed a mathematical formulation of Cohesion, which enables any social environment to be compared with any other with respect to an operationally defined characteristic which is tentatively identified as social cohesion.[9] This conceptualization was at first entirely theoretical; but it later appeared that both the Westgate study and the University Village sudy provide a framework within which this measure may be empirically applied.

Findings

Micro-Ecology. In the pilot study of 134 non-selected neighborhoods, the mean rating of relationships with each respondent family's ten closest neighbors was 1.47, barely above a casual greeting relationship, although the mean length of occupancy of respondents' dwelling units was 12.2 years. There were moderate but significant correlations between the mean rating and various indices of the "quality" of the residential district derived from the age of buildings, density of population, and median rent. Districts of single-family houses showed marked advantages in neighboring over apartment house and mixed districts.

The negative findings were more striking. Above a minimum length of residence of one year, there was no discernible relationship between length of residence and the closeness or intensity of neighboring relationships. A variety of social factors such as age of children, possession of a car, ownership or rental tenure and size of family, showed no correlation with neighboring, except that similarity to a neighbor in any of these respects contributed somewhat to a closer relationship.

The block selected in University Village differs most sharply from these diversified neighborhoods in three respects: the uniformity of dwelling units; the relatively short length of residence, with consequent high mobility; and the social homogeneity of the population.

Figure 1–1 illustrates the arrangement of units in a block of 5 double rows. As will appear below, the experientially meaningful aspect of this

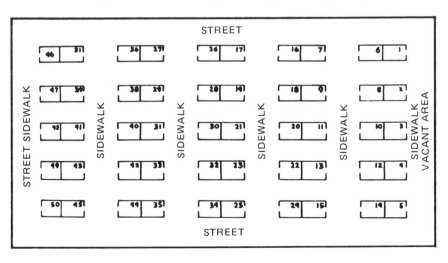

Figure 1–1   University Village-Plan of the Sample Block

arrangement is the division of the block into 4 interior lanes of 10 units each, and 2 exterior lanes of 5 units.

The mean length of residence for the 50 Village respondents was 14.86 months. The maximum length of residence was 23 months; the minimum 1 month.[10] The mean scale rating of the association between each family and the 9 nearest families was 2.89—conspicuously higher than that found in the diversified neighborhoods where the average length of residence was about ten times as great.

While the test-tube is not unflawed, a surprising number of social variables were controlled by the selection of University Village tenants. With one exception (a widower and two children) each family in our sample consists of a husband, wife, and at least one minor child. There are no servants or relatives in the households. All of the husbands are students, all family heads are between the ages of 21 and 39; all of the husbands are veterans and all of the wives, including 8% who work outside the home, are housewives. By far, the larger number of both husbands and wives are native-born residents of Minnesota, and all residents are white. It was not possible, for administrative reasons, to secure exact data on income, but at least half of the families report no source of income besides the $120 government allowance.

In discussing the implications of this homogeneity, at least one qualification should be inserted. Both University Village and Westgate are characterized by high morale and a high measure of reported satisfaction with both the physical facilities and the social opportunities. It is curious that in both projects, the phrase "we're all in the same boat" appeared again and again in connection with expressions of satisfaction. Undoubtedly, the homogeneity of the community accounts in part for the high morale, but other conditions—the more or less imminent goal of graduation, and the expectation of future mobility—should not be overlooked. It is conceivable, at any rate, that homogeneity in a prison colony might be less conducive to favorable adjustment than it appears to be here.

The total amount of social interaction within the block is enormous. This may be derived in two ways. We may consider the score for each family to be the sum of all the ratings it gives to relationships between itself and others (Out-Score); or we may use instead the sum of all the ratings given to it by others (In-Score). The means are almost identical, being respectively 46.74 and 45.78, but the In-Scores—being in effect the combined ratings of a group of "judges"—have a somewhat smaller standard deviation. If we consider relationships with a scale value of 1 to be minimal, and those with a scale value of 4 to be reasonably close, it is obvious that the Village resident engages in an amount of neighboring roughly equivalent to a minimal relationship with each of the other families in the block, or to a close relationship with more than ten of his neighbors. In fact, the mean number of other families known was 17.

8. The total amount of interaction (score) in either form represents a combination of 2 dimensions of association—the number of families known, and the average closeness of the association (mean rating). It might be plausibly suggested that these two components of the total score would be interrelated; more specifically, it was expected that as the number of families known increased, the average intimacy of all reported relationships would decrease. This did not prove to be the case. The intercorrelations are as follows:

Mean Rating with No. of Ratings	+.15	±.14
Number of Ratings with Total Score	+.80	±.05
Total Score with Mean Rating	+.53	±.11

An extension of the social circle in this milieu apparently involves a *net* increase in social interaction. Conversely, there does not appear to be any "fund" or "lump" of sociability, to be exhausted by intimate and exclusive relationships.

If this interpretation is correct, we might expect that the effect of long residence would be to expand the circle of acquaintance rather than to increase the intensity of association. This, indeed, appears to be the case. The product-moment correlation between number of months in the dwelling unit and Neighborhood Interaction Score is $+ .52 \pm 10$. But the correlation of length of time in the unit with mean rating is only $+ .08 \pm 14$. In other words, the increase in neighboring score with length of residence is entirely attributable to an increase in the *number* of acquaintances made. This is consistent with our finding in the pilot study that intensity of relationship did not increase with length of residence; and it supports the hypothesis that more symbiosis is unlikely to lead to intimacy in the residential neighborhood. Although new families in the Village associate with relatively few of their neighbors, these relationships apparently become quite intimate within a matter of weeks.

If time be considered, in some sense, as an "elementary" ecological factor, then distance is another, and distance involves both simple distance and routine accessibility. It will be seen from Figure 1–1 that the 10 units in each of the 4 interior lanes, and the 5 units in each of the end lanes, open on to a common sidewalk. The use of this footway for ordinary traffic, and the obstruction of passage between lanes by mud, snow, laundry lines, and sundry other obstacles, give each of the lanes considerable identity as social units. The degree of in-lane association is so high that it may almost be taken for granted that any two families in the same lane are acquainted. A comparison of the mean rating of relationships within the lane and the mean rating of the relationships in the nearest contiguous lane for each of the 50 families produces the following table (after combination):

FREQUENCY OF MEAN LANE RATINGS

	0 — 1.9	2.0 — 2.9	3.0 plus
Own Lane	6	14	30
Contiguous	35	10	5

The chi-square obtained was 45.53. For 2 degrees of freedom, a chi-square of 11.34 is significant at the 1% level. The derived contingency coefficient was .57. Because there were no mean lane ratings greater than 2.0 for more distant lanes, the analysis in this direction could not be carried further. This fact itself, however, demonstrates the overwhelming influence of propinquity.

Within the lane, a further distinction may be made between units immediately adjacent or opposite and those farther away. A comparison of ratings given to families in nearest and farthest units of the same lane by the method used above gives us a contingency coefficient of .48.[11]

Community Structure. The sociometric diagrams, Figures 1–2 and 1–3, are based upon close and "verified" relationships; that is, a line is drawn between families who mutually rated their relationship as 4 or higher.[12] Figure 1–2 shows all such close relationships within the block (the distance and arrangement of the units have been distorted for ease of presentation, but the relative position of the units is unchanged).

It is at once apparent that the block is an integrated community. Only 2 of the 50 families are isolates: all of the others are involved in a network of fairly intimate relationships which extends from one end of the block to each other. The maximum chain-distance between any two families involves eight steps, but there are ready channels of communication between each lane and every other.

The presentation of the diagram immediately raises several vital questions. To what extent is the integration of the block attributable to the participation of a group of leaders? Does the integration of so large a group inhibit or promote the formation of cliques? What evidences can be found for formal stratification? These questions will be taken up in order.

There are five families which have 7 or more close relationships with other families in the block. A sixth family, having only 6 such relationships has 3 of them with these "stars." Together, the six families (Numbers

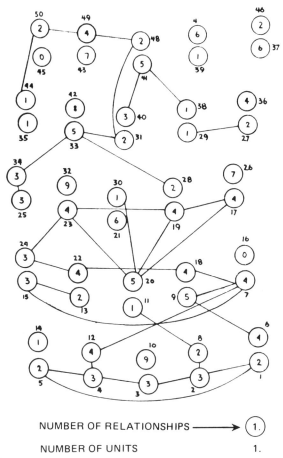

Figure 1–2   Sociometric Relationships in University Village,
All Close Relationships within the Block

10, 26, 32, 42, 43, 47) may be considered to occupy "star" positions on the sociometric diagram. It will be seen from Figure 1–2 that these six families have close associations with twenty families besides themselves, and that these associations form a network covering the entire block.

That the selection of these "stars" is not entirely fortuitous is illustrated by a variety of characteristics which these six families have in common. All of the six have some measure of formal participation, although thirty-one of the families in the block have no formal social participation at all. The husbands in five of the six families have part-time jobs taking 16 or more hours a week. All six families have at least close associations with at least one Village family outside the block. Five of the six "stars" have lived in the block for more than a year, and four have lived there since the block was opened. The "stars" reported more use of the Village Community

29

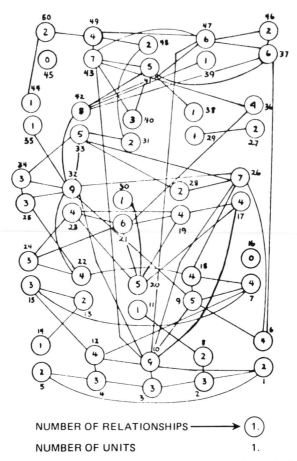

Figure 1–3 Sociometric Relationships in University Village, Relationships between Families Having Only Five or Less Close Relationships

center, and of automobiles, than most of their neighbors. Thus, instead of finding that participant activity in one area tends to reduce the energy available for other forms of participation, we see that the "star" families show high levels of activity in most of the areas open to them.[13] This is consistent with the general findings reported above as to the relationship between number of acquaintances and intimacy of relationship.

Figure 1–3 shows the relationships among families having fewer than 6 close relationships. Reference to the figure suggests that even with the "stars" removed the block would be definitely structured and channels of communication would exist from each line to every other. While position as a "star" is by no means equivalent to formal leadership, there is a hint here that the adequately integrated group may be integrated, in a sense, at two different levels. Indeed, in the long run it must be, if it is to survive changes in its membership without serious damage.

In a group of this size with its very high level of personal interaction, common sense or at least common cynicism would anticipate the formation of cliques. A reasonable operational definition of a clique in the milieu being studied would be a group of families all having close relationships with each other and none having close relationships with other families in the block. This definition would not, of course, eliminate more casual associations with other neighbors.

However, inspection of Figure 1-2 reveals that there are no families which meet even this rather elastic criterion. As a matter of fact, there are only three groups of four families each of which exhibit all possible inter-relationships, and two of these involve a total of only five families (the 2 configurations centered on Family #21). This aggregation of five families comes fairly close to being an independent structure or clique, but the other close relationships which its members have within the block clearly prevent it from being a closed system.

While no causal relationship has been demonstrated between the integration of the complete block on two separate levels and the absence of clique formation, it is here presented as an hypothesis that the existence of cliques as autonomous structure is inhibited by the integration of the larger group.[14]

The third and perhaps most important phase of community structure to be considered is the evidence of stratification. There is at least a suggestion in many of the more recent community surveys of the inevitability of stratification, and the suggestion has been made explicit by Form in a recent study of Greenbelt. He concludes that, "Large status differences should not be expected in settlements whose populations are selected on the basis of their homogeneity. Nevertheless, despite efforts to limit stratification, some of it appears inevitable."[15] Because this proposition, if valid, has serious implications for democratic social planning, it deserves close examination.

In the first place, it must be noted that University Village is considerably more homogeneous than Greenbelt where the occupations of residents ranged from physician and college professor to truck driver and janitor. Moreover, Form points out that ". . . the planned nature of Greenbelt was responsible for a situation which gave particularly high status to the politically powerful." With two strong factors operating to produce stratification, it is not difficult to see how it arose in Greenbelt, "despite efforts to limit" it. But the Greenbelt experience appears to us to present no conclusive evidence of a general strain toward stratification in the homogeneous community.

On the basis of a careful examination of the evidence, we are unable to detect any status stratification in University Village. That its existence was denied by a number of residents who were graduate students in the social sciences and presumably qualified observers is merely suggestive.[16] What is more significant is the outcome of a number of tests for stratification which could be applied. Two of these tests are summarized below.

In the event of distinct stratification, we would expect that some or all of the "star" families would be of high status. To anticipate otherwise would be to disregard the entire massive evidence on the relationship between status and social participation. But in such case, the tendency for other families to exaggerate their association with the status bearing families should be as marked as it has been in other studies and would be reflected by the "star" families having higher In Scores than Out Scores. In other words, if the "star" families were of higher status, they would presumably report less interaction with their neighbors than their neighbors claimed with them. On the contrary, it was found that only one of the six "stars" had a higher In Score than Out Score.

A second test for stratification was made with the level of living scale used in the study. Although we are reluctant to lean very heavily upon this unvalidated instrument, it is a perfectly straightforward numerical summation of important visible possessions, and we know of no instance where such a scale has not reflected status in a stratified community. Yet when we compare level of living with total interaction, mean intensity of relationships, or a measure of social expansiveness derived by comparing ratings, given and received, the chi-square test gives us no probability significant at the 5% level.

Some Implications

It was suggested at the outset that the pilot study seemed to us to raise questions far more significant than the original hypotheses about mobility.

There is distinct evidence in the foregoing pages that the assumption so frequently found in the literature of urban sociology[17]—that mobility is the *cause* of non-association—is, at the very least, oversimplified. The University Village sample—as mobile a family population as can be discovered in the urban milieu—has a rate of interaction about as high as one would expect in an isolated farming community. Perhaps it would be more reasonable to assume that those factors—the substitution of interest for primary groupings, the increasingly fine ramifications of status systems, the failure of communication channels to develop in the larger community—which are likely to elicit a high degree of spatial mobility also tend to inhibit association on the basis of proximity. In somewhat different terms, we may say that where the neighborhood and the interest group coincide, there will be a high degree of association, regardless of whether the milieu is urban or rural, stable or mobile. Conversely, isolation and immobility do not of themselves foster social participation.

The findings which seem to us to go beyond the question of mobility are (1) the degree of interaction in University Village, which is extraordinarily high in absolute amount; (2) the almost mechanical effect of accessibility upon intimacy, and of time upon the number of relationships; (3) the absence of any observable "automatic" stratification; (4) the apparent tendency of neighborhood integration to inhibit the formation of cliques; (5) the presence of a group structure integrated on the level of the "leaders" and again of the "followers"; (6) the tendency for high participation in one area to be accompanied with high participation in other areas.

It is at once apparent that the characteristic which we have called "homogeneity" is of crucial importance in group formation. We have no reason to suppose that the psychological variability of Village residents is especially low; nor can we characterize them as having a common culture, except to the extent that Americans in general may be so characterized. Nevertheless, the type of informal organization which has been described is, in its essentials, closer to the *sacred* than to the *secular* community.

The students at the University Village are, of course, not literally living in a *sacred* society. The absence of traditional sanctions, and their thorough involvement in the metropolitan milieu, make such a notion ludicrous. All that is claimed is that the type of organization they have developed rests essentially upon what Durkheim described as mechanical solidarity, rather than upon the complicated interdependence of differential statuses which is characteristic of modern society at large.

Much of the recent discussion about group formation has been tinged unconsciously with the experience of the middle-class citizen in organizing small voluntary interest groups, so that we have come to think of social participation as something grudgingly offered and easily withdrawn. Nevertheless, there is a wealth of material on the play-group, the informal organization in industry, and the association of institutional inmates, which suggests that only very powerful inhibiting factors can prevent intensive and intimate interaction among persons of similar status wherever opportunity affords.[18]

Among these status differentials, perhaps the most significant are those arising from differences in occupation, level of living, and family composition. The effects of ethnic, religious and racial differences are equally important, but it is notable that most urban neighborhoods tend toward homogeneity on these factors.

What makes University Village diverge so strikingly from the run of urban neighborhoods is the accidental but thorough elimination of the first three of these status differences. Occupations, we have noted, are identical. The design and furnishing of the dwelling units have the effect of reducing differences in level of living, and family composition is by the rules of eligibility standardized. With these obstacles removed, neighborhood interaction rises to an extremely high level and organizes itself with almost molecular simplicity in terms of the spatial pattern of the community.

Research in this field has barely begun, but it is already apparent that the processes of group formation may be more amenable to analysis than has been supposed. Certainly it is evident that the selection of intimate associates is in large measure a function of a social situation rather than of individual whimsy, and is therefore capable of being predicted in some detail.

NOTES

1. Theodore Caplow, "Residential mobility in a Minneapolis sample," *Social Forces,* Vol. 27, May 1949.

2. Rural sociologists use the term *neighborhood* chiefly in this sense. It is defined by Davies as "a small geographic area inhabited by a cluster of families with a sense of local identification and unity." See Vernon Davies, "Neighborhoods, townships and communities in Wright County, Minnesota," *Rural Sociology,* Vol. 8, March 1943, which includes citations to the relevant literature.

3. Cooley considered it to be one of the three basic primary groups, comparable to family and play group. See his *Social Organization,* 1909.

4. Cf. R. D. McKenzie, *The Neighborhood: A Study of Columbus, Ohio,* University of Chicago Press, 1923; E. V. Zorbaugh, *The Gold Coast and the Slum,* University of Chicago Press, 1929.

5. The most extensive study is that of Jessie Bernard, "An instrument for the measurement of neighborhood with experimental applications," *South Western Social Science Quarterly,* September 1937, pp. 145–160. A somewhat different approach was used by Frank L. Sweetser, "A new emphasis for neighborhood research," *American Sociological Review,* Vol. VII, 4, August 1942, pp. 525–533.

6. This is a sociometric scale in the sense set forth by F. S. Chapin in "The Relation of Sociometry to Planning in an Expanding Social Universe," *Sociometry,* Vol. VI, 1943, p. 235. "Sociometry . . . may then be defined as the science of social measurement." More specifically, the Neighborhood Interaction Scale is similar to the scales

developed by Moreno and his associates in that it permits the diagramming of relationships and the graphic analysis of group organization. It differs, however, in being a presumable report of actual behavior rather than of subjective preference. In practice, both methods may produce similar results in any given group, although they are based on different assumptions. At least two other sociometric studies concerned with related problems have used reports on interactional behavior rather than interactional preferences. See Paul Deutschberger, "Interaction Patterns in Changing Neighborhoods: New York and Pittsburgh," Beacon House, *Sociometry Monographs*, No. 18, 1947, and Charles P. Loomis "Political and Occupational Cleavages in a Hanoverian Village, Germany," Beacon House, *Sociometry Monographs*, No. 16, 1947.

7. Leon Festinger, Stanley Schachter and Kurt Back, *Social Influence*, Harper & Bros., 1950.

8. Stuart C. Dodd, Ruth A. Inglis, and Robert W. O'Brien, "Interracial and Other Tensions in a Public Housing Project," Washington Public Opinion Laboratory, mimeographed, 17 pp. See also, "A Measured Wave of Interracial Tension: Partially testing the interactance hypothesis," mimeographed, 24 pp., same source.

9. The gist of this concept is that an appropriate measure of the individual's social environment is the amount of interaction among the persons with whom he interacts. This may be expressed for any individual by taking the ratio of actual to theoretical combination-pairs found in a sociometric diagram which includes all of the persons with whom he sustains interaction above a designated minimum level. The ratio will approach zero for the anomic urban individual, and unity for the member of an isolated folk-society. The group average of such individual ratios may be tentatively considered as a measure of social cohesion.

10. The maximum length of residence in Westgate was even less, being 15 months in one section of the project, and 5 months in the new addition, at the time of interviewing.

11. These findings are exactly parallel to those of the Westgate study. Table 13, for example, shows the ratio of choices given to possible choices in a number of categories.

Own Court	.133
Adjacent Court	.025
Other Courts	.007
Other part of project	.001

Table 14 shows the relationship of sociometric choices to physical distance among the houses in row (roughly comparable to a lane in University Village).

Units of approxi-mate Physical Distance	Ratio of actual to possible choices
1	.271
2	.083
3	.042
4	.000

Social Influences, op. cit.

12. A rating below 4 signifies a relationship in which neither family *makes an effort* to interact with the other, the association being confined to situations where they encounter each other in the course of other activities. A rating of 4 or more implies a deliberate attempt to associate. It is this type of relationship which will hereafter be designated as "close."

13. The theory of limited social expansiveness, which this finding contradicts, is set forth by Lundberg and Steele who note that, "The conspicuous tendency to make a few choices offers some support to the theory of limited social expansiveness. Aside from possible motives of expediency . . . it is also possible that the diffusion of one's social energies among a large group may weaken the intensity of one's emotional bonds with selected smaller groups." ("Social Attraction Patterns in a Village," *Sociometry*, Vol. I,

1937.) It is possible that this conclusion would have been reversed if their data had been able to differentiate degrees of intensity of relationships.

14. While the Westgate study contains a good deal of data on clique, formation, the matter is too complex to be summarized here. In general, their findings seem to us consistent with this hypothesis.

15. William H. Form, "Status Stratification in a Planned Community," *American Sociological Review* X (October 1945), 613.

16. Courtney B. Cleland, "Personality Interaction in the University Village," Unpublished manuscript, University of Minnesota, 1947.

17. A typical expression of this viewpoint is found in Noel P. Gist and L. A. Halbert, *Urban Society*, Thomas Y. Crowell Co., 3rd ed, 1948, pp. 272–273: "Wherever mobility takes the form of frequent changes of residence, neighborhood life tends to decline because individuals and families have insufficient time to become socially established and thereby develop an interest in persons living near them."

18. Cf. Georg Simmel, "The Sociology of Sociability," (tr. E. C. Hughes) *American Journal of Sociology*, Vol. LV, November 1949. "While all human associations are entered into because of some ulterior interests, there is in all of them a residue of pure sociability or association for its own sake."

2

WILLIAM FOOTE WHYTE

SOCIAL ORGANIZATION
IN THE SLUMS

For many decades sociologists have been studying the slums in terms of social disorganization. It is my purpose to make a critical examination of some of the literature in this field and to suggest a different approach to the analysis of slum social life.

Interest in the slums seems to have stemmed from two sources: (1) an urge to bring about social reforms, and (2) an effort to reach an understanding of the process of urbanization. The studies of Charles Booth[1] and B. Seebohm Rowntree[2] are representative of the reform interest. Being preoccupied with poverty and related problems, these men provided a mass of valuable data upon working class standards of living, but they had little to say about the social life of slum dwellers.

The urbanization studies provide a closer approach to the analysis of social behavior in this area. The contrast between primitive or peasant society and the urban community has prompted many eminent social scientists to formulate theories upon the nature of social relations in the two environments. Henry Maine[3] put the contrast in terms of *status* and *contract*, Ferdinand Tönnies[4] used the concepts of *Gemeinschaft* and *Gesellschaft*, and Émile Durkheim[5] talked of *mechanical* and *organic solidarity*. While the ideas of these men differed in detail, they all agreed that the evolution of the modern city out of the primitive or peasant society involved a movement from a homogeneous social organization based upon familial relations and supported by sacred sanctions toward a heterogeneous, individualized, and secularized society. All three scholars recognized that their dichotomous formulations represented ideal types. There is no society in which the personal relations are all of one type.

Reprinted with permission from *American Sociological Review* 8 (1943): 34–39.

Nevertheless, these concepts serve to draw attention to certain general differences between rural and urban social life.

Georg Simmel[6] turned his attention directly to the social life of the city, analyzing it in terms of the predominance of the money economy and the development of rational and impersonal social relationships. His contribution has had a great influence upon subsequent thinking in this line.

Noting the breakdown of primary group controls in city life, certain sociologists have undertaken to analyze the resulting situation in terms of the concept of social disorganization. Probably the best known definition of this concept is given by W. I. Thomas and Florian Znaniecki who write that social disorganization is to be observed in a *decrease of the influence of existing social rules of behavior upon individual members of the group.*[7]

If the city represents the highest development of individualization and hence of social disorganization, some scholars have thought to find in the slums the most striking manifestations of these phenomena that exist within the city. The following quotation from R. D. McKenzie expresses the orthodox views in the field:

Slums have been characterized as "areas of lost souls and missions," areas where individuals and family groups are living in enforced intimacy with people whom they naturally shun and avoid; areas where there are no standards of decency or social conduct except those imposed by outside authority. In such an environment the individual has no status, there is no representative citizen, the human desires for recognition and security remain unsatisfied.[8]

Some sociologists, notably Robert A. Woods,[9] Thomas and Znaniecki,[10] Robert E. Park and H. A. Miller,[11] and Louis Wirth,[12] have pointed to the existence of indigenous organizations in the slums, but the conflict between their findings and characterizations such as McKenzie's has gone largely unnoticed and attention has remained centered upon social disorganization.

Since Harvey Zorbaugh's volume, *The Gold Coast and the Slum*,[13] has assumed a prominent place in the literature, we shall examine it as an illustration of this type of approach. Zorbaugh begins with this general statement upon the slum:

The slum is an area of freedom and individualism. Over large stretches of the slum men neither know nor trust their neighbors. Aside from a few marooned families, a large part of the native population is transient: prostitutes, criminals, outlaws, hobos. Foreigners who come to make a fortune, as we used to go west, and expect to return to the Old Country as soon as they make their "stake," who are not really a part of American life, and who wish to live in the city as cheaply as possible, live in the lodging-houses of the slum.

Here, too, are the areas of immigrant first settlement, the foreign colonies. And here are congregated the "undesirable" alien groups, such as the Chinese and the Negro.[14]

Zorbaugh sees no difficulty in making generalizations upon the various slum areas which he lumps together in this paragraph. They are all unorganized. But then he goes on to discuss the manner in which the immigrant community *is* organized:

. . . as the colony grows, the immigrant finds in it a social world. In the colony he meets with sympathy, understanding, and encouragement. There he finds his fellow-countrymen who understand his habits and standards and share his life-experience and viewpoint. In the colony he has status, plays a rôle in a group. In the life of the colony's streets and cafes, in its church and benevolent societies, he finds response and security. In the colony he finds that he can live, be somebody, satisfy his wishes—all of which is impossible in the strange world outside.[15]

Zorbaugh continues:

. . . the life of this area is far from unorganized. The Gold Coast has its clubs; intimate groups gather in "village" studios; the foreign areas have numerous lodges and mutual benefit societies; the slum has its "gangs." . . . And these groups may play an enormously important rôle in the lives of their members.

But these groups, with the exception of the clubs of the Gold Coast, are interstitial groups, not only from the point of view of the larger society, but also from the standpoint of the local community. They represent communities in the process of disorganization. They are segmental rather than communal expressions of the life of the local area. The horizon of interest of the clubs of the Gold Coast, on the other hand, is city-wide and local issues rouse but faint echoes in the ballroom of the Casino or the lounges of the Racquet Club.[16]

Having thus disposed of the evidences of organization, Zorbaugh presents the orthodox conclusion:

Throughout the Near North Side, then, community life, where it has not already disintegrated, is in process of disintegration. Community institutions are ceasing to function. The church, the school, the family, the occupational group, government, and the news have ceased to bear any direct relationship to local life. Behavior is individualized in the extreme. There is little or no public opinion. There is no common interest or cultural background. The greater part of the area is incapable of political action. What government there is on the Near North Side is in the hands of the social agency and the police. But neither the social agency nor the police meet with any degree of success. Life is highly disorganized—lived without the law, and without the mores of the larger society. The Near North Side is a section of the old frontier transplanted to the heart of a modern city.[17]

Apparently Zorbaugh began his study with the conviction that the slum represents the *Gesellschaft* ideal type. It is this idea which is expressed in the first and last paragraphs quoted. His discussion of the evidences of social organization does not fit the ideal type. However, by calling them interstitial phenomena, he manages to dismiss them from further consideration. When he has stated that lower class people do not profess the community-wide loyalties which are expected of respectable middle and upper class people, he finds it unnecessary to take lower class groupings into account in his generalizations upon the social organization.

The political organization is disposed of in the same way:

> Politics on the Near North Side is nothing more than a game, a game played without well-defined rules, a game played only incidentally in the local community and bearing little or no relationship to the problems—they can scarcely be called issues—of local life.[18]

To illustrate the undesirable nature of this situation, Zorbaugh contrasts it with that obtaining in Hyde Park and Woodlawn (middle class areas) where politics is purportedly organized around community "issues."

Zorbaugh is simply saying that politics in the slum district is not like politics in the middle class district. Since it does not meet middle class standards, it is "nothing more than a game." The author apparently made no attempt to study the political organization in order to see how it fitted into community life.

In case it is argued that the evidences of lower class organization observed by Zorbaugh were transitory and unimportant so that they do not vitiate his generalizations, we need only refer to the recent literature on the Near North Side Area Project. This part of the area discussed by Zorbaugh was selected as the first section in which a community project was to be organized under the auspices of The Chicago Area Project on the assumption that it had an organized social life which could support such a program. Dr. A. J. Lendino, a life-long resident of the Near North Side and one of the leaders in the community program, writes:

> Our Italian neighborhood . . . has unusual unity and strength. Perhaps nowhere else in the city is there to be found a neighborhood where as many people know each other as they do in our district. We have to a very great extent the same kind of warmth, friendliness and intimacy in our community life that was to be found in the small towns of Sicily from whence our parents came.[19]

Dr. Lendino goes on to describe the highly organized social life of the area and then discusses the manner in which the community program was adopted and carried on by the *already existing* social groupings. No one who reads this document or who is otherwise familiar with the activities of The Area Project on the Near North Side can help but conclude that Zorbaugh has neglected to see some of the most significant features of the life of this area.

The criticisms thus far offered cannot be met by slight alterations in the character of slum research. A fundamental reorientation seems to be required. The first essential is the establishment of clear distinctions between different types of slum districts. On the one hand we have the rooming house district which has been well described by Zorbaugh.[20] Since members of the rooming house population have very little contact with one another, it is accurate to say that such a district is largely lacking in social organization. On the other hand, we have the area of immigrant settlement, described by Dr. Lendino. Here people live in family groups and have built up an elaborate social organization. These two areas resemble each other in congestion of population, poor quality of housing, and low income of the inhabitants, but such physical and economic indices do not provide us with the discriminations needed for sociological analysis. The social life differs so fundamentally from one district to the other that any attempt to lump the two together and make generalizations upon this basis is bound to be fruitless and misleading.[21]

I am concerned primarily with the slum family area, and my discussion of the reorientation of slum studies is restricted to this type of district. To give this discussion concrete form it will be necessary to outline some of the significant characteristics of the social organization of such districts. My data are drawn from a three and a half year study of the Italian slum district of "Cornerville," which I have reported upon in detail in the book, *Street Corner Society*.[22] Discussions with those involved in the Chicago Area Project indicate that my conclusions apply in a general way to other immigrant family settlements.

It has frequently been pointed out that immigrant family groups tend to become disorganized as the children are drawn away from the standards of their parents. The conflict here is a real one, and many instances of family disorganization have been cited to emphasize this point. However, concentration upon cases of disorganization introduces an element of distortion into the picture. I knew many families in Cornerville which retained the most intimate ties of loyalty; adjustments on both sides minimized the conflict between generations. Dr. Lendino presents the same picture when he comments upon the strength of family ties in his area. For too long sociologists have concentrated their attention upon individuals and families that have been unable to make a successful adjustment to the demands of their society. We now need studies of the way in which individuals and groups have managed to reorganize their social relations and adjust conflicts.

Furthermore, preoccupation with the study of family disorganization has led some sociologists to underestimate the degree of organization of any kind found in the slums. Implicitly the assumption is made that the family is the only group capable of organizing intimate personal relations and controlling individual behavior. In discussing the problems of juvenile delinquency, Thomas and Znaniecki say:

> . . . there is a large proportion of immigrant children—particularly in large cities—whose home and community conditions are such that their behavior is never socially regulated, no life organization worthy of the name is ever imposed upon them. Their status is, exactly speaking, not that of demoralization—for demoralization presupposes the loss of a moral system and they never had any moral system to lose—it is simple and plain "a-morality." If personal character is the product of social education acting upon a given temperamental foundation, such individuals in the most radical cases have no character, good or bad.[23]
>
> If now a practically a-moral boy who has no efficient life-organization inculcated in him is put in contact with the complex life of an American city, it is only natural if he simply follows his instincts and moods.[24]

This would lead one to believe that the boy, freed from the control of his parents, simply went out and committed delinquencies as an individual in response to individual whims. The studies of Frederic Thrasher,[25] Clifford Shaw[26] and others have shown that this is not the case. Nearly all delinquencies are committed by groups of boys. In other words, the boy's behavior is not unorganized; it is organized—by the gang.

It does not necessarily follow that a looseness in family ties involves disorganization throughout community life. Some of the Plains Indian tribes had a system of age-graded societies in which the individual purchased membership in the society of his immediate seniors in part by turning over his wife to the man who sold the membership. At the expense of family ties, the age societies assumed the dominant role in community activities.[27] Different peoples emphasize different parts of their social organizations, and we have no right to assume that the family must always and everywhere be relied upon to provide the primary cohesive and organizing force.

While the family does not play the role in directing slum life that it assumes in peasant European communities, other groupings have arisen to provide organization. The corner gangs, well described by Thrasher, mobilize the young men of the district, and, as Thrasher and John Landesco[28] have pointed out, they form the building blocks of the community wide organizations of the rackets and politics. The informal ties of the corner gang provide a network of personal relations and mutual obligations upon which these larger organizations are based.

The sociologist who dismisses racket and political organizations as deviations from desirable standards thereby neglects some of the major elements of slum life. He fails to see the role that they play in integrating and regulating the smaller and more informal groupings of the district. He does not discover the functions they perform for their members. The Irish and later immigrant peoples have had the greatest difficulty in finding places for themselves in our urban social and economic structure. Does anyone believe that the immigrants and their children could have achieved their present degree of social mobility without gaining control of the political organization of some of our largest cities? The same is true of the racket organization. Politics and the rackets have furnished an important means of social mobility for individuals, who, because of ethnic background and low class position, are blocked from advancement in the "respectable" channels.

If social disorganization involves a "decrease of the influence of existing social rules," and the rules referred to are those of the peasant society from which the immigrants came, then the slum is certainly disorganized. However, that is only a part of the picture. It is fruitless to study the area simply in terms of the breakdown of old groupings and old standards; new groupings and new standards have arisen. A large majority of the young men of the district participate in the social world dominated by politics the rackets, and the corner gang. That is their social world, and they understand it. While there is competition for positions within this orbit, the competition is conducted according to indigenous standards. Those who do not accept these standards face a conflict within the district, but such individuals represent proportionately a small minority. The major conflict is that between the organized life of the slums and organized, "respectable" middle class society.

Many years ago Charles Booth wrote this paragraph upon the relations between rich and poor in a London parish:

> . . . their poverty has met with compassion, and those who visit in the name of Christianity seek to relieve the distress they find. The two duties seem to be naturally, and even divinely, combined. The heart is softened, gratitude is

felt, and in this mood the poor are pointed to God. Sin is rebuked, virtue extolled, and warning words are spoken against drunkenness, extravagance and folly. Advice, assistance and rebuke are all accepted, and the recipient is urged to turn to where alone strength can be found and to no longer neglect the observances of religion.[29]

Booth applied without question the standards of middle and upper class society to his lower class population. Subsequent students in this field have been more sophisticated in their terminology, but it is the thesis of this paper that many of them have been applying, implicitly, the same normative approach. Terms such as "good" and "evil" have been supplanted by terms like "interstitial" and "disorganization," but the underlying ideas have been the same. I do not deny that there is a legitimate place for the terms, "interstitial" and "disorganization"; I am only objecting to their use as a means of avoiding consideration of evidences of organization in the slums. The character of slum social organization cannot be understood until more sociologists shift their emphasis from social disorganization in order to investigate the process of social reorganization.

The reorientation of study here proposed can be expressed in broader terms relating to the conceptual schemes of Maine, Tönnies, and Durkheim. It is not argued that their schemes have no application to the process of urbanization. I am simply pointing out that the slum family area is not to be confused with the Gesellschaft ideal type. We may analyze the situation in terms of the in-group and the out-group. Within the in-group, personal relations are of the intimate Gemeinschaft type. Relations of an individual with an outgroup are of the impersonal Gesellschaft type. In a small primitive or peasant society, all of the society may in a sense be called the in-group, although there are of course varying degrees of intimacy in the personal relations. In a highly populous, heterogeneous, urban society, only a small fraction of the population can be in the in-group for any individual.

While urban society has become generally more individualized than that of the primitive tribe, it is not made up simply of an aggregate of individuals. Man lives a group life—even in the city. The problem of sociology in the slum (as elsewhere) is to determine the inter-relations of individuals within the in-group and then to observe the relations between the groups that make up the society. This requires that the sociologist become a participant observer of the most intimate activities in the social life of the slums. Proceeding by this route, he will find many evidences of conflict and maladjustment, but he will not find the chaotic conditions once thought to exist throughout this area.

44

NOTES

Prepared for the Thirty-seventh Annual Meeting of the American Sociological Society, December 1942.

1. *Life and Labour of the People of London.* London: Macmillan & Co., 1892–1904.

2. *Poverty: A Study of Town Life.* London: Macmillan & Co., 1901.

3. *Ancient Law* (4th American edition). New York: Henry Holt, 1884, pp. 163–165.

4. *Fundamental Concepts of Sociology* (translated and supplemented by Charles P. Loomis). New York: American Book Co., 1940, pp. 37–39.

5. *The Division of Labor in Society* (translated by George Simpson). New York: Macmillan & Co., 1933.

6. *Die Grossstadt und Das Geistesleben* (translated by Edward A. Shils). Second Year Course in the Study of Contemporary Society, University of Chicago, selected readings, 8th ed., 1939.

7. *The Polish Peasant in Europe and America.* Boston: Richard C. Badger, 1920, IV, 2.

8. "The Neighborhood: A Study of Local Life in the City of Columbus, Ohio," *American Journal of Sociology,* XXVII, 506, 1922.

9. *The City Wilderness* and *Americans in Process* (Boston: Houghton Mifflin & Co., 1898 and 1902).

10. *Op. cit.*

11. *Old World Traits Transplanted.* New York: Harper & Bros., 1921.

12. *The Ghetto.* Chicago: University of Chicago Press, 1928.

13. Chicago: University of Chicago Press, 1929.

14. *Ibid.*, p. 128.

15. *Ibid.*, p. 141.

16. *Ibid.*, pp. 192–193.

17. *Ibid.*, pp. 198–199.

18. *Ibid.*, p. 194.

19. Unpublished manuscript.

20. *Op. cit.*, p. 82.

21. Of course, these two types do not exhaust the possible variations in slum social organization. Other types need also to be investigated and characterized.

22. Chicago: University of Chicago Press, to be published.

23. *Op. cit.*, V, 295.

24. *Ibid.*, V, 313.

25. *The Gang.* Chicago: University of Chicago Press, rev. ed., 1936.

26. Clifford Shaw, Henry D. McKay, Leonard Cottrell, and Frederick M. Zorbaugh, *Delinquency Areas.* Chicago: University of Chicago Press, 1929.

27. R. H. Lowie, *Plains Indian Age-Societies: Historical and Comparative Summary.* New York: Anthropological Papers of the American Museum of Natural History, XI, part XIII, 1916, p. 919.

28. *Organized Crime in Chicago; Part III of the Illinois Crime Survey.* Chicago: Illinois Association for Criminal Justice in Cooperation with the Chicago Crime Commission, 1929.

29. *Life and Labour of the People of London,* Third Series, *Religious Influences,* VII, 45. London: Macmillan & Co., 1904.

3

H. LAURENCE ROSS

THE LOCAL COMMUNITY: A SURVEY APPROACH

The model of the local community was proposed by Robert E. Park and Ernest W. Burgess as a framework for the description of social structure in American cities. The original model underlies several more recent investigations of urban life. Among the distinctive features of this model are the divisibility of the city into "natural" areas delimited by "natural" boundaries, the recognition of the areas as communities by their inhabitants, and the organization of social life within the areas around distinctive local facilities. This paper reports on a study using survey methods to investigate these aspects of the local community model. A further concern of the study was the status-ascriptive function suggested for named areas in the work of W. Lloyd Warner.

The research attempted, first, to determine whether named and bounded areas are recognized by a sample of urban residents who were asked to name and bound their own area of residence and to identify other named areas within the city. Second, the status-ascriptive functions were investigated through analysis of free responses to the stimuli of selected area names. Third, the residents were questioned concerning the location of various common activities that appeared to be relevant to the local community model. The results of this paper both amplify and qualify portions of the original model.

The Local Community Model

In the industrial metropolis, depicted by Simmel as a collection of overstimulated, blasé, and reserved individualists, Robert E. Park and his colleagues noted many regions where social life was intense, informal, and

Reprinted with permission from *American Sociological Review* 27 (1962): 75–84.

intimate. Prototypical of such regions was the immigrant ghetto, integrated by the institutions of a quasi-folk society and isolated from other parts of the metropolis by language barriers and prejudice. The limits of the immigrant colonies were often marked by physical barriers to travel, such as elevated railway walls and watercourses. Impressed by the fact that the entire urban landscape was divided into small areas by the network of transportation and industry, these early ecologists put forward a model in which the interstices of this network, termed "natural areas," contained the units of urban social structure, which they called "local communities." Starting with a map of Chicago containing the expected natural boundaries, they began a search for "the correspondence, if any, between this physical formation of the city . . . and the currents of the economic and social life of the city." The latter were determined by the following tests:

(1) Well-recognized historical names and boundaries of local communities and the changes which these have undergone.

(2) Dividing lines that are at present recognized by the residents, as when on one side of the street persons state that they live in one community and persons on the other side of the street state that they live in another community.

(3) Boundaries of areas claimed by local organizations as businessmen's associations, by local newspapers, and by improvement associations, and in cases of dispute checking claims by plotting memberships of these groups.

(4) Plotting membership or attendance or patronage of local community institutions or enterprises and noting the effect of barriers like parks and railroad lines.

(5) Plotting the distributions and the movements of cultural groups like immigrant colonies and noting the effect of these barriers.[1]

According to Burgess, the model was appropriate to Chicago. On the other hand, simultaneously with this effort to demonstrate that the metropolis is made up of community areas segregated by natural boundaries, students following Park's research suggestions were noting certain limitations of the model, especially in some central city areas. Among these was Zorbaugh, who, after studying the Near North Side "community" in Chicago, stated:

. . . the older organization of the community, based on family ties and local associations, is being replaced by an organization based upon vocational interests and attitudes. This vocational organization cuts across local areas; defines itself spatially as city-wide; and takes much of a person's life out of the local community.[2]

In American cities of the fifties and sixties, many of the cultural differences that once distinguished among, and isolated, the local communities appear to have diminished. The large immigrant ghettoes of the early twentieth century have declined in size and have been reduced in variety and number, and the association "based on vocational interests and attitudes" appears increasingly prevalent. The question arises: can one identify today entities analogous to the local community as described by Park and his colleagues? Furthermore, if such entities are found, what functions do they serve in modern urban life?

Several recent urban studies imply the finding of local areas with properties similar to those given by the model cited above. Janowitz' concept of the community of limited liability represents a conditional confirmation of the model, in which he cites the proliferation of local communications media as evidence of residents' orientation to a local community, but stresses the partial and selective character of this orientation. This perspective is confirmed in Greer's studies of outlying urban areas. Greer stresses the local press, local organizations, and informal interaction as local community characteristics.[3] A somewhat similar approach appears in the "social areas" tradition of Shevky, Williams, Bell, and their students. This tradition is based on the demonstration of socially homogeneous areal units in several cities, and it offers a convincing typology for these units that has been found useful by other researchers.[4] On the other hand, some investigators, following the lead of Paul Hatt, have found a lack of homogeneity within small areal units, and a lack of congruence between reasonable alternative criteria of local organization, leading them to reject or to severely qualify the community model.[5] In the field of city planning, many writers take for granted the possibility of creating a community-like structure in the urban plan, but differ in their opinions as to whether a corresponding social organization can or should develop from such a plan.[6] In short, the local community model is still employed in much current urban theory and research, but with various degrees of confirmation arising from different empirical tests. The principal purpose of this paper is the submission of selected parts of the model to a new test through the use of survey techniques.

Recognition of Named Areas

With rare exceptions,[7] surveys concerned with the identification of a local community, in terms of respondents' naming and bounding an area in which their residences are located, have been unsuccessful. Typical are the findings of Riemer[8] in Milwaukee, Bloch *et al.*[9] in Chicago, Foley[10] in Rochester, McKenzie[11] in Columbus, and Smith, Form and Stone[12] in Lansing.

The present study was initiated on the assumption that these negative findings were in large part the result of methodological weaknesses, including the use of the ambiguous term "neighborhood" and the placement of questions concerning the name and boundary of the area at the end of questionnaires concerning "your block" or "the area within five blocks from home." Therefore, the first question asked of respondents in this study was, "What is the name of this part of [the city]?" There followed a request to state the boundaries of the area so named. The hypothesis to be tested was that residents agree on the name and boundaries of the area in which they live, and it was arbitrarily decided in advance that the criterion of "agreement" would be a simple majority.

A census tract in central Boston[13] was chosen for study. The choice was made in order to depart as much as possible from the ghetto prototype of the local community. The tract in question was an apartment house area. It contained population of mixed class and ethnic background. Because of a large proportion of young, unmarried people, the area had a very high mobility rate. Two hundred fifty respondents, representing 87 per cent of a random sample of households,[14] participated in the study.

Tables 3–1 and 3–2, presenting the distributions of names and boundaries given in answer to the above questions, show that there was a great deal more agreement in this study than in previously cited studies that the respondents lived in a certain named and bounded area of the city. Majority agreement was found on a name for the area and on three of four boundaries. Moreover, the boundaries were those predicted in advance

TABLE 3-1

Distribution of Names Ascribed to the
"Part of Town" by Respondents in the Study Area

NAME	PER CENT USING NAME
Beacon Hill	68%
Modified form of Beacon Hill[a]	6
West End	23
Other name	2
D. K.	1
Total	100% (250)

[a] e.g., "the Back Side of Beacon Hill," "Bohemian Hill," etc.

49

TABLE 3-2

Distribution of Boundaries Ascribed to the "Part of Town" by Respondents in the Study Area

Northern Boundary		Southern Boundary		Eastern Boundary		Western Boundary	
Street	Per Cent	Street	Per Cent	Street	Per Cent	Street	Per Cent
Cambridge	80%	Beacon[a] or Boston Common	81%	Joy	12%	Charles St., Charles River and Embankment[c]	87%
		Myrtle or Pinckney	5	State House and streets bordering	43		
				Scollay and Tremont[b]	21		
Other	9	Other	3	Other	9	Other	5
D.K., vague	11	D.K., vague	11	D.K., vague	15	D.K., vague	8
Total	100% (250)	Total	100% (250)	Total	100% (250)	Total	100% (250)

[a] Combined because Beacon Street forms the near border of the Boston Common.
[b] Combined because Tremont Street begins at and forms an extension of Scollay Square.
[c] Combined because the Embankment is a park that follows the Charles River, and Charles Street parallels and borders the Embankment in the immediate vicinity of the census tract studied.

from natural area considerations. To the north, the boundary was a heavily traveled street, and to the south and west the boundaries were parks, major streets, and a river.

The presence of a second name for the area, on which a minority agreed, was not expected. It was noted that the boundaries given by respondents terming the area "the West End" tended to include territory lying farther north than the region defined by respondents using the name "Beacon Hill," and the hypothesis was advanced that the respondents might be living in a border region between two more clearly defined areas. In order to test this hypothesis, two small samples of people in tracts adjacent to the study area were asked the same questions. To the north, 24 respondents agreed unanimously that they lived in the West End. To the south, 22 of 23 agreed that they lived in Beacon Hill. Thus, the border region nature of the study area appears to explain the bimodal distribution of names among the original sample.

The question was raised whether areas of the metropolis other than the area of residence were commonly identifiable by name. A previous study by Kevin Lynch,[15] using a small and non-random sample of well-informed Bostonians, had located several named areas by asking the respondents to describe the city. Among these were three—the Back Bay, the North End, and the South End—that had also been recognized by Firey in his study of symbolism in ecology.[16] Professor Lynch sketched the boundaries obtained for these three areas from his respondents on a map prepared for the present study. The Beacon Hill-West End sample was asked if they knew the areas by name (no map was shown) and, if so, to name a street in each. The hypothesis that some[17] areas of the metropolis, in addition to the area of residence, are known as named areas, was tested according to the criterion that a majority of the respondents must be able to name a street within the boundaries sketched by Lynch. As many of the respondents were new to the city, and no measure of the accuracy of the Lynch boundaries (as against those determined by questioning a random sample of residents) was available, this could be expected to be a difficult test of the hypothesis. Yet the percentages of respondents correctly naming a street within the boundaries drawn by Lynch were 66 per cent for the North End, 80 per cent for the Back Bay, and 57 per cent for the South End. The hypothesis was therefore rather strongly confirmed.

In summary, it can be said that residents of the area studied regard themselves as living in a named area of the city, and agree on the boundaries of their area in all but one direction. The criterion of majority agreement was satisfied despite the fact that the study happened to be conducted in a border region formed by the intersection of two clearly defined named areas. Furthermore, residents of this region can correctly identify several other named areas within the city. These results were achieved in spite of the fact that many residents were new to the city, and that the census tract studied was highly urbanized, being central to the city and heterogeneous in population.

Functions of the Named Area in Ascribing Status

Some sociologists, not primarily concerned with the study of local communities, have found the concept of named urban areas to be useful in other respects. One important use that has been made of area names is in ascertaining the social class of an individual. Warner's instructions for scoring the Index of Status Characteristics are illustrative:

> By previous knowledge or interview, establish the major social areas and their relative ranking . . . make a map of the areas and indicate the value of each area by putting its rating after its name on the map. Sub-areas of higher and lower ranking should be delineated and ranked. People living in the area know the differences.[18]

While these instructions, quoted in their entirety, are not very precise, Warner seems to be proposing the interview as a method for determining the named areas and finding out the degree of prestige associated with each area name. This technique would presumably be increasingly useful in large cities, where ratings that depend on intimate knowledge of individuals (for instance, Evaluated Participation) are less feasible.

Others have suggested that what is useful to the sociologist is also useful to the average man. Shevky and Williams write:

> In urban-industrial society, the unfailing indicators of the social position of others readily accessible to everyone are houses and areas of residence. As every occupation is evaluated and generally accorded honor and esteem on a scale of prestige in society, so every residential section has a status value which is readily recognized by everyone in the city.[19]

Consideration of such names as Chinatown, Little Italy, Kilgubbin and Harlem suggests that ethnic connotations as well as status connotations are conveyed by the names of areas. A possible conclusion from these considerations is that area names play an important role in identifying the status and ethnicity of individuals, in a manner resembling that of occupational title for social class and family name for ethnicity. If area names are to perform this function in large cities, the names must be well-known, and the connotations they bear concerning class and ethnicity must be appropriate to the population of the areas. The diffusion of knowledge of area names in different parts of the metropolis was suggested in the previous section of this paper. Evidence concerning the appropriateness or accuracy of the connotations evoked by names of urban areas will be presented in the following paragraphs.

In the study by Lynch cited above, certain parts of the named areas were designated core areas because of very high agreement on them by his respondents. The core areas were smaller than, and central to, the wider areas containing them. A census tract approximation of Lynch's core areas was used to determine selected demographic features for each of the named areas. Indices of social class and ethnic composition for the areas are presented in Table 3–3. Residents of the studied tract were asked to give a description of the three distant areas. Respondents denying knowledge of an area or citing a street not within the wider boundaries given by Lynch were not counted in the following tabulations. The descriptions, coded for mentions of class and ethnicity, were compared with the demographic indices for each area. Among the three areas, it was expected that the Back Bay would be described as white-collar, in contrast to the other areas; that the South End would be seen as Negro; and that the North

TABLE 3-3

Indices for 1950 of Class and Ethnicity for Five Named Areas in Boston

	NAMED AREA				
INDEX	NORTH END[a]	BACK BAY[b]	SOUTH END[c]	BEACON HILL[d]	WEST END[e]
Percentage professionals, proprietors, managers, and officials in the labor force	8.0%	39.0%	9.7%	34.0%	13.8%
Percentage laborers and operatives in the labor force	46.2	3.7	27.5	6.4	31.3
Percentage of population foreign born	18.9	14.0	11.6	15.5	26.3
Percentage of population non-white	0.0	0.6	22.2	0.9	1.1

[a]Tracts F-2, F-4, and F-5.
[b]Tracts K-3 and K-5.
[c]Tracts I-1, I-2, I-3, I-4, L-1, L-4, and L-5.
[d]Tracts K-1 and K-2.
[e]Tract H-1.
Source: *United States Census of Population: 1950. Vol. III, Census Tract Statistics.* Chapter 6.

End would be seen as Italian, since 96 per cent of its foreign-born were from Italy. Tables 3–4 and 3–5 support these expectations. Given the very open nature of the question,[20] the absolute number of class and ethnic symbols mentioned is evidence that these associations are among the first to be made to the stimulus of an area name.[21]

A similar pattern appears in Table 3–6, in which respondents thinking of themselves as living in Beacon Hill are compared with those thinking of themselves as living in the West End. In this tabulation, direct questions[22] were asked of the respondents about the class and national origin of the people in the area named, so the proportions mentioning class and ethnic composition cannot be taken as an index of the salience of these characteristics. The respondents speaking of Beacon Hill thought of it as an upper- and middle-class area of North European Protestant stock.

TABLE 3-4

How Respondents Characterize Three Named Areas in Terms of Status

	PERCENTAGE OF THOSE DEMONSTRATING KNOWLEDGE OF THE AREA WHO MENTION CLASS						
COMMUNITY	WHITE COLLAR	BLUE COLLAR	BOTH	TOTAL	NO MENTION	GRAND TOTAL	N
North End	1%	14%	1%	16%	84%	100%	166
Back Bay	33	4	3	40	60	100	199
South End	1	45	1	47	53	100	142

TABLE 3-5

How Respondents Characterize Three Named Areas in Terms of Ethnicity

PERCENTAGE OF THOSE DEMONSTRATING KNOWLEDGE OF THE AREA
WHO MENTION ETHNICITY

COMMUNITY	NEGROES	ITALIANS	OTHER ETHNIC	TOTAL	NO MENTION	GRAND TOTAL	N
North End	a	67%	1%	68%	32%	100%	166
Back Bay	a	a	4	4	96	100	199
South End	37%	a	7	44	56	100	142

aNot coded separately.

Those speaking of the West End thought of it as a working- and lower-class area of ethnic stock. These characterizations are supported, for the cores of these areas, by the census statistics presented in Table 3–3.

The preceding paragraphs have shown that accurate characterizations of class and ethnicity of the residents are among the salient connotations of area names. It follows that these names are available for use in social interaction between non-intimates in defining their respective statuses, as suggested by Shevky and Williams. This study is not able to supply proof

TABLE 3-6

*Differences in Characteristics Attributed to the Area
Among Respondents Identifying with Beacon Hill
and West End*

CLASS DESIGNATION OF AREA	RESPONDENTS SPEAKING OF BEACON HILL	RESPONDENTS SPEAKING OF WEST END
Upper or middle	70%	31%
Working or lower	27	66
Both, or D.K.	3	3
Total	100% (169)	100% (58)
Ethnic Designation of Area		
North European Protestanta	54%	7%
Ethnicb	24	81
Both, or D.K.	22	12
Total	100% (169)	100% (58)

aOld Yankee, English, Scottish, German, Dutch, Scandinavian origin.
bAll other countries of origin.

that these names are actually used for this purpose, but one of the tabulations made suggests that people act as if this were so. The study took place in a border region between two named areas with different status connotations, and residents of the region had a choice between the names of Beacon Hill and the West End. If people are socially typed by the name of their area of residence, those with a choice may be expected to choose the name with status connotations corresponding most closely to their own self-conceptions. Thus, in the present case, people conceiving of themselves as upper- and middle-class should tend to choose Beacon Hill as the name of their residence area, whereas people conceiving of themselves as working- and lower-class should choose the West End, allowing a margin of error for working-class people who would like to "rise" to Beacon Hill and for middle-class people who do not accept the stereotype of the West End as working-class.

The results of the survey support the predictions. Among the respondents describing themselves as upper- and middle-class, 81 per cent "chose" Beacon Hill as their area of residence, compared with 58 per cent of the respondents thinking of themselves as working- and lower-class. A similar situation exists with respect to national origin. Among the North European Protestants, 76 per cent "chose" Beacon Hill, as against 65 per cent of the ethnics. Proximity to the cores of the respective areas was found to be associated with this decision, but cartographic analysis revealed that proximity operated independently, and that at any distance from the cores of the communities, working- and lower-class individuals were more likely to "choose" the working- and lower-class West End label for their area of residence.

The Named Area as a Community

The concept of community has several different meanings in sociology. According to a classical definition, "wherever any group, small or large, live together in such a way that they share, not this or that particular interest, but the basic conditions of a common life, we call that group a community."[23] Definitions of local community implicit in empirical investigations focus on both interaction and institutions. The former focus, prominent in the work on suburban communities, is exemplified by such criteria as friendship, neighboring, participation in informal organizations, and orientation to communications media.[24] The latter focus, prominent in the Chicago tradition of concern with ethnic and central city communities, is exemplified by such criteria as membership in formal organizations and intensive use of distinctive local facilities.[25] Thus, the literature on local communities furnishes various criteria that could be framed as hypotheses concerning properties of named areas. This study investigated one of these criteria, the usage of local facilities.

Two studies of peripheral urban areas by Donald Foley served as a background and source of specific hypotheses for this work. While inspection of Foley's designs suggests that he never came to grips with what constituted "local" for his respondents, the parallel between his results and the findings in central Boston supports the general applicability of both.

Foley's first study[26] concerned a lower-middle-class area in northwestern St. Louis, containing elementary schools, churches, movie theaters, and "other facilities" as well as industries. Not available within the district were public high schools, large parks, and, aside from movies, professional entertainment facilities. A representative sample of families was polled to ascertain the location of various facilities used by all members of the family. Usage within the boundaries of the arbitrarily defined district was classified as local. Foley found that local food outlets and churches were used by the residents of this area, with 69 per cent and 77 per cent of the total uses, respectively, being local. On the other hand, only 5 per cent of clothing, household equipment, and furniture shopping was local, and only 18 per cent of employment was local, despite the presence of industry. A study of a peripheral area in Rochester[27] revealed a similar pattern, where "local" was defined as "within five blocks from home."

The data from Boston are shown in Table 3-7. Because of the border nature of the census tract, both Beacon Hill and the West End were considered local, and the most liberal boundaries available (those sketched by

TABLE 3-7

Distribution of Facilities Used by Respondents According to Location of Facility

FACILITY	BEACON HILL AND WEST END	DOWNTOWN	OTHER	DON'T USE OR D.K.	TOTAL	
Food shopping	80%	a	18%	2%	100%	(250)
Clothing shopping	2	75	21	2	100	(250)
Furniture shopping	5	63	24	8	100	(250)
Work	22	28	34	16	100	(250)
Entertainment	22	37	34	7	100	(250)
Church	36	17	27	20	100	(250)

aLess than ½ of 1%.

Lynch) were used. All major categories of facilities were available within the area, although in variety and quality of stores the area was inferior to the adjacent central business district. Despite the differences between this area and those studied by Foley, and the different criteria of what is "local," the pattern is quite similar. Food shopping and church attendance are modally local, but all other facilities usages were found to be predominantly non-local. While the adjacent downtown area accounts for much non-local usage, it is noteworthy that non-local facilities usage *apart from the downtown area* far exceeds local facilities usage in all categories investigated except food shopping and church attendance. The non-local and non-downtown usage was fairly widespread throughout the metropolitan area. Respondents expressed preferences for suburban discount houses, for furniture and clothes from fashionable streets in the Back Bay, for roadhouse entertainment, and a host of items available in isolated locations or in specialized business centers serving the entire metropolis.

In view of the support lent to the pattern found here by Foley's work, the proposal that the local community is organized around distinctive facilities must be strongly qualified. The nature of the qualification can be illustrated by considering the kinds of facilities that are locally used. While only food shopping and church attendance are modally local in these studies, the distribution of retail outlets in the city suggests that drugs, some kinds of banking, purchasing at variety stores, and other similar activities, are also typically local. This type of activity can be characterized as convenience shopping, involving goods which are used in small quantities and purchased fairly often, in which price differentials are not very important, and which are relatively highly standardized. It is, in other words, precisely in those lines in which goods are *not* strongly differentiated that local shopping is done. Goods and corresponding outlets that are distinctive appear to require a larger market than that supplied by a typical named area.

These data indicate that the local facilities usage of the modal urbanite, in the areas studied in this project and in Foley's previous work, tends to be confined to convenience goods. However, it should be kept in mind that local facilities usage in almost all categories appears greater than a chance model would predict, especially considering the absence of opportunities in the area.[28] Furthermore, a supplementary analysis revealed a slight tendency for some residents to use various local facilities more than other residents, supporting a model proposed by Merton in which the relevant community may be different for different people living in the same general locality.[29]

Summary and Conclusions

The research reported here supports the proposition, contained in the local community model of the metropolis, that the city is perceived by its residents as containing named areas, bounded by such barriers to travel as parks, rivers, and large streets. On the background of many studies yielding negative evidence, this study succeeded, using a new method that avoided the ambiguity of the term "neighborhood" and presented definitional questions at the beginning of the questionnaire.

The names of areas apart from the one of residence were found to be well-diffused in this study. Furthermore, these names were shown to have class and ethnic connotations that were in harmony with indices derived from the census. This evidence can be interpreted as support for the proposition that one function of named areas is the attribution of class and ethnic positions in the secondary social relations typical of the city.

An investigation of the proposition that residents of a named area use distinctive local facilities yielded generally negative results. Little use was made of local facilities except in items commonly termed convenience items, which are similar from area to area.

These results, based on a sample of households in one census tract in Boston, are statistically generalizable only to the census tract sampled. However, there is evidence to indicate that the results are not entirely due to peculiar local conditions in Boston and in the study area. In pre-tests of the questionnaire used in this study, residents of three Chicago "local communities" as defined by the Chicago Community Inventory—South Shore, Near North Side, and New City—were asked to name and bound their part of Chicago. Agreement on name and boundaries in these areas compared favorably with that found in the Boston case, although residents of New City uniformly used the more pungent name of Back-of-the-Yards in referring to their area of residence. Similar results were found in a secondary analysis by the author of data gathered in outlying areas of Boston by Morton Rubin of Northeastern University. Consciousness of living in a named and bounded area thus does not appear to be confined to residents of high-status and historic areas of an old city. With respect to the other findings in this paper, Warner's use of the Index of Status Characteristics in various cities supports the characterization of named areas as a source of statue ascription, and the previously noted similarity between areas in Boston and St. Louis and Rochester supports the generalizability of the results reported for use of facilities.

This study supports the local community conception of the city by demonstrating that named units with "natural" boundaries are recognized by residents of an urban area. It further suggests that named areas have a status-ascriptive function not stressed in the original model. The research qualifies an aspect of the model concerning the usage of local facilities. Other features of the local community model, such as the presence of participation in local organizations and a network of local friendships, were not specifically tested in this study, and await further research.

NOTES

1. Ernest W. Burgess, "Basic Social Data," in T. V. Smith and Leonard D. White, editors, *Chicago: An Experiment in Social Science Research*, Chicago: University of Chicago Press, 1929, pp. 47–66; see particularly p. 58.

2. Harvey Zorbaugh, *The Gold Coast and the Slum*, Chicago: University of Chicago Press, 1929, p. 241.

3. Morris Janowitz, *The Community Press in an Urban Setting*, Glencoe, Illinois: Free Press, 1952; Scott Greer, "Urbanism Reconsidered: A Comparative Study of Local Areas in a Metropolis," *American Sociological Review*, 21 (February, 1956), pp. 19–25; and Scott Greer, "Socio-Political Structure of Suburbia," *American Sociological Review*, 25 (August, 1960), pp. 514–526.

4. A general guide to work in the social areas tradition appears in Wendell Bell, "Social Areas: Typology of Urban Neighborhoods," in Marvin B. Sussman, editor, *Community Structure and Analysis*, New York: Thomas Y. Crowell, 1959, pp. 61–92.

5. Paul Hatt, "The Concept of Natural Area," *American Sociological Review*, 11 (August, 1946), pp. 423–427. See also William H. Form, Joel Smith, Gregory P. Stone, and James Cowhig, "The Compatibility of Alternative Approaches to the Delimitation of Urban Sub-Areas," *American Sociological Review*, 19 (August, 1954), pp. 434–440.

6. See, on the favorable side, Judith Tannenbaum, "The Neighborhood: A Socio-Psychological Analysis," *Land Economics*, 24 (November, 1948), pp. 358–369. The chief critic is Reginald Isaacs. See "The Neighborhood Theory," *Journal of the American Institute of Planners*, 14 (Spring, 1948), pp. 15–23.

7. One exception is contained in Shirley Star, "An Approach to the Measurement of Interracial Tensions," unpublished Ph.D. dissertation, University of Chicago, 1950. She notes in passing that 81 per cent of the residents in one local community and 49 per cent of those in a second used the names attributed to the areas by the Chicago Community Inventory. The finding is vitiated by the fact that interviewers introduced the study as one of Grand Crossing or Auburn-Gresham, thus providing a set for questions on area name. Bell (*op. cit.*, p. 75) implies the use of names employed by residents in social area analysis. Scott Greer, in an unpublished research report, found that 98 per cent of residents of a part of Saint Louis County gave a distinctive name to their residential area. Names have been assigned to areas in countless studies in urban sociology, perhaps implying positive findings concerning agreement of residents to the name. An impressive example is in Calvin F. Schmid, "Urban Crime Areas: Part I," *American Sociological Review*, 25 (August, 1960), pp. 527–542, Figure 1, p. 528.

8. Svend Riemer, "Villagers in Metropolis," *British Journal of Sociology*, 2 (March, 1951), pp. 31–43.

9. Donald Bloch, *et al.*, "Identification and Participation in Urban Neighborhoods," unpublished M.A. thesis, University of Chicago, 1952.

10. Donald L. Foley, "Neighbors or Urbanites?", mimeographed manuscript, Rochester: University of Rochester, 1952.

11. Roderick McKenzie, *The Neighborhood: A Study of Local Life in the City of Columbus, Ohio*, Chicago: University of Chicago Press, 1923.

12. Joel Smith, William H. Form, and Gregory P. Stone, "Local Intimacy in a Middle-Sized City," *American Journal of Sociology*, 60 (November, 1954), pp. 276–284.

13. Tract K-1, between Cambridge Street and Myrtle Street, Joy Street and the Charles River.

14. Twenty-nine refusals and nine non-contacted persons made up the rest of the sample. A check of age, sex, and occupational distributions of the respondents against census statistics for the tract showed no significant differences between the sample and the population on these variables.

15. Kevin Lynch, *The Image of the City*, Cambridge, Mass.: Technology Press, 1960.

16. Walter Firey, *Land Use in Central Boston*, Cambridge, Mass.: Harvard University Press, 1947.

17. The sample of areas was not random, so no statistical generalization can be made.

18. W. Lloyd Warner *et al.*, *Social Class in America*, Chicago: Science Research Associates, 1949, p. 238.

19. Eshref Shevky and Marilyn Williams, *The Social Areas of Los Angeles*, Berkeley, Calif.: University of California Press, 1949, pp. 61–62.

20. "Tell me a little about the North End as you see it. What kind of a place is it? What makes it different from other neighborhoods in Boston?"

21. In contrast, the same comparison made on the variable of family status revealed little salience. In no case did as many as a quarter of the respondents mention age and/or marital status variables in their descriptions of the communities, although the Back Bay contains unusually large numbers of young, single people, and great stress could have been placed on this fact.

22. The question on class was based on that used by Richard Centers in *The Psychology of Social Classes*, Princeton, N. J.: Princeton University Press, 1951. It read: "When [the area] is mentioned, do you think first of the middle class, the lower class, the working class, or the upper class?" The question on national origin was, "When [the area] is mentioned, which of these groups do you think of first?" A card listing eleven broad national groups was presented with the question.

23. R. M. MacIver, *Society: A Textbook of Sociology*, New York: Farrar and Rinehart, 1937, pp. 8–9.

24. The works of Greer, Bloch *et al.*, and Janowitz, cited above, are examples of this focus.

25. This focus is illustrated by several of the studies in the Chicago Sociological Series, most notably Louis Wirth, *The Ghetto*, Chicago: University of Chicago Press, 1928, and Zorbaugh, *op. cit.* See also Foley, *op. cit.*

26. Donald L. Foley, "The Use of Local Facilities in a Metropolis," *American Journal of Sociology*, 56 (November, 1950), pp. 238–246.

27. Donald L. Foley, "Neighbors or Urbanites?", *loc. cit.*

28. The term "opportunities" is used as in Samuel A. Stouffer, "Intervening Opportunities: A Theory Relating Mobility and Distance," *American Sociological Review*, 5 (December, 1940), pp. 845–867.

29. For instance, about half the respondents with working- and lower-class self-descriptions, and half of those over 45 years of age, used local churches. See Robert K. Merton, "Patterns of Influence," in Paul Lazarsfeld and Frank Stanton, editors, *Communications Research 1948–1949*, New York: Harper, 1949.

4

SCOTT GREER

〰〰〰〰〰〰〰〰〰〰〰〰〰〰〰〰〰〰〰〰〰〰〰〰〰〰

URBANISM RECONSIDERED:
A COMPARATIVE STUDY OF
LOCAL AREAS IN A METROPOLIS

The investigation of the internal differentiation of urban population has been concerned chiefly with economic rank and ethnic diversity, and with the differences which accompany variations in these factors. Such studies throw little light upon the broad, non-ethnic, cultural differences generated in the metropolitan environment, i.e., upon "urbanism as a way of life." While there has been much concern, theoretically, with the effects of the metropolitan ambit upon all social relationships, most of the empirical basis of urban theory has been the study of small "natural areas" or the study of gross regularities in census data, arranged spatially for analysis.

Perhaps the best evidence bearing upon this larger question of "urbanism" has been the study of urban neighborhoods. The work of Donald Foley, for example, indicates that in a sample of Rochester residents (1) the neighborhood pattern still exists to some degree, but, (2) many individuals do not neighbor and do not consider their local area to be a social community.[1] Such studies approach the propositions that urban society is functionally rather than spatially organized and that urbanites are mobile, anonymous, and lacking in identification with their local area.

To gauge the generality of Foley's conclusions, however, one needs to know where the neighborhoods he studied fit in an array of neighborhoods. Because wide variation exists, the relation between the area studied and others is crucial for the hypothesis tested; most of Rochester may be much more neighborhood oriented, or much less so, than the area studied.

The Shevky-Bell typology of urban subareas is useful in this connection, for it allows any census tract to be located in three different arrays by

Reprinted with permission from *American Sociological Review* 21 (1956): 19–25.

means of three indices constructed from census data.[2] It is hypothesized that these represent three dimensions within urban social space, each statistically unidimensional and independent of the others. The dimensions are social rank, segregation, and urbanization.[3] The last largely measures differences in family structure, and, it is assumed, indicates corollary differences in behavior. Thus, when social rank and segregation are controlled, differences in the index of urbanization for specific tract populations should indicate consistent variations in social behavior. One purpose of the present research was to determine the nature of such corollary differences, and particularly differences in social participation.

This report is based upon a pilot study of differences in social participation between sample populations in two Los Angeles areas (census tracts 35 and 63).[4] The two tract populations are nearly identical with respect to two of the indices (social rank and segregation) and differ on the third, urbanization. For simplicity in presentation the tract with the higher urbanization index score (tract 63) will hereafter be called the high-urban tract, the other (tract 35) the low-urban tract.

The two sample tracts compare as follows. *History:* the low-urban tract is in an area that thirty years ago was separately incorporated for a brief time; the high-urban tract has always been a part of Los Angeles proper. *Location:* the low-urban tract is approximately fifteen minutes from the city center by auto; the high-urban tract is about half as far. (The low-urban tract is adjacent to the competing centers of Glendale and Pasadena.) *Social rank:* both tracts fall within the large middle range, being slightly above the median for the County. The social rank index for the low-urban tract is 68, for the high-urban tract, 66, as of the 1950 census of population, based upon the standard scores developed by Shevky with 1940 census data. *Ethnicity:* in neither tract does the foreign-born and non-white population amount to more than 5 per cent. *Urbanization:* the two tracts represent the extremes of the middle range of the urbanization index, within which a majority of the Los Angeles County census tracts lie. The low-urban tract had an urbanization index of 41, the high-urban tract, 57. There are much more highly urban tracts at middle rank, and much lower ones, in the County. The sample is weighted against the instrument, so that if striking and consistent variations appear in this middle range, they probably indicate more extreme variations at the poles.

The Field Procedure and the Sample

The field study included scheduled interviews on the participation of adult members of households in formal organizations, neighboring, cultural events, visiting, domestic activities, the mass media, the kin group, and other social structures.

Visiting was measured by questions concerning friends or relatives who were visited regularly at least once a month. The respondent was asked to give the address of the residence visited, both as a control over the accuracy of the information, and as a clue to social space position in the Shevky-Bell typology. Neighboring was measured by Wallin's "Neighborliness Scale," which was developed for a similar population in Palo Alto, California.[5] The scale assumes that neighborliness is unidimensional and can be measured by a small battery of questions referring to the degree of interaction with neighbors. The reproducibility for the present sample has not yet been determined. Cultural events were recorded and categorized in the manner devised by Queen, in his studies of social participation in St. Louis.[6] Individuals were asked about their attendance in the past month at movies, classes and study groups, athletic contests, lectures and speeches, museums and exhibits, musical events, and stage shows. They were also asked the location of the event and who accompanied them. Special schedules of questions were developed for the purpose of describing participation in formal organizations of various sorts, definitions of the local area, domestic participation, neighborhood play of children, and other aspects of participation which will not be reported here.

An area random sample was interviewed in each tract, with 161 respondents in the low-urban tract, 150 in the high-urban tract. These households represented approximately 7 per cent of the populations of the two census tracts chosen. The housewife was the respondent, and the response rate was over 85 per cent, being higher in the low-urban area. Interviewers were advanced and graduate students at Occidental College, and the average interview time was approximately one hour.

The two samples of households compare as follows.

Income: 20 per cent of the households in each area had less than $3,000 annually; 37 per cent in the low-urban area and 31 per cent in the high-urban area had annual incomes between $3,000 and $5,000; 35 per cent in the low-urban area and 38 per cent in the high-urban area had over $5,000 annually. Those who did not know or declined to state were 8 per cent in the low-urban area, 11 per cent in the high-urban area. The chief difference was a preponderance of middle income households in the low-urban area, with somewhat more heterogeneity in the high-urban area.

Occupation: using the blue collar-white collar break, the samples were identical. In both areas, 72 per cent of the employed respondents were white-collar. Seventy-two per cent of the husbands in each area were in clerical jobs or higher.

Education: if education is divided into three classes, elementary or less, some high school or completed high school, and some college or more, the low-urban sample is slightly more homogeneous. Both respondents and husbands are 60 per cent high-school educated, with approximately 15 per cent below and 25 per cent above this class. In the high-urban sample the middle category accounted for only 50 per cent, with approximately 25 per cent below and 25 per cent above this class.

Such differences are not great but seem to indicate a consistent tendency towards somewhat more heterogeneity in the high-urban sample. It includes a slightly higher proportion of low-income, low-education persons, and also a slightly higher proportion of high-income, high-education persons. The high-urban sample is also more heterogeneous with respect to ethnicity. Although the percentage of non-white and foreign-born is similar in the two samples (9 for the low-urban sample, 11 for the high-urban) differences in religious affiliation indicate more ethnic diversity in the high-urban sample.

The low-urban area sample is much more homogeneous and Protestant in affiliation and preference. The high-urban sample, however, includes sizeable representations of the minority American religious beliefs: Jews and Roman Catholics are, together, only 20 per cent of the low-urban sample; they are 37 per cent of the high-urban sample. This heterogeneous and non-Protestant population in the high-urban sample is probably, to a large degree, made up of second and later generation ethnic individuals. Since the census tracts with high indexes of segregation in middle economic ranks are usually found in the more highly urbanized areas of the Shevky-Bell grid, it is likely that "later generation ethnics" (not identified in census data) are also concentrated in the more highly urbanized tracts of the middle social rank.

Such a correlation between second and later generation ethnic populations and urbanization, however, does not allow the reduction of the urbanization dimension to the ethnic component. In truth, many of these individuals are in process of leaving their ethnic status behind. Instead, it may be said that one of the attributes indicated by the urbanization index is apt to be the presence of second and later generation ethnics in the midst of acculturation. Such heterogeneity between faiths and within faiths is one of the conditions that give highly urbanized populations their particular characteristics.

Empirical Findings

Table 4–1 gives differences in participation between two areas with respect to the localization of community. The low-urban sample differed sharply and consistently in the direction of more participation in the local community. Their neighboring score was higher, they were more apt to have friends in the local area, and these constituted a larger proportion of all close friends, i.e., those visited at least once a month. They were more apt to go to cultural events such as movies, athletic contests, stage shows, and study groups, in the local area, and they were more apt to use local commercial facilities of certain types.

The low-urban sample had a higher rate of membership and participation in formal organizations other than church, and, more important, a larger proportion of their organizations were local in nature. A large majority of the respondents' organizations held meetings in the local area, and although the husbands' organizations usually met outside the area, still a much larger proportion met locally than did in the high-urban sample. Furthermore, the members of formal organizations to which the low-urban sample belonged were more apt to live in the immediate local community. In the high-urban sample other members were most apt to be scattered over the metropolis as a whole.

Further indication of the differential importance the local based organization had for these two samples is the greater familiarity of the low-urban sample with local community leaders. (See Table 4–2.)

While the samples were equally able (and unable) to name Los Angeles leaders, there was a significantly higher proportion who could name local leaders in the low-urban area sample. This probably indicates a uniform engagement of the middle-rank populations in the affairs of the metropolis as a whole, but definite variations in their interest and involvement with respect to local affairs.

It is sometimes stated, almost as an axiom, that the urban milieu results in the extreme attrition of kin relations. The present study indicates this to be questionable. The most important single kind of social relationship for both samples is kinship visiting. A large majority of both samples visit

65

TABLE 4-1

Local Community Participation in Two Urban Areas

TYPE OF SOCIAL PARTICIPATION	LOW URBAN*	HIGH URBAN*
Per cent of respondents with high neighboring scores		
(Scale types 2 through 5)	67†	56†
N of respondents	(162)	(150)
Per cent of respondents with friends in the local area	50	29
N of respondents	(162)	(150)
Per cent of all respondents' friends who live in local area	41	25
N of all friends	(441)	(316)
Per cent of respondents attending cultural events in local area, of those attending any cultural events	45	18
N attending any events	(101)	(92)
Per cent of respondents' formal organizations which meet in:		
Local area	62	26
Other areas	35	71
No response	3	3
N of organizations	(126)	(67)
Per cent of respondents' formal organizations with the majority of members residing in:		
Local area	57	33
Other area	18	18
Scattered over the city	23	45
No response	2	4
N of organizations	(126)	(67)
Per cent of husbands' formal organizations (as reported by respondent) which meet in:		
Local area	21‡	5‡
Other areas	73	86
No response	6	9
N of husbands' organizations	(104)	(57)
Per cent of husbands' formal organizations (as reported by respondent) with the majority of members residing in:		
Local area	25	10
Other area	23	12
Scattered over the city	45	77
No response	7	1
N of husbands' organizations	(104)	(57)

* P $(x^2) < .01$, with exceptions noted below.
† P (x^2) slightly above .05 level: $x^2 = 3.77$.
‡ P (x^2) between .01 and .02 levels.

TABLE 4-2

*Respondents' Ability to Name Leaders
of the Local Area and of Los Angeles*

	LOW URBAN	HIGH URBAN
Per cent of respondents who could name at least one local leader	32*	21*
N of respondents	(162)	(150)
Per cent of respondents who could name at least one Los Angeles leader	38†	37†
N of respondents	(162)	(150)

* P (x^2) between .02 and .05 levels.
† Difference not significant.

their kin at least once a month, and *half of each sample visit their kin at least once a week.* These data, reported in Table 4–3, are consistent with the findings of Bell in his comparable study of social areas in the San Francisco Bay Region.[7]

Both samples indicated complacency with their neighborhood and said they were satisfied with it as a home, but in giving their reasons for liking it, they tended to differ. The low-urban sample described their area as a "little community," like a "small town," where "people are friendly and neighborly." The high-urban sample, on the other hand, most frequently mentioned the "convenience to downtown and everything," and spoke

TABLE 4-3

Kin Visiting in Two Urban Areas

PER CENT VISITING KIN	LOW URBAN*	HIGH URBAN*
Once a week or more often	49	55
At least once a month, but less than once a week	24	21
A few times a year, but less than once a month	11	8
Never	5	9
No kin in Los Angeles	11	7
N of respondents	(162)	(150)

*No significant difference between low and high urban area samples.

often of the "nice people" who "leave you alone and mind their own business." The high-urban sample seemed less committed to remaining in their present area—a higher proportion stating that there were other neighborhoods in the city in which they would rather live.

A tendency toward differential association with populations at a similar level of urbanization is indicated in the visiting patterns of the two samples outside their local areas. The residences of close friends and the meeting places of social circles are almost mutually exclusive for the two samples. Furthermore, when the census tracts in which are located the homes of the friends they visit are categorized by urbanization scores, clear differences appear. The low-urban sample is more apt to have friends in other low-urban areas, while the high-urban sample is apt to visit in other high-urban areas. (See Table 4-4.)

When it is recalled that these two samples are almost identical with respect to social rank and segregation, the importance of the urbanization dimension is underlined. These visiting patterns refer to well structured friendship relations of probable importance. Such differential association may result from proximity, as well as selective visiting by levels of urbanization. The relative importance of proximity will be measured through the use of the intervening opportunities model. However, even if such differential association is to a large degree a function of spatial proximity, its significance in certain respects would remain. For, if populations at given levels of urbanization interact more intensely within those levels than with other

TABLE 4-4

Residence of Friends Visited, Outside of the Local Area, by Urbanization Index Score *

	LOW URBAN†	HIGH URBAN†
Per cent of friends living in tracts with urbanization index score of		
1-20	13	12
21-40	35	25
41-60	41	33
61-80	8	19
81-100	3	11
N of friends visited	(180)	(162)

*Friends' addresses which could not be coded (80 in the Low Urban area, 65 in the High Urban) are excluded.
†P $(x^2) < .001$.

populations, such interactions should result in fairly stable networks of informal communication and influence. The content of such communication should vary with urbanization.

Summary and Interpretation

In order to investigate empirically the complex of notions surrounding the nature of urban social behavior, the Shevky-Bell typology, applied to sub-areas in Los Angeles County, was used to select two neighborhoods which differed clearly on the index of urbanization. Social rank was not used as the chief factor accounting for differential social participation, as was the case in the studies of Komarovsky, Goldhamer, and others.[8] Instead, rank was controlled, and the urbanization dimension was tested for broad differences in social participation.

It should be noted that this study investigates the effects of urbanization at a *particular* level of rank and segregation; at other levels, the effects of urbanization remain problematical. It is hoped that future studies will clarify, for example, the effects of differential urbanization at higher and lower social ranks, as well as in segregated populations. The Shevky-Bell typology, based upon a three dimensional attribute-space model of urban society, calls attention not only to three separate factors, but also to the possibility that the particular effects of one may be transformed as either or both of the others vary.

However, the urbanization dimension was the focus of the present study. It was not identified with the older notion of urbanism which implies that all city populations are changing in the direction of atomistic, mass society.[9] Instead, it was assumed that there is a continuum of alternative life-styles at the same economic level and that these are concentrated in different urban sub-areas. In this framework, the low-urban areas are just as characteristic of modern urban society as are the high-urban areas. Both types continue to be alternatives in the urban complex. In this view, the Shevky-Bell index of urbanization is a putative means of identifying such variations in "ways of life." Instead of concentrating on urbanism as *a* way of life, the present study was focused upon the variations possible.

Two social aggregates, inhabiting tracts with similar economic rank and ethnicity but varying with respect to the urbanization index, were sampled. The sample populations were then studied by means of reported social participation.

The findings are consistent with the hypothesis that, where rank and ethnicity are equal, differences in the urbanization index will indicate differences in social behavior. Had the index identified populations not significantly different, doubt would have been cast upon its utility at the level of individual social behavior, for the urbanization dimension of modern society, as conceived by Shevky in his theoretical structure, implies such differences in social behavior.[10] However, the present study indicates that the index, constructed primarily with items related to family structure, does identify differences in social participation which are associated with variations in family structure but not derived solely from them. The general validity of the hypothesis must rest upon further studies in Los Angeles and other urban complexes. Although this study and that of Bell indicate the urbanization dimension does affect social participation to an impressive degree, the regularity with which these differences form a continuum at this intersection of social rank and segregation, and the nature of the hypothesized continuum, remain to be spelled out. Still, in the interpretation of the findings here reported, the following implications come to mind.

1. The local area in the contemporary American metropolis may be viewed as attracting population, not only by the economic rank and ethnic composition of the population already in the area, but also by the degree of urbanization characteristic of the area—the way of life common to the older inhabitants.

2. Such areas may attract populations on at least two different functional bases: (1) the demographic and the cultural characteristics of the older settlers, who give the area its "tone," may attract people, as seems true in the low-urban sample, or, (2) the area as a socially neutral, but convenient, base of operations for various segmental interests, may attract people as in the high-urban sample. Such different principles of attraction would tend to produce greater homogeneity of background and interest in low-urban areas, and from this similarity a higher degree of community-type behavior and of conformity would be expected.

3. A continuum is hypothesized for non-segregated, middle-rank areas. At one pole lie the local areas which select a predominantly "old American" population with similar jobs, aspirations, incomes, who wish to raise children, neighbor, participate in local community groups, and, in brief, carry on a life in many ways similar to that of the small towns described by Warner and his associates.[11] At the other pole lie those areas of the city which are more heterogeneous, with fewer children and little interest in the local area as a social arena. Such areas may approach, in many ways, the ideal type of urban environment hypothesized by Wirth.[12]

4. In this perspective, the local area is important as a framework for

interaction, as a "social fact," just where it is least representative of the total urban society. The small community, as studied by Warner and others, is a very poor example of the urban complex, since it will include the fewest elements of urban society as a whole. At the same time, the high-urban tract as a sample of urban society is only slightly less biased, for in it the local area as a social fact disappears altogether. Thus it is not possible to use either the model of a small, spatially enclosed community or the stereotype of the continually more atomistic mass society in describing social participation in the contemporary metropolis.

There are, however, certain common structural threads running through the fabric of modern society. As Paul Hatt noted, the indices developed by Warner and others to measure social status may be generalized to the total society, since the various methods correlate highly with one universal attribute—occupation.[13] The present approach is, then, to ask: How does this attribute become defined and organized, how does it influence participation, in different sub-areas of the metropolis?

A tentative answer is that the individual's social position is defined differently and his social participation is patterned differently as the focus shifts from the low-urban populations to the high-urban populations. One may envisage the low-urban areas as somewhere between the small town and the conventional picture of metropolitan living. Where the local area is a social fact, where common interests and associations obtain, generalizations derived from small community studies may have validity. For here the individual's status will result, in part, from participation in a known and used local organizational structure and from family ties that are publicly understood.

When, however, high-urban populations are considered, social participation is organized around position in other organizational contexts, as for example, the corporation, politics, the labor union, or perhaps, as Riesman has suggested, categories derived from the popular culture of the mass media.[14] Here also are many individuals whose life, aside from work, is ordered by participation in small informal groups, and informal groups only, floating within the vast culture world of the market and the mass media. In such populations the locally defined community is largely irrelevant to status and participation, Associations are spread geographically, but ordered and concentrated in terms of selected interests. Family, in this context, is still important. It is slightly more important in the high-urban sample described. But it is probably much more private in its reference. In fact, kin relations may be seen as growing in importance just because of the diminished reliance placed upon neighborhood and local community.

What has been sketched above is a tentative model which will allow the use of contributions from earlier research, (studies of small cities, natural areas, the apartment house family, the suburban fringe) within a framework which integrates and orders them in relation to one another. Such a frame of reference also relates, eventually, to the increasing importance of large-scale organizations in a society which allows many alternative life patterns for individuals at the same functional and economic level.

NOTES

Revised version of paper read at the annual meeting of the American Sociological Society, September, 1954. The study was carried out by the Laboratory in Urban Culture, a research facility of Occidental College, with the support of the John Randolph Haynes and Dora Haynes Foundation. I wish to express gratitude to Ella Kube, Research Associate, for assistance in the computation and analysis upon which the report is based.

1. Donald L. Foley, "Neighbors or Urbanites? The Study of a Rochester District," *The University of Rochester's Studies of Metropolitan Rochester*, Rochester, New York, 1952.

2. Eshref Shevky and Wendell Bell, *Social Area Analysis*, Stanford, California: Stanford University Press, 1955. See also, Eshref Shevky and Marilyn Williams, *The Social Areas of Los Angeles*, Berkeley and Los Angeles: University of California Press, 1948.

3. For a description of the statistical analysis and testing of the typology, see Wendell Bell, "Economic, Family, and Ethnic Status," *American Sociological Review*, 20 (February, 1955), pp. 45–52.

4. The extension of the study to include two additional sample tracts will be reported later; results are generally consistent with the findings reported here. Rank and segregation are the same in the added tract samples, but the new tracts extend to the extremes of the urbanization index within middle economic rank.

5. Paul Wallin, "A Guttman Scale for Measuring Women's Neighborliness," *American Journal of Sociology*, 49 (November, 1953), pp. 243–246.

6. Stuart A. Queen, "Social Participation in Relation to Social Disorganization," *American Sociological Review*, 14 (April, 1949), pp. 251–256.

7. Wendell Bell (with the assistance of Maryanne Force and Marion Boat), "People of the City," (processed) Stanford University Survey Research Facility, Stanford, California, 1954.

8. Mirra Komarovsky, "The Voluntary Associations of Urban Dwellers," *American Sociological Review*, 11 (December, 1946), pp. 868–896; Herbert Goldhamer, "Voluntary Associations in the United States," unpublished Ph.D. thesis, University of Chicago, 1942.

9. See Louis Wirth, "Urbanism as a Way of Life," *The American Journal of Sociology*, 44 (July, 1938), pp. 1–24.

10. Shevky and Bell, *op. cit.*, especially Chapter II.

11. See, for example, W. Lloyd Warner and associates, *Democracy in Jonesville*, New York: Harper and Brothers, 1949.

12. Wirth, *op. cit.*

13. Paul K. Hatt, "Stratification in the Mass Society," *American Sociological Review*, 15 (April, 1950), pp. 216–222.

14. David Riesman, in collaboration with Reuel Denny and Nathan Glazer, *The Lonely Crowd, A Study of the Changing American Character*, New Haven: Yale University Press, 1950, especially Chs. X, XI, XII.

5

WENDELL BELL AND MARYANNE T. FORCE

URBAN NEIGHBORHOOD TYPES
AND PARTICIPATION
IN FORMAL ASSOCIATIONS

This paper reports part of a study of social participation conducted in San Francisco in the spring of 1953. The investigation rested upon two main notions:

First, that the major social roles which an individual occupies regulate the amount and nature of his participation in society. For example, if one knew a person's economic, family, and ethnic status, his age and sex, his aspirations or expectations regarding the roles he might achieve, and his status history with respect to these types of statuses, one should be able to predict closely that person's participation in the various activities of society.

Second, that the social type of neighborhood in which an urbanite lives is an efficient indicator of his social participation and may be a significant factor in its own right in shaping his social participation. It has been contended, for example, that social differences between the populations of urban neighborhoods can be conveniently summarized into differences of economic level, family characteristics, and ethnicity.[1] It is our hypothesis that neighborhood populations having different configurations with respect to these three variables will have different patterns of social participation.

This paper will be limited to an examination of the relationship between amount of formal association participation and certain of the above mentioned individual status and neighborhood differences. Other papers are in preparation dealing with additional aspects of individual social participation.

Following Komarovsky, all formally organized groups are included in our definition of formal associations ". . . except economic concerns

Reprinted with permission from *American Sociological Review* 21 (1956): 25–34.

(stores, corporations), governmental agencies, and schools."[2] Thus, all non-profit formal organizations are included unless they are part of the governmental body. "Their functions are characterized by explicit regularity and standardization—such as being identified by a name, or having officers, or having a written constitution, or having regular meetings."[3] This follows generally accepted definitions of "voluntary associations," "formal organizations," or "formal groups."

Description of the Sample

Selection of the Neighborhoods. Using the census tract scores given in *Social Area Analysis*[4] four census tracts were selected in San Francisco in which to conduct the study of social participation. The identifying place names, census tract designations, and index scores for the four tracts selected are given in Table 5-1. It was decided to hold ethnicity constant as far as possible, so all four of the tracts selected contain relatively few non-whites and few members of foreign-born groups, as indicated by their relatively low scores on the index of ethnic status. Census tracts N-8 (located in the Mission district) and M-6 (located in the Outer Mission district) have low scores on the index of economic status relative to the scores of the other census tracts in the San Francisco Bay Region. The Mission population, however, is a rooming-house district with a relatively low score on the index of family status, having a low fertility ratio, many women in the labor force, and few single-family detached dwellings. The

TABLE 5-1

Identifying Place Names, Census Tract Designations, and Index Scores for the Four Study Tracts *

INDEX	MISSION (N-8)	PACIFIC HEIGHTS (B-6)	OUTER MISSION (M-6)	ST. FRANCIS WOOD (O-7)
Economic status†	46	96	43	92
Family status‡	28	9	67	70
Ethnic status§	14	7	20	6

* Index scores can vary approximately from 0 to 100.
† Composed of measures of occupation and education.
‡ Composed of measures of fertility, women not in the labor force, and single family detached dwelling units.
§ Per cent of persons in the census tract who are nonwhite or foreign born white from Southern and Eastern Europe, Asia, and French Canada.

population of Outer Mission has a relatively high score on the index of family status and is characterized by high fertility ratios, few women in the labor force, and many single-family detached dwellings. Census tract B-6 in the Pacific Heights district and is a high-rent apartment house area, having a relatively high economic level, but a low score on family status. Census tract O-7 contains the district known as St. Francis Wood and, like Pacific Heights, contains a population having high economic status, but like Outer Mission is a single family home area characterized by a high score on family status.

Selection of the Respondents. A probability area sample was selected for each of the study census tracts. First, a complete list of dwelling units in each of the tracts was compiled by means of standard block listing procedures. Second, a sampling interval (k) was established for each tract, and a sample of dwellings drawn by taking a random number from 1 to k and selecting every kth dwelling unit thereafter. Third, within each sample dwelling one male over the age of 21 was selected as the respondent, thus eliminating from this study social participation differences resulting from the differential requirements of the roles of the two sexes. Dwellings containing no males over age 21 were removed from the sample, and in those which contained two or more males over age 21 one male was selected randomly from a respondent selection table provided on each interview schedule. In order to assure randomness in the sample no substitutions were allowed.

Response Rates. St. Francis Wood (high family and high economic status) had the highest per cent of completed interviews with 90.8 per cent of the number of qualified respondents in the sample fully completing their interviews. Pacific Heights (low family and high economic status) had a response rate of 84.9 per cent, Mission (low family and low economic status) had 83.9 per cent, and Outer Mission (high family and low economic status) had 83.3 per cent. Refusal rates were higher in the two low economic status neighborhoods than in the two high economic status neighborhoods, but refusals accounted for most of the loss in completed interviews in all four neighborhoods. People seemed to be more suspicious of the interviewers in Outer Mission than in the other tracts, although a recent robbery in Mission influenced several respondents not to open the doors to their rooms until they had made certain of the identity of the interviewer. The resistance occurred in spite of several articles in the metropolitan papers describing the study, television programs featuring a discussion of the study, advance letters to the respondents, official credentials carried by each interviewer, and the co-operation of the Police Department in identifying *bona fide* interviewers to the householders.

Amount of Participation by Neighborhood

Number of Formal Group Memberships. One measure of formal group participation used in many previous studies and employed in this study is the sheer number of memberships in formal associations. Table 5–2 contains the per cent of persons in each neighborhood who belong to a certain number of formal organizations.[5] From Table 5–2 it can be seen that in each of the different neighborhoods more than 76 per cent of the men belong to at least one formal group. This finding is comparable to the findings of other studies of formal group membership in urban areas. Goldhamer[6] in his study of Chicago residents found that 70 per cent of the men belonged to one or more formal groups, and Axelrod[7] found that 80 per cent of the men in his Detroit sample belonged to at least one formal group.

However, these figures indicate considerably higher membership in one or more formal associations than is given in some other studies of formal participation among urban dwellers, especially among those men who are blue-collar workers. Komarovsky,[8] for example, reports that 60 per cent of the working class men belong to no formal associations. Dotson[9] presents similar findings for a later period in New Haven. It is not clear whether the inconsistency of our findings with those of Komarovsky and Dotson is due to regional differences, Komarovsky's low response rate (29 per cent of the questionnaires were returned), Dotson's small sample of men ($N = 50$), or variations in degree of unionization. (If memberships in labor unions were not counted in our two low economic level neighborhoods, then our findings would correspond to theirs.)

Although the data shown in Table 5–2 support the contention that the formal association is widespread throughout diverse social groupings in an urban environment, only about a third or less of the men in every neighborhood, except St. Francis Wood, belong to three or more formal associations.

Comparing the tracts with respect to the number of formal group memberships, we find that the high economic status tracts contain relatively more men who belong to a greater number of formal associations than do the low economic status tracts. The largest percentage (66.1 per cent) of men belonging to three or more associations is in St. Francis Wood, and the next largest percentage (35.6 per cent) is in Pacific Heights. The two low economic level neighborhoods at each level of family status have significantly ($p < .01$) lower percentages of men who report that they

TABLE 5-2

Per Cent of Men Having Membership in a Certain Number of Formal Associations

NUMBER OF GROUPS	LOW FAMILY LOW ECON. (MISSION) PER CENT	LOW FAMILY HIGH ECON. (PACIFIC HEIGHTS) PER CENT	HIGH FAMILY LOW ECON. (OUTER MISSION) PER CENT	HIGH FAMILY HIGH ECON. (ST. FRANCIS WOOD) PER CENT
Seven or more	1.7	11.0	0	19.0
Six	0	2.6	0	4.2
Five	1.2	3.2	1.2	11.9
Four	2.3	7.3	2.9	13.7
Three	11.6	11.5	8.8	17.3
Two	22.1	23.0	22.4	13.7
One	37.8	19.9	44.7	13.1
None	23.3	21.5	19.4	7.1
Not ascertained	0	0	0.6	0
Total	100.0	100.0	100.0	100.0
Number of cases	(172)	(191)	(170)	(168)

belong to three or more associations with 16.8 per cent so reporting in Mission and 12.9 per cent so reporting in Outer Mission.

Differences between neighborhoods having different family status, holding economic status constant, are not consistent, although at the high economic level St. Francis Wood, having high family status, has a much larger percentage of men who belong to three or more associations than does Pacific Heights, the low family status neighborhood. Pacific Heights also contains a larger percentage of men who belong to no associations than does St. Francis Wood.

Attendance at Formal Group Meetings. The mere number of memberships does not give adequate information regarding the amount of participation in formal associations, since membership in some cases may be only nominal. Table 5–3 contains the frequency of attendance at all formal association meetings for these men who report belonging to at least one such organization.[10]

In St. Francis Wood only 5.8 per cent, in Mission 12.1 per cent, in Pacific Heights 14.1 per cent, and in Outer Mission 17.5 per cent of the members of formal groups do not attend meetings. Thus, the vast majority of the members in each of the neighborhoods, in excess of 82 per cent, attend at least one meeting a year.

This finding is fairly consistent with those of Axelrod[11] who found that 22 per cent of the men who belong to formal groups in Detroit attended

TABLE 5-3

Per Cent of Formal Association Members Who Attend a Specified Number of Meetings

FREQUENCY OF ATTENDANCE	LOW FAMILY LOW ECON. (MISSION) PER CENT	LOW FAMILY HIGH ECON. (PACIFIC HEIGHTS) PER CENT	HIGH FAMILY LOW ECON. (OUTER MISSION) PER CENT	HIGH FAMILY HIGH ECON. (ST. FRANCIS WOOD) PER CENT
More than once a week	8.3	30.9	6.6	26.9
About once a week	8.3	15.4	10.9	14.1
A few times a month	28.8	17.4	16.1	23.1
About once a month	17.4	6.7	16.1	6.4
A few times a year	19.0	12.1	25.5	19.9
About once a year	6.1	3.4	6.6	3.8
Never	12.1	14.1	17.5	5.8
Not ascertained	0	0	0.7	0
Total	100.0	100.0	100.0	100.0
Number of members	(132)	(149)	(137)	(156)

no formal group meetings during a three month period, although Dotson[12] found that of the number of memberships held by men in his sample in New Haven as many as one-third were inactive.

When the members in the four neighborhoods are compared with respect to the frequency of formal association attendance, marked differences between neighborhoods appear. Again, the greatest amount of formal participation occurs among the persons who live in the high economic status neighborhoods. Men living in St. Francis Wood and Pacific Heights who belong to formal associations attend more frequently than those living in Mission and Outer Mission. In Pacific Heights 30.9 per cent of the members attend meetings more than once a week compared to only 8.3 per cent in Mission (p < .01); in St. Francis Wood 26.7 per cent of the members attend meetings more than once a week compared to only 6.6 per cent in Outer Mission (p < .01).

Considering those men who belong to formal associations but who attend only about once a year or less, it may be noted that Pacific Heights, the high economic, low family status neighborhood, has almost as large a percentage of men who are relatively isolated from social contacts in formal groups as the two low economic status neighborhoods. Since Pacific Heights, Mission, and Outer Mission are the neighborhoods with the largest percentages of men who do not belong to formal groups, it is evident that sizeable segments of the population in these three neighborhoods are socially isolated from this form of participation. This is consistent with the general conclusion of Komarovsky who says with respect to formal group participation that a large segment of the population, particularly the lower social and economic level ". . . is cut off from channels of power, information, growth and a sense of participation in purposive social action."[13] We would add to this generalization that even on the higher economic levels a significant segment of these men living in neighborhoods of low family status are similarly isolated.

Office Holding in Formal Associations. Generally, holding positions of leadership in a formal association denotes more active participation in the group than not holding positions of leadership. Thus, a third measure of formal association participation used in this study, and one which indicates the relative power position of the individual within the association, is whether or not the individual holds office in the formal associations to which he belongs. Table 5–4 contains a summary presentation of this material. Consistent with our other findings, the high economic status neighborhoods contain a larger percentage of members who hold office in a formal association than do the low economic status neighborhoods at each level of family status. Pacific Heights (24.5 per cent) contains a larger percentage than Mission (13.0 per cent) (p. < .05), and St. Francis Wood (34.8 per cent) contains a larger percentage than Outer Mission (11.6 per cent) (p < .01).

Although no difference appears between the two low economic status neighborhoods, the relative number of office holders is somewhat higher in St. Francis Wood (high economic and high family status) than it is in Pacific Heights (high economic and low family status). Our findings consistently show that the higher economic status neighborhoods contain relatively more men who belong to formal associations, more members who frequently attend meetings, and more members who hold office in

TABLE 5-4

Per Cent of Formal Association Members Who Hold Offices

HOLDS OFFICE	LOW FAMILY LOW ECON. (MISSION) PER CENT	LOW FAMILY HIGH ECON. (PACIFIC HEIGHTS) PER CENT	HIGH FAMILY LOW ECON. (OUTER MISSION) PER CENT	HIGH FAMILY HIGH ECON. (ST. FRANCIS WOOD) PER CENT
Yes	13.0	24.5	11.6	34.8
No	86.3	74.8	87.7	65.2
Not ascertained	0.7	0.7	0.7	0
Total	100.0	100.0	100.0	100.0
Number of cases	(131)	(151)	(138)	(155)

formal associations when compared with neighborhoods of a lower economic level.

The differences by family status are not so large nor so consistent, although at the high economic status level, the lower family status neighborhood contains a higher percentage of men who are socially isolated with respect to formal association participation by all three measures of participation used here than the higher family status neighborhood contains.

Individual and Neighborhood Characteristics

Education, Occupation, and Income. Thus far in the analysis the discussion has been limited to the formal association participation of men as that behavior is related to the social type of neighborhood in which the men live. In effect, we have been assigning to each man his neighborhood scores for economic and family status, and relating his formal association behavior to these scores. However, the neighborhoods are not completely homogeneous with respect to economic and family status; that is, each man by some measure of his own individual economic or family status does not necessarily have a score which equals the average for his neighborhood. A neighborhood's score has been referred to as a unit variable, and an individual's own score as a personal variable.[14] In this section we wish to explore further the relationship between economic position and formal association by tabulating these two types of variables simultaneously.

Since the most significant and consistent findings concern economic and not family status, the study neighborhoods have been grouped so that the two low economic status neighborhoods, Mission and Outer Mission, are together, and the two high economic status neighborhoods, Pacific Heights and St. Francis Wood, are together. Education, occupation, and annual family income were taken as measures of personal economic status. As is shown in Table 5-5, the high economic status neighborhoods contain relatively more men with higher education, with white collar occupations, and with higher incomes; and the low economic status neighborhoods contain relatively more men with lower education, blue collar occupations, and lower incomes. However, there is a small percentage of men living in the high economic status neighborhoods who have either relatively low education, blue collar jobs, or relatively low incomes, that is,

TABLE 5-5

*Per Cent of Men Having Selected Socio-Economic
Characteristics by Neighborhood*

SOCIO-ECONOMIC CHARACTERISTICS	NEIGHBORHOOD CHARACTERISTICS	
	LOW ECONOMIC STATUS (MISSION AND OUTER MISSION) PER CENT	HIGH ECONOMIC STATUS (PACIFIC HEIGHTS AND ST. FRANCIS WOOD) PER CENT
Education		
Some college or more	9.6	50.4
Completed high school only	24.6	25.6
Some high school	23.7	13.1
Grade school or less	42.1	10.9
Not ascertained	0.0	0.0
Total	100.0	100.0
Number of cases	(342)	(359)
Occupation		
Profs., mgrs., props., and offs.	12.9	67.4
Sales, clerical, and kind. workers	8.5	21.2
Craftsmen, foremen, and operatives	57.0	8.6
Service workers and laborers	21.6	2.5
Not ascertained	0.0	0.3
Total	100.0	100.0
Number of cases	(342)	(359)
Income		
$10,000 and over	2.0	41.5
6,000–9,999	18.4	28.7
3,000–5,999	65.0	20.9
0–2,999	14.0	5.3
Not ascertained	0.6	3.6
Total	100.0	100.0
Number of cases	(342)	(359)

who would be classified as low economic status on the basis of personal variables even though they are living in high economic status neighborhoods. Similarly, there are in the low economic status neighborhoods small percentages of men who would be classified as high economic status on the basis of their personal ratings on education, occupation, and income. The question arises whether differences in amount of formal association participation between high and low economic status neighborhoods still exist when controls are introduced for personal economic status.

Table 5–6 shows the per cent of men who attend formal association meetings frequently by the average economic status of the neighborhood and by the respondent's own education, occupation, and family income. Comparing the percentages *within each neighborhood*, the general tendency is for relatively more frequent attenders to have higher education, white collar occupations, and higher incomes. This, of course, is consistent with the findings of many studies which have related such measures to formal association participation.

Of particular interest here, however, is the comparison of amount of formal association participation between neighborhoods, holding personal education, occupation, and income constant. For example, a larger percentage of the men who have been to college are frequent attenders in the high economic status neighborhoods than in the low economic status neighborhoods. This is also true of the men in the less educated categories. At each of the educational levels the men living in the higher economic status neighborhoods are more likely to be frequent attenders than are the men living in the lower economic status neighborhoods. ($\Sigma\chi^2 = 15.78$, p < .01)

Although not statistically significant, a similar tendency can be seen when personal occupation and income are held constant. Men with high occupations are more likely to be frequent attenders if they live in the high economic status neighborhoods. The same is true for the other occupational groups. For example, men who are service workers and laborers are more likely to be frequent attenders if they live in the high economic status neighborhoods. A similar tendency occurs between the two neighborhoods when comparing men who have similar incomes. Those who live in the high economic status neighborhoods are somewhat more likely than those who live in the low economic status neighborhoods to be frequent attenders at formal association meetings. Thus, differences in formal association participation still exist when comparing the low with the high economic status neighborhoods, even when certain measures of personal economic status are controlled.

There seem to be at least two explanations for these findings. First, the neighborhood characteristics may be an index to the self image of the individual, and second, the type of neighborhood in which a person lives may itself be a factor in the kinds of pressures which are brought upon the individual to participate in formal associations.

In the first instance the lower economic status persons who live in high economic status neighborhoods and the higher economic status persons who live in low economic status neighborhoods may be the "deviants" who are found in many stratification studies; that is, they may be those

TABLE 5-6

Per Cent of Men Who Attend Formal Association
Meetings Frequently by Neighborhood and Individual
*Socio-Economic Characteristics**

INDIVIDUAL SOCIO-ECONOMIC CHARACTERISTICS	NEIGHBORHOOD CHARACTERISTICS	
	LOW ECONOMIC STATUS (MISSION AND OUTER MISSION) PER CENT	HIGH ECONOMIC STATUS (PACIFIC HEIGHTS AND ST. FRANCIS WOOD) PER CENT
Education		
Some college or more	27.3 (33)	46.4 (181)
Completed high school only	14.5 (83)	28.3 (92)
Some high school	17.3 (81)	30.4 (46)
Grade school or less	7.6 (144)	23.1 (39)
Occupation		
Profs., mgrs., props., and offs.	32.6 (43)	42.7 (241)
Sales, clerical, and kind. workers	20.7 (29)	26.3 (76)
Craftsmen, foremen, and operatives	9.3 (194)	22.6 (31)
Service workers and laborers	10.8 (74)	33.3 (9)
Income		
$10,000 and over	0.0 (4)	53.4 (148)
6,000–9,999	16.9 (65)	29.1 (103)
3,000–5,999	13.1 (222)	20.0 (75)
0–2,999	12.5 (48)	15.8 (19)

*Men were classified frequent attenders if they attended meetings 37 or more times per year. The total number of cases on which the percentage is based is given in parentheses in each case.

whose objective class position does not seem congruent with their own placement of themselves. The economic characteristics of the neighborhoods in which they live, however, may give important objective clues regarding their group identification and, thereby, give indications of certain kinds of behavioral and attitudinal correlates.

The second case would involve the effect of the neighborhood in determining the role expectations of the individual after the individual became a part of the neighborhood. For example, persons living in high economic status neighborhoods may come under much greater pressures to participate in certain types of associations than do persons living in low economic status neighborhoods. Neighborhood improvement associations, civic groups, welfare and charitable organizations, etc., are more likely to have members from high economic status neighborhoods than from low economic status neighborhoods.

Family Characteristics. Within each of the four neighborhoods the number of formal association memberships, as well as the frequency of attendance at formal association meetings, was tabulated against marital status, age of children, employment status of wife, and type of dwelling (single family detached vs. two or more family dwelling). Although other writers report relationships between formal association participation and these variables, we find no consistent trends when making comparisons within each of the neighborhoods.

Age Differences. Many writers have investigated the relationship between age and formal association participation. Axelrod,[15] for example, in his Detroit study finds that formal association membership starts out relatively low in early adulthood, reaches a peak in the forties, and then declines to a new low by the sixties. He also finds this same pattern for the very active participants. Goldhamer found that when participation is measured by frequency of attendance, the young men tend to exceed the older men and that participation tends to decline in the oldest age group (fifty and over).[16] From this study of persons aged 65 and over living in a California community of retired people, McKain noted that formal association participation declined with advanced years; about 50 per cent of those over age 65 reported that they gave less time to associations than they did when they were 50 years of age, only 1 per cent said that their social activities had increased.[17] These findings have been interpreted by some as indicating a structural relationship between the adult life cycle and formal association participation: *ties within formal associations preventing many formal associations in the twenties;* consolidation of occupational position, a home and a family leading the individual to join associations in the thirties; formal associations becoming an end in themselves in the forties and occupying more time; children grown to adulthood, retirement, and loss of physical stamina and vigor resulting in less and less formal association participation at the older age groups.[18]

Annual formal association attendance by age is given in Table 5–7 for

TABLE 5-7

Annual Formal Association Attendance by Neighborhood and Age *

| | AGE | | |
| | 21—39 PER CENT | 40—59 PER CENT | 60 AND OVER PER CENT |
NEIGHBORHOOD			
Low family, low econ. (Mission) Attendances per year:			
37 or more	18.9	7.3	16.2
5—36	33.9	54.9	10.8
0—4	47.2	37.8	73.0
Total	100.0	100.0	100.0
	(53)	(82)	(37)
Low family, high econ. (Pacific Heights) Attendances per year:			
37 or more	28.3	35.6	43.9
5—36	32.6	19.6	17.5
0—4	39.1	44.8	38.6
Total	100.0	100.0	100.0
	(46)	(87)	(57)
High family, low econ. (Outer Mission) Attendances per year:			
37 or more	10.4	16.7	16.7
5—36	29.9	37.5	16.7
0—4	59.7	45.8	66.6
Total	100.0	100.0	100.0
	(67)	(72)	(30)
High family, high econ. (St. Francis Wood) Attendances per year:			
37 or more	21.4	38.0	53.1
5—36	53.6	33.3	25.0
0—4	25.0	28.7	21.9
Total	100.0	100.0	100.0
	(28)	(108)	(32)

*The numbers on which the percentages are based are given in parentheses.

each of the four study neighborhoods in San Francisco. These data require a revision of the above view, and constitute some evidence of the degree of difference in life styles of segments of the population at different levels of economic status. In each of the high economic status neighborhoods *the per cent of men who are active participants increases with increasing age.* No such relationship, however, occurs between age and formal association participation among the men who live in the low economic status neighborhoods. On the contrary, in these neighborhoods the smallest percentage of men who attend meetings "seldom or never" is in the middle age group and the largest percentage, who are thus "socially isolated," is in the older age group. Thus, the relationship between age and formal association participation in the low economic status neighborhoods approximates that found by most other writers, but we find an entirely different pattern in the high economic status neighborhoods.

There is some corroboration of our findings in Webber's study.[19] In Orlando, Florida he found that the older age group, which he defined as 70 or older, had a slightly greater nonmembership and slightly lower incidence of membership in two or more associations. However, he found the opposite relationship in a generally higher economic status community, West Palm Beach, where those under age 70 reported considerably higher nonmembership, and somewhat lower proportions in one or more associations. He also found that persons over age 70 in the latter community were more likely to attend five to nine meetings per month.[20]

In addition (see Table 5–7) the reported relationships between participation and neighborhood still hold within the three different age groups. The largest percentages of men who are frequent attenders live in Pacific Heights and St. Francis Wood, and Pacific Heights has a relatively larger number of men who attend seldom or never than does St. Francis Wood.

Summary

This paper has attempted to relate amount of formal association participation to some of the social types of neighborhoods in which men live and to certain social roles which men occupy. A brief review of the findings follows:

1. Although the four urban neighborhoods studied were widely divergent with respect to economic level and extent of family life, over three-fourths of the men hold membership in at least one formal group, and a relatively small percentage of these are inactive.

2. Men living in the high economic status neighborhoods belong to the greater number of associations, attend more frequently, and hold office more than men living in low economic status neighborhoods.

3. Comparing the two high economic status neighborhoods, the low family status neighborhood contains relatively more men who belong to no formal associations, who never attend meetings if they do belong, and who do not hold office than does the high family status neighborhood. No such relationship appears when comparing the two low economic status neighborhoods.

4. Within each of the neighborhoods persons of higher economic status, as indicated by their own individual educational level, income, and occupation, generally have a greater amount of associational participation than do individuals of lower economic status. However, holding individual economic status constant, persons living in the high economic status neighborhoods still have more associational participation than those living in the low economic status neighborhoods. Thus the economic characteristics of the neighborhood population as a unit may be an important indicator of the economic reference group for those living in the neighborhood, and may define a set of general societal expectations with respect to associational behavior for the residents.

5. It was reported that individual family status characteristics within each of the neighborhoods, such as marital status, age of children, employment status of wife, etc., showed no consistent relationship to formal association participation.

6. Finally, the relationship between age roles and associational participation depends upon economic level. In the high economic status neighborhoods the percentage of frequent attenders increases with increasing age, but in the low economic status neighborhoods no such trend exists. In fact, in the latter type of neighborhoods the relationship between age and participation tended to follow the pattern most often reported in other studies with the older aged persons being the most isolated and the middle aged persons the least isolated.

NOTES

The writers wish to express their appreciation to the Carnegie Corporation of New York and the Stanford University Committee for Research in the Social Sciences who furnished funds for the execution of the study of which this report is part. Harry V. Kincaid and Marion D. Boat made important contributions to this study, and we gratefully acknowledge their aid.

1. Eshref Shevky and Wendell Bell, *Social Area Analysis*, Stanford: Stanford University Press, 1955.

2. Mirra Komarovsky, "A Comparative Study of Voluntary Organizations of Two Suburban Communities," *Sociological Problems and Methods*, Volume 27, Publications of the American Sociological Society, 1933, p. 84.

3. Morris Axelrod, "A Study of Formal and Informal Group Participation in a Large Urban Community," unpublished Ph.D. dissertation (microfilmed), University of Michigan, 1953, pp. 14–15.

4. Shevky and Bell, *op. cit.*, pp. 61–66.

5. General church membership is not included, but memberships in church-connected groups are included throughout this paper.

6. Herbert Goldhamer, "Some Factors Affecting Participation in Voluntary Associations," unpublished Ph.D. dissertation (microfilmed), University of Chicago, 1942.

7. Axelrod, *op. cit.*

8. Mirra Komarovsky, "The Voluntary Associations of Urban Dwellers," *American Sociological Review*, 11 (December, 1946), pp. 686–698.

9. Floyd Dotson, "Patterns of Voluntary Association Among Working-Class Families," *American Sociological Review*, 16 (October, 1951), pp. 687–693.

10. General church attendance is not included here or elsewhere in this paper, but attendance at meetings of church-connected groups is included.

11. Axelrod, *op. cit.*

12. Dotson, *op. cit.*

13. Komarovsky, 1946, *op. cit.*, p. 698.

14. Paul F. Lazarsfeld and Allen H. Barton, "Qualitative Measurement in the Social Sciences: Classification, Typologies, and Indices," in Daniel Lerner and Harold D. Lasswell (editors), *The Policy Sciences*, Stanford: Stanford University Press, 1951, pp. 187–192.

15. Axelrod, *op. cit.*

16. Goldhamer, *op. cit.*

17. Walter C. McKain, Jr., "The Social Participation of Old People in a California Retirement Community," unpublished Ph.D. dissertation, Harvard University, 1947.

18. Axelrod, *op. cit.*

19. Irving L. Webber, "The Organized Social Life of the Retired in Two Florida Communities," *American Journal of Sociology*, 59 (January, 1954), pp. 340–346.

20. Foskett has recently reported similar findings for two Oregon communities. See John M. Foskett, "Social Structure and Social Participation," *American Sociological Review*, 20 (August, 1955), pp. 431–438.

6

H. LAURENCE ROSS

UPTOWN AND DOWNTOWN: A STUDY OF MIDDLE-CLASS RESIDENTIAL AREAS

One of the fundamental propositions of traditional urban sociology is that the character of social life varies with distance from the urban core. Evidence supporting this proposition appears in the wealth of studies that have accumulated since 1925 in confirmation of the Burgess Zonal Hypothesis and similar models of the city.[1] Although some aspects of the Burgess formulation have been strongly criticized, and negative results have occasionally been published,[2] the weight of the evidence appears to be heavily in its favor.

A current version of this general proposition distinguishes between the central city and the suburb, viewing the latter as a kind of midway point between urban and rural communities.[3] The suburb may be conceived either as a paradise of stable institutions or as a provincial backwater, but observers of either persuasion agree that there are differences between the suburb and the city. The issue now is whether these differences are inherent in the nature of city and suburb (i.e., whether distance from the urban core is an independently causal variable), or whether these differences merely reflect the well-known distinctions among social classes, ethnic groups and people of varying family status, drawn to city or suburban residences by such considerations as the availability of suitable housing. The latter suggestion has appeared in the work of human ecologists, modern researchers in the "community" tradition, and members of the "social areas" school of urban research.[4]

This paper reports the results of an effort to identify life-style differences between residents of a neighborhood close to the urban core and residents

Reprinted with permission from *American Sociological Review* 30 (1965): 255–259.

of a peripheral area, holding constant social class, ethnicity and family status. Although the character of the sample makes the conclusion very tentative, the data suggest that city-suburban differences in life style are primarily the product of underlying differences in class, ethnicity and family status.

Method

Since distance from the urban core was to be the principal independent variable, and its relation to class, ethnicity and family status was to be controlled, the study was designed to compare two residential areas approximately similar in class and ethnic composition, situated at different distances from the core of New York City. (It was not possible to hold constant family status in selecting the areas for study.) The areas selected were a portion of the East Side of Manhattan, and Riverdale, a neighborhood in the Bronx.[5] Both are high-status areas, virtually without non-white residents, and each contains many large new high-rise apartment houses. The downtown or Manhattan area is within the census-defined New York central business district, though the immediate vicinity is largely residential. In contrast, Riverdale is located adjacent to the city limits, approximately 11 miles from the core, and is notoriously inconvenient to cheap public transportation. Impressionistically, the downtown area is part of the asphalt jungle, its streets choked with traffic and its multi-story buildings packed closely together, while the uptown area is spacious and suburban, with many single-family houses and much greenery.

Random sampling within the areas was not feasible for two reasons. First, there were insuperable difficulties in gaining admission to a large number of Manhattan apartment houses, guarded by doormen and elevator operators instructed to exclude interviewers.[6] Second, rentals in the high-rise buildings of Riverdale, although higher than in any comparable uptown neighborhood, were on the whole lower than those in the high-rise buildings of the downtown area, creating an undesirable class difference. The sample was therefore drawn from only one apartment house in each area. Both were designed by the same architect, managed by the same firm, and they were closely matched on rent level.[7] The downtown building contained 195 adult residents and the uptown building 236. An attempt was made to interview all individuals living in both buildings during April, May and June of 1962; 114 interviews were completed in Manhattan and 108 in Riverdale.[8] As the selection of buildings and of residents within buildings was not representative and systematic, inferences from the data are suggestive only and will not support tests of statistical significance.

Status Characteristics

Indices of social class and ethnicity in each area were compared to verify the extent to which the attempt to control these variables succeeded. The two groups could be considered equivalent in class and ethnicity when these variables were defined in gross terms, but further analysis revealed some subtle differences. Thus, with the exception of the resident custodian in Riverdale, all the respondents in both areas were engaged in white-collar occupations. These white-collar jobs were held in different industries, however: almost 45 per cent of the downtown group were in arts and communications, compared with 13 per cent of the uptown group. Similarly, the Riverdale sample included a relatively high proportion of free professionals such as physicians and lawyers (18 per cent, compared with 4 per cent in Manhattan), as well as a high proportion of proprietors, managers and officials outside arts and communications (43 per cent, compared with 18 per cent). No Negroes were interviewed in either building, but the proportion of Jews among the Riverdale respondents was more than double that in Manhattan (56 per cent, compared with 24 per cent); Catholics were 19 per cent of each group. Although these differences in occupation and religion are probable not due to chance, they did not strongly affect the relations reported below between centrality and the other variables studied.

Whereas a control for class and ethnicity was introduced in selecting the areas for study, no such control was possible for family status. The data in Table 6–1 show that the two groups differed considerably in this respect. So large a proportion of the Riverdale group were married couples that no separation by marital status was justifiable for the purpose of further analysis. The Manhattan group in contrast occupied a variety of marital statuses. The selectivity described here is confirmed in the Census as characteristic of the areas, rather than peculiar to the buildings studied. In spite of this difference in marital status, however, school-aged children were not very much more common in Riverdale: 68 per cent of the Riverdale respondents, compared with 89 per cent in Manhattan, reported no school-aged children. Likewise, the differences in marital status were not associated with marked difference in age distribution: approximately

TABLE 6-1

*Marital Status in the Riverdale and
Manhattan Samples (in percentages)*

MARITAL STATUS	MANHATTAN	RIVERDALE
Single	39.5	7.4
Married	46.5	90.7
Widowed	3.5	0.9
Divorced	7.9	0.9
No answer	2.5	—
Total	99.9	99.9
(N)	(114)	(108)

75 per cent of the respondents in both areas were between 20 and 49 years of age.

Life Style

The rationale of the study was the expectation that residents of a central area in a metropolis would display a more cosmopolitan style of life than people of the same class and ethnic status residing in a peripheral area. Specifically, residents of the central area were expected to rate as important the qualities of excitement, opportunity and privacy commonly attributed to highly urbanized environments; to be less likely to have friendship and institutional ties in the local community; to express greater tolerance of deviants and minorities; to show greater exposure to "quality" media of communication; and to make greater use of the specialized leisure facilities found only in close proximity to the urban core.

In general, these expectations were only weakly supported by the data. Illustrative results from pre-coded questions are presented in Table 6–2. For example, nearly identical majorities of each group rated the "urban" virtues of privacy, opportunity and excitement as important features desired in their residential environment, though the Riverdale residents were more apt to declare the "rural" virtues of friendliness and cleanliness important. With regard to friends and other bonds in the neighborhood the similarities between the areas were more impressive than the differences, although the latter were generally in the expected direction. In both areas the mean number of acquaintances was relatively high (greater than six), while local facilities usage was minimal. A projected comparison of

TABLE 6-2

Selected Indices of Life Styles:
Riverdale and Married Manhattan Samples
(in percentages)

ITEM	MANHATTAN (N = 53)	RIVERDALE (N = 108)
Aspects of community environment considered important:		
Friendliness	32.1	55.6
Cleanliness	77.4	95.4
Privacy	83.0	78.7
Opportunity	83.0	74.1
Excitement	62.3	64.8
Ties to local community:		
Knows 7 or more people	66.0	74.0
Knows manager of grocery	11.3	23.1
Has local charge account	39.6	44.4
Likes idea of Negro friend	30.2	18.5
Reads quality newspaper	92.6	97.2

local as against midtown shopping preferences failed to yield meaningful information because such facilities as existed in Riverdale were not comparable to those available in the Manhattan area.

A projected comparison of tolerance towards deviance, based on the Stouffer scale,[9] was abandoned in the pre-test because both groups were concentrated at the extremely tolerant end of the scale. An attempted revision, substituting more extreme situations, was a failure. The item reported in Table 6–2, concerning favoring the idea of a Negro friend, however, was in the predicted direction. Quality newspaper readership (*Times* and *Herald-Tribune*) was very high in both areas.

Use of specialized leisure facilities is a relatively direct index of life style. Most of the leisure facilities mentioned in the survey schedule are available only in large metropolitan areas,[10] and common experience indicates that they tend to be relatively centralized within these areas. The hypothesis that downtown residents make greater use of these facilities seems eminently reasonable under the assumption that the discomforts of downtown living, including high rentals, select as residents people who are particularly attached to the centralized facilities, or even under the less stringent assumption that people tend to devote their leisure time to more, rather than less convenient, activities.

Ten types of specialized leisure facilities were mentioned to the respondents, who were asked to state whether they had used such a facility within the previous month. Table 6–3 presents the percentage of the

TABLE 6-3

Use of Specialized Leisure Facilities:
Riverdale and Manhattan Residents
(in percentages)

| | MANHATTAN | | | | |
| | UNDER 40 | | | | |
ITEM	UNMARRIED (N = 38)	MARRIED (N = 41)	40 AND OVER (N = 31)	TOTAL (N = 114)*	RIVERDALE (N = 108)
Museum	55.3	53.7	32.3	46.5	47.2
Play	71.1	70.7	45.2	63.2	51.9
Opera, Concert	44.7	29.3	38.7	36.0	25.0
First Run or "Art" Film	86.8	75.6	54.8	73.7	54.6
Public Lecture	15.8	19.5	16.1	16.7	24.1
Night Club	50.0	51.2	16.1	41.2	29.6
Indoor Spectator Sports	31.6	48.8	32.3	38.6	28.7
Outdoor Spectator Sports	5.3	17.1	6.5	10.5	12.0
Specialty Shopping	84.2	80.5	64.5	78.1	75.9
Hotel Events (Dances, etc.)	44.7	36.6	32.3	37.7	49.1

*Sum of previous columns plus 4 cases not included there.

groups named who had used the various facilities at least once during the previous month.[11]

Comparison of the Riverdale sample with the total Manhattan sample yields little support for the hypothesis. In four of the ten comparisons, a higher proportion of the uptown than of the downtown group had used the facility in question. Moreover, the absolute level of participation and the general pattern of activities are similar in both groups. Facilities that draw a high proportion of Manhattanites also draw a high proportion of Riverdalers, and vice versa.

The initial expectation, that downtown residents would actively utilize specialized leisure facilities however, was quite true of the younger unmarried subgroup.[12] These were definitely the "doers" among the respondents. At least half of them had been to museums, plays, major film theaters, night clubs and specialty or department stores during the previous month. Nonetheless this is a selective pattern of activities, for it did not extend to such items as outdoor spectator sports, or public lectures. Less congruence with the expectation of downtown participation occurred among the younger married and particularly among the older Manhattanites.

In the light of the relatively infrequent use of specialized leisure facilities among the older and married downtown residents, the high degree of

94

participation by the Riverdale residents is somewhat surprising, as they were nearly all married and were not significantly younger than the downtown population. A distance of 11 miles apparently is not an insuperable barrier to high-status people in their enjoyment of leisure facilities located at the urban core. Conversely, the relative convenience of some facilities to Riverdale (e.g., several stadiums) is not reflected in any appreciable preference for their use.

In sum, this test of the hypothesis that life style in a downtown residential area is more cosmopolitan than that in an uptown area yielded but weak support when social class and ethnicity were held constant. Both downtown and uptown, residents of these upper middle-class apartment buildings gave evidence of a highly cosmopolitan life style, particularly in the use of specialized leisure facilities. Within the downtown group, though, life style varied considerably, according to differences in age and marital status. These results seem to support the contention that differences between city and suburban life styles are but the reflection of class, ethnic and family status differences. In addition, the differences among Manhattanites point to the fact that downtown populations, unlike many suburban populations, are extremely complex and heterogeneous, and therefore maintain a variety of life styles not possible in a homogeneous population.

Residential Origins and Destinations

A subordinate hypothesis with a somewhat happier empirical experience was that uptown and downtown residents differ in their residential origins and future residential destinations. In particular, residence in Riverdale was conceived as a step in a series leading from central New York City residence to the suburbs. The downtown area was conceived as a reception center for in-migrants, youths from suburban families and newcomers from outside the area. Plans to move directly to the suburbs were thus expected to be less common in the downtown than in the uptown group.

The residents of the two areas did differ in the type of community in which they grew up. Approximately two-thirds of the Riverdale group, compared with 40 per cent of the Manhattanites, grew up in a large city; apparently this was usually New York, though no direct question was asked to that effect. Older unmarried residents of Manhattan most often originated in a small city or town on a farm, and these origins were more common among Manhattanites generally than among the Riverdale residents.

Immediate residential origins (location prior to the last move) also differentiated the two groups. Of the Manhattan residents, 17 per cent came from the New York suburbs, and 8 per cent came directly from places outside the metropolitan area, compared with 11 per cent and none at all, respectively, of the Riverdale residents. And although 54 per cent of the uptown residents were now living in larger quarters than before, only 31 per cent of the downtown residents were in larger quarters, and 45 per cent at their last change of residence had moved to *smaller* quarters. (Whether the new quarters were larger or smaller than the old, they were nearly always more expensive.)[13]

Critics of the suburbs might not be surprised to learn that the uptown residents were noticeably less likely to be satisfied with their neighborhood: 78 per cent in Riverdale and 92 per cent in Manhattan expressed satisfaction. Among those planning to remain within the New York area but to leave the neighborhood,[14] well over a third of the uptown residents, expressed a desire to move to the suburbs.

Summary

A survey was made among the residents of two similar apartment houses in upper middle-class, all-white neighborhoods in New York City, in an effort to isolate some life-style correlates of residence in central and peripheral parts of a city. Differences in life style between residents of the two buildings were small in magnitude and inconsistent in direction; more impressive were the differences among sub-groups of the downtown population based on age and marital status. Younger single people were active users of specialized leisure facilities, whereas older and married people were not. The uptown and downtown groups differed in their residential origins, satisfaction with the neighborhood, and plans for future moves.

Since the sample does not represent central and peripheral residential areas in general, the results are merely suggestive. They support the position that the importance of the distinction between city and suburban residence lies mainly in the selectivity of these areas with respect to social class, ethnicity and family status, major statuses already recognized as important in social area analysis and similar approaches. In addition they remind us that downtown residential areas, even when segregated by rental, contain heterogenous populations, with a wide variety of life styles.

NOTES

I wish to express appreciation to Sheldon Messinger for advice and comments on this manuscript; to Mr. Henry Weitzer and the Heights Academic Computing Facility for aid in data processing; to the Faculty Research Fund of New York University for financial support; and to the Rosedale and Kibel Management Corporations for their kind cooperation in facilitating this study.

1. The classical zonal hypothesis was suggested by Burgess in "The Growth of the City," in Robert E. Park and Ernest W. Burgess (eds.), *The City*, Chicago: University of Chicago Press, 1925. A series of doctoral dissertations at Chicago provided confirmatory data; they are summarized in Ernest W. Burgess and Donald J. Bogue (eds.), *Contributions to Urban Sociology*, Chicago: University of Chicago Press, 1964, esp. Pt. IV.

2. The most well-known critiques are Milla Alihan, *Social Ecology*, New York: Columbia University Press, 1939, and Maurice R. Davie, "The Pattern of Urban Growth," in George P. Murdock (ed.), *Studies in the Science of Society*, New Haven: Yale University Press, 1937.

3. See Anselm Strauss, *Images of the American City*, New York: Free Press of Glencoe, 1961.

4. See, respectively, Leo Schnore, "The Socioeconomic Status of Cities and Suburbs," *American Sociological Review*, 28 (February, 1963), pp. 76–85; Herbert J. Gans, "Urbanism and Suburbanism as Ways of Life: A Reevaluation of Definitions," in Arnold M. Rose (ed.), *Human Behavior and Social Processes: An Interactionist Approach*, Boston: Houghton, Mifflin, 1962, pp. 625–648; and Wendell Bell, "Social Choice, Life Styles and Suburban Residence," in William Dobriner (ed.), *The Suburban Community*, New York: Putnam, pp. 122–131.

5. The principal variable investigated in this study was distance from the urban core. The other defining variable of the city-suburban distinction, political independence, was deliberately excluded from consideration by the choice of Riverdale as the peripheral neighborhood; both neighborhoods are, politically, part of New York City.

6. See H. Laurence Ross, "The Inaccessible Respondent: A Note on Privacy in City and Country," *Public Opinion Quarterly*, 27 (Summer, 1963), pp. 269–275.

7. Both buildings had only recently been completed, and both represented current trends in the construction of middle-class apartment houses in New York City generally. The Manhattan building was in the area where expensive high-rise apartments are totally replacing outmoded lower-class tenements. The Riverdale building is one of several built on vacant land or on the sites of single-family homes on the bluff overlooking the Hudson River. Because of rapid change in the areas, data from the 1960 Census are only approximate for the time at which the study was undertaken. The block containing the Manhattan building had a 1960 median rental of $164 for apartments averaging three rooms in size. Only eight dwelling units are listed in the entire tract containing the Riverdale building, but an adjacent tract had a median rental in excess of $150 (exact amount unspecified) for apartments averaging 3.9 rooms in size.

8. These proportions are lower than is usual in survey research, reflecting the difficulty of finding apartment-dwellers of this social class at home. A minimum of three call-backs was specified.

9. See Samuel A. Stouffer, *Communism, Conformity and Civil Liberties*, New York: Doubleday, 1955.

10. See Otis Dudley Duncan, "The Optimum Size of Cities," in Paul K. Hatt and Albert J. Reiss (eds.), *Reader in Urban Sociology*, Glencoe, Ill.: Free Press, 1951, pp. 632–645.

11. The ten unmarried Riverdale respondents were not analyzed separately. Likewise, division of the Riverdale population into older and younger yielded few notable differences and is omitted from Table 6–3 for the sake of simplicity.

12. The decision to dichotomize the population at age 40 was made in advance on the grounds that at this age those who are unmarried are likely to remain so. Regrettably, the number of older respondents in either marital status was very small.

13. Compare this finding with Peter H. Rossi's (*Why Families Move*, Glencoe, Ill.: Free Press, 1955) to the effect that moves in four types of residential communities were most frequently to larger quarters, as a consequence of adding family members.

14. These respondents were 20 percent of the Manhattan group and 31 per cent of the Riverdale group.

PART II

Enclaves and Ghettos:
The Concentrated and
the Segregated

7

ROBERT BIERSTEDT

THE SOCIOLOGY
OF MAJORITIES

A casual but not uninterested observer of the current sociological scene
could not fail to notice the serious concern within the field for problems
of minorities and minority groups. If he pauses to reflect upon this phenomenon the thought may occur to him that nowhere is there a similar or
even comparable concern for majorities and majority groups. Systematic
treatments of this latter subject are distinguished by their scarcity, and this
may seem doubly strange in view of the fact that some of the societies in
which sociology has reached its highest development accept as almost
axiomatic the political principle of majority rule.

The proposition that majorities have been neglected requires no more
than negative evidence. Even those sociologists like Simmel,[1] von Wiese,[2]
and MacIver,[3] who have touched upon the subject, have done so largely
in a political rather than a sociological context.[4] Without implying that
political and sociological concerns are mutually exclusive, it may nevertheless be suggested that the latter might be broader in significance than
the former and may present issues which a political emphasis obscures.
Some of these issues we should expect to see treated in sociography.
When we turn to the sociology of groups, however, a subject which
has properly been regarded as of central and indeed of pivotal concern,[5]
we find an almost infinite number of classifications of types of groups, but
no mention of majorities. There are open groups and closed groups,
organized groups and unorganized groups, primary groups and secondary
groups, "A" groups and "B" groups, in-groups and out-groups, "real" groups
and "nominal" groups, horizontal groups and vertical groups, voluntary
groups and involuntary groups, large groups and small groups, long-lived
groups and short-lived groups, "unibonded" groups and "multibonded"

Reprinted with permission from *American Sociological Review* 13 (1948): 700–710.

groups, and many others in terms of sociological form, and others still, such as age, sex, ethnic, occupational, economic, educational, class, religious, linguistic, territorial, and so on,[6] in terms of sociological content.[7] In all these classifications the majority-minority distinction is conspicuous by its absence. If not in sociography at least in the general texts on sociology one would expect the majority-minority distinction to have achieved some prominence, particularly in view of the heavy emphasis upon minorities, but again the distinction fails to appear, and there is no discussion of majorities as such. Finally, one would expect to find treatments of majorities in texts on social control, but once again a cursory examination leaves the expectation unfulfilled.[8] Social control is treated almost exclusively in terms of such cultural factors as folkways, mores, institutions, laws, and so on, rather than in terms of such social factors as the influence of majorities. It is almost as if sociologists had unanimously agreed to leave the subject of majorities to the devices of political scientists.

The subject, however, is worth considering for several reasons. The first of these is that number is a necessary category in sociology and that phenomena of many different kinds change not only in degree but also in their nature as they vary in size. Certainly small groups, for example, are different from large groups in other ways than that the former are small, the latter large.[9] In like manner, majorities differ from minorities in other ways than that they are larger, and it is these other ways that it is instructive to analyze. Differences of this kind have an intrinsic sociological interest and, difficult as they may be to discern, comprise an integral part of group theory. In this connection von Wiese has the following comment:

> "It is difficult to assign the proper place to the concepts of majority and minority. They are primarily expressions of a purely numerical relation, and they therefore belong among the other colorless terms here discussed [swarm, band, pack, and herd]. The social relationships between majority and minority, however, play an extremely important part in many plurality patterns. . . . The circumstance that these two categories taken in conjunction denote a proportion and not a mere summation makes them sociologically important. Majority and minority are not primarily or usually plurality patterns, but in certain situations they may become groups, and hence should receive attention for this reason as well."[10]

Secondly, it is apparent that the majority-minority distinction differs in principle from distinctions based upon number and size. As von Wiese says in the passage quoted immediately above, a proportion is different from a summation. Groups of whatever size differ from other groups of the same size when the former are majorities and the latter are not. Furthermore, it is obvious that a majority may be relatively small, a minority relatively large, although not, of course, when they are in opposition in the same context. It is also obvious that majorities may vary considerably in size, in relation to their conjoint minorities, without ceasing to be majorities. In a group of 100, 51 and 99 both constitute majorities. For these reasons the majority-minority distinction is not comprehended by any other formal categories of groups and the distinction is, in fact, unique.

In the third place, majorities and minorities are universal in all societies and in all groups, except those which have an even number of members evenly divided and those which are unanimous. In all complex societies, where integration is imperfect and unanimity non-existent, majorities and minorities are constant phenomena.

A fourth reason for studying majorities has both theoretical and practical consequences, and the latter outweigh the former. For it has often been observed by writers concerned with oppressed minorities that the problems are essentially not minority problems at all, but majority problems. Writers on the Negro in the United States, for example, and especially Myrdal, have insisted that there is no such thing as a Negro problem, that the problem is actually a "white" problem. In a sense, of course, this is only a manner of speaking, but there can be no doubt that the problem, whether Negro or white, would have a dramatically different impact upon American life if (a) the Negro population were not so large as it is, (b) the Negro population were not so small as it is, (c) the white population comprised not a majority but a dominant minority, (d) the Negro population were the same size but comprised a dominant minority, (e) Northern whites were not a majority and Southern whites not a minority, and so on through many diverse combinations. Whatever the way in which the issue is phrased, it is easy to agree that there is something about majorities which causes and creates minority problems and that a knowledge of the nature and characteristics of the former may contribute to an understanding of the latter. We know, for example, that people become prejudiced not through contact with minority (*i.e.*, oppressed) groups, but through contact with prevailing attitudes toward minority groups.[11] Attitudes "prevail" in a society when they are held by majorities.

Finally, as suggested above, a sociological approach to the subject of majorities may assist in discerning attributes and properties which are not insignificant for the purposes of political science and which tend to be obscured in the latter approach. It may be suggested, for example, that political majorities and what we are unfortunately forced to call societal majorities (*i.e.*, the majority of all the people in a society) do not necessarily coincide, either in personnel or in political predilections. Even under conditions of universal suffrage a political majority may represent only a small societal minority. Of even greater significance, however, is the fact that majorities have so often been conceived of in purely political terms that the broader sociological nature of the subject has suffered neglect. Political majorities are only one kind of majority and, even if they are the most important kind, it does not follow that other kinds are unimportant. Nor does it follow that the nature and characteristics of majorities in general can be discerned in an investigation of political majorities or, for that matter, of any particular kind of majority. In other words, as in most cases affecting the relationships between sociology and the other social sciences, certain phenomena appear which have a more generic and universal significance than can be grasped in any inquiry more specialized than the sociological. It is not inconceivable that a general sociological analysis of majorities may illuminate some of the more special political implications of majorities.[12]

These five reasons, among others, support the opinion that the subject merits attention by sociologists. In the present place it is naturally not possible to inquire into all of the problems presented by majorities, but it is at least desirable to indulge in some preliminary observations of a formal and necessarily hypothetical nature.

A preliminary analysis may begin with the recognition that majorities, like other groups, may be large or small (both absolutely and relative to their conjoint minorities), open or closed, primary or secondary, active or inactive, cohesive through one or many bonds, relatively permanent or relatively impermanent, and so on. Indeed, many additional adjectives of this polar kind may be attached to them. These adjectives will not, however, contribute anything substantial to an investigation of their specific characteristics. One aspect of groups, on the other hand, is significant. This is the aspect which determines whether the group, or the majority, is organized or unorganized. There has been a tendency in sociology, not dominant perhaps but nevertheless discernible, to consider organized groups, often called associations, to be of greater significance than unorganized groups. Attention to majorities may help to dispel the opinion that this is always, or even usually, the case. For majorities, in many situations of interest to sociology, are unorganized, and this absence of organization does not diminish their significance.

The distinction between organized and unorganized groups, however, is insufficiently discriminating when applied to majorities. It is doubtful, in fact, if it is wholly satisfactory when applied to groups. A consideration of majorities illustrates that there are four general kinds, as different one

CLASSIFICATION OF GROUPS

	Organization	Social Relations between Members	Consciousness of Kind
A. Statistical	No	No	No
B. Societal	No	No	Yes
C. Social	No	Yes	Yes
D. Associational	Yes	Yes	Yes

from the other as the kinds of groups of which they are a part. In attempting to delineate these kinds one is embarrassed, as so often in sociology, by the paucity of terms with which to label them and by the consequent necessity of utilizing words already burdened with connotations. In spite of this hazard, we may distinguish four kinds of groups as exhibited in the accompanying somewhat crude "table." These four may be called the statistical, the societal, the social, and the associational. Statistical groups are synonymous with logical classes. They have only an "analytical" existence and are "formed," if one may be permitted the expression, not by people themselves but by people who write about people—in other words by sociologists, statisticians, demographers, and so on. Whether they have members or not is immaterial, and we may accordingly have null groups in sociology in the same sense in which we have null classes in logic. Statistical groups, therefore, have no social organization, they have "members" in a logical but not in a sociological sense; and consciousness of kind, in the absence of a social stimulus to evoke it, is only potential. Similarly, the "members" do not enter into social relations with each other on the basis of the trait in terms of which they constitute a group. They may have one or several traits in common, but they have no interests in common, nor any like interests.[13] Examples of such statistical groups are right-handed persons, red-headed persons, persons fifty years of age, persons who are five feet tall, persons who have had the measles, persons who have died of tuberculosis, persons who prefer soap operas to Italian operas, and so on.

Societal groups differ from statistical groups in that they do have members and these members are conscious of their kind, of the similarity or identity of traits they all possess. There are no null groups here and the trait itself may be single or multiple. Here appear external signs by means of which the members recognize each other, such as skin color, language, accent, grammar, response to patriotic symbols, appearance, and so on. The members, in short, are or may easily become "visible" to each other. They have like interests but not common interests. They do not, however, in the absence of a social stimulus, enter into social relations with each other. Examples of societal groups are males, females, Negroes, whites, Southerners, New Yorkers, golfers, the blind, college professors and indeed all occupational groups, and so on.

Social contact and communication appear in the third category. The social group differs from the societal group in that its members have social relations with one another and from the statistical group both in this respect and in that consciousness of kind is present. Social relations are the distinguishing additional characteristic. The members may have like but not common interests, common but not like interests (*e.g.*, an assortment of persons on a life-raft after a shipwreck), or both like and common interests. Examples are groups of acquaintances, relatives, cliques, audiences, spectators, crowds, mobs, passengers on board a small ship, and many other unorganized groups discussed in the texts.

When a group has these characteristics and is, in addition, organized, we have the fourth kind of group indicated above, the associational group or, more simply, the association. Examples are a fraternity, a lodge, a club, a team, an orchestra, a committee, and so on. In these groups it is the formal organization which is the prominent characteristic and membership in them in itself confers consciousness of kind and generates social relations in accordance with procedural norms. Here, finally, the members usually have both like and common interests.

Before commenting upon its uses, it is necessary to say that this is not an inclusive classification. Some groups find no place in these categories; for example, groups which involve social relations but no necessary consciousness of kind, and groups comprised not of individuals but of other groups. It should also be recognized that none of these groups is stable, and that in the process of social life they may become transformed into groups in other categories under the impress of events. Red-headed people, a statistical group, would become a societal group with the improbable passage of legislation taxing them, a social group if they entered into social relations on the basis of the color of their hair and attended a meeting, for example, to which only red-headed people were invited, and an associational group if they organized a Red-Headed League for the purpose of resisting the legislation. Finally, the classification is a logical but not a temporal continuum; a statistical group may become an association immediately, without passing through the intervening categories; and the reverse could happen on the occasion of the dissolution of an association.

When we return from this digression on group classification in general to the question of majorities in particular, an interesting reflection emerges. For it immediately appears that all four of these groups, the statistical no less than the associational, have sociological significance when they are majorities. And in many cases it is only because they are majorities that they acquire general social significance in the societies in which they occur. This significance can be illustrated by a number of examples. Consider the significance of the majority first of all when it is a statistical group, where no social relations are involved. A society or group in which the majority of the population were of age fifty and above would be a different kind of a society from one in which the majority were fifty and below. Substitute any age categories and the generalization retains its cogency. Similarly, societies differ when or if right-handed persons or left-handed persons are in the majority, urban-dwellers or rural-dwellers, literates or illiterates, and so on. In other words, statistical groups do have sociological significance when they are majorities. They determine to an extensive degree the general characteristics of a society and of a social group. Statistical majorities always have more than a statistical significance. It is therefore a mistake to limit sociology, as formal sociologists are sometimes inclined to do, to a study of social relationships as such, if that term implies social contact and communication between people. For it is apparent that many phenomena of the highest import for sociology, those responsible for the character of an entire society, are determined by the juxtaposition within it of majorities whose members have never met, who do not know each other, and who may, in fact, be unaware of the individual existence of each other.[14]

Comparable observations are relevant to the role of societal majorities. Men's college communities are different from women's college communities, and the differential status of "faculty wives" in the two situations is striking. Of more importance, however, is the fact that minority group problems, problems involving ethnic and national minorities, appear in societies when consciousness of kind and consciousness of difference characterize majority and minority groups. Tension in such situations, in the absence of compensating factors, is directly proportional to the size of the minority and inversely proportional to the size of the majority. That is, majority-minority tension appears to be least when the majority is large, the minority small, and greatest when the minority threatens, by increase in size, to become the majority. Meanwhile, ethnic minorities are oppressed largely in proportion not to their absolute but their relative size. Conversely, a very small minority, again relatively speaking may suffer the satiric sanction but no specific social disability. This point unfortunately requires more development than can be offered here, but it is noteworthy that it is amenable to empirical research.

The social group also, the group that is unorganized but in which social relations occur, is dependent for its function upon a majority. Whether a group of friends goes to a play or to a musical comedy, to an expensive nightclub or to an inexpensive tavern, drinks coffee or beer on a given occasion, and so on, depends, often unconsciously, upon majority desires. Similarly, in larger groups, a lynching can occur only if it is at least tacitly sanctioned by a majority of those present, and a panic can occur only if a majority of the persons involved in a situation fail to "keep their heads." A clique clearly operates under the influence of the majority of its own members and an elite, although a minority, suffers no discrimination only because it embodies social values of which the majority approves and would like to emulate.

It is in the organized group, the association, in which majorities seem, on the surface, to have the least significance. As social organization introduces an hierarchical structure into a group the significance of numbers, and therefore of majorities, diminishes in proportion. The more highly organized the association the fewer functions belong to the majority. Here majority action is, in fact, constrained and limited by organization, by rules and regulations, and by the creation of authority. It would be an error to assert that the majority exercises any official influence in a tightly organized, hierarchically ordered association like, for example, the Roman Catholic Church, the United States Navy, or the Communist Party, three associations which, whatever their diverse goals, exhibit a remarkable sociological similarity in internal organization and structure.[15] There are many more priests than cardinals, seamen than admirals, and party-workers than members of the Politburo, and it is the latter, not the former, which possess the power. This, of course, is true in varying extent of all associations, even the most "democratic." The power structure is always pyramidal.

But even here majorities play a role. This role appears with the recognition that all associations have two types of organization, a formal organization and an informal organization,[16] and that, while majorities exercise no formal function whatever—except when they constitute a legitimate party[17]—they often exercise covert and sometimes even overt informal control in associations. Utilizing only the most extreme and rigid cases for illustration, that is associations in which majorities would seem to have the least influence, it can be demonstrated that they are not immune from the pressures of majorities. A clear example is afforded by the Navy during the recent war. Not even the highly inflexible rules and regulations of the service, enforced by Regular Navy officers in command positions, were impervious to the pressure of the large majority of Reserve officers who considered some of the niceties of naval etiquette, particularly with respect to salutes, ceremonies, and relations with enlisted men, to be more than a little ridiculous. The exodus of Reserve officers after the war, their declining majority and ultimate minority, contributed increasing conformity to the rules and reduced the discrepancy between the formal and informal organization.[18]

The Roman Catholic Church offers another illustration in a totally different sphere. The long struggle with "modern errors" began in 1543 with the publication of *On the Revolutions of the Celestial Orbs* by Nicolai Copernicus and became intense when Galileo was summoned once in 1616 and five times in 1633 to the bar of the Inquisition. This story is well known. What is not so well known is that a license to print a book espousing the heliocentric hypothesis was refused as late as 1820 and that not until September 11, 1822 was the following decree quietly issued by the Holy Office:

"There is no reason why the present and future Masters of the Sacred Palace should refuse license for printing and publishing works treating of the mobility of the earth and the immobility of the sun, according to the common opinion of modern astronomers."[19]

What scientific evidence was unable to accomplish, majority and "common" opinion finally did, even though several centuries were consumed in the process.[20] One is tempted to say that no association, no matter how rigidly organized, is able to withstand the permanent pressure of a majority and that an organized majority is the most potent social force on earth. There is a certain authority in a majority which no hierarchy can wholly obliterate.

From these instances and others another principle can be induced. It concerns the nature of formal and informal organization in any association and the role of majorities with respect to these two forms of organization. First, however, it is appropriate to clarify the meaning of these terms which have appeared in preceding paragraphs. The formal organization of an association consists of the formally recognized and established statuses of the members in accordance with the rank of the offices and other positions they occupy, together with the rules and regulations which set out the obligations, duties, privileges, and responsibilities of these positions. The status of non-office holding members, their duties and privileges, is also, of course, a part of the formal organization—formal because formally recognized and concurred in as a condition of membership. Social relations between the members are conducted formally in terms of these statuses, in conformity with explicit norms, and in accordance with "extrinsic" and "categoric" evaluations of persons. In the formal organization, statuses have differential prestige in independence of the persons who occupy them.

Since this independence is difficult if not impossible to maintain in the dynamics of associational life, however, an informal organization arises to exist coevally with the formal. The informal organization consists of roles rather than statuses, of patterns of dominance and ascendancy, affection, hostility, or indifference of the members in accordance with their intrinsic and personal evaluations of each other. These role patterns may or may not coincide with or conform to the status hierarchy of the formal organization. In the informal organization social relations occur on the basis of the esteem which the members have for one another in independence of their statuses. In short, in formal organization social relations proceed in terms of the prestige of statuses in accordance with explicit associational norms; in informal organization they proceed in terms of the esteem for persons in accordance with implicit societal (*i.e.*, extra-associational) norms. Prestige attaches to statuses; esteem to persons.[21] The former is a component of formal organization, the latter of informal organization.[22]

Now it is apparent that in some associations there may be a close coincidence between the formal and the informal organization and that this coincidence may be relatively permanent. In such cases the statuses which carry the greatest prestige are occupied by the persons who are held in the highest esteem. On the other hand, an association may exhibit a wide discrepancy between its formal and informal organization. In these cases the prestige continues to attach to the status while esteem is withheld from the person who occupies the status and who thereupon becomes a figurehead. The officers then have the formal authority of their positions but not the informal authority sustained by esteem. Now, whether or not offices are filled by "democratic" vote, it is within the power of the majority to confer actual as well as statutory authority upon the officers or to retain authority residually in the informal organization. Similarly, it is within the power of the majority to determine whether social relations in the association shall proceed only in terms of the formal rules and regulations, which are explicit norms, or in terms of informal norms which may or may not coincide with the former. Here then is the principle to which attention is invited, that the discrepancy between the formal and informal organization of any association will be least when the majority gives full support and sanction to the former and greatest when this support is for any reason or in any particular withheld. That this power of determination is a function of the majority rather than of any aspect of social organization itself is clear from the consideration that it is prior to social organization and determines the form which social organization takes.

Finally, it is the support of the majority which sustains the association, the absence of this support which moves it in the direction of change or of ultimate dissolution.

We may now inquire whether some of these observations have a similar relevance in the larger society. Here the problem becomes involved in the more general question of the nature and kinds of social power, especially when we attempt to probe the source of the power which the majority exercises. Unfortunately, the subject of social power is not one which has received a comprehensive analysis in the literature, and to discourse on majorities in terms of power is like pronouncing the words of a language one does not fully understand.[23] MacIver defines it variously as "the capacity in any relationship to command the service or the compliance of others,"[24] and "the capacity to control the behavior of others either directly by fiat or indirectly by the manipulation of available means."[25] Among the sources of power MacIver lists property, status, office (apart from status[26]), special knowledge, managerial and executive function, financial resources, artistic, religious or other eminence, publicity, and so on. It is clear from his discussion that social power, whatever its sources and manifestations, is "responsive to the *mores* of the society."[27] And it is the majority which sustains the mores. Here then we find the authority which lies "beyond the realm of government," the authority which community and society retain, which they may or may not confer upon the state, and which, even when it is wrested from the community, wells up again and restrains the actions of governments. Not even an autocrat can remain unresponsive to the will of a majority.[28]

It would, of course, be highly unrealistic to assert that the power of the majority always manifests itself, or is always successful when it does. Majorities are frequently inert and frequently too have no means of expression. Indeed, it is one of the lessons of history that majorities of one kind or another have long suffered oppression. Nevertheless, it is of sociological significance to note that majorities remain the source of so much residual power, even in these situations, that autocrats and oligarchs bend every effort to prevent them from organizing. It is the power of a majority which gives meaning to the imperial command, "Divide and rule."

We find, thus, in the larger society the same principle which was found in the association. Where there is no organization, the majority determines. In the absence of stratification, likewise, the majority determines. When there is formal organization there is also informal organization, and in the latter the majority plays an important role. Indeed, society itself is an informal organization, the state a formal organization; the laws belong to the formal structure, the mores to the informal. It is the majority which sustains the mores, the minority which initiates changes in them which are then either resisted or finally sanctioned by the majority. In all societies of any complexity there is a discrepancy between the laws and the mores. This discrepancy will be wide or narrow depending upon the position of the majority. Where it is wide it will be found that the majority supports the mores, a minority supports the laws. It is the role that majorities play in societies which gives point to what is one of the most profound and cogent of all sociological principles—"When the mores are adequate, laws are unnecessary, when they are inadequate, laws are useless." The mores are adequate when they are supported by a large majority; they are inadequate when they lack this support. There is a power in the majority which can contravene any law.

It is the majority, in short, which sets the culture pattern and sustains it, which is in fact responsible for whatever pattern or configuration there is in a culture. It is the majority which confers upon folkways, mores, customs, and laws the status of norms and gives them coercive power. It is the majority which guarantees the stability of a society. It is the majority which requires conformity to custom and which penalizes deviation— except in ways which the majority sanctions and approves. It is the majority which is the custodian of the mores and which defends them against innovation. And it is the inertia of majorities, finally, which retards the processes of social change.

Throughout the preceding discussion we have, except for several incidental references, omitted from consideration the question of the size of majorities. Here it is possible to note only one implication of size, one which relates to the general problem of social and cultural integration. Reflection upon majorities enables us to see that cultural integration is a function of the size of the majority which conforms to a single set of patterns, which subscribes to the same myths, and which aspires to attain the same societal goals. When this majority is large, the culture is integrated, no matter how extensively the society is stratified. When it is small the culture lacks integration. When it dissolves into competing minorities all vestiges of integration disappear. A culture is in fact dependent upon the existence in a society of a majority. Without it the society is split into partial and fragmented cultures. Whatever the value of the cultural approach in sociology, when used exclusively it sometimes obscures the *social* factors which create and sustain a society and which determine both its coherence and its cohesion.

What, finally, is the ultimate ground for the power which the majority exercises? The answer is so deceptively simple as to discourage ready acceptance. It rests in the elemental fact, a fact so formidable as to seem incontrovertible, that the majority is stronger than the minority or, in Simmel's words, "dass die Vielen mächtiger sind als die Wenigen."[29] It is certainly incontrovertible that two men can force one man to do what they want, and that ten men can do it even more easily. Given the same organization, the larger number can always control the smaller, can command its service, and secure its compliance. This, incidentally, is a social and not a cultural fact.[30]

In summary, we have noted the neglect of majorities in contemporary sociology and have introduced, in a very preliminary fashion, some hypotheses which a sociology of majorities might subject to further investigation. We have observed that the majority-minority distinction is a distinction *sui generis* which requires inclusion in any comprehensive group theory; that majorities play significant roles in both organized and unorganized social groups, and particularly in the informal aspects of the former; that majorities play a similar role in the larger society; that majorities constitute a residual locus of social power; that they sustain the mores; and that they are responsible for whatever cultural integration a society exhibits. Majorities doubtless have in addition multifarious characteristics and functions which we have neglected to mention. But these will suffice to show that the subject merits sustained sociological analysis.

NOTES

1. "Exkurs über die Überstimmung," in *Soziologie*, Leipzig: Duncker & Humblot, 1908, pp. 186–197.

2. Leopold von Wiese and Howard Becker, *Systematic Sociology*, New York: Wiley, 1932, pp. 267–268, 431–432, 598.

3. See *Leviathan and the People*, Baton Rouge: Louisiana State University Press, 1939; *The Web of Government*, New York: Macmillan, 1947; and *The Elements of Social Science*, London: Methuen, 1921, pp. 174–176.

4. Political treatments of the principle of majority rule embrace almost the entire literature of political philosophy, and particularly the philosophy of democracy. For an excellent recent discussion, with carefully selected bibliography, see Willmoore Kendall, *John Locke and the Doctrine of Majority Rule*, Urbana: University of Illinois Press, 1941. Kendall suggests that while in one sense no political scientist can avoid the problem of majorities, in another sense it is the " 'dark continent' of modern political theory" (p. 16). See also von Gierke, "Über die Geschichte des Majoritätsprinzipes," *Schmollers Jahrbuch für Gezetsbegung Verwaltung und Volkswirtschaft im Deutschen Reiche*, 39: 565–587, 1915; and Ladislas Konopczynski, "Majority Rule," *Encyclopedia of the Social Sciences*, 10:55–59.

5. For a comprehensive summary of this subject see Logan Wilson, "The Sociography of Groups," in *Twentieth Century Sociology*, Gurvitch and Moore, eds. New York: Philosophical Library, 1945, pp. 139–171. Also Florian Znaniecki, "Social Organization and Institutions," *Ibid.*, pp. 172–217; Wiese-Becker, *op. cit.*, pp. 488–555; G. A. Lundberg, *Foundations of Sociology*, New York: Macmillan, 1939, pp. 339–374, and

"Some Problems of Group Classification and Measurement," *American Sociological Review*, 5:351–360 (June, 1940).

6. For a recent discussion of the problem of group classification see P. A. Sorokin, *Society, Culture, and Personality*, New York: Harper, 1947, pp. 145–255.

7. In view of the difficulty of finding a *fundamentum divisionis* for a logically rigorous classification of groups, the question arises as to whether a classification can serve any useful purpose, even if an adequate construction could be achieved. Ogburn and Nimkoff, for example, contend with some cogency that all such classifications are of limited usefulness. See *Sociology*, Boston: Houghton Mifflin, 1946, p. 251. In support of this view it may be said that a good deal of so-called formal or structural sociology, whatever its intrinsic merit or logical appeal, has little or nothing to do with sociological theory. Taxonomy is not theory, although the two are often confused. Sociological taxonomy belongs to methodology, sociological theory to sociology itself; taxonomy deals with the logical relations between sociological concepts; sociological theory deals with the spatio-temporal and causal relations between social variables. Logical order is the goal of the former inquiry, scientific truth of the latter; the former issues, ideally, in a modified Tree of Porphyry; the latter in universal propositions. On the other hand, in opposition to the view of Ogburn and Nimkoff, classifications, like nominal definitions, are, if not systematically necessary, at least a desirable propaedeutic to the construction of sociological theories.

8. On this subject see L. L. Bernard, *Social Control*, New York: Macmillan, 1939; Paul H. Landis, *Social Control*, Philadelphia: Lippincott, 1939; Jerome Doud, *Control in Human Societies*, New York: Appleton-Century, 1936; E. A. Ross, *Social Control*, New York: Macmillan, 1916, (Ross notes, however, that "The prestige of *numbers* gives ascendancy to the crowd," p. 78); and Joseph S. Roucek and Associates, *Social Control*, New York: Van Nostrand, 1947. On the other hand, there is relevant material in William Albig, *Public Opinion*, New York: McGraw-Hill, 1939, although not couched specifically in terms of majorities and minorities. See especially Chapters I, II, and XVI.

9. On the influence of number and size upon social groups see Simmel, *op. cit.*, pp. 47–133, and Wiese-Becker, *op. cit.*, pp. 498–501.

10. Wiese-Becker, *op. cit.*, pp. 431–432. These few lines, under the section on "Concepts and Categories: Numerical," are unfortunately all these authors have to say about majorities, with two minor exceptions.

11. There is a vast literature which can be invoked in support of this point. See, for example, Murphy, Murphy, and Newcomb, *Experimental Social Psychology*, New York: Harper, 1937; Murphy and Likert, *Public Opinion and the Individual*, New York, 1938; Theodore M. Newcomb, "The Influence of Attitude Climate upon Some Determinations of Information," *Journal of Abnormal and Social Psychology*, 41:291–302, 1946; Arnold Rose, *Studies in Reduction of Prejudice* (mimeographed) Chicago: American Council on Race Relations, 1947; Robin M. Williams, Jr., "The Reduction of Intergroup Tensions," *Bulletin* 57, Social Science Research Council, 1947; and Robert M. MacIver, *The More Perfect Union*, New York: Macmillan, 1948. For psychological studies of the influence of majorities in the formation of opinion see H. E. Burtt and D. R. Falkenburg, Jr., "The Influence of Majority and Expert Opinion on Religious Attitudes," *Journal of Social Psychology*, 14:269–278 (1941); and C. H. Marple, "The Comparative Suggestibility of Three Age Levels to the Suggestion of Group vs. Expert Opinion," *Journal of Social Psychology*, 4:176–186 (1933). These last two studies, unfortunately, were made with very small groups and are not conclusive. In short, the experimental evidence on the influence of majorities upon opinion is meager.

12. Kendall, for example, says that Simmel's "Excursus," cited *infra*, note 1, is "a discussion which no student of the social sciences can read without subsequently

paying to it the unusual compliment of wishing that it had been many times as long." *Loc. cit.*, p. 27.

13. For a distinction between the like and the common see R. M. MacIver, *Society*, New York: Farrar & Rinehart, 1937, pp. 28, 30.

14. It is similarly a mistake to emphasize the role of organized groups in a society at the expense of the unorganized, and especially of those in the latter category which are only statistical groups, *i.e.*, as defined above, groups the sociologist himself constructs in the process of classifying people in various ways. It may be safe to say, incidentally, that the conclusions of demographers have not been integrated into formal sociology and that chapters on population remain somewhat logically separate from those on social structure, even though frequently bound together in the same book.

15. One interesting similarity, among others, is that the distinction between "associational" and "private" statuses of the functionaries tends to disappear and extraassociational statuses have little importance. Such associations differ in this respect from the "corporate groups" delineated by Max Weber which exemplify "rational-legal" authority and in which distinctions between official and private statuses are maintained. On this point see *Max Weber: The Theory of Social and Economic Organization*, edited by Talcott Parsons, New York: Oxford, 1947, pp. 324ff, and especially Parsons' Introductory essay, "The Institutionalization of Authority," pp. 56–77. See also E. T. Hiller on the professions and on the office, *Social Relations and Structures*, New York, Harper, 1947, pp. 544–596.

16. Although E. T. Hiller has not used these concepts, his distinctions between intrinsic and extrinsic valuations of persons and between personal and categoric social relations are directly relevant. See *Ibid.*, pp. 191–213; 631–645. The interrelations between formal and informal organization represent an important junction of formal sociology and social psychology and require, perhaps, more intensive analysis than they have as yet received.

17. In sociological terms a party is a device for recruiting a majority and can, as Max Weber suggests, exist only within an organized group or association (Weber: *Verband*; Parsons: "corporate group"), even though it operates, as do political parties in the United States, without specific constitutional sanction. See Max Weber, *loc. cit.*, p. 407. See also R. M. MacIver, *The Web of Government*, *op. cit.*, pp. 208–224 and especially p. 213.

18. For an excellent analysis of formal and informal organization in the Navy see Charles H. Page, "Bureaucracy's Other Face," *Social Forces*, 25:88–94, October, 1946. For an implicit fictional treatment of the same theme see *Mister Roberts*, by Thomas Heggen, Boston: Houghton Mifflin, 1946.

19. Quoted in Preserved Smith, *A History of Modern Culture*, New York: Henry Holt, 1930, Vol. I, p. 58.

20. Illustrations for the third example, the Communist Party, are more difficult to exhibit because of lack of information. It is possible, however, that increasing antisemitism in the high councils of the Party in Russia, as reported by Drew Middleton in articles in the New York *Times* in February, 1948, may be concessions to majority opinion even though in direct opposition to both constitutional and doctrinal orthodoxy.

21. The writer is indebted to Professor E. T. Hiller for this distinction between prestige and esteem.

22. It is not altogether clear in what respect it may be appropriate to refer to these informal elements in terms of "structure" or even "organization." In some respects they may be antithetical to organization and in that case the concept "informal organization" becomes an oxymoron. This is particularly true because it is these informal elements which are susceptible to frequent change in contrast to the formal which are, by comparison, relatively stable.

23. R. M. MacIver observes that "There is no reasonably adequate study of the nature of social power," although he himself contributes some highly pertinent remarks. See *The Web of Government, op. cit.*, p. 458, and especially Chapter 5, "The Pyramid of Power," pp. 82–113. E. A. Ross's discussion, while short, is still suggestive. See *Social Control, op. cit.*, pp. 77–88.

24. *Ibid.*, p. 82.

25. *Ibid.*, p. 87.

26. That is, the power which proceeds from the *possession* of status.

27. *Ibid.*, p. 98.

28. In an eloquent passage, MacIver has described this situation as follows: "The authority of government does not create the order over which it presides and does not sustain that order solely by its own fiat or its accredited power. There is authority beyond the authority of government. There is a greater consensus without which the fundamental order of the community would fall apart. This consensus plays a different role under different forms of government. Sometimes it has nothing to do with the processes that make or unmake the princes or potentates who rule the people. Sometimes it has no mode of expression, should the ruler get out of hand and violate the fundamental order he is presumed to protect, save the rare violence of revolution. Sometimes it is alert and sensitive to all that government does and sets its seal of approval or disapproval on the policies that government pursues. But always, whether mainly acquiescent or creatively active, it is the ultimate ground on which the unity and the order of the state repose." *Ibid.*, p. 85.

29. *Loc. cit.*, p. 190.

30. For an expansion of this thesis see John Dollard, "Culture, Society, Impulse, and Socialization," *American Journal of Sociology*, 45:53–56 (July, 1939).

8

RICHARD A. BALL

~~~~~~

A POVERTY CASE:
THE ANALGESIC SUBCULTURE
OF THE SOUTHERN APPALACHIANS

Despite the presence of a tradition of vigorous dissent and considerable evidence to the contrary, conventional sociology still tends to assume an essentially rationalistic view of man. Reminiscent of the eminently cool and calculating "economic man" of classical economics, the model of modern "sociologic man" is on the order of an almost perfectly programmed android, operating in accordance with the dictates of his culture. Any injudicious behavior on his part is typically attributed to "conflicts" or conditions of "anomie" in the cultural program, and only ritualistic lip service is paid to Thomas's (1928:572) early emphasis on the idiosyncratic "definition of the situation," to Wrong's (1961:187–193) more recent criticism of the "over-socialized conception of man," or, in fact, to any of the other prominent expressions of minority opinion. Even when the criticisms are granted, they are really accepted as peripheral considerations rather than as central theoretical propositions. Observations suggesting that man's most basic attribute may be his capacity for inexpedience are largely ignored by sociological theory and systematically suppressed by contemporary methodology.

Apprentice sociologists are taught that they may discern more clearly what a man believes by observation of his behavior in critical situations than by easy acceptance of his vocalizations. If this assertion is to any degree correct, it follows that the best single test of the accuracy of the charge made here lies in close scrutiny of sociologists' behavior as they handle the critical task of applying their discipline to the diagnosis and treatment of "social problems." Such an examination clearly supports the

Reprinted with permission from *American Sociological Review* 33 (1968): 885–895.

allegation. That is, considerations of the nonrational qualities of human behavior, lip-serviced in theory, have been widely ignored in favor of the underlying assumptions of rationalism. That this is true in spite of the fact that efforts at directed social change ought to benefit from greater recognition of nonrational qualities constitutes powerful evidence of intellectual rigidity. Actually, the origin, development, and continued survival of many "problem" subcultures can be explained in terms of reasonably predictable, albeit "nonrational," responses to environmental circumstances. The failure of planners to understand and deal with them serves to illustrate the inadequacy of their rationalistic assumptions when put to the test.

One of the more serious failures has been the inability of social planners to understand and deal with widespread, apparently "irrational" recalcitrance among the very people whose lives they are attempting to "improve." These "target groups" represent rather general social categories such as the elderly, the Negro, and the poor. The categories are surprisingly heterogeneous, but one major thread running through the experience of most constituents is intense and prolonged frustration. The present thesis holds that, to explain, predict, and alter their behavior, one must recognize the extent to which it reflects that institutionalized nonrational response to frustration which is here termed *the analgesic subculture*.

Although its application is obviously regarded as more general, the analgesic subculture concept will be limited in the following analysis specifically to the condition of the poor. Since, however, this is a remarkably heterogeneous category in itself, the intention here is to be even more specific by a focus upon only one of the many manifestations of poverty—the "folk subculture" of the Southern Appalachian Mountains. This particular example must not be considered a representative case; it is instead almost an "ideal type" illustration in support of the thesis.

The Frustration-Instigated Behavior Concept

The distinction between frustration-instigated behavior and motivation-instigated behavior first came about as a result of Maier's (1949) experiments with rats. In most of the reported experiments, the Lashley jumping apparatus was used. This device consists of a small stand facing a wall in which there are two apertures. Each "window" is covered with a card printed with its respective symbol. The animal, placed on this platform, is forced to choose one card by jumping at it and striking it with his body. If the correct card is struck, the card falls over and the animal lands on a feeding platform (reward). If the incorrect card is struck, the card remains locked in place and the animal receives a thump and falls into a net below (punishment). When one of the cards is consistently locked, and is changed to both a right and left position on different trials, the animal develops a preference for one card so that it consistently chooses the card that leads to reward and avoids the other—regardless of the side on which the reward card is placed. In experiments in which the cards are changed from side to side, and either the left or right card is consistently made correct, the animal disregards the symbol and responds in terms of position. These choices Maier regards as learned preferences representing goal-oriented or goal-motivated responses.

If, however, the cards are locked at random, then there is no systematic response which will permit escape from punishment. In such cases, the animal usually shows a stage of variability in its choices, and soon thereafter it refuses to jump. This resistance to jumping may be overcome by an electric shock, prodding with a stick, or blowing a blast of air on the animal. Maier speaks of this situation as the "insoluble problem" and regards it as frustrating, both because it is a problem that cannot be solved and because pressure is applied to force a response.

The behavior of the animal in these circumstances is instructive. After a short while in the "insoluble" situation, and with pressure applied to force jumping, the rat develops a response which has no "adaptive" value in the sense that it is adequate to the situation or in the sense that it is superior to any number of any other possible responses. Thus, an animal may respond by always choosing the card on its right, in spite of the fact that this *position-stereotyped* choice is punished on half the trials. Other animals respond by developing a *symbol-stereotyped* preference for one of the two cards, regardless of its position. The stereotype adopted by any given animal will be maintained rigidly, without the animals once attempting an alternative, despite the fact that the response is punished half the time. *Even more striking is the observation that the animals will not abandon their stereotyped responses when punishment is instituted on every trial.*

Maier maintains that such behavior cannot be adequately accounted for by ordinary learning theory. His hypothesis is that motivation and frustration are qualitatively different instigators of behavior and must therefore be described by different principles. "In order to make the distinction between motivation and frustration clear, we shall use the term *motivation* to characterize the process by which the expression of behavior is determined or its future expression can be influenced by consequences to which such behavior leads." (Maier, 1949:93). Motivation-instigated behavior is properly approached on the basis of learning theory; it is flexible and adaptive. The behavior is goaloriented, and the learner profits from experience. Frustration-instigated behavior, in contrast, is not goal-oriented behavior in the usual sense. "In distinguishing between motivation and frustration, therefore, it is important to recognize that the consequence of the action is not a factor in the selection of behavior under frustration." (Maier, 1949:94).

Since there is no apparent goal in frustration-instigated behavior, such behavior appears senseless when regarded from the typical motivational point of view. But behavioral science researchers and social change agents are typically products of backgrounds in which goal-orientation is a dominant theme. They find it difficult to think in terms of less rationalistic assumptions and tend to overlook the possibility that behavior resulting from extreme frustration may represent a terminal response to the frustration itself rather than a means to any end. The possibility that satisfaction simply comes in temporary relief and tension-reduction would explain the observation that, although frustration may be a result of deprivation, it often produces behavior logically unrelated to alleviation of the frustrating conditions. According to Maier, there are essentially four classes of such frustration-instigated behavior. These seemingly irrational responses are fixation, regression, aggression, and resignation.

One is constrained to repeat the common caution against over-generalizing the results of rigidly controlled experiments with rats to account for what may be "infinitely more complex" human behavior. It is also true that laboratory experiments are structured in pure "ideal type" situations which no one expects to encounter in "real life." Thus, humans encounter reward and frustration simultaneously and in varying degrees, partly as a result of a complexity of objective life circumstances and partly because of differences in individual perceptions and definitions of similar situations. Still, to admit that the laboratory is not life, and that rats are not men, is not to dismiss the real connections within these pairs.

Conclusions based on the behavior of infrahuman species can serve as valuable hypotheses in a study of man's behavior. It is ironic that the rationalistic bias, by no means restricted to sociology, has interfered with a rational evaluation of contributions such as Maier's, based on hundreds of controlled experiments spanning decades. As Yates (1962:2) remarks, "There is no doubt that the lasting value of his work has been obscured by sheer prejudice and *a priori* convictions."

Actually, support for the principle of frustration-instigated behavior is really much broader than might initially appear to be the case. First, there is the fact that the concept proves extremely useful in the interpretation of controlled experiments using *human* subjects. Secondly, the approach partly explains the failure of conventional, rationalistic methods of behavior modification. It also provides a rationale for new techniques. Finally, it is significant to the present thesis that these arguments for a less rationalistic posture are supported by one of the grand speculative theories of social change—that of Arnold Toynbee. That such different sets of foci and method as those of Maier and Toynbee result in such mutually reinforcing conclusions implies the need for a more temperate reassessment of their core ideas.

Environmental Challenge and Cultural Response

Toynbee is another who, although his writings have hardly been ignored, has found himself subjected to unusually vehement criticism, the most essential of which refers to "his claim that A *Study of History* is based upon empirical methods." (Cahnman and Boskoff, 1964:55.) Such a claim must be denied if the phrase, "empirical methods," is employed in anything but the loosest sense. There is, however, empirical evidence relevant to the theories, and it exists in some of the most rigorous forms available in the behavioral sciences. While these data, of which Maier's is illustrative, will certainly not substantiate the more sweeping speculations, they do suggest that Toynbee's ideas ought not to be rejected out of hand. Furthermore, Toynbee's work is of special relevance to the problem of subcultural origin and change as "a magnificent example of the possibilities of cultural case-study in historical sociology" (Barnes, 1948:729), particularly if his concepts are regarded as sensitizing rather than as definitive.

Toynbee (1946), of course, views the development of civilization itself as a "response" to "challenges" in both the social and natural environment. There is considerable similarity between his idea of the impossible challenge and Maier's concept of the "insoluble problem" situation, but even more significant is the close correspondence between the historian's speculations on human responses and the experimental psychologist's observations of reactions in laboratory animals. Toynbee argues, for example, that the basic contributions to the building of American civilization came from those living in the coastal region bounded by the Mason-Dixon Line to the south and a line through New England to the north. He maintains that the environmental challenge below the Mason-Dixon Line was generally insufficient to produce an energetic response, while in

Maine, on the other hand, the challenge was actually too great. In his analysis of historical responses to overwhelming challenges, Toynbee (1946:147) refers to Maine as a "museum piece," remarking that, "Maine today is at once one of the longest-settled regions of the American Union and one of the least urbanized and sophisticated."

These words describe almost exactly conditions in the Southern Appalachian Mountains. In fact, closer study of the latter region discloses an even more striking congruence between Toynbee's generalizations and the results of Maier's experiments. If the frustration-instigated behavior hypothesis is correct, the response similarities can be explained by the observation that the historical challenges faced in Appalachia approximated even more closely the conditions of Maier's experiments than did the problems encountered in Maine. Life in the Southern Appalachians has been for many almost a model of "insoluble problems," "impossible challenges," and overwhelming frustrations.

The Problems of Appalachia

Toynbee (1946:149) has set forth his view of the Appalachian challenge and the human response in no uncertain terms. He writes as follows:

> Let us next consider an instance in which the challenge has been not exclusively physical but partly physical and partly human. . . .
>
> The modern Ulstermen, however, are not the only surviving overseas representatives of this stock, for the Scottish pioneers who migrated to Ulster begat Scotch-Irish descendants who reimmigrated in the eighteenth century from Ulster to North America, and these survive today in the fastnesses of the Appalachian mountains, a highland zone which runs through half a dozen states in the American Union from Pennsylvania to Georgia. . . . Obviously, this American challenge has been more formidable than the Irish challenge in both its aspects, physical and human. Has the increased challenge evoked an increased response? If we compare the Ulstermen and the Appalachian of today, two centuries after they parted company, we shall find that the answer is once again in the negative. The modern Appalachian has not only not improved on the Ulstermen; he has failed to hold his ground and has gone downhill in the most disconcerting fashion. In fact, the Appalachian "mountain people" today are no better than barbarians. They have relapsed into illiteracy and witchcraft. They suffer from poverty, squalor, and ill health. They are the American counterparts of the latter-day white barbarians of the Old World— Rifis, Albanians, Kurds, Pathans, and Hairy Ainus; but, whereas these latter are belated survivals of an ancient barbarism, the Appalachians present the melancholy spectacle of a people who have acquired civilization and then lost it.

Toynbee has, of course, overstated the case. A closer look will usually show more differentiation than is apparent from afar, and many Southern Appalachian mountaineers have cause to resent such a blanket condemnation. Toynbee's words are more accurate when limited to what may be designated as the "folk subculture" of the area. Writers who deal with Appalachia unintentionally devote most of their attention to this particular portion of the regional population—partly because it is a sizable contingent, partly because its existence has been defined as a "social problem," and perhaps partly because the bulk of the region's people are too much like most Americans to be considered "interesting."

These mountaineers have been subjected to a history of unremitting physical, economic, and social frustration. They have been repeatedly blocked, pressured, and defeated by their environment. The history of their frustration is described vividly in the following passages from Caudill's (1962:ix–xi) *Night Comes to The Cumberlands:*

> . . . Their past created the modern mountaineers and the communities in which they live, and resulted in a land of economic, social, and political blight without parallel in the nation. . . . Coal has always cursed the land in which it lies. When men begin to wrest it from the earth it leaves a legacy of foul streams, hideous slag heaps, and polluted air. It peoples this transformed land with blind and crippled men and with widows and orphans. . . .
>
> But the tragedy of the Kentucky mountains transcends the tragedy of coal. It is compounded of Indian wars, Civil war, and internecine feuds, of layered hatreds and of violent death. To its sad blend, history has added the curse of coal as a crown of sorrow. . . .
>
> In the 1960 preferential primary, Senator—now President—John F. Kennedy campaigned across West Virginia and saw at first hand the conditions existing in the coal fields of that state. The spectacle of mass misery and of mass surrender to it appears to have deeply impressed him, because in the general election campaign he repeatedly referred to the hunger and depression he had seen there. . . . However, the fact is that a million Americans in the Southern Appalachians live today in conditions of squalor, ignorance, and ill health which could scarcely be equalled in Europe or Japan or, perhaps, in parts of mainland Asia.

Certain typical responses have resulted from these conditions. Ford (1962:9–34), interpreting data from the most comprehensive general survey of the Southern Appalachians ever conducted, lists the principal cultural themes as (1) individualism and self-reliance, (2) traditionalism and fatalism, and (3) religious fundamentalism. Weller (1965), specifically describing what he calls the "folk class" as *Yesterday's People,* gives special emphasis to individualism, traditionalism, fatalism, action-seeking, fear psychology, reference-group domination, and familism. There is now a wealth of descriptive data, and it clearly substantiates such portraits of the folk subculture. The task of explanation has proved more difficult, for the bland assertion that the subculture represents "tradition" is not in fact an explanation at all. There remains the problem of the origin and persistence of this way of life; to maintain that it persists because it is traditional is more than a bit tautological.

The Analgesic Subculture

Prominent research attention has been directed toward Appalachia in recent years, and specifications of the content of the Appalachian folk subculture are fairly complete, but most of the authors of these descriptions, and particularly the regional planners, admit to difficulty in understanding and dealing with the values they have described. The conduct of these people seems to them even more senseless than that of most "hard core" poverty groups. Why, it is asked, are they so little interested in improving their lives? How can they resign themselves to acceptance of minimal welfare payments and then adopt the "dole" as a permanent way of life? Why aren't they more eager to leave their hopeless environment for urban areas of greater opportunity? What, in short, explains their lack of ambition, their "episodic" view of life, and their inability to arouse themselves to sustained efforts? Admittedly, their past has been bleak and hopeless, but why should this prevent them from responding to the opportunities of the present?

As is often the case, the inability of students of Southern Appalachia to comprehend the behavior of their subjects is rooted less in faulty logic or inadequate observation than in the implicit acceptance of dubious assumptions about human behavior. One of these is the assumption that all behavior is rational or motivation-instigated. The stubborn recalcitrance of the mountaineer simply resists explanation in these terms. Nor can one explain fatalism and apathy as sensible adaptations to contempory learning situations. What the highly motivated and remarkably adaptive observer cannot easily understand is the daily experience of inexorable pressure, "insoluble problems," and absolutely overwhelming frustration. These are the life experiences of the poor generally, but they have been experienced with special intensity by the mountaineer, and it is this fact which makes his particular plight of more general relevance.

These life conditions provide the major key to the origin, development and continued existence of the Southern Appalachian folk subculture. The subculture represents to a significant degree *the institutionalization of frustration-instigated behavior*. The principal values, beliefs and implementing norms, formed during a history of protracted misfortune, are supported by the internal nature of the subculture and by the external pressures of contemporary life. These shared understandings are transmitted across generations; the young learn to anticipate defeat and to perform the subcultural rituals which reduce its impact. The frustration-instigated behaviors observable in laboratory experiments have become a thoroughgoing way of life, justified by religious doctrine and sustained by a social order. The result of this process, viewed in terms of its functional properties, may be conveniently labeled the *analgesic subculture*. It is a prototype of which the Appalachian folk subculture is only one manifestation. In whatever form, the analgesic subculture is possessed of considerable durability, for not only is the expectation of defeat a self-fulfilling prophecy, but the relief behaviors predicated by the subculture tend in the long run to produce additional problems. More than a vicious circle, the consequence resembles a descending spiral.

Principal Components of the Analgesic Subculture

The concept of the analgesic subculture implies that the principal components of the subculture can be subsumed under Maier's four response categories. Applying the thesis to the specific test case, one might predict that the Appalachian folk subculture would be dominated by symptoms of fixation, regression, aggression and resignation. Seldom is an expectation more completely fulfilled.

Fixation as a Subcultural Pattern. If fixation is defined as an abnormally strong and persisting response, without ascribing any psychoanalytic meaning, the stereotyped behavior of the rats in Maier's experiments represents a clear illustration. More extreme examples are to be found in additional experiments which indicate that, even when the fixated animals have actually learned which card punishes and which does not, they are unable to practice the required response. Maier notes that this property of the fixation makes it appear as a form of *compulsion*. That is, the animal executes an unadapted response even though it "knows better." The compulsive nature of the fixation is apparent, for example, when one places the negative card on the side to which the animal is fixated, and the other window is left open with a dish of food placed in plain view near the opening. In this case the animal orients itself toward the open window and sniffs toward the food; it then turns and jumps "forcibly" at the locked card representing the stereotyped (fixated) response. Such behavior can hardly be described as rational or goal-oriented. It is important to recognize, however, that the fixation does appear to provide *a sort of adjustment* to the situation, thereby reducing "emotional tensions" in the animal. The fact that resistance to jumping in the "insoluble problem" situation declines, when stereotyped responses appear, supports the view. The conclusion is further reinforced by the observation that animals developing a fixation response thereafter suffer fewer seizures under pressure. Apparently the "abnormal" fixation gives the animal a way of responding to the insoluble problem, without which such situations would have remained unbearably stressful.

Much of the obstinate traditionalism of the Southern Appalachian folk subculture may be interpreted as the stereotyped behavior of people seeking relief from insoluble problems. What has long been criticized as an adherence to old ways which is "stubborn, sullen and perverse to a degree that others cannot comprehend" (Kephart, 1913:23) becomes more understandable in terms of the soothing qualities of ritual. Critics who complain that the tenacious adherence to custom limits the adaptability of the subculture are quite correct, but Maier's experiments indicate that such nonrational behavior may be temporarily effective in reducing anxiety. The result is that, although the opinionated, dogmatic, and argumentative behavior of the mountaineer may multiply his problems, he persists in it nevertheless. If, in the vernacular of the subculture, he frequently "cuts off his nose to spite his face" by stubbornly insisting upon actions which are clearly against his rational self-interest, this "irrationality" is at least comprehensible as a frustration-instigated action.

Regression as a Subcultural Pattern. The frustration-instigated behavior concept also leads one to predict that the Appalachian folk subculture will be typified by patterns of regression, aggression and resignation. As Maier points out, the early work of Barker et al. (1941), in which regression is conceptualized as a simplification of behavior rather than as a retracing of the individual's past, has clearly linked conditions of frustration with regression responses. Since this early research, a considerable number of studies have discovered additional connections (Yates, 1962: 113–138).

Many of the behaviors commonly cited in descriptions of the folk culture can be construed as examples of regression induced by frustration. These characteristics would include the lack of aesthetic appreciation, anti-intellectualism, the preference of anecdote over abstraction, the insistence upon a literal interpretation of the Bible, the entanglement of religious fundamentalism with deep superstition, the improvident squandering which often accompanies "pay day" or a welfare check, the tendency for self-pity, and the conversion of the "sick role" into what local physicians sometimes half-seriously term a "chronic passive-dependency syndrome" (Caudill, 1962:283). Use of the term "regression" to describe these circumstances is congruent with Toynbee's conclusion that the mountaineer has "failed to hold his ground," that he has "gone downhill in a most disconcerting fashion," and that he has "relapsed" into conditions of barbarism.

Two particular manifestations of regressive behavior stand out as major problems of Appalachia. One of these may be called the Welfare Syndrome. The other is the occasionally neurotic dependence upon kin which is manifested in extreme Familism. Space limitations preclude more than a summary of the Welfare Syndrome. Many of the members of the folk subculture have regressed to a state of social dependency. Although what has been intended as a temporary assistance has been converted into a way of life, the explanation of this behavior is not to be sought in standard concepts of rational motivation. There is nothing particularly "sensible" about living on welfare payments little above subsistence when opportunities for goal-directed behavior are, if not abundant, at least in many cases available. To one who proceeds solely on assumptions of rationalism, permanent reliance upon public welfare seems to be an inexplicable use of means (of temporary assistance) as ends (or terminal adaptations). The frustration-instigated behavior concept supplies an explanation of such behavior, for frustration-instigated behavior is characteristically a *terminal response to frustration* and not a means to an end. Without intending a play on words, one may say that the satisfaction which occurs from frustration-instigated behavior is precisely in the form of relief rather than of goal-attainment.

Just as the Welfare Syndrome may be interpreted as a form of regression, so may exaggerated Familism. The literature on Appalachian life consistently points to an intensive *emotional dependence* on kin. Some young people simply never establish themselves as separate individuals. Nor are they encouraged to do so by their parents. Both parents and children maintain what may be termed a "clinging behavior" which may be based less upon genuine affection and shared activities than upon neurotic emotional entanglements characterized by a mutual resentment. Grown offspring who hate their parents cannot bear to be away from them. Migrants who have finally broken away suddenly and curiously return home at the slightest misfortunes. The subculture not only condones this behavior, but *it functions to institutionalize it.*

Aggression as a Subcultural Pattern. Of the four characteristic frustration-instigated responses described by Maier, neither fixation nor regression has received the research attention accorded to the frustration-aggression combination. Since the initial publication of *Frustration and Aggression,* (Dollard et al., 1944) intensive study has been pointed toward an elucidation of the connection between these phenomena (Yates, 1962:66–112). One may, of course, accept the evidence for a relationship between frustration and aggression without assuming that behaviors other than aggression are excluded as possible frustration responses. Maier maintains that the frustration-aggression hypothesis, in its less extreme form, could be integrated with this theory of frustration-instigated behavior. Dollard and his colleagues have recognized that aggression is not necessarily directed to the point which obstructs problem-solving and that the results of the aggression may even be such as to aggravate the frustration. Maier contends that this sort of aggression is characteristic of frustration-instigated behavior generally. Again, the response is an end-product rather than a means to an end. The expression of aggression may be interpreted as a tension-reducing response against available targets rather than as a rationally motivated, goal-directed activity, and Maier (1949:103–107) himself cites research on human subjects in support of this contention.

Much of the otherwise "senseless" conduct of the mountaineer is comprehensible in terms of an analgesic subculture theory. Herein may lie the explanation for the imfamous mountain feuds. Feuding behavior is an excellent example of subculturally patterned aggression which, while providing the momentary satisfactions of revenge, serves no rational purpose. As some unsuccessful mediators have dimly perceived, the feud was not developed as an intelligently designed means to an end, nor even as an accidentally effective instrument. It is an end in itself. Had the McCoys been unavailable, the Hatfields would have probably (to use another insightful expression) "taken it out on" some other target.

Resignation as a Subcultural Pattern. In addition to fixation, regression, and aggression, the frustration-instigated behavior concept would lead one to predict considerable resignation to the hostile conditions of Southern Appalachian life. Seldom is an expectation more fully realized. Resignation, apathy, and fatalism are rarely so prominent as among the members of the mountain folk subculture. Since resignation consists in giving up, it is not representative of goal-oriented action. In fact, goals have receded from reality and motivation seems largely absent. Resignation has, in short, the attributes of the other frustration-instigated behaviors. It is not a means to anything; it is an "end of the line" behavior. Such a response may be difficult for the motivation-oriented observer to comprehend, but it is quite likely to provide relief from the tensions of extreme and prolonged frustration.

Conclusion

To maintain that man's conduct is frequently "unreasonable" is by no means to argue that it can never be explained or predicted. There are patterns to his anomalies, and these must be rigorously traced, empirically verified, and systematically applied to sociological theory and to social action programs. The delineation of the analgesic subculture is one step in that direction. Students of socially thwarted minorities would have less difficulty understanding the normative orders they describe if they would recognize the extent to which such systems represent the institutionalization of basic frustration responses. The reactions will be expressed somewhat differently in various subcultures, depending upon the particular nature of the obstacles and the available tradition, but the underlying processes are essentially identical. The responses are perhaps most vivid with the mountaineer since his impoverished condition is coupled with a hostile environment and historical tragedy.

The Southern Appalachian folk subculture is certainly easier to understand in terms of the thesis presented. Responding to a given configuration of "insoluble problems," the mountaineer has developed a way of life emphasizing stereotyped behavior, dependency, belligerence and fatalistic resignation. Admittedly, these reactions are not "adequate adaptations to the situation." They do not represent "effective coping with the environment." Nevertheless, the responses are in a limited sense functional, for they provide relief from the pains of frustration.

Such subcultures are, however, complicated wholes maintained by internal linkages as well as by their capacity to deflect environmental pressures. One would expect them to survive for some time even if the circumstances which produce them were eliminated entirely. This persistence is based on the "autostability" of the system. This phenomenon, neglected by the more rationalistic functionalists, may be observed whenever an obsolete technology is maintained by vested interest, or a policy rendered inexpedient by change is compulsively persevered in by the system constructed for its implementation. The process involves a two-step sequence. In the first stage the system, receiving "feedback" as to its effectiveness, adjusts and maintains itself in terms of its principal functions. Various aspects of the whole develop and integrate to that end. The result, under appropriate conditions, is a system which "runs itself" on the basis of what in mechanics is called autostability.

The analgesic subcultures are generally perpetuated by such autostability as well as by their intrinsically functional properties. One explanation for their durability, for example, lies in the very fact that they have developed as nonrational responses to frustration rather than as rewarding solutions to environmental problems. It is entirely possible that these are among the most rigid of all subcultures. Such implications follow from certain basic data.

Animals that have previously developed stereotypes in a given situation are less likely to learn a simple reward response than animals that have previously acquired a reward response and then must learn another. Thus, it seems to be more difficult to substitute a reward response for a stereotype than to substitute one reward response for another. . . .

. . . The stereotyped response developed in the insoluble problem situation is more stable than a similar response required through systematic reward. This greater persistence of a response developed in the insoluble problem occurs despite the fact that under this condition the assumed response is one that is punished as frequently as it is rewarded (Maier, 1949:31–32).

The consequences are truly paradoxical in terms of rationalistic assumptions. The strength of the analgesic subculture is apparently in large part a product of its failures. Formed as a response to defeat, and offering no "adaptive" solutions to environmental problems, it virtually assures the persistence of the problems, and thereby becomes more deeply entrenched. Even if the problems were suddenly solved by outside intervention, Maier's data suggest that the responses built on years of stress would be extremely difficult to alter. The rigidity of any analgesic subculture seems inherent in its nature.

Each individual subculture may be expected to develop additional autostabilizing components. Again, the Appalachian folk subculture provides convenient illustrations of the more general process. The subculture's punitive child-rearing practices may be cited as a case in point. One of the clearest distinctions between motivation-instigated behavior and frustration-instigated behavior is seen in the effects of punishment with regard to the latter. From the rationalistic point of view, one would assume that punishment tends to force abandonment of proscribed behavior. In terms of the frustration-instigated behavior hypothesis, on the other hand, one might postulate that punishment aggravates frustration and that punishment would therefore tend to strengthen the stereotyped behavior. Maier's experiments support the latter conclusion. His data indicate, in fact, that punishment on all trials is even less likely to transform an animal's stereotyped response than is irregular punishment. He concludes that punishing a stubborn, undesirable response may not only fail to alter it but may actually increase its persistence and consequently make future corrections more difficult. The folk subculture offers evidence of this relationship, for Weller (1965:65–66) reports that discipline is "punishment-based" and that children are taught to obey through fear.

Furthermore, the subculture generally renders the mountaineer more susceptible to frustration-instigated behaviors by incorporating practices which impede the development of frustration tolerance. It is not customary to praise children judiciously or to reward effective conduct in any systematic fashion. Caudill (1962:73) notes the absence of "a quality which is almost never encountered in the highlands to this day: willingness to commend a person openly for a favor done or for some desirable skill or trait," and he points out that "the mountaineer was literally starved for compliments and for some outward show of appreciation." This is still the case, and one apparent result is a low frustration threshold. There is no history of reward to balance future frustrations, and there are few pleasant memories to assist one through periods of stress. The effect is to reinforce the subculture, for it becomes even more attractive to the vulnerable.

It is small wonder that these subcultures are so resistant to change. Exhortations against the symptoms of frustration will not eliminate the causes. Maier's experiments indicate instead that to teach people to restrain their frustration-instigated reactions without also attacking the source is to force them into a state of intolerable anxiety. Those who would modify such subcultures must realize that they may be for some the only emotional refuge available. They must also realize that to stigmatize such practices may simply reinforce them.

The impoverished mountaineer finds himself in a situation not unlike that of other minority groups. Despite the fact that he has been provided with gradually increasing opportunities, he is faced with increasing frustrations based on the sense of relative deprivation and the growing demand that he solve his problems. The experience of relative deprivation is forced upon him through increased physical contact with other people and by way of the mass media. These convey to him an image of the "good life," and in contrast with this image his own existence appears more bleak and hopeless than before. His frustrations are also deepened by those who urge him to self-help and increase his expectations for improvement, for they may succeed in increasing his desire for a "better" life. Unless this goal is attained quickly, the problem often becomes even more frustrating simply because the motivation to solve it is intensified.

This analysis should not be interpreted as a repudiation of planned social change. The argument is rather that social action might be more effectively undertaken after reappraisal of fundamental assumptions regarding human behavior. Since one important rationalistic misconception is the assumption that such behavior is predominantly goal-directed, admission of the (psychological) concept of frustration-instigated behavior and the (sociological) hypothesis of the analgesic subculture represents a modest but extremely significant concession to those who insist that values, norms and behaviors may be less than wholly rational. There is evidence that these concepts may be very effective tools in understanding and dealing with social problems such as "hard-core" poverty; many of the implications are apparent.

The tentative and still inexact nature of the analgesic subculture thesis is obvious, and contemporary sociological training is such as to incline one toward more cautious assertions. Certainly less controversial hypotheses are always in demand, and it is with some reluctance that one submits incompletely developed notions to demanding audiences. It remains to be seen whether the premises in the argument are justified, but this must be resolved empirically. Overgeneralizations must be identified and corrected, impressions must be quantified, and assumptions must be tested. The argument, however forcefully it may be put, is regarded as an opening statement.

REFERENCES

Barker, R. T. Dembo and K. Lewin.
    1941   Frustration and Regression. Iowa City: University of Iowa Press.
Barnes, H. E., ed.
    1948   An Introduction to the History of Sociology. Chicago: University of Chicago Press.
Cahnman, Werner J. and Alvin Boskoff, eds.
    1964   Sociology and History. New York: Free Press.
Caudill, Harry M.
    1962   Night Comes to the Cumberlands. Boston: Little, Brown.
Dollard, J., N. E. Miller, L. W. Doob, O. H. Mowrer and R. R. Sears.
    1944   Frustration and Aggression. London: Kegan Paul.
Ford, Thomas R., ed.
    1962   The Southern Appalachian Region. Lexington: University of Kentucky Press.
Kephart, Horace.
    1913   Our Southern Highlanders. New York: Outing Publishing.

Maier, Norman R.
1949   Frustration. New York: McGraw-Hill.
Thomas, W. I.
1928   The Child in America. New York: Knopf.
Toynbee, Arnold J.
1946   A Study of History. New York: Oxford University Press.
Weller, Jack E.
1965   Yesterday's People. Lexington: University of Kentucky Press.
Wrong, Dennis H.
1961   "The oversocialized conception of man in modern sociology." American Sociological Review 26 (April):187–193.
Yates, Aubrey J.
1962   Frustration and Conflict. New York: Wiley.

9

JAMES B. WATSON AND JULIAN SAMORA

SUBORDINATE LEADERSHIP IN A BICULTURAL COMMUNITY: AN ANALYSIS

It is held in the present paper that the ability of a subordinate group to generate effective leadership in its relations with a dominant alien people is a critical aspect of dominant-subordinate group relationships. The subordinate group in question here is the Spanish of the Southwest. We wish to see Spanish leadership in its autonomous setting, to see it in relation to the intercultural system which is emerging between Spanish and Anglo-Americans, and to consider leadership and some of its acculturational consequences.

Regional Background of the Case

The Spanish-speaking people are one of the largest United States ethnic minorities, and are concentrated principally in the southwestern part of the nation. Those whose forefathers were in the area in 1848 when the United States acquired the territory are also among the oldest ethnic groups, although many others have entered the region from Mexico over the intervening years. The Spanish-speaking are not powerful politically, a fact closely related to the perennial lack of leadership among them. They are seen by some authorities as surprisingly undifferentiated, compared to other large American ethnic groups, in schooling, in occupation, in income, and in degree of acculturation.[1] Perhaps the most outstanding fact about the Spanish, besides their lack of leadership is their low rate of

Reprinted with permission from *American Sociological Review* 19 (1954): 413–421.

acculturation. The special historical status of the Spanish may have a bearing upon the two facts, and the broad historical context suggests linkages between the leadership question and that of low assimilation.

The Southwestern Spanish[2] were a separate society when they came into contact with, and in a sense were conquered by Anglo-Americans, or "Anglos." Speaking a separate language and practicing separate customs, they were highly visible culturally. They represented nevertheless a modified branch of European civilization, unlike the Indians from whom they had received many influences, and unlike African slaves. In contrast to many Europeans who migrated to the United States, however, they had not voluntarily elected to adopt the lifeways of the dominant group. Moreover, they were more "native" and ecologically more adapted to their habitat in the Southwest than the dominant group. In these two respects they were more like Indians than immigrants. In the growing similarity of their goals with those of the dominant group, the Spanish are comparable to the present United States Negro, though their cultural similarity to Anglos is much less. In the sense of being a "conquered people" enslaved by their conquerors, the Spanish are somewhat like colonial people but more strictly comparable to the French of Canada. They differ from the French, however, in having smaller numerical strength relative to the dominant group, and they did not occupy the beachhead and focal areas of the Anglo-American culture and society. Their relative isolation (1650–1900) from the parent culture as well as from the Anglo culture is also an important factor with respect to assimilation.

Hence, historically having less motivation toward assimilation and deeper environmental and traditional roots than most U. S. immigrants, less commitment to and a less exclusive need for identification with the dominant cultural system than U. S. Negroes, but smaller numerical strength and less strategic position than the Canadian French, the Spanish as a group might be expected, more than others, to sense ambivalences about assimilation. Again, beside the fact of an increasing struggle for status in the Anglo system, one must place the opposing fact—peculiar to the Southwestern Spanish—that they have at their backs an effective reservoir of Spanish language and national Mexican culture to help reinforce and stabilize any tendency toward cultural separatism.

All of these broad, contradictory factors probably play their part in the default of Spanish leadership, as well as the more specific factors discussed below. In the larger Southwestern setting ambivalence about nativism vs. assimilation would obscure the direction Spanish leadership should take and thus hamstring the development of effective leadership.

Turning to the present, there is singularly little controversy concerning whether Spanish leadership is weak, regardless of the point of view of different commentators. Agreement is all but unanimous among scientific investigators,[3] among social workers and public and private agencies interested in the Spanish-speaking people, among Anglo politicians, and among the people themselves. The Spanish of "Mountain Town," the subject of the present paper, are no exception.

The Community Studied

In the summers of 1949 and 1950, students from the Department of Sociology and Anthropology of Washington University, under James B. Watson's direction, carried out part of an intended long-range study of a small Anglo-Spanish community. Samora further pursued field work in the community, relating particularly to the question of Spanish-speaking leadership and organization, in the spring and summer of 1952.[4] It is largely with the findings from this bi-ethnic community that we propose to explore the question of weak leadership, but with the general background of the region always in mind.

Mountain Town, as we have called the community, is located in a high mountain valley of southern Colorado. It is at about 7000 feet above sea level, in an area of mixed truck farming and cattle and sheep ranching. Its 1950 population was close to 2500, comprising approximately 58 per cent Spanish-speaking and 42 per cent Anglos. (Hence the Spanish-speaking are not numerically a "minority" in the community itself, and will not be so called.) Founded around 1870, Mountain Town developed as a community of Anglo miners, storekeepers, and homesteaders. There were at the time but few "Old Spanish" families in the area, and they did not precede the Anglos by more than a decade or two. Mountain Town, hence, developed differently from the older established Spanish communities to the south which Anglos have come to dominate. The difference may have a bearing in the discussion which follows.

Descendents of original Spanish settlers still live in or near Mountain Town. It is probable that at least some of them could have been classed as *Patrón* families. Two or three are still landowners. However, the vast majority of Spanish-speaking families in Mountain Town came at a later date, many possibly around 1920. Much of this migration was from the Spanish villages of northern New Mexico, and kinsmen can often still be traced to or from that area. Practically none of these people are landowners, except for house plots; nor are they often proprietors in any other sense. The largest number are still seasonal wage workers, unskilled or semiskilled "stoop labor." Some of the women work as domestics, but many more work in the fields or produce-packing sheds. As a group, the Spanish-speaking depend for employment on the prosperity of local agriculture.

While the foregoing generalizations stand, some Spanish are now making their way slowly up the socioeconomic ladder as store clerks, garage or filling station employees, a few as operators of small groceries or oil stations, and several as salaried clerical personnel. There has been a gradual increase over the last 25 years in the number of Spanish-speaking who have eighth grade schooling, and gradually more go on or complete high school.[5] The war industries of the Pacific Coast attracted a number from Mountain Town and materially raised their economic level, and service in the armed forces broadened the ethnic outlook of not only Spanish but also of some Mountain Town Anglos. There is no question of palpable Spanish acculturation. Bilingualism, to mention an important facet, now prevails among a majority of the Spanish and increasingly one finds older people the only strict monolinguals.

Many older Anglo residents of Mountain Town feel that they have seen a definite change in the social and economic status of the Spanish-speaking, but there is no denying that traditional attitudes and traditional ethnic relationships still generally prevail. The Anglo and Spanish-speaking groups are sharply distinguishable as to religion, economic status, occupational status, language, surnames, residence, and usually physical appearance. Ethnic distinctions along these lines are made by nearly all members of both groups. The Spanish are nearly all nominally Catholic and the Anglos are nearly all nominally Protestant. Political and economic control of the community is in the hands of the Anglos. There is not the slightest question of their superordinate position in relation to the Spanish as a whole, though certain individuals of Spanish background clearly receive personal respect and prestige well above that of many Anglos.

The Anglo-Spanish relationship has some of the properties of a caste system. Spanish and Anglo are practically endogamous. Religious participation is mostly along ethnic lines, and many Anglo Protestants would not want the conversion of non-Protestants at the expense of any sizeable Spanish attendance in their churches. Although somewhat ill defined, there is residential distinctness in Mountain Town, and distress is felt by some Anglos at having close "Mexican" neighbors. The Spanish are excluded almost completely from Anglo social and civic organizations (*e.g.*, lodges, Volunteer Firemen, Chamber of Commerce, Junior C of C, Rotary), except, to some extent, the P.T.A. and a veterans' group. In the cases of many of these organizations, the vast majority do not qualify for membership (*e.g.*, in Rotary), but the lack of qualifications appears to be largely incidental. Parties, dancing, picnics, and visiting are uniformly intraethnic, as are bridge, sewing circles, teas, and bazaars. As in a true caste system, obviously the sharp differentiation of interaction is not simply the will and doing of one group by itself. The Anglos, for example, find out, when they decide to broaden the membership of the Parent-Teachers Association, that it is not easy to enlist Spanish parents or to have them assume office.

Spanish Disunity

The disunity among the Spanish group is quite evident in Mountain Town. Disunity does not mean the existence of factionalism, it refers, rather, to the lack of common action and to limited group cohesion. When an issue of import to the members of the group comes up, few people will do anything about it. This has been proved many times in such things as politics, school segregation, employment, arrests, welfare aid, and in general discrimination.

Considering the distinctness of sociocultural boundaries, the disunity of the Spanish group is striking, for the rigid exclusiveness of the Anglos might theoretically be a strong factor in their cohesion. Nor can Spanish disunity find its explanation in any wide socioeconomic disparity within the group. Nevertheless, Spanish cohesion seldom transcends such verbalizations as *nosotros* ("we") or *la raza* ("our people"), a generalized resentment of Anglo dominance and discrimination, and a readiness to perceive injustice in Spanish-Anglo dealings.

Disunity is a large factor in the lack of political power of the Spanish. In Mountain Town numbers do not explain the failure of the subordinate group—a majority—to put people they trust into critical offices. The Spanish are not wholly indifferent about certain elective offices, the sheriff, for example, who, if prejudiced, may enforce the laws quite one-sidedly. The school board offices are also thought to be ethnically critical or sensitive because of constant fear of segregation. But the election of an avowedly pro-Spanish candidate is rare indeed. Perhaps few Anglo politicians have understood the basic disunity of the Spanish, but a good many have at least recognized it. Occasionally, however, a direct appeal is made to the Spanish as Spanish. The results in Mountain Town bear out the cynical who feel it is better to ignore the ethnic issue. "They will not even vote for their own people" is commonly asserted, and this is bitterly conceded by most Spanish.

The failure of unity and leadership in politics is not the only type of weakness of the Spanish group. There is, of course, a more informal type of leadership in interethnic relations. The spokesman, as he is often called, is a leader to whom politicians or others may turn for advice and commitments on matters seen as affecting the interests of the ethnic group. There are two or three Spanish individuals in Mountain Town—one in particular—whom most Anglos consider to be spokesmen. The same individuals were cited by the majority of the Spanish when asked by Samora who were the leaders of their group. Yet these individuals usually make commitments for their group only at great risk. Actually, they generally refuse to do more than express an opinion or give very general advice. Investigation failed to show that any individual among the Spanish, including those most mentioned as leaders by Spanish and by Anglos, was willing to assume the responsibilities of a real spokesman for the group. There was no reason to believe that any of the persons mentioned could actually keep significant commitments if he made them.

But if a distinction is made between the inter-ethnic leadership described above and intra-ethnic leadership,[6] is the picture of the latter more favorable? Investigation was made by the junior author and his wife of 16 *sociedades* and *mutualistas*, lodges and mutual benefit organizations, which exist in Mountain Town with exclusively Spanish membership and objectives, as well as of lay societies ancillary to the Roman Catholic Church. The findings, reported in detail elsewhere, were rather uniform.[7] On the whole, the non-church associations were characterized by ineffectual leadership, very poor attendance, irregularity of procedure and schedule, lack of decisive action—even in inducting new members—and often a precarious existence. Careful comparison of the church-sponsored sodalities (*e.g.*, Altar Society, Family Society) revealed the priest as central to their direction and probably instrumental in their better showing compared to the secular groups. Even when the priest tried to play a less prominent role, circumstances, if not his own inclinations, tended to thrust him into a position more beside than behind the figure in the chair. Lay leadership, by the priest's admission, from observation of the members, and by their testimony, was not considered adequate.

The facts about the Mountain Town Spanish suggest deficiency, then, both as to leadership in inter-ethnic relations and as to leadership of purely ethnic organizations, except those ancillary to the Church. Yet strong factors for cohesion unmistakably exist—Anglo exclusiveness, a relatively undifferentiated Spanish group, a common ethnic tongue, Spanish group concepts, recognition of group-wide grievances, their majority voting position, and even some Anglo political attempts to unify the Spanish vote. In the light of such factors, we may ask why leadership is so ineffectual among the Spanish.

The Hypothesis of Leadership Deficiency

It is the contention of this paper that four principal conditions account for the inadequacy of Spanish leadership in Mountain Town and probably to some extent among the Spanish of the larger Southwest.

(1) Traditional forms (patterns) of leadership, which functioned well enough in pre-Anglo-Spanish culture, have been unadaptable and possibly a handicap to the development of adequate patterns of group leadership in the contact situation.

(2) Increasingly, the status goals of the Spanish group as a whole lie in the direction of Anglo culture; for the achievement of such goals, hence, leaders relatively well adapted to the Anglo system are increasingly indicated.

(3) General ambivalence and suspicion are accorded individuals of Spanish background who are "successful" since the terms of success are now largely Anglo terms (viz. (2) above), and it is widely assumed that success is bought by cooperation with the outgroup and betrayal of one's own.

(4) Although caste-like enough to give sharp definition to the two groups, Anglo structure is relatively open to competent Spanish and thus permits the siphoning off of potential Spanish leadership, individuals relatively well adapted to the Anglo system.

The net result of these conditions is that, in the lack of adaptable traditional types, the only potential leaders who might be qualified to provide the kind of leadership indicated today are by virtue of their very qualifications absorbed into the larger body politic and are disqualified in the minds of their own fellows.

Discussion

(1) The conclusion is widespread that what can be said about traditions of authority in Mexico, and even Latin America, applies on the whole to the Spanish of the Southwest. If so, the pre-Anglo-Spanish picture was

one of strong authoritarian roles, the padre, the *patrón*, and the *jefe de familia*.[8] The *caudillo* is of course a classic Latin American type. In fact, a suggestive interpretation can be made of these roles in Spanish culture as variations on the same fundamental theme, strong and decisive authority, and F. Kluckhohn has commented that the Spanish-American is quite systematically trained for dependence upon such authority.[9] Such a pattern would scarcely appear by itself to be an impediment to the existence of effective Spanish leadership in inter-ethnic relations.

But the traditional pattern of local, secular authority among the Spanish is of the wrong kind. First, in many places, the *patrón* pattern was simply unable to survive the innovations of Anglo contact. In Mountain Town the *patrón-peón* relationship has no strong personal relevance for the majority of Spanish. They probably still possess some cultural adjustments to the pattern, but many lack deep roots in the community and hence lack any long-standing familial connection with local *patrón* lineages. Moreover, there is relatively little tenant or even employee relationship nowadays except with Anglo landlords or employers. Crew bosses and labor middlemen exist, to be sure, but these intercultural agents are usually themselves committed to Anglo employers.

Yet there are two *patrón*-like figures in Mountain Town, and these were the ones most often mentioned as leaders by the Spanish Samora interviewed. There was some ambivalence about them, however. Many who named these "leaders," apparently in default of anyone else, declared that they could not be counted on in a pinch or that they would not do all that they could for the Spanish people.[10] Investigation showed that these pseudo-*patrones*, when called upon, usually served their fellow Spanish in limited and personal ways. They might give an individual help in the form of advice or instructions. They sometimes helped him fill in an official form or make out an application. They might, though rarely, intercede, using their personal influence with some governmental (*i.e.*, Anglo) agency, typically the County Welfare bureau. Intercession in these cases would almost never be insistent; in fact, it is ordinarily reluctant. The pseudo-*patrones* were not reported by anyone as ever attempting to organize their people for some lasting and broadly based social action.

Interestingly enough, leadership in approximately these limited terms matches fairly well the authors' understanding of the older *patrón* pattern. The *patrón* did not form committees, found organizations, or often refer formally to his followers for common assent to social decisions. He bound them to him on a personalistic basis, with advice and counsel and by providing assistance to those lacking other resources. Such paternalistic leadership could function in the status system of colonial Mexican culture;

141

it cannot function very extensively where the *patrón* cannot assure his followers of security in reward for their loyalty—they work for Anglos— and where even the status of the *patrón* himself is guaranteed by no *latifundium* manned with loyal retainers. Too often his status depends— even more than that of successful Anglos, he feels—upon the sufferance and approval of those in dominant positions. In such a situation erstwhile leader and follower can do little for each other in the traditional terms which were the very core of the *patrón-peón* relationship.

It may be relevant to add that the *patrón* himself was usually identified with the same general social class as those who held most of the important formal offices in the government. Ties of kinship were traditionally common between *patrón* and official. It is probably not going too far to suggest that the *patrón* himself tended in many instances to act informally as an agent of government in relation to the *peones*—"His word was law." To the extent that *patrón* status was adjusted to fit such an identification with and informal extension of governmental authority, it would likely not be an adaptable form of leadership when kinship and status identification with the dominant group were made ambivalent or impossible through their replacement by aliens.

It will be recalled that the church-sponsored societies in Mountain Town are generally the most effective ones among the Spanish. The lack of inter-ethnic leadership by the church certainly cannot be blamed, like that of the *patrón*, on any local restriction of the church's ability to function, nor probably on any intrinsic maladaptation of church leadership. Rather, the reason is probably that the Roman Church in the United States is only indirectly political and that not all its communicants are Spanish. In any event the church does not attempt to provide local leadership for the Spanish as a group in their common struggle for status. A special factor in Mountain Town is the national origin of the priests, who come from Spain. This factor may be of no consequence, however, as Southwestern Spanish parishes with American-born priests may have no greater church leadership than Mountain Town in inter-ethnic relations.

(2) No attempt will be made to argue that traditional Spanish culture everywhere in the Southwest approximates that of Anglos in all its basic values. The case to the contrary has been effectively presented elsewhere, *e.g.*, concerning time orientation and the value attached to formal schooling.[11] Even with only superficial observation it is clear that "go-getter" tendencies are much less typical of Spanish than of Anglos, and there may be some basis in fact for other traits ascribed to the Spanish in the Anglo stereotype, as well as *vice-versa*.

Nevertheless, it is possible to carry the emphasis of Spanish-Anglo cultural differences to the point where certain obvious and growing similarities of goal and value are overlooked or omitted. Generalizing, necessarily, the Spanish in Mountain Town are interested in better jobs, better pay, and more material things, such as automobiles, housing, and appliances. There is increasingly a concern for having children complete at least grammar schooling and learn at least moderately fluent English. Measures taken by the school system, which either are, or are interpreted by the Spanish to be, attempts at segregation (such as a special first grade for English-deficient children), are strongly resented, as is discrimination in hiring and firing in employment, and alleged inequality in the administration of Old Age Pensions. The Spanish in Mountain Town, however, as we are emphasizing, are not very effective in changing conditions as they would.

It may be that the Mountain Town Spanish differ somewhat as to goals from those in some other parts of the Southwest. They are almost entirely landless, and are predominantly low-paid agricultural labor, a kind of rural proletariat. Yet they are resident, not essentially a migratory group. However, we are not convinced that Mountain Town is markedly unrepresentative of Spanish elsewhere in the Southwest.

The Spanish goals sketched lie in the direction of Anglo goals and for their realization a mastery of Anglo techniques and behavior patterns is necessary. Insofar as advancement toward such goals involves groupwide status, Spanish leader qualifications must necessarily include such skills as literacy, relatively high control of the English language, and knowledge of social, political, and legal usages primarily based on the dominant culture. Few Spanish in Mountain Town possess such thorough adjustment to and broad familiarity with Anglo culture, dependent as it largely is upon extensive schooling.

(3) Only a handful of eight Spanish individuals in Mountain Town possess the necessary qualifications in markedly higher degree than their fellows. As a matter of fact, it is essentially individuals with proven ability in Anglo culture who are singled out for mention as "leaders" in the survey conducted by Samora. What, then, if anything, keeps these persons from exercising the leadership functions so generally desired by the Spanish? As was mentioned, a good deal of ambivalence exists concerning these people (almost all men) in the minds of most Spanish questioned. It is often stated that these "leaders" will not really accept an active part in directing a struggle for Spanish equality; they will only do such things for their fellow Spanish as they think will not antagonize the Anglos. They are even frequently accused of working for the Anglos and not for *la raza*. And not a few feel that such leaders could only have achieved their—

usually modest—socioeconomic position at the expense of "selling out to the Anglo" or "by climbing over their own people." They are referred to as "proud" (*orgullosos*). Another adjective has been coined in Spanish especially to describe such relatively successful members of the Spanish community. Samora found that they are called *"agringados"*—"gringo-ized."

Here, then, is the dilemma: that the very traits which would qualify an individual to provide the sort of leadership called for are such as to cast suspicion upon his loyalty in the eyes of many he would lead. Is it that the qualified "leaders" make little effort to lead effectively because they feel—perhaps correctly—that they would have difficulty in getting an effective followership? Or is it that they get no effective following largely because of their own reluctance to exert leadership? No simple answer to the question will do, of course, particularly as leadership and followership are reciprocal roles and the lack of either precludes the other. It may be hard to say if there is a causal priority in Mountain Town between the two factors, but something more like a vicious circle is suggested by the frequent testimony of Mountain Town Spanish: many agree, on the one hand, that the relatively assimilated "leaders" are "proud" (*orgullosos*) but admit, on the other, that the people are "envious" (*envidiosos*) and are themselves unable to "follow" (*seguir*) anyone. It appears to be the case both that the hypothetical leaders are unwilling to lead and that the hypothetical followers are unable to accept followership.

(4) The factors so far suggested for the default of Spanish leadership clearly have their inter-cultural aspects, though they appear in some respects intrinsic to the Spanish culture. The fourth factor is more completely extrinsic to the Spanish side of the picture. It is that the ranks of the Anglo social structure are not completely closed to the exceptional Spanish individual who achieves appreciable mastery of Anglo culture. There is obviously no question about discrimination against individuals of Spanish background for equally competent Spanish and Anglos do not have an equal probability of success. But Anglo discrimination is paradoxically not rigid enough, in a sense, for the "good" of the Spanish as a group. That is, those able to deal with Anglos on their own terms frequently have a chance to do so—as individuals. Hence, they are not completely frustrated, embittered, or thrust back into their own group where they must either quit the struggle altogether or turn their energies and skills to leading their people in competition with the Anglos. Instead, although against greater obstacles than an Anglo, the unusual person frequently achieves a degree of success to some extent commensurate with his abilities relative to those of his fellows.

From the standpoint of leadership the Spanish situation is not helped by Anglo mythology. The Anglo social myth recognizes two racial types among the Spanish-speaking. One is the "Real Spanish," with higher intelligence, industry, and dependability, while the other is the "Mexican," a term frequently preceded by opprobrious adjectives according to the context. The latter type, according to the Anglo, lack amibition, and generally possess just the qualities which lodge them where they are found in the social order.

The Spanish themselves make no distinction between "Real Spanish" and "Mexicans." When referring to themselves in Spanish they use the term *"mejicanos"*; when referring to themselves in English they use the term "Spanish." When the Anglos refer to them, the Spanish prefer that they use the term "Spanish" rather than "Mexican," because of the derogatory connotation of the latter term.

There is greater social acceptance of the "Real Spanish" by Anglos, particularly when they show mastery of Anglo culture—which tends to corroborate the myth. This divisive effect of Anglo mythology on the Spanish group, although difficult to assess, is nonetheless real.

The net result of these characteristics of the Anglo system is to lower the motivation of qualified persons to lead, and perhaps to contaminate the successful individual in the view of his group. His partial acceptance by the Anglo gives seeming verification to Spanish suspicions of disloyalty. The intercultural source of this effect on subordinate leadership is dramatically underscored by the Mountain Town evidence.

The three most overtly successful Spanish individuals in Mountain Town confirm in every major respect mentioned what has been said above. They are much more competent and successful in the Anglo system than most Anglos; they are given a social acceptance by the Anglo group which, although far from unqualified, sets them markedly apart from the great majority of the Spanish; they are predominantly regarded by Anglos as "spokesmen" for the Spanish group, although by no means are they themselves willing to play the role intensively; they are mentioned with the highest frequency by the Spanish interviewed as "leaders" and the only people of their own to whom one could turn for certain kinds of assistance; but they are complained against as *orgullosos*, as being unwilling to do as much for the *raza* as they easily might, and as being subservient to the Anglo and unwilling to risk offending him. These individuals are, then, leaders largely by default and would not otherwise be mentioned as leaders. Although almost uniquely qualified in some respects to lead, they do not. In a situation where adequate inter-ethnic leadership would call for the exercise of organizing skill and close identification of the destinies of leader and follower, these individuals largely limit themselves to personalistic functions roughly comparable to those of the *patrón* of yore, and a social distance tends to be kept which is in some respects as great as between *patrón* and *peón*. Though the comparison with traditional patterns is suggestive, we need not, as has been discussed, hark back to the *patrón* system to explain everything in the situation found today. Inter-cultural factors in the Spanish relationship with Anglos are of strategic importance in explaining leadership deficiency.

NOTES

1. Leonard Broom and Eshref Shevky, "Mexicans in the United States: A Problem in Social Differentiation," *Sociology and Social Research*, 36 (January, 1952), pp. 150–158.

2. The term "Spanish," used throughout the paper refers to "the Spanish-speaking people."

3. Cf. Robert C. Jones, "Mexican Youth in the United States," *The American Teacher*, 28 (March, 1944), pp. 11–15; Olen Leonard and C. P. Loomis, *Culture of a Contemporary Rural Community, El Cerrito, New Mexico*, Washington: USDA, BAE, 1940; R. W. Roskelley and C. R. Clark, *When Different Cultures Meet*, Denver: Rocky Mountain Council on Inter-American Affairs, 1949; George I. Sanchez, "The Default of Leadership," in *Summarized Proceedings IV*, Southwest Council on the Education of the Spanish-Speaking People, Fourth Regional Conference, Albuquerque, New Mexico, January 23–25, 1950; Ozzie G. Simmons, *Anglo Americans and Mexican Americans in South Texas, A Study in Dominant-Subordinate Group Relations* (Ph.D. Thesis, Harvard University, 1952); Ruth D. Tuck, *Not With The Fist: Mexican-Americans in a Southwest City*, New York: Harcourt, Brace and Company, 1949.

4. Julian Samora, *Minority Leadership in a Bi-Cultural Community* (Ph.D. Thesis, Washington University, St. Louis, 1953).

5. James B. Watson, *Preliminary Observations Based On the Community of Mountain Town* (Unpublished manuscript, Washington University, St. Louis, n.d.).

6. Julian Samora, *op. cit.*, p. 52.

7. *Ibid.*, pp. 13–51.

8. Cf. R. L. Beals, *op. cit.*, pp. 8–10; and O. Leonard and C. P. Loomis, *op. cit.*, p. 15.

9. F. R. Kluckhohn, "Dominant and Variant Value Orientations," in C. Kluckhohn and H. A. Murray, *Personality in Nature, Society, and Culture*, 2nd ed. rev., New York: Knopf, 1953.

10. Julian Samora, *op. cit.*, pp. 74–76.

11. Cf. F. R. Kluckhohn, *op. cit.*, pp. 352–354; R. L. Beals, *op. cit.*, pp. 5–13. Arthur Campa, "Mañana is Today," in T. M. Pearce and A. P. Thomason, *Southwesterners Write*, Albuquerque: University of Mexico Press, 1947.

10

PETER A. MUNCH

SOCIAL ADJUSTMENT
AMONG WISCONSIN NORWEGIANS

From the point of view that culture, in the broadest sense of the word, is the total *adjustment* of human society to its physical and social environment, it is evident that no specific form of culture can be transplanted from one environment to the other without a more or less radical change. Unless the two environments are exactly alike in every respect—and no two environments will be found to be exactly alike—the migrating group will have to *re-adjust* to the new environment, i.e., it will have to discard certain value attitudes and patterns of behavior and replace them by others that better answer the new situation.

Especially, in a complex cultural situation like that of the United States, where several groups of different racial and cultural backgrounds are thrown together in one geographical area, participating in the same political and economic system, we would have to expect rather drastic cultural changes to be involved in the process of adjustment between all these different groups.

Besides, when the European immigrants of the 19th century came to this country they found an already established society, with its own form of culture, with its own values, norms, and patterns of behavior that, in some respects, were vastly different from their own. And they were immediately put under a heavy social and cultural pressure to conform to the new culture, a pressure that seems to have increased as the new society was more firmly established with always more comprehensive and efficient institutions. As a matter of well-known fact, great efforts have been made in order to bring about this cultural conformity of the American people—through organized propaganda, "Americanization" programs, and, especially, through indoctrination in the compulsory school. The ideological

Reprinted with permission from *American Sociological Review* 14 (1949): 780–787.

rationalization of this activity is the well-known concept of the United States as a cultural "melting pot" that should produce an "amalgamation" of all the divergent culture forms that have been brought over to this country from all parts of the world.

Along with this organized and officially sanctioned pressure on every alien culture group, the immigrants of the 19th century were also put under a social pressure from the Old American groups, who seem generally to have assumed an exclusive and superordinate status in relation to the more recent immigrants and their descendants. This unofficial pressure, based on economic standing and a long family history in the country, was mainly exercised through the formation of exclusive associations and a formal, rather refined, social life where more recent immigrants and their descendants were not accepted on a basis of equality.

Finally, as time went on, the immigrants were also exposed to the pressure of a certain part of their own kinsfolk and former associates, namely those individuals, groups, and factions who submitted to the American way of life and became more American than the Americans—even in that respect that they refused to accept for full association those groups and individuals who stayed loyal to their original culture groups.

In fact, the "melting pot" was rather conceived of as a "smelting furnace" that was supposed to burn out the alien culture elements like slag from the pure metal of American culture.

And yet, ethnic groups still exist in this country, easily discernible by various traits characteristic of each particular group and, above all, by a special loyalty that keeps them together as groups and isolates them more or less from other groups. Evidently, as one writer puts it, the "melting pot" has failed to reach the melting point.[1]

Although these ethnic groups are very conspicuous in most cases, they have been paid little attention in general descriptions of American culture in the past. And in local, state, and federal administration there has been a deliberate tendency to neglect their existence: they have hardly been paid any attention at all except maybe as a phase in the development of the nation that would be overcome in time. Administrators as well as scholars seem to agree to regard these ethnic groups as a "cultural lag," a "hard core" of each group having failed, so far, to adjust itself to the new environment in accordance with the "melting pot" theory.

However, looking at the various ethnic groups in the United States, it appears that some of them actually have very little in common with their original culture. In comparison with the people of their respective countries of origin, they clearly stand out as Americans, which is brought to a very conspicuous evidence every time an American visits his "old country."

Yet they have a special *loyalty* within the group that makes it stand out clearly as an ethnic group. Truly, this loyalty is very often brought to overt expression through the cultivation of certain culture traits by which the group distinguishes itself from other groups. These distinguishing culture traits, however, are not necessarily of an aboriginal nature. They have very often been acquired in this country and would have to be described as truly American. This is true, for instance, of the "Sons of Norway" lodges of the Norwegians, or the cultivation of tobacco which has almost become a symbol of Norwegianism in certain parts of Wisconsin. In some cases, it seems, the immigrant group has made a thorough adjustment to the new environment without losing its identity as an ethnic group. An almost complete *cultural* assimilation has not always been followed by the expected *social* assimilation.

The social differentiation of ethnic groups in the United States can hardly be explained in terms of a "cultural lag." It is evidently not due to a "lack of adjustment" to the new social order. In human society, there are forces working both ways, both towards assimilation and towards differentiation of groups. And the existence in this country of easily distinguishable ethnic groups, even after more than a hundred years' residence, through three or four or even five generations, under a tremendous social pressure, suggests that here there have been *positive* forces working towards a *differentiation* of groups on the basis of ethnic origin.

From this point of view, the Norwegian settlements in Vernon County, Wisconsin, are of particular interest. In this area there are two distinct Norwegian settlements. One is situated in the northern central part of the county, on the plain known as Coon Prairie, and extending strongly into Coon Valley and other adjacent valleys. The other settlement occupies the southern central part of the county with its center of gravity around Folsom, in the town of Franklin, and in West Prairie, in the town of Sterling. It spreads heavily to the south into Crawford County, where Soldiers Grove forms another center. Between these two Norwegian settlements, in the central part of the county, there used to be a strong settlement of Old American stock. This settlement is older than any of the Norwegian settlements and had already at the time of the Norwegian immigration created an important trade and business center in the city of Viroqua, which was likewise dominated by the Old Americans. This city is now the county seat.

The two Norwegian settlements in this area have many important traits in common. In the first place they are equally old. Both settlements were founded about 1850. And both of them were first formed, not by direct immigration from Norway, but by expansion of the Koshkonong settlement in southeastern Dane County. Furthermore, the two settlements were both situated at an equal distance, about 5-10 miles, from the city of Viroqua which formed a convenient and natural prospective trade center for both of them. With respect to the social situation, they were both under the dominance of the Old Americans in and around Viroqua who controlled the economic life of the area through their business and banking system. These Old Americans gladly accepted the Norwegians as labor hands and as housemaids—in fact, it was reported that once it was quite fashionable for a Viroqua family to have a Norwegian housemaid. But they did not accept the Norwegians in their social life and thus exercised a social pressure on the subordinate groups of Norwegians.

However, in one very important respect, there is a great difference in the socio-ecological situation of the two settlements. As already stated, when the Norwegians first came to this area the central part of the county was already occupied by a settlement of Old Americans. This settlement, however, extended strongly to the south into the town of Franklin. Besides, in the northern part of Crawford County a strong Irish settlement developed, with centers of gravity in Soldiers Grove and in Rising Sun, just south of the county line. Thus, while the Coon Prairie Norwegians settled in a practically empty space, the ones who settled in the southern part of the county had to squeeze in between other settlers. Consequently, from the very beginning, the Norwegians who settled in the Folsom-West Prairie area had, relatively, a much more extended line of contact with non-Norwegian groups than the ones who settled in the northern part of the county.

Moreover, this initial difference in the socio-ecological situation of the two settlements was stressed to a marked degree through the later developments. A comparison of existing plat maps of the county shows that the Norwegian settlements in this area have expanded in the course of time. Part of this expansion is due to the arrival of new Norwegian immigrants who, somewhere around 1880, came directly from Norway and formed a third Norwegian settlement in the area between the two already in existence. But, apart from this new immigration of Norwegians, there has also been a strong expansion of the southern settlement, the Norwegians in this area having gradually made their way into the Old American settlement and partly outcrowded the original settlers. The Coon Prairie settlement, on the other hand, has hardly had any outward growth of territory for the last 70 or 80 years at least. In this settlement the development has rather been one of spatial consolidation, the tendency having been to get rid of foreign elements within the area of the settlement itself rather than expanding into new areas.

Thus, the development in the Folsom-West Prairie settlement has been towards an extension of the line of contact with non-Norwegian groups, whereas the Coon Prairie settlement has shown a tendency towards an always stronger consolidation with a corresponding contraction of the line of contact.

This difference in spatial development already implies a marked difference in the form of adjustment of the two settlements to the new environment. And further investigation reveals that there are even other remarkable differences in the cultural and social adjustment of the two groups which are clearly correlative to the difference in spatial growth just described.

What actually happened is this: From the Folsom-West Prairie settlement the Norwegians have made their way into the Old American community around Viroqua, not only in a spatial, but even in a social and economic respect. Not only did they expand their settlement into the rural area around Viroqua; they even invaded the city itself, established businesses, and took an active part in the economic functions of the city. Today, about half the population of Viroqua is of Norwegian descent. (See Figure 10–1.)

The Coon Prairie settlement, on the other hand, through its spatial and socio-economic consolidation, has been able to build up an independent and socially self-sufficient community of its own. In the city of Westby, which is about 95% Norwegian, it has even created its own community center with most of the economic, social, and cultural services that are usually allotted to such a center in a community of that size. In this way, the Norwegians in this settlement have actually managed to withdraw the whole area from the economic and social control of the "Yankee" dominated city of Viroqua.

In accordance with what might be expected from these conditions, the Coon Prairie settlement is even culturally and socially a very solid Norwegian community which appears to have had relatively little contact with, or influence from, other ethnic groups as well as the American society, although it is not uninfluenced by American ideology. The Norwegian language is still used in daily conversation, even by the third and fourth generations, and certain Norwegian customs and values have been preserved strongly. This is more true for the rural area. But even in the city of Westby it is true to some degree, although the city is definitely American in its outer appearance as well as in its socio-economic functions. This community is very hard to break into, as is felt strongly by everyone who has tried it. There is a strong loyalty to the community and a correspondingly strong social pressure against any deviation from the accepted

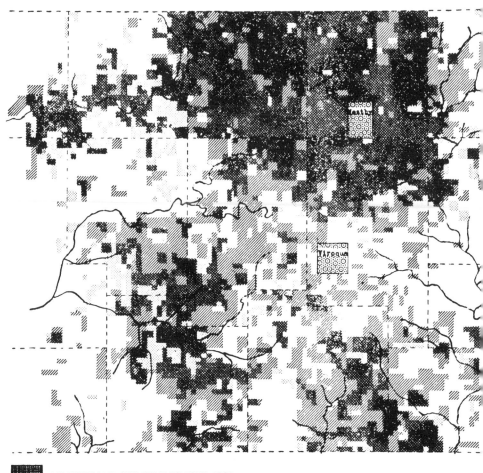

 NORWEGIAN OWNERSHIP 1878-1930

 ACQUIRED 1878-1930

LOSS 1878-1930

Figure 10–1   The Central Part of Vernon County, Wisconsin,
Land Owned by Norwegians in 1878 and in 1930

152

local pattern. What foreign elements have come in have either been assimilated completely to the cultural pattern of the community or they have been isolated socially until they preferred to leave. A few German farmers who have come in from the neighboring German settlement in the lower part of Coon Valley have had to learn the local dialect of the Norwegian language and speak it fluently.

In sharp contrast to these conditions, the Norwegians in the southern settlement seem to be quite adaptive to the American way of life. And, as the situation is today, they are definitely more acceptable to, and actually accepted by, the non-Norwegian group. What is taking place in the city of Viroqua seems to be a perfect acculturation process with a free interchange of culture patterns. Even this city is definitely an American city, and Norwegians as well as non-Norwegians submit quite freely to the process of urbanization which is commonly mistaken for "Americanization." In certain respects, on the other hand, Norwegian patterns have put a definite stamp on the community, the non-Norwegian group having conformed to certain rural Norwegian customs, such as food habits, the forenoon and afternoon coffee hour, etc. Nationality differences are seldom stressed. The ideology of the community is outwardly indifferent to national origin. People do not usually talk or think in terms of nationalities, and there is no longer any recognized difference of social status between the nationality groups. Norwegians and non-Norwegians mix freely in clubs and other secular organizations. Intermarriages are quite frequent, and so are partnerships in business and work across nationality lines. Outwardly, the Norwegians do not mark themselves off from the rest. The use of Norwegian language in public situations is negligible, and it seems obvious that it will die out as a means of communication with the present older generation.

Thus there is a marked difference in the form of adjustment of these two Norwegian settlements. And the most likely explanation seems to be pointing to the difference in the social situation that each of them had to respond to.

However, when we analyze the social structure of the two settlements more closely, it appears that there is a difference more in form than in principle of adjustment between the two groups.

In the first place, the Coon Prairie settlement is not merely a Norwegian community transplanted. In one respect, it has been very adaptive to the pattern of American society or rather to its ideology. The Norwegians who settled down in this area obviously came with the definite idea of establishing a democratic society on the basis of the genuine American ideas of liberty and equality. Most of them came from the dependent social class of *husmenn*, or cotters, who did not own their land in the old country, but had to work on the farm of the landowning *bonde* in return for the right to use a small piece of his land, large enough to feed one or two cows. But whether they came from this class or from the more fortunate class of the landowning *bönder*, they seem to have agreed to abandon this social distinction in their new community. This spirit is still very strong in the settlement. Even in the second and third generations there is a strong traditional recollection of the social distance between *bönder* and *husmenn* that used to be very pronounced in the rural communities of Eastern Norway in the 19th century. And there is still a rather emotional resentment of these conditions and a strong and conscious will to establish and maintain a thoroughly democratic society in the new country.

However, by bringing these ideas into effect the Coon Prairie settlement segregated itself culturally and socially, not only from its Norwegian mother society, but also from the factual American society, especially as it manifested itself in the neighboring Old American community in Viroqua, with its distinctions of social status and its discrimination of nationalities.

In this respect the Coon Prairie settlement has acquired some of the characteristic traits of Utopia. As mentioned before, there is a strong loyalty to the community and its local pattern, and the unbroken tradition of democratic equality of status is the all-important focus of this loyalty. The people feel that this community, which is their own creation, is their "America," and they are proud of it. This loyalty—in connection with certain Norwegian patterns, such as a strong attachment to the family—has created a rather strong exclusiveness towards *any* outsider, whether he is of Norwegian origin or not, and has increased the social and cultural isolation of the community.

In Viroqua, on the other hand, the adaptiveness to the more conspicuous traits of American life is greater. But when it comes to certain nonmaterial values of social life, there is a definite cleavage between the Norwegians and the non-Norwegian group even there. Even in this community there is a strong persistence of certain values and attitudes that belong specifically to the Norwegian group. And, like in Westby, there is a strong social pressure exercised by the group, claiming conformity to the Norwegian values on the part of anybody who wants a more close association with that group.

In the first place, the Norwegians are strongly identified with the Lutheran Church. According to common usage, "Norwegian" is almost synonymous with "Lutheran." The exclusiveness of the Norwegian group on this point is revealed by the fact that Norwegians who have joined the Methodist or any other church are no more considered as Norwegians—

which is simply a consequence of the fact that, by quitting the Lutheran Church, they have cut themselves off from a very important part of the social life of the Norwegian group.

Another important focus of loyalty among the Norwegians even in this community is the family, especially the extended family which is often referred to as the "clan." Here is where another important part of the social life of the Norwegian group takes place in the form of visiting, celebrations, and regular family reunions. Of course, this is again a social activity from which the non-Norwegians are excluded although they are freely accepted in case they are married into the clan—which happens quite frequently—and assume a certain loyalty to the clan.

Finally, a marked distinction seems to prevail between the Norwegian and the non-Norwegian groups in certain principles and values in connection with the determination of social status. In this respect, the Norwegian group adheres very strongly to a pattern that prevailed in Norway in the 19th century and still is the valid pattern in the least urbanized rural areas of Norway. According to this pattern, a group of professionals, state officials, and patrician business people distinguished themselves from "the common people," namely, *bønder* and *husmenn*, by a certain family background with education, alertness in behavior, and "culture," i.e., interest and knowledge in literature, music, and art, acquired through several generations of strong family tradition. A Norwegian élite of this kind once was very strong in Westby, but has now almost disappeared. In Viroqua, however, it is still in existence and is recognized by the Norwegian group. This élite is a very small group and rather exclusive, especially to the non-Norwegian élite of successful business people by whom it is accused of being "snobbish." Yet, this Norwegian élite has certainly retained a high recognition in the Norwegian group by stressing such values as family tradition, education, and "culture" rather than the accumulation and conspicuous display of wealth of the present non-Norwegian élite.

Thus, the Norwegian group in Viroqua has actually counterbalanced the social pressure from the Old American group by establishing an adverse pressure from the Norwegian group. Consequently, the city of Viroqua itself is an interesting example of a pronounced dual community, with a dualism that can be traced through the whole of the social prestige scale from top to bottom. The split between the two groups seems to be most pronounced at the top of the scale. The two élites are rather exclusive to each other, although the withdrawal seems to be stronger on the Norwegian side. It is in the middle and lower social strata where we find the most free association between the two groups. But, again, the strong family ties of the Norwegians tend to exclude non-Norwegians from the more intimate social activities of the Norwegian group.

On the whole, the Norwegian group seems to be the more exclusive of the two. Thus, while the non-Norwegian group is apparently open for the Norwegians to join in whenever they like, the Norwegian group is pretty much closed. Norwegians will participate in the usual clubs and organizations, such as lodges, the American Legion, Kiwanis, etc., almost in proportion to their number in the community. Norwegian Lutheran women will even take part in the Methodist Ladies' Aid. But the opposite is never found, and the only way that a non-Norwegian by descent can be included and fully accepted in the social life of the Norwegian group seems to be by marrying into a Norwegian clan and conforming to certain Norwegian values and customs, such as family ties (applied to the Norwegian clan), certain food habits, and, first of all, Lutheranism.

With all their conspicuous differences in the form of adjustment, however, in one respect these two Norwegian settlements have made a parallel adjustment to their social situation in the new society: they have both built up a social system of their own, rather firmly knit through a strong loyalty within the group, and with a sharp bounding outwards towards the encompassing society. There is no doubt in my mind that this reaction is a response to the social situation in which the groups found themselves in the New World. Feeling that they were not fully accepted in the new society they had no choice other than trying to provide for the satisfaction of the social needs of their members within their own group, unless they wanted to submit to a rather subordinate status in the society. And they were able to do it because they were large enough and had an élite of their own that was morally strong enough to withstand the pressure, but first of all because they adjusted to the pressure by assuming an increased solidarity within the group and a sharpening of the outer social bound coupled with a strong adaptiveness to certain American culture patterns.

Whether these observations can serve as a general explanation of the social differentiation of ethnic groups in the United States is very uncertain at the present stage. Great variations are found in the form of adjustment that is made, not only by the various nationalities but even by different settlements of one and the same nationality group. For that reason, one should be very careful in making any general statement about the form of adjustment, or the degree of persistence, of any particular nationality in the United States. Besides, the problem of adjustment is pretty much the same whether the immigrant group is of German, Polish, Italian, or Norwegian origin. The main problem of any immigrant group is not how to preserve as much as possible of the original culture, but how to be *accepted* in a social configuration in the new social environment. And the form and direction that the adjustment takes in each case is not only determined by the form and contents of the original culture but probably more so by the particular *social situation* that the group has to respond to in each particular case.

However, there is at least one trait in the social situation that the European immigrants of the 19th century met in this country that is common to them all. They were all, more or less, under the same social pressure from the American society. In the case of Vernon County, Wisconsin, this social pressure proved to be instrumental in creating an intensive solidarity of an immigrant group over against the American society and thereby became fatal to a complete assimilation of that group. And it is quite possible that, even in other cases, this pressure may be the ultimate reason why the cultural "melting pot" of the United States so often has failed to "reach the melting point." Under a too heavy pressure, the process has turned out to be a hardening rather than a melting process.

NOTE

1. Lowry Nelson, *Rural Sociology*, New York: American Book Company, 1948, pp. 189–196; "Speaking of Tongues," *American Journal of Sociology*, 54 (November 1948), 202–210.

11

GUY B. JOHNSON

PERSONALITY IN A
WHITE-INDIAN-NEGRO COMMUNITY

Scattered throughout the South, there are over a hundred groups of people who are classified by the Census Bureau as "Indians." Some of these groups, like the Catawba and the Eastern Cherokee of North Carolina, the Seminoles of Florida, and the Choctaws of Mississippi, are of relatively pure Indian stock and are recognized as such by the government, but the majority are "Indians" by courtesy. They represent varying mixtures of white, Negro, and Indian blood, but as a rule the white strain predominates, and Indian culture is either very weak or extinct.

Most of these groups are small, but there were at least thirty which had 100 or more members in 1930, and there was one, the so-called Croatan Indian group centering in Robeson County, North Carolina, which totaled nearly 15,000 members.

Although these mixed-blood communities differ in numerous minor ways, there is one thing they all have in common: they have a social status which is intermediate between that of whites and Negroes. This results from two factors: their own determination not to be classed as Negroes, and the white people's determination not to accept them as white. Thus, suspended as they are between the white man's world and the Negro's world, they must live in a social world of their own, and it is this fact which brings them to our attention for sociological study.

To delimit the scope of this paper, I use this tentative classification: 1. Those groups which are disintegrating and are being absorbed primarily into the Negro group; 2. Those which are being assimilated chiefly into the white group; 3. Those which have established some degree of accommodation to the larger white and Negro worlds and are, for the present at least, functioning as intermediate groups. All of these groups have cer-

Reprinted with permission from *American Sociological Review* 4 (1939): 516–523.

tain things in common, but those of the third type are more unique and more interesting because they are exceptions to the rigid biracial system in the South. Maintaining such groups involves a great deal of strain and it should be of some interest to observe problems of personal adjustment to which this gives rise. This paper is based upon field work among the largest and most significant of these groups, the so-called Croatan Indians of Robeson County, North Carolina.

A glimpse at the history of the Robeson County Indians is essential to an understanding of their present situation. Their early history is uncertain. Their origin goes back to early colonial days. In fact, they have been connected by some historians with America's greatest historical mystery, namely, the fate of Sir Walter Raleigh's Lost Colony of Roanoke Island (1587). The name, Croatan, which they once proudly claimed but which has fallen into disrepute among them (for reasons which I shall explain later) was derived from the Croatoan Indians, an Algonkin tribe which lived on the North Carolina coast in the sixteenth century and which befriended the Roanoke Island colonists. According to legend, the survivors of the colony mixed with the Croatoan Indians and moved inland to the swamps of Robeson County where the family names of some of the Roanoke colonists survive to this day.

Whether this story is true or not, it cannot account for the heterogeneous group now known as Indians in Robeson County. Much could have happened in the 140 years between the disappearance of Raleigh's colony and the settlement of Robeson County by Scotch and English. When the white people entered the area in the 1730's, they found a mixed-blood people inhabiting the swamps, living by fishing, hunting, and small farming, speaking an English dialect, and having an English type of culture. Mention of these people in colonial records was scarce, but when they were mentioned, they were referred to as "a roving band of mulattoes," or "a mixed and motley crew." They were listed in the early federal Censuses as "free colored." It seems safe to say that during the period of slavery the original nucleus, which may have been white-and-Indian, was augmented by runaway slaves, free Negroes, remnants of Indian tribes, and by all sorts of white adventurers. Only thus can we account for the heterogeneity of the present-day Robeson Indians.

These mixed, despised, and nameless people were classed as colored by the white people, but they cherished an intense desire to escape this stigma and be recognized as white. When the state constitution was revised in 1835, they were deprived of the suffrage, along with the free Negroes, and they were told that they could not attend the public schools for whites. Resentful, some of them built little one-room schools of their own, or kept their children out of school, rather than send them to school with Negroes.

The Civil War brought about a crisis which has much to do with the subsequent fortunes of these people. The white people tried to draft the Indians into the service of the Confederacy, assigning them to heavy duty along with Negroes. The Indians would express their resentment by going home. Bad feeling increased. One day in 1864, a group of Home Guards decided to make an example out of some of the Indians. They arrested three men of the Lowry family for desertion, took them into the woods, made them dig their own graves, and shot them down in cold blood. A younger member of the family, Henry Berry Lowry, is said to have witnessed the shooting from his hiding place. He organized a band of kinsmen and friends to avenge the killing of the Lowrys and history records that he was unusually successful. It was not until nearly eight years had passed and Robeson County had become the laughing stock of the nation that Henry Berry Lowry and his outlaw gang were killed. The truth was that Lowry was something of a Robin Hood; he had many friends among the whites.

In a sense, Henry Berry Lowry was the making of the Indians. He was their martyr and hero, and he focused attention upon their grievances in a dramatic way. A prominent white man took up their cause, discovered their legend of descent from the Lost Colony, and proposed a legislative solution to their problem. The legislature of 1885 passed an act which read in part as follows:

> Whereas the Indians now living in Robeson County claim to be descendants of a friendly tribe who once resided in eastern North Carolina on the Roanoke River, known as the Croatan Indians; therefore,
> *The General Assembly of North Carolina do enact:*
> Section 1. That the said Indians and their descendants shall hereafter be designated and known as the Croatan Indians.
> Section 2. That said Indians and their descendants shall have separate schools for their children, school committees of their own race and color, and shall be allowed to select teachers of their own choice, . . .

Thus the Croatans were set apart as a separate people, were given "a local habitation and a name." Their little social world developed remarkably. Schools, churches, and lodges prospered. The state even provided a special teachers' college for them. Their enumerated population grew by leaps and bounds, from 174 in 1890 to 3877 in 1900, and to 12,404 in 1930.

Today, Robeson County is a unique triracial laboratory. Its 66,000 population is distributed as follows: white, 47 percent; Negro, 34 percent;

Indian, 19 percent. If these Indians were *bona fide* Indians, the situation would not be unique, but since they have no trace of Indian culture and have a very small proportion of Indian blood, they constitute a glaring exception to the southern white man's dictum that a drop of Negro blood makes a man a Negro. The very existence of such a group is something of an anachronism.

We are now ready to enquire into the problem of the personality of the mixed bloods who form the middle caste in this triracial society. What are the points of strain and what personal adjustments are made?

The keystone in this problem is, of course, the white man's determination not to accept the Indian as his equal and, as far as possible, to put him into the same category as the Negro. In all of his relations with white people, this principle is either expressed or implied. The Indian is restricted to his own schools, and he is forbidden to marry a white person. He is supposed not to enter a white man's front door. He is not addressed as "mister" by white people and if he attends a theatre, he has to choose between one which provides a three-way segregation and one which seats him with Negroes. There is not an eating place in the country which permits him to enter the front door and eat with the white people. In numerous subtle ways, by glances, gestures, and intonations, he is reminded by whites and Negroes of the unmentionable stigma which attaches to him.

The Indian, then, is forever on the defensive. He feels that there is always a question mark hanging over him. His wish to escape the stigma of Negro kinship, and thus to be identified with the white man, is uppermost in his mind. It is this wish which dominates his behavior and determines his modes of personal adjustment to the other races.

One of the chief sources of mental conflict in the Indian arises from his Negroid physical traits. In 1885, when the Indians were legally declared a separate race and were named Croatan, they faced the problem of deciding just who was Indian and who was not. They wanted to weed out those who were considered "undesirables," but it was difficult for them to draw the line. They evidently fell back on a sort of pragmatic definition, viz.: an Indian is a person called an Indian by other Indians. It was as if they had said, "All right, everyone who is already in can stay in, but woe unto anybody with Negro blood who tries to get in hereafter." At their request, the legislature passed two laws which strengthened their position. One of these provided "that all marriages between a Croatan Indian and a Negro, or between an Indian and a person of Negro descent to the third generation, inclusive, shall be utterly void." Another provided "that there shall be excluded from such separate schools for the said Croatan

Indians all children of the Negro race to the fourth generation." The Indians themselves were to be final judges on matters of genealogy.

It is certain that very little new Negro blood has found its way into the group in recent times. However, the Croatans today are undoubtedly one of the most heterogeneous groups ever brought together under one name. They range from pink skin, blue eyes, and flaxen hair to unmistakably Negroid color, hair, and other features. Many could pass for white anywhere else, and many would be taken for Negroes anywhere else. Even in the same family, the children often have a wide range of color and hair types. Every growing child notices these things and ponders over them. He learns that it is taboo to discuss such things. He learns that the ultimate insult that anyone can give an Indian is to intimate that he has Negro blood. He stands ready to defend his personal honor and the honor of his whole group from such intimations from any source. So intense is the feeling on this subject that one can only conclude that there is present in many persons a certain "sense of guilt" which arises from the observed reality and which calls for constant denial of the reality.

As might be expected, the strength of this color prejudice varies with the physical types. The whiter Indians seem to worry less over this matter. While they resent any attacks on the "purity" of the Indians as a group, they feel less than the darker people the necessity for personal justification. They travel about a good deal and find that they are taken for white or for Indian-white mixtures. Their very appearance is a badge of security. Indeed, they feel that if all of the Indians were like them there would be no problem. They blame the dark Indians for the stigma attached to the group and they hate them for it, but their hatred must be kept below the surface.

The darker Indians, on the other hand, are apt to be more sensitive on the matter of physical features. Their chances for unpleasant experiences are, of course, greater, and they feel more keenly the impulse to "whiten" their ancestry. Furthermore, they are jealous of the whiter Indians. Thus there is an incipient but never openly admitted cleavage between the darker Indians and the lighter ones.

The hypersensitiveness of the Croatans has led them on several occasions to drive out people who were offshoots from the main body and who came in from adjoining counties to take advantage of the Indian schools. The excuse was always, "We can't be sure about these people. We think they have Negro blood." Incidentally, some of these rejected people petitioned for a special set of schools for their benefit, but school officials threw up their hands and declared that three school systems were enough.

Another aspect of the Croatans' struggle for a status of respectability is their concern over their history and their group name. When the legislature of 1885 gave them the name "Croatan" and, by implication, recognized their Lost Colony legend, it was trying to present them with a proud past and a good name, but the name "Croatan" soon went sour. For the first time, the whites and Negroes had a term which they could apply to these hitherto nameless people. They pronounced it with a sort of sneer or they shortened it to "Cro"—with the all too obvious implication. It soon became a fighting term, and for many years it has been virtually taboo in the presence of Indians.

Now the Indians were divided for a time over the merits and demerits of "Croatan," but the majority of them finally embraced a theory that there was really nothing to the Lost Colony legend and that "Croatan" was not their true name. Accordingly, they got the legislature in 1911 to strike out the word "Croatan," leaving their name simply "Indians of Robeson County." Thus, they were willing to give up their Lost Colony legend for the removal of the curse of "Croatan."

The vagueness of the word "Indian" was a challenge to them, because it was in a way an admission that they did not know what they were. So a new theory of history came to the front: they were really Cherokee. They again asked the legislature for help, and in 1913, over the protest of the Eastern Cherokee of the Great Smoky Mountains, they were legally named "Cherokee Indians of Robeson County." The law bore the flattering title, "An act to restore to the Indians of Robeson and adjoining counties their rightful and ancient name." But no one ever calls them Cherokee, and the problem of the name keeps gnawing at their consciousness. Lately, there has been a shift in tactics. Some of their more literate men have searched history and ethnology and have concluded that the group originated from the remnants of the Siouan tribes which once lived in central North Carolina. For several years now they have been begging Uncle Sam to name them "Siouan Tribes of Lumber River" and to take them under his wing as wards of the federal government. This, according to one young Indian, would settle the problem once and for all.

In various other ways, the Indians are striving to construct a history which will do them justice. Most significant is their attitude toward Henry Berry Lowry and the outlaw years. They reject the picture of Lowry as murderer and outlaw and substitute a picture of a warm-hearted, courageous man who chose to fight in order that his people might not forever be oppressed, and what is more striking, some of the Indians have refused to let Lowry die. They contend that he escaped from Robeson County in 1872 and that he still lives in some faraway secret place. Others admit

that he was killed in 1872, but they insist that he killed himself accidentally with his own gun.

The situations which I have discussed thus far are largely situations
which can be met by subjective adjustments. The Indian can deny or
affirm this or that, can invent theories to fit the exigencies of the situation,
but what does he do when the realities of the caste structure call for more
overt behavior? Apparently, he takes some of the sting out of the realities
of caste by avoiding as far as possible those situations which are most
heavily charged with caste meaning. Here, again, the answer seems to be
that he "corrects" the reality in accordance with his wish. In so far as
possible, he conducts himself in such a way that the unpleasant reality is
negated. He avoids theatres where his only choice is to sit with Negroes.
If he must eat in town, he either takes along a lunch or patronizes an
open-air "hot-dog" stand rather than sit with Negroes in the back room of
a cafe.

In his work, the Indian's aim is to have as little to do with white people
as possible. He thereby reduces his chances of being insulted. His economic outlook is greatly restricted because he will not engage in various
menial tasks which Negroes engage in. His ideal is to own a farm and be
his own master. With the exception of a handful of teachers, preachers,
and small shopkeepers, the Indians are all farmers. They are especially
expert in tobacco culture. When they are tenants for white farmers they
advertise their difference from the Negro by refusing to take the subservient
role of the Negro. I asked an Indian tenant how he got along with his
landlord. "Oh, all right," he replied, "I don't have any more to do with
him than I have to. I never go to his house, because I don't want to have
any trouble with him." By this, he meant that if he went to the white
man's house the white man would expect him to go to the back door—
then there might be trouble. The white farmers, for their part, recognize
this independence of the Indian when they say, "If you want a tenant to
take care of your land and make money, get an Indian. *But don't try to
boss him.* He wears his pride like a sore thumb."

Thus, the Indian avoids some caste situations and bring about some
degree of modification in others by sheer pride and belligerence; but he
cannot avoid or negate everything. He knows well enough that the restrictions and prohibitions are there, whether he tests them out or not, and he
carries a constant sense of frustration and tension.

In civic and political affairs the Indian meets with further frustration.
He sees his vote count for almost nothing because of the wiles of the
County Democratic Machine. He sees his one little town, Pembroke, his
social center and seat of his normal school, taken over largely by white

merchants. He sees the selection of town officers removed from his own control and placed in the hands of the legislature so that white people can be appointed. He has been, from Reconstruction days until the past year, without representation on any jury in Robeson County. He sees instances of brutality on the part of officers of the law. He sees many things which make his blood boil, and he feels utterly powerless to do anything about them. He feels that his little world is carefully guarded, controlled, and exploited by the white man. He is blocked at every point, yet he cannot give up the struggle, for to do so would be to admit that he is no better than the Negro. So he lives in this continuing state of compromise between the world of the white man and the world of the black man.

It might be expected that a group which has to meet the situations which the Croatans face would produce a great many bitter, aggressive, and desperate persons who would strike back at the white man in various ways, but this is not the case,—at least, up to the present. Minor altercations occur occasionally, but assaults and homicides against white persons are rare. The Indian is noted for his restraint in this respect. It has long been said in Robeson County that whatever else may be said about the Indian he never molests a white woman. In November 1938, when an Indian was convicted of rape on a white woman, the judge of the county court delivered a dramatic denunciation of the prisoner for having broken this long and enviable record. If the situation of the Indian produces bitterness toward the white man, it also produces caution and a sense of the futility of violence except as a last resort.

In the Indian's own world, there seems to be some evidences of the disorganizing effect of his anomalous social position. There are certain families and certain neighborhoods which are known as "tough," and these produce an unusual amount of drunkenness, assault, and homicide. Whether this represents a primary result of caste status is difficult to say, but I am inclined to believe that it is in some measure correlated with the frustration experiences of the Indian and with certain cleavages in the Indian community.

These cleavages are probably of major importance for the understanding of interpersonal relations within the Indian community. They are roughly correlated with physical traits, and yet it is probable that the latter have no genetic significance. At the bottom of the social scale are the darker Indians. They are on the whole poorer than the others, they are conscious of what others think of their appearance, and they are jealous of the lighter Indians. They are credited with a good deal of what is sometimes called "hell-raising." Next come the intermediate Indians. They are a little too dark to pass as white and they are especially sensitive to physical appearance. They envy the lighter ones and resent the darker ones, and they incline to be the militant, agitating type. Finally, there are the "white" Indians. They could pass for white almost anywhere. On the whole, they have a better economic status, a better education, and higher prestige. These color cleavages are a tabooed subject with the Indians, and yet they permeate the whole society. They are no doubt at the bottom of much of the violent crime of Indian against Indian. They also have something to do with the lack of strong group solidarity, the presence of factions, and the timidity of leaders.

I should not leave the impression, however, that the Indians are typically disorganized and unstable. On the contrary, most of them lead relatively calm, moderate, and industrious lives. They have a strong sentimental attachment to their native soil, and in spite of all their troubles, relatively few of them seek escape through permanent migration. They are perhaps one more example of the well-known adaptability of the human personality. Apparently, when people have work to do, have strong community institutions and a few things to be proud of, they can adjust their thoughtways and behavior so as to absorb a great deal of emotional strain.

This situation, however, is by no means static. It is difficult to conceive of a community like the Croatan community surviving indefinitely. It seems likely that the Indian will rebel more and more against his caste status. Education, wider travel, and reading, are already beginning to have their effects. The changing situation will produce personalities who no longer see virtue in patience and compromise. The Indians are becoming more group conscious. They have recently demanded the right to serve on juries, they are talking of running for political office, and they are saying among themselves that "if things don't get better we may have to start killing." The future holds interesting and unpleasant possibilities.

12
MELVIN TUMIN

RECIPROCITY AND STABILITY OF CASTE IN GUATEMALA

The situation I wish to report here concerns the pueblo of San Luis Jilotepeque, a small, relatively isolated community in the interior of Guatemala, about 90 miles from Guatemala City, inhabited, at the time of my studies there, by about 3500 people of whom some 1100 were Ladinos, or people of presumptive Spanish descent, and 2400 of whom were Indians (or mixed-Indian and Ladino) of Maya-Quiche descent.[1]

Intrinsically, the community is no more nor less significant or interesting than any other community which might be chosen at random. It does have considerable sociological significance of a sort, however, for it represents one of those "Pango-Pango" situations, of which some anthropologists are so fond, because it can be cited as a local exception to some generally prevailing hypotheses. For instance, it is generally agreed that here is a situation of caste-relations between people of different genetic and cultural origins where there is a minimum of conflict. Moreover, the superordinate caste, the Ladinos, are in a distinct numerical minority. Furthermore, the socially subordinate Indian caste has a lifeway which appears to be intrinsically far more satisfying for them than is the Ladino lifeway for the Ladinos. Numerous other such local variations on general themes can be documented. But for our present purposes they are irrelevant.

The initial fact of importance is that there are a very limited number of ways to perform the functions traditionally considered prerequisite to societal survival and continuity. In Linton's terms, the universals are dominant, with the alternatives occupying only a relatively insignificant role.

Reprinted with permission from *American Sociological Review* 14 (1949): 17–25.

Thus, for instance, almost without exception, every San Luis family is directly or indirectly dependent upon the successful growing of corn and beans for survival. Additionally, religion is overwhelmingly Roman Catholic and highly standardized in ritual (with certain notable Indian "idiosyncratic" interpretations prevailing). The discrepancies between the citizens in knowledge and skills are relatively minimal. Magic and witchcraft are widespread throughout both Ladino and Indian groups, but are limited in the kinds of practices which are respected and thought efficacious. A common government is shared by both groups, and there prevails a core of relatively common definitions of community interest and significance. The groups are somewhat ghettoized in their living accommodations, yet they share a physical proximity which allows for high visibility of social acts between and within the two strata. Gossip, expectedly, is the principal means of communication within and between the castes, with character-assassination and ego-expansion being the principal topics.

In spite of this closely shared and restricting institutional framework, it becomes apparent to the observer in relatively short order that the Ladinos and Indians are sharply separated by a relatively rigid caste line, with Ladinos occupying, by all tokens, the superordinate position. Breaking through the caste-bars on intermarriage is a rare phenomenon (I know of only one documentable case—and this of short duration), and commensalism is apparently even rarer. There is, however, plenty of "mixed" sexual intercourse, resulting not too infrequently in half-breed children who almost invariably assume the status of their Indian mothers.

In addition to this observable sharp caste separation, the observer is also quickly struck by the fact that despite the narrow range of possible alternative life styles, Indian and Ladino culture patterns can be described in sharp distinction one from the other, and very different attitudes toward the community and its life are also notable.

This sharp distinctiveness between life style and culture patterns raises some immediate questions: (a) What are the instances of joint participation of Indian and Ladino in the overall social life of San Luis? (b) What are the instances of separate participation? (c) What are the principal distinctions between the two classes of participation? (d) How much and what kind of reciprocity is there in the joint and separate participations? (e) How stable is the structure of differential participation?

A. THE JOINT PARTICIPATIONS

It is possible to list most briefly the major relationships in which Indians and Ladinos jointly participate. They are: (1) employer-employee; (2) seller-buyer; (3) landowner-tenant; (4) godparent-godchild and *com-*

padres (*compadre* is the generic term of reference as between the parents and the godparents of a child); (5) Indian prostitute-Ladino patron; (6) co-worshipping at religious affairs; (7) co-participation in voting and everyday governmental affairs; (8) co-attendance of children at the same schools; (9) military drill of the Home Guard; (10) casual meetings on street corners, in stores, in the plaza, etc.

B. THE SEPARATE PARTICIPATIONS

In contrast to these, the situations of separate participations include the following: (1) housing location and housework; (2) funerals, weddings, wakes; (3) participation in street corner gatherings; (4) leisure time pursuits (soccer, fishing, mule-back trips, picnics, swimming parties, etc.); (5) extracurricular school functions; (6) local and national public celebrations; (7) social visits and exchange of meals; (8) friendship units; (9) private social affairs, such as parties, dances, etc.; (10) Indian religious affairs; (11) courtship and marriage.

C. THE DISTINCTION BETWEEN JOINT AND SEPARATE PARTICIPATIONS

When we attempt to contrast and compare the two sets of participations, we find, first, that the joint participations are easily classifiable into four major categories, into none of which do the separate participations fall, all this being "for the most part." The four categories are as follows:

1. Those situations in which Ladinos and Indians are mutually dependent upon each other for the success of the effort around which the situation is constructed. Into this class fall the employer-employee, seller-buyer, and land-owner-tenant relationships.

2. Those situations in which one of the groups needs the other or desires and profits from the participation of the other without the latter incurring any loss. Included in this class are the godparental relationships and those between prostitutes and their patrons.

3. Those situations in which joint participation is not required for the success of the effort, nor particularly desired by either or both groups, but in which there is a force or custom, external to and compulsive upon both groups, which determines that they shall participate jointly rather than separately. In this class we find the religious, educational, governmental and military co-participations.

4. Those situations in which joint participation is neither required nor desired and in which the meetings are largely accidental and transitory, and interaction is at a minimum. Here we refer to the temporary encounters at street corners, in the stores, and the like.

It is perhaps reasonable to state, in view of the foregoing classifications, that the joint participations are distinguishable as a class from the separate participations by the presence in the former of a distinctive degree of necessity and in the latter, of a distinctive degree of choice. As we shall see later, in almost all cases the choice is the prerogative of the Ladino, and is almost without exception exercised in the direction of separatism.

It is also reasonable to distinguish the joint and separate participations by the fact that the latter are situations where, for the most part, the interaction is likely to be intimate and personal, and in which there would be required equalitarian treatment of all involved if they were to continue to be motivated to repeat the situations.

By contrast, the joint participations are characterized by the fact that they can be structured in a superordinate-subordinate fashion, and interaction can be limited to clearly defined and well-known roles, largely circumscribed beforehand, in many instances, by contractual definition. An analogy to the relations between enlisted men and officers in the United States Navy does not go far off here.

D. HOW MUCH AND WHAT KIND OF RECIPROCITY IS PRESENT?

To answer this question, we have chosen to inquire in some detail first into the structure of relations and then into the attitudes attached to the co-participation of Indians and Ladinos in the godparental complex. (We choose this complex because it is a vital segment of the social structure and because, as we shall soon see, the choice of a Ladino godparent for an Indian child involves the attendance at the same party or celebration —in the formal role of equal participants—of both Indians and Ladinos. To my knowledge this is the only such instance in all of San Luis social life.) In its formal structure, the godparental complex may be described as follows:

1. Ladinos serve as godparents for Indian children, at the request of the Indian parents, in a fair number of cases.
2. Ladinos never ask Indians to serve as godparents for Ladino children, and there are, therefore, no discoverable cases of this relationship.
3. The Ladino godparents, and whichever Ladino friends the godparents care to invite, usually attend the baptismal party given by Indian parents for the newly-baptised child.
4. At these parties, Ladino men may and do dance with single Indian girls, but no Ladino woman, single or married, ever dances with an Indian man.
5. When not dancing, the Indians tend to keep to one side of the house and Ladinos to the other, so that for all intents and purposes the separateness of the two groups is clearly marked and preserved.
6. Except in the case of the Indian girls who are asked to dance by the Ladino men, all the observable merrymaking is engaged in only by Ladinos.

7. When the time for serving food arrives, the order of eating is as follows: Ladino women, Ladino men, Indian men, Indian women. There have been no observed cases at any time of joint eating. Nor does this separatism get broken in the case even of the Indian parents of the child.

8. One other aspect of the situation is worth describing. But since it refers largely to the "tone" of the situation as impressionistically interpreted by this observer, it is offered here not as incontrovertible evidence but only as additional data which may give a more rounded picture of the situation. The "tone" appears to be that of the Ladinos "taking over" the baptismal party, as though it were simply an excuse for getting free food and drinks and having a marimba paid for, to which they may dance. The Indian contingent, by contrast, fades into insignificance so far as merrymaking goes, and usually is to be found either running around fulfilling "requests" of the various Ladinos, or out in the backyard watching the Indian women cook. The Ladinos, always seem ready to remind the Indians that they are, after all, doing them a great honor and service by consenting to have a Ladino couple serve as godparents, in the first place, and consenting to grace an Indian house with Ladino presence, in the second.

After observing such parties, one naturally begins to wonder why the Indian ever asks the Ladino, and why the Ladino ever consents to serve as godparent for Indian children. The answers to these involve finding out (1) what concrete benefits, if any, the Indians and Ladinos derive from having Ladinos as godparents for Indian children; (2) how both groups feel about this kind of joint participation.

The Benefits. It is quickly discoverable that there are concrete benefits for the Indians. They are of the following order: (1) The Indian godchild gets his baptismal clothes and sometimes his baptismal fee and a little present paid for by his Ladino godparents. He would get them paid for by Indian godparents as well, of course, except that Indians show a well-known and well-appreciated reluctance to accept the invitation to be godparents because of the expense involved. (2) The Indian parents fall into a special relationship with the Ladino godparents which carries some prerogatives both for the Indian male and the female which they otherwise would not have. For the female, the prerogative is largely that of being permitted to use the water fountain in the house of the Ladino godparent instead of having to go and wait on line at the public fountain in the central plaza. For the male, the prerogative is that of getting some kind of priority right to rental of land for farming from the Ladino landowner-godparent. Since farming-land is very scarce, this is no mean prerogative.

Both of these prerogatives, of course, presume that the Ladino family is

wealthy, for only the wealthiest Ladino families have private water foun-
tains and enough land to rent out for farming. This should mean that a
few Ladino families should have a large number of Indian godchildren.
This turns out to be the actual case with at least two Ladino families each
having over 100 Indian godchildren to their credit.

(3) An additional prerogative refers to some kind of expectable patron-
ization by the Ladino godparent of the Indian parents in case of trouble
with the law or with other Ladinos. It is difficult to tell how effective this
is, but it nevertheless is cited by both Ladinos and Indians as one of the
presumed benefits.

(4) A further advantage acquired is that of protection and patroniza-
tion of the Indian godchild by his Ladino godparents to the extent of
being superficially looked after in case of the death of one or both of his
own parents. In at least a few cases, I can document this to be a working
advantage, but I do not actually know how generally widespread it is.

(5) A fifth general advantage is an observable, marked attenuation of
the discourteous and gruff treatment Ladinos traditionally hand out to
Indians. The Indian parents and their children may expect, in most cases,
a rather softened and sometimes actually warm, yet always transitory,
interaction with their Ladino godparental relatives. Since the godparental
relationship also throws all the children of both families into an acknowl-
edged special status with reference to each other, a considerable number
of Indians and Ladinos are thereby placed in special categories where, at
odd moments during their regular life-cycles, the usual Indian-Ladino kind
of caste behavior is somewhat attenuated. It is my impression that this is
one of the saving graces in the social structure, helping to keep a kind of
low level of quasi-equalitarian human interaction functioning in a situation
which would otherwise be much harsher for the Indians. In any event,
Ladinos sometimes "apologize" for being nice to special Indians by indicating that they are related in the godparental complex.

Concretely, these five instances describe the kinds of advantages which
Indians derive, or can derive, from having Ladinos act as godparents for
their children. But what about Ladinos? Why do they consent to serve at
all? What advantages, if any, do they acquire? Here the query leads us in
less observable paths to a more impressionistic answer.

For here we have to attempt to impute motivations, as carefully as
possible, to be sure, but based more on general impressions about covert
cultural needs than on any specific overt cases. What we refer to is the
fact that in San Luis, a man's "reputation" is a highly valued thing and is
based in part on the amount of "service" he can point to: how many

poor people he has helped, how kind he is to the Indians, etc. One of the accepted ways in which to acquire the reputation of being a man *de servicio* is to serve as godparent for Indian children. It is relatively inexpensive, and carries no lengthy obligations which are not easily taken care of, and at the same time provides a boastworthy dossier of sorts. It is the transmutation of the "Good deed for the day" concept. In San Luis, where character approbation and assassination are the main foci of conversation, and where a man has virtually nothing else by which to distinguish himself except his "character," it is not unimportant to be known as a man who renders service to the less fortunate. Additionally, it is considered bad taste if you refuse to serve, when requested, without good reason. It is also considered a limited religious honor of sorts, and Catholicism holds sway in San Luis.

I have no evidence which permits imputation of any other motivation. But when we add these considerations to the additional facts that the Ladinos can virtually control the entire situation, structuring it as they wish, and lose virtually nothing by their participation, their service as godparents for Indian children does not offend the prevailing logic of the Ladino culture pattern.

Attitudes Involved. The kind of image of the situation which is carried by each of the participating groups gives some necessary insight into the dynamics of the situation and allows for some estimate as to its significance as part of the caste situation, as well as for social change in general in the community.

Questionnaires administered to a 10 per cent sample of male heads of households in both Indian and Ladino groups revealed some interesting data with regard to how both groups view the situation.

Briefly summarized, they are as follows:

LADINOS (22 MALE HEADS OF HOUSEHOLDS)	
Might ask Indian to serve as godparent	3
Might ask Ladino to serve as godparent	19
Would never ask Indian to serve	16
Would never ask Ladino to serve	0
Thinks it possible for Indians to serve for Ladinos	9
Thinks it impossible for Indians to serve for Ladinos	11

A rough content analysis of the reasons Ladinos gave for never asking Indians to serve as godparents for Ladino children reveals the following:

REASON GIVEN	NO. OF TIMES MENTIONED
"The people would make fun and criticize."	10
"The people would say one is a fool."	3
"The people would say it was shameful."	2
"One doesn't want to lower one's category to that of the Indians."	1
"The people would say that one didn't have friends he could have asked."	1
"The Indians are disrespectful; they address one as 'vos' (highly familiar or highly formal, depending on the situation, but in the case of the Indian, simply a function of ignorance) instead of 'usted.' "	1

As reasons for why they thought it impossible for Indians to serve as godparents for Ladino children, the Ladinos offered the following:

REASON GIVEN	NO. OF TIMES MENTIONED
"We don't ever ask them."	5
"The Indians are looked on as lesser people."	5
"It's not the custom."	3
"I don't know why."	2
"It's the custom."	2
"For their class."	2
"Because the castes are divided."	1
"Indians are 'apart.' "	1
"The Indians don't like to."	1
"The Indians don't understand the affair."	1
"One's godparent should be able to substitute for one's father."	1
"The Indian *caste* (my emphasis) is looked on as lesser."	1
"The Indians are less civilized."	1
"Ladinos always ask Ladinos; they understand."	1
"We are better than they."[2]	1

As far as those Ladinos who said they might ask Indians, or thought it possible for Indians to serve as godparents for Ladino children, the following are some of the necessary conditions which they imposed:

Three said that it depends on the friendship one has with an Indian.

One said he would ask a well educated and well dressed Indian if he wanted him.

One said that if an Indian had a bachelor's degree [only two people in town had bachelor's degrees; the interviewee in question himself had had only two years of school, could read only printed letters and could only sign his name], he might ask him, if he were friends with him; the people wouldn't make fun then.

One said he might ask an Indian if he had the preparation and the honorableness.

One said he might ask an Indian if he were "good type."

One said that it is possible because poor Ladinos will sometimes ask wealthy Indians, even though he knows of no cases yet that had happened.

Now, it will be noted that almost without exception Ladinos explain the separatism between themselves and the Indians on the grounds of (1) shame to lower oneself and fear of ridicule; and/or (2) the inferiority or some other undesirable attribute of the Indians; and/or (3) the differences in customs; and/or (4) the existence of a custom which urges them to "seek their own kind." A comparative view at the same data from the Indians is most instructive with regard to the degree of reciprocity in group image and mutual understanding and acceptance of the definitions of the situation.

INDIANS (49 MALE HEADS OF HOUSEHOLDS)	
Might ask Indian to serve	49
Might ask Ladino to serve	47
Would never ask Indian to serve	0
Would never ask Ladino to serve	2
Thinks it possible for Indians to serve for Ladinos	4
Thinks it impossible for Indians to serve for Ladinos	42

In addition, the Indian interviewees were asked one question which was not asked of Ladinos, namely, whether they thought it was *better* to have Ladino or Indian godparents for Indian children. The answers were as follows:

Better to have Indian godparents	29
Better to have Ladino godparents	12
No preference	8

Note that a far larger proportion of Indians (47 out of 49) might "theoretically" ask Ladinos to serve, than the comparable proportion of Ladinos (3 out of 22) who might ask Indians to serve. The actual figures of mixed godparentalism for the group questioned are as follows:

175

LADINOS (22 MALE HEADS OF HOUSEHOLDS)

Had Ladino godparents	22
Had Indian godparents	0
Had Ladino godchildren	16
Had Indian godchildren	16
Wife had Ladino godparents	15
Wife had Indian godparents	0

INDIANS (49 MALE HEADS OF HOUSEHOLDS)

Had Ladino godparents	9
Had Indian godparents	41
Had Ladino godchildren	0
Had Indian godchildren	23
Wife had Ladino godparents	9
Wife had Indian godparents	36

It will be noted that Ladinos had as many Indian as Ladino godchildren, but that no Ladinos had Indian godparents. By contrast, no Indian had Ladino godchildren, but 18 out of the 88 Indians (husbands and wives) had Ladino godparents.

We may turn back now to the figures on Indian attitudes, and inquire further into the reasons offered by Indians for some of their answers. In answer to the question as to why they thought it was impossible for them to serve as godparents for Ladino children, the Indians answered as follows:

REASONS GIVEN	NO. OF TIMES MENTIONED
"Ladinos don't ask; I don't know why."	13
"Ladinos don't want Indians."	8
"Ladinos never ask Indians."	6
"Ladinos don't ask us because we are poor."	3
"Ladinos think they're better."	2
"They are Ladinos and we are Indians."	1
"The Ladinos are more lively than we are."	1
"We are Indians, they say."	1
"That's the way it is; that's our custom from old."	1
"It doesn't please the Ladinos."	1
"That's their custom."	1
"Because one is an Indian."	1
"Because Ladinos are ashamed to ask Indians."	1
"Because of the difference in clothes."	1
"Ladinos don't ask because they're Ladinos."	1
"Ladinos don't ask and we can't offer."	1
"Because we do not have enough money to handle matters."	1
"Because we are Indians."	1
"Because we don't mix with Ladinos."	1

In answer to the question as to why they thought it was better to have Indians serve as godparents for Indian godchildren, the Indians answered as follows:

REASONS GIVEN	NO. OF TIMES MENTIONED
"That's the custom."	7
"There is less expense involved."	7
"We have the same customs."	5
"Indians give advice to godchildren about the customs."	3
"Because we are Indians."	3
"Indians treat their godchildren better."	2
"For the religion."	1
"One has more confidence in them."	1
"We can speak together in the language."	1
"Indian godparents help out all during one's life."	1
"There are some who don't like to speak Spanish."	1
"That's my taste."	1
"Our customs are different."	1
"The Ladinos have a different law; it's not the same."	1
"It's better among the same kind of people."	1
"Indian godparents help out fathers and mothers in need. Ladino godparents do not help out their compadres."	1
"When one is poor, one always asks an Indian to serve."	1

In answer to the question as to why they thought it better to have Ladinos serve as godparents for Indian children, the 12 who thought so offered reasons in the following table.

As we compare the answers from Indians and Ladinos we can note a marked asymmetry between the reasons offered by each for the separatism between them. Whereas the Ladinos persistently offer the fact of inferiority of the Indians, the Indian confines himself for the most part to reasons of plain difference or "greater comfort," e.g., one can speak the Indian dialect with fellow Indians but not with Ladinos, etc. The few instances of Indian deprecation of Ladinos referred to the facts that (a) Indians treat their godchildren better; and (b) one has more "confidence" in Indians. Without wishing to brush away the second instance, it should be noted that "confidence," as used by the Indian, is most variable in its meanings, and often refers to the comfort one feels at being with "one's own kind" more than anything else. In general, however, it may reason-

REASONS GIVEN	NO. OF TIMES MENTIONED
"If one gets orphaned, he gets better care from Ladinos."	4
"Because Indians talk a lot and make false stories."	3
"Indians live in a funny way; they are backward."	1
"Because the customs are different."	1
"Ladinos clothe their godchildren well; Indians do not."	1
"It is more gallant to speak Spanish."	1
"Ladinos can teach their godchildren what Indians do not."	1
"Ladinos teach their orphaned godchildren Spanish and send them to school."	1
"They are of other customs; are not so sensitive; one can greet them better and more easily on the street."	1
"Ladino godparents give you good advice, Indians don't. Indians tell you not to beat a wife but what should one do with a bad wife who drags you off to the mayor?"	1
"You can borrow money from Ladino compadres; you can't from Indians because we are poor."	1

ably be said that the Ladinos keep distance from the Indians because they are contemptuous and/or disdainful of the Indian, whereas the Indian keeps distance because the Ladino insists on it and/or each wishes to be with "his own kind."

Some general observations about reciprocity and mutuality are immediately suggested by these data:

1. The situation is definitely structured in terms of superiority and inferiority of social position, with the Ladinos, by their own definition and that of at least some of the Indians, occupying the superior stratum.

2. Only some Indians are sensitively aware of the exploitative implications of the situation and of the derogatory attitudes held by the Ladinos toward them.

3. A much larger proportion of the Indians are either indifferently aware of the invidious aspects of the situation, or profess ignorance of any reasons for the separation and stratification other than "custom."

4. Whatever joint social participation of a voluntary or quasi-voluntary nature does exist in the godparental complex is, for the most part, initiated by the Indians, and participated in by the Ladinos with largely an attitude of *noblesse oblige*.

5. The group images of each other which the two groups carry are neither complements nor obverses. Rather, we have a situation here where one group looks down upon, openly exploits and derogates the other, while the latter, in turn, is only insignificantly aware of the situation; in large part, is unaware

of it; in small part, is sensitive to it; in the largest part, does not seem to be distressed by it, and does not generally, in turn, tend to deprecate the upper group, nor to envy it, nor attempt to emulate it or acquire membership within it.

Conclusions

E. HOW STABLE IS THE SITUATION?

In answer to this question, it seems important to note first the marked asymmetry relative to each other of the social images of the two groups in contact. This asymmetry might ordinarily be assumed, *a priori*, to be a source of tension, conflict and change. But our inquiry into reciprocity reveals that the forces of custom and traditionalism ("that's the custom;" "that's the way things are;") tend to promote a general unawareness of and indifference, on the part of the exploited and deprecated groups, to these invidious aspects of the total situation. And, where awareness is present, these forces tend to reduce the quotient of sensitivity present in the awareness and thereby recommend to the Indian the passive acceptance of the *status quo*. In so doing, these forces of traditionalism and ignorance help to perpetuate the underprivileged situation of the Indian. But they compensate for this, in part, by making his lot tolerable.

Conversely, if the Indian were to be more sensitively aware of the invidious status he occupies, the possibilities of social change would increase. By the same token, however, there would most likely be an increase in Indian discontent and dissatisfaction such as is not now present. One might reasonably generalize, therefore, that traditionalism and ignorance combine here to produce, for the Indian, short term profits and long term losses, whereas a change toward non-traditionalism and an increase in knowledge might be expected to produce short term losses but probable long term profits. It may thus be said that a prime sociological function of traditionalism and ignorance here, as in most other cases, is to provide guarantees of the stability of the status quo.

We can see this situation, moreover, as one in which the continuity of the society demands the co-participation of both groups in certain critical situations, and, over the course of time, has resulted in a working arrangement. By this we do not mean to imply that the prevailing arrangement is by any means the only possible one, nor that the present situation is a predictable response to certain teleological impulses in social structure. We do mean to state, however, that the caste system, as presently constituted, allows for the performance of the functional and structural prerequisites of societal continuity. And, additionally, it gives itself added guarantees of stability by generating, in its operations, a spirit of traditionalism and a marked ignorance which then serve to reinforce the system of which they were themselves expectable consequences.

A later monograph will document in more detail the unequal share of the available social rewards received by the Indians for their contribution to the continuity of the described social system. Their acceptance of their invidious situation, without any signs, overt or covert, of change-producing tensions, seems to me to be additional support for the contention that it is not possible to judge from a formal structural analysis alone the probable points, times, and levels of reaction of a people in an exploited situation. Humans will apparently endure much more than we, with our quasi-democratic projections, are able to envisage. We tend to set rather high levels of sensitivity and reaction to social exploitation and degradation. But our judgments in these cases seem to be a function more of our own time- and space-bound ideas than of objective insight into the inherent necessities of social structure. To put it bluntly, we know remarkably little about such inherent necessities.

It is important to note, in conclusion, that our judgment as to the stability of the described case could not have been determined from an analysis of the formal structure of relations alone, but required an empirical determination of the quotient of reciprocity operative in the situation. That empirical investigation enables us to state that here we have a case of a relatively stable social equilibrium which, supported by traditionalism and ignorance and the attitudes which derive from them, has much promise of long life. For, at least in the situations described, there are no discernible stresses and strains pushing toward rapid or basic social change.[3] Additionally, in those areas where co-operation or co-participation is indispensable to the continuity of the social order, the caste arrangement is sufficiently flexible to permit a clearly defined, hierarchically-structured cooperation[4] which for a variety of reasons, is mutually acceptable to both groups. Moreover, the caste system has institutionalized certain release valves, such as the godparental complex, which seem to function to reduce, in anticipation, any tensions which might arise.

NOTES

The materials in this article are part of the field data collected as a pre-doctoral fellow of the Social Science Research Council, to whom acknowledgment is here made. I am also indebted to my colleagues, Professors Harry Bredemeier, William J. Goode,

Paul K. Hatt, and Wilbert E. Moore, who have helped me clarify the ideas contained in the article.

1. The most recent article on the community is John Gillin's "Race Relations Without Conflict: A Guatemalan Town," *American Journal of Sociology*: LIII, 5, March 1948, pp. 337–343. This is in some measure derived from my field notes and my previous articles, the most recent of which is "Culture, Genuine and Spurious: A Re-Evaluation," *American Sociological Review*: X (April, 1945), pp. 199–207. I am in process of preparing a full length analysis of the system of social relations existing in the community. This present paper contains a brief consideration of some materials which will be dealt with in much greater detail in the forthcoming monograph.

2. The answer of one Ladino interviewee is richly enlightening. He is among the five wealthiest men in town; is considered by most of the Indians as one of the five best friends of the Indians; is held by the Ladinos to be among the five most important men. From all indications during his interview and before and after it, I take him to be a magnificent liar. But I quote verbatim his remarks on the godparental business. The reader will note where, though not explicated, a question from me had been put. "Yes, it is possible for an Indian to serve as godparent for a Ladino; many have so served; they are all Christians and have the same rights; but they don't like to serve; and they wouldn't serve; it isn't their custom; they don't have the facilities; they would have to refuse; they don't have the money. It is possible because there is much affection between us (my note: i.e., between Indian and Ladino); but they have other customs; a godfather is a second father to a child; if they raised a child of ours, it wouldn't be very seemly; they don't have aspirations; even if a Ladino is poor, he won't live in a *ranchito* like they do. At least a Ladino will rent a decent house. They live like animals. They don't have aspirations for a good house or a bed or to eat well. Rigoberto? (My note: this was the Ladinoized-Indian secretary [former] of pueblo). No, I wouldn't ask him. You see, an Indian with a little aspiration thinks he's a great person; but the Indian always has to be a little below. God help us if they were above us; the torture would never stop. Naturally, I have aspirations to visit the United States, for instance; the biggest spot you have there, I would like to go to. But the Indians? No, they don't have aspirations."

3. It is certain, however, that there are some tensions and strains in the social structure. These have largely been ignored in the present paper, since the going society is characteristically stable. A forthcoming paper, however, will examine in some detail the role of changing bases of land tenure as a source of actual discontent at present, and as a probable source of later social change of a significant degree.

4. See Jos. W. Eaton, "A Conceptual Theory of Cooperation," *American Journal of Sociology*: LIV, (Sept., 1948), p. 133.

13

CHRISTEN T. JONASSEN

CULTURAL VARIABLES
IN THE ECOLOGY
OF AN ETHNIC GROUP

The attempt to discover, describe, and explain regularities in man's adaptation to space has long been a matter of concern to social scientists and sociologists. In the United States the ecological school of sociology, depending primarily on the observation of man in an urban environment, has concerned itself with this problem. Since Alihan's shattering critique[1] of the Parkian ecological theory a decade ago, two schools of thought seem to have emerged. Their discussions have sought to determine whether or not a science of ecology is possible without a socio-cultural framework of reference. The crux of the problem seems to center around the relative influence of "biotic," strictly economic, "natural," and "sub-social" factors on the one hand, and socio-cultural elements on the other hand. Those stressing the former as causative factors have been referred to as the "classical" or "orthodox" ecologists,[2] while those emphasizing the latter factors might be called the "socio-cultural" ecologists.[3]

Perhaps the best if not the only way to determine where the correct emphasis should lie is by empirical research. It is hoped that the results of a research project[4] reported in this paper may contribute toward that end.

One writer suggests "that the time has come when we should study the influence of the cultural factor in the phenomena sociologists have defined as ecological."[5] The study of an ethnic group in an American urban environment seems particularly suitable for such a project. Such a group has a distinct culture which can be described and characterized, and the reaction of such a group to the American environment is more readily

Reprinted with permission from *American Sociological Review* 14 (1949): 32–41.

observed since it is set apart from the general population in the Census and other governmental reports.

The Norwegians in New York have a continuous history[6] as a group since about 1830 when they formed their first settlement and community in Lower Manhattan. Since that day the community has moved until it is now located in the Bay Ridge section of Brooklyn.[7] The first location was .25 mile from City Hall, the center of the city; the present location is about ten miles from that point. From 1830 to the present time six fairly distinct areas of settlement may be observed.

I. The Problem

We shall be primarily interested in the mobility of the Norwegian community. Why did the group first settle where it did, and why did it move from this area to another? We shall want to know why it moved in one direction and not in another, and we shall be interested in the rate and type of movement. And if we are able to suggest some answers to these questions, we shall be able to ascertain if the distribution of the Norwegian group in New York and the movement of its community can be explained in terms of factors that are "non-cultural," "sub-social," "impersonal," and "biotic," as the classical ecologists and their followers would contend; or if causality must be referred to cultural and social factors to explain the movement of this community in New York, as the "socio-cultural" ecologists would maintain.

II. Cultural Background of the Settlers

If we are to ascertain the comparative influence of culture in determining spatial distribution, it becomes necessary to sketch briefly the cultural background of this group so that their values and cultural heritage may be indicated. The Norwegians who created this settlement, unlike those who pioneered in the Western states, came for the most part from the coastal districts of Norway. Norway was in those days underdeveloped industrially and its main means of livelihood were agriculture, lumbering, fishing and seafaring. Many individuals would combine all of these occupations and especially fishing and agriculture which were carried on in the innumerable fjords and inlets of the long indented shoreline of Norway. In these districts a culture based primarily on the sea as a means of transportation and a source of food combined with a little farming has flourished for centuries since the Viking days. The people are trained from their earliest youth in skills necessary to make a living in such an environment. The men and women who founded and continued the Norwegian settlement in New York originated in such environments, and many men joined the colony by the simple expedient of walking off the ships on which they worked as sailors.

Norway, of all the civilized countries in the world, has one of the most scattered populations, the density being only 23.2 persons per square mile as compared to 750.4 for England and 41.5 for the United States.[8] Norway does not have very large cities and its people never live far from the mountains, the fjords, and the open sea. They are for the most part nature lovers and like green things and plenty of space about them.

III. Settlement and Movement of Norwegians in New York

The first Norwegian community which has an unbroken connection with the present one was located about 1830 in the area now bounded by the Brooklyn Bridge, the Manhattan Bridge, and the East River.[9] At that time, along this section of Manhattan were located docks where ships from all parts of the world loaded and unloaded, and here were also located the only large drydocks in New York, capable of repairing large ocean-going vessels. Here also were found the offices of shipping masters, vessel owners, and other seafaring occupations. In this atmosphere of salt water and ships, men familiar with the sea could feel at home. And within walking distance of their homes they found plenty of work as carpenters, shipbuilders, sailmakers, riggers, and dock and harbor workers.

Across the East River lay Brooklyn, a town of some 3,298 inhabitants in 1800. It grew rapidly and became an incorporated city in 1834, and by 1850 it had grown to 96,850 inhabitants. In 1940, the Borough according to Census figures had a population of 2,698,284. Brooklyn gradually superseded New York as a shipbuilding, ship repairing, and docking center. There was the New York Navy Yard in Wallabout Bay. But the center of shipping activity became Red Hook, that section of Brooklyn jutting into the New York harbor, across from the Battery. The Atlantic Docks were completed here in 1848. It also became the terminus of the great canal traffic that tapped the vast resources of the American continent. Here large grain elevators were built to hold grain for ships that came from all parts of the world to load and discharge. In 1853, the famous Burtis Shipyard already employed 500 men, and in 1866 a great celebration was held when the John N. Robbins Company opened two huge graving docks and three floating docks in Erie Basin.[10] These docks could build and float the largest vessels and they were the only such docks in New York outside those in the Navy Yard. Red Hook became a humming yachting, shipping, and ship-building center.

The Norwegians living in New York found the journey by horsecar and ferry tedious and time-consuming. They soon began to settle in Red Hook and the next Norwegian settlement developed in the area immediately adjacent to and north of Red Hook, where a small group of Norwegians settled in 1850. By 1870 the invasion of Brooklyn was gathering speed.

A horsecar, travelling along South Street in Manhattan, took Norwegian ship workers to Whitehall. Here they boarded the Hamilton Ferry to Hamilton Avenue, Brooklyn. Between 1870 and 1910, Hamilton Avenue became the most Norwegian street in Brooklyn and New York.

The colony developed to the north of Hamilton Avenue. The churches moved over from New York and new churches were established. In the Nineties, this section was one of large beautiful homes and tree-shaded streets. The section became better as one went north and became very exclusive at Brooklyn Heights where the grand old families lived. This section occupied in those days a functional relation to the downtown section of Manhattan that Westchester, Connecticut, and Long Island do today. A contemporary wrote, ". . . the greater part of the male population of Brooklyn daily travels to Manhattan to work in its offices. . . . The very fact that Brooklyn is a dwelling place for New York . . . a professional funny-man long ago called it a 'bed chamber.' "[11] It was actually as the saying went "a city of homes and churches."

Norwegian immigrant girls coming to New York found jobs as domestics in these beautiful homes and Norwegian men, skilled in the building, repair, and handling of ships of all kinds, found plenty of work for their hands in Erie and Atlantic Basins a short distance to the south. The section therefore became a logical location for the development of a Norwegian immigrant community. It offered them everything they needed. The Irish and Germans also moved into this neighborhood, and as it grew more and more crowded the old families moved out. Just as the New Englanders had forced out the Dutch, so now Norwegians, Irish, and Germans were forcing out the New Englanders. The stately old homes were converted to two- and three-family houses, and some to boarding houses. In this neighborhood the Norwegian colony flourished for some decades up to the beginning of the Twentieth Century.

At the time that certain members of the New York community moved away to settle in this area of Old South Brooklyn, others migrated across the river to Greenpoint in another part of the Brooklyn waterfront.[12] This section was also connected to the old Manhattan community by ferry. There was some shipping activity along this side of the waterfront but it offered only limited opportunity for the particular skills of the Norwegian immigrants. The area was soon invaded by new immigrants from the south of Europe and by factories of various kinds. It is rather significant that unlike the settlement in Old South Brooklyn this community did not move to adjacent territory, and after some years it ceased to exist, its inhabitants scattering in all directions.

The inexorable growth of the city continued. In old South Brooklyn, open places became fewer and fewer and green grass and trees disappeared. Old large one-family houses were torn down to give place to tightly packed tenements. Then it came the turn of the Norwegians, Irish, and Germans to be invaded and succeeded by the southern Europeans, mostly Italians from Sicily.

By 1890, many old downtown families purchased fashionable homes a little further out near Prospect Park, in the Park Slope section, as "a means of getting away from the thickly populated section of Brooklyn," the incentive being the scarcity of houses, plenty of wide open spaces and an abundance of trees and garden spots in the Park Slope area.[13] The residents of the area used to be known as the brownstone people who lived in beautiful mansions, paid their bills monthly, and ordered from the store by telephone. In the beginning of the century, the Norwegians also started to move out of the downtown area and into this section. This became the next center of the Norwegian colony in Brooklyn.

But the city continued to push its rings of growth further and further out and the same process repeated itself all over again. By 1910, the Norwegians were on the move again, this time to the adjoining area of Sunset Park. The docks and shipyards were extended all the way out to Fifty-ninth Street. And in 1915, the Fourth Avenue subway was completed. Electric cars running on Ninth and Fifteenth Streets and Third Avenue and Hamilton Avenue provided transportation to the shipping center at Red Hook.

The center of the Norwegian colony remained in Sunset Park district up to about 1940. The exodus of Norwegians from this section and into Bay Ridge and other outlying sections is now in progress. It is the sections of Sunset Park and Bay Ridge which now constitute the area of the settlement. The present Norwegian settlement is located on the high ground overlooking New York Harbor. For the most part it is a section of one- and two-family houses with small lawns, backyards, and tree-planted streets. The nature of this area was determined by indices which have proved reliable in characterizing urban neighborhoods. Indices of economic status, rents, condition of housing, density of population, mobility rates, morbidity and mortality rates, demographic characteristics, standardized rates of crime and juvenile delinquency, dependency, poverty and desertion rates were also employed. From the cumulative evidence of such data it is apparent that the area in which the Norwegians live is, when compared with other areas of New York and Brooklyn, one of the best, and no part of this area according to this study displays the characteristics of a slum district. However, a detailed study of the various parts of the area shows that it can be divided into areas that, on the basis of the indicated indices, may be designated as "poor," "medium," and "best." The distribution of Norwegians living within these areas is as follows: ten per cent live in "poor" sections, fifty-four per cent in "medium," and thirty-six per cent in "best" areas. The "best" areas include parts of Bay Ridge and Fort Hamilton which contain some of the best residential areas in New York, while the "poor" areas in the northwestern part of the Sunset Park district have some sections that border perilously on slum conditions.

An analysis of population movements within the area of the Norwegian settlement indicates that the Norwegians are moving out of the northern and western census tracts of the Sunset Park district and into the southwestern census tracts of Bay Ridge and Fort Hamilton. Italians and Poles are moving in from the northeast and Russian Jews are taking over the sections of the northern and eastern periphery of the area vacated by the Norwegians and other Scandinavians.

From the ecological and historical study of the characteristics of the Norwegian community over a period of more than a hundred years, it appears that it has maintained rather consistent characteristics and a functional position in New York since the community was established. Like all other groups, native and foreign, the Norwegians were unable to prevent change of the character of their neighborhood, nor were they able to prevent invasion by other land use and lower status groups; they could maintain the things they valued only by retreating before the inexorable development of the city to new territory where conditions were more in harmony with their conceptions of a proper place to live.

It is apparent from the data of this study that numerous causative factors have operated in determining the location and movement of the

Norwegian community in New York: the economic and social conditions of Norway, the economic and social conditions of the United States, the rate and direction of New York City growth, the condition of the neighborhood, available lines of communication between the cultural area and the location of the economic base, and attitudes and values of the Norwegian heritage. Where they were to settle and the rate and direction of movement were thus largely determined by elements of the immigrants' heritage and the character and needs of the host society of the United States.

Neither one of these factors was *the* determining one. The Norwegians' reaction to this urban environment resulted rather from a judicious balance of all these factors. It is clear from old maps that transportation to Bay Ridge was available as early as 1895, if they had wanted to live there. But this was slow transportation by horsecar in the early days, and the downtown area evidently presented agreeable enough conditions. As the city grew, however, these conditions became less desirable to people who valued plenty of space around them and nearness to nature.

It is apparent that the Norwegian immigrants broke away from the original economic base to a certain extent later. This development depended on the advance of lines of transportation and new technological and economic development and on the fact that the Norwegian culture was becoming ever more industrialized, which gave later emigrants new skills and knowledge that they could apply here. The erection of skycrapers and use of steel construction in New York gave Norwegian sailors jobs as structural steel and iron workers. They were used to working aloft and their experience as riggers made them particularly valuable for this work. In the Twenties, the great building boom provided skilled carpenters with plenty of work.

Figure 13–1 shows the sections the Norwegians have inhabited at various times. The dotted lines represent lines of transportation. Figure 13–2 is the same map with its salient factors consolidated and simplified. The progression of the Norwegian cultural area, as can be seen, may be represented as a series of interlocking circles, the centers of which are the centers of the cultural areas at the times specified. The path of this progression is the locus of the centers of the interlocking circles, and it represents in reality the lines of communication.

At each stage, the cultural area presents definite ecological characteristics. It has a center, a clustering of ethnics. The center attracts and repels (repulsion and attraction here are considered as functions of the choice of individuals in relation to the realities of the environment); it repels some who move out and establish the basis for a new center farther out along

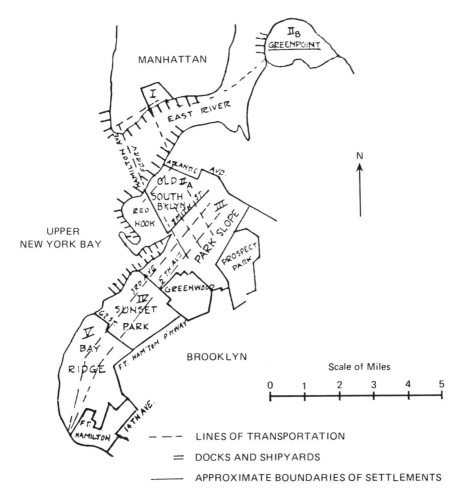

Figure 13–1   Norwegian Settlements, 1850–1947

the path of advance, and it attracts others to it who are lagging behind. The lagging areas, shaded on the map (Figure 13–2), are created at the stage when the colony is breaking up to advance again; they represent transitional areas in process of invasion by other land use and lower status groups. They are therefore the least desirable sections of the settlements to which those who are economic failures gravitate. The advance guard of the new cultural area settled new territory or mingled with native Americans, and these Norwegians in turn formed a center for a new Norwegian cultural area. The process is a continuous one, and change from one area to another must be measured in decades rather than in years. It is a seepage-like movement rather than a sudden mass change.

189

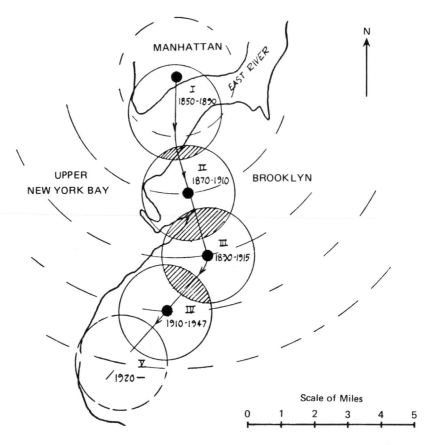

Figure 13-2   Movement of Norwegians, 1850–1947

IV. Some Implications of This Study for Ecological Theory

The change of location of the Norwegian community was produced by persons breaking away from the old area and individually choosing a new habitat. Because of its concerted progression in a certain direction to a certain place, the illusion of a directed mass movement is created. But this ecological behavior arises out of the interaction of the realities of the New York environment with the immigrants' attitudes and values. The resulting actions of many individuals are very much alike since they are motivated by very similar attitudes created in conformity with the cultural pattern of Norway. *It is therefore indicated that the movement of these people must be referred to factors that are volitional, purposeful, and personal and that these factors may not be considered as mere accidental and incidental features of biotic processes and impersonal competition.*

It has been stated that immigrant colonies are to be found in the slums or that immigrants make their entry into the city in the area immediately adjacent to the central business district.[14] From the data of this study we are fairly certain that the Norwegian colony has not existed in an area with the characteristics of a slum, and we can be certain that it does not occupy such an area today even though it is the habitat of recently arrived immigrants. It would therefore appear that the statements referred to above can not be taken as generalizations, but apply to certain ethnic or racial groups only.

The cause of the Norwegians' settling where they did and in no other place around New York is not at all clear if we refer the explanation to biological, sub-social, and non-cultural factors. It is logical to assume that as biological creatures interested primarily in sustenance and survival, the Norwegians could have survived in any number of other places. But if we refer the explanation of the location of their community to cultural factors it becomes so obvious as to be banal. It is clear that their cultural heritage had given them the tools whereby they were able to elicit meaning and values from this particular environment. Other sections of New York, for example the financial section, the clothing manufacturing sections, etc., had little meaning for them in terms of survival or satisfaction. To the Jew from a crowded Ghetto in the center of Poland the realities of the harbor district would probably have no values and meaning, or they might have different values and meanings, perhaps negative values. But to the Norwegian, socialized in the coast culture of Norway, this environment had meaning and value in terms of sustenance and psychological satisfaction. The very method by which he could compete and sustain himself was inherent in the cultural heritage which he brought to this country, and whether or not this cultural heritage should ever find expression and be useful to him depended on the cultural pattern of the United States and the cultural artifacts of that country.

The objective realities of New York thus presented the Norwegians with a multitude of environments to which they might have reacted. It is significant that they reacted primarily to those aspects of the New York milieu that had meaning in their value system. Thus the environmental facts were of little significance *per se* and only as they were incorporated into the value-attitude systems of the Norwegian immigrants.

The movement of the group, when compared with the movements of other ethnic groups in New York and other American cities, assumes some significance. Studies of Italians[15] and Jews[16] reveal different developments. The usual situation in these groups is one in which an area of first settlement is established which stays in one place, and continues to receive new arrivals. As the old immigrants become assimilated and the second generation grows up, they move out to an area of "second settlement," usually far removed from the first in space and time. Thus Italian and Jewish communities in New York are still found in many of the areas, such as the Lower East Side of Manhattan and downtown Brooklyn where they were first established. But there is hardly a trace of any Norwegians in the areas of New York and Brooklyn which they originally inhabited. Furthermore, the development and progression of Norwegian cultural areas in New York show a continuum of space and time and result from the unique character of their heritage in interaction with their new environment. It does not therefore seem possible to generalize as to the type of movement that all immigrant groups in urban areas will exhibit; rather the type of movement, its rate and direction will depend on the interaction of the particular heritage of each immigrant group with the urban environment in which the immigrants live. The different rates of movement of different ethnic groups[17] from the center of cities might find a more satisfactory explanation on this basis.

The area of the Norwegian community was described in terms of indices of various kinds. These might be regarded as objective measures of the values which Norwegians have in regard to the environment in which they want to live. Thus the amount of crowding within the home and congestion without, and other conditions indicated by crime, delinquency, health, and population statistics, have for Norwegians apparently reached an intolerable point in certain census tracts. Other tracts present them with conditions that they find more favorable, and it is to these areas that they move as soon as they are able to do so.

It is probable that the Norwegian community has been able to maintain its solidarity for over a hundred years and in spite of constant moving, because the variable factors that determined its existence were favorable. The dissolution of the Greenpoint settlement indicates what happened when the factors that sustained it were unfavorable. But for the community that did survive and move, there was, when conditions reached an intolerable state, always an appropriate area immediately adjacent to the old area; so the community was able to move from Manhattan to old South Brooklyn, to Park Slope, to Sunset Park, and finally to Bay Ridge. Norwegians have not been segregated from native whites, nor is there any evidence that they have been discriminated against in any way as far as choosing a home is concerned. The clustering within the area is therefore voluntary.

However, there is no place having the characteristics which Norwegians require adjacent to the present settlement in Bay Ridge. The city is moving in on them from north and west, and there is only water to the east and south. The area is also being invaded by other ethnic groups. Nor is the type of buildings within this area entirely of their liking. It is still predominantly a neighborhood of single- and two-family houses, but a great number of large, high class apartment houses have been built, and the land value has increased so tremendously that wherever zoning permits, this is the type of housing that is erected. It would seem that the Norwegian community in Brooklyn is making its last stand in Bay Ridge with its back to the sea. Its final dissolution is a matter of years and will be brought about because the balance of variables that determined its development cannot be maintained much longer. As long as the values of their heritage could be integrated and harmonized with conditions of the developing city, the community grew and flourished; when this integration is no longer possible it will disintegrate and its members disperse.

This development has already commenced. Census figures and the changes of addresses for subscribers to *Nordisk Tidende* indicate that many Norwegians are moving to Queens, Staten Island, New Jersey, and Connecticut, where new settlements are forming in environments which are more in harmony with the values of their heritage. Some of these settlements have started as colonies of summer huts, and finally developed into all-year round communities.

The peculiar interplay of a plurality of motives that goes into the determination of ecological distribution of Norwegians is well illustrated by these informants:

I like it here (Staten Island) because it reminds me of Norway. Of course, not Bergen because we have neither Fløyen nor Ulrik, nor mountains on Staten Island, but it is so nice and green all over in the summer. I have many friends in Bay Ridge in Brooklyn, and I like to take trips there, but to tell the truth when I get on the ferry on the way home and get the smell of Staten Island, I think it's glorious. However, I'm taking a trip to Norway this summer, and Norway is, of course, Norway—and Staten Island is Staten Island.[18]

A man states:

I arrived in America in 1923, eighteen years old. I went right to Staten Island because my father lived there and he was a ship-builder at Elco Boats in Bayonne, New Jersey, right over the bridge. I started to work with my father and I am now foreman at the shipyard where we are building small yachts— the best in America. I seldom go to New York because I don't like large cities with stone and concrete. Here are trees and open places. . . .[19]

Another tells what he likes about his place in Connecticut:

I like the private peace up here in the woods. There is suitable space between the cabins so that we do not have to step on each other's toes unless we want to get together with someone once in a while. Since I started to build this house, it is as if I have deeper roots here than in the city. This is my *own* work for myself. . . .[20]

And a woman says:

. . . . It is a real joy to get out of the city with all its wretchedness. I go down to the brook where I have a big Norwegian tub. There I sing lilting songs and wash and rinse clothes. Everything goes like play, and before you know it, the summer is over, and all this glorious time is gone and I could almost cry.[21]

One who has moved to Staten Island weighs the advantages and disadvantages:

It is countrylike and quiet here with plenty of play room for the children. But I must admit I am homesick for Brooklyn once in a while, perhaps often. Then I take the ferry and visit friends and acquaintances there.[22]

The assumption that "in general, living organisms tend to follow the line of least resistance in obtaining environmental resources and escaping environmental dangers" has been used as the basis for hypotheses of human distribution in space.[23] Such a statement in the light of this study seems too mechanistic, too simple, and therefore inadequate as an explanation of the distribution of this group in New York. Men need not merely to survive, require not only shelter or just any type of sustenance; they want to live in a particular place, in a particular way. A better description of man's distributive behavior might be: *men tend to distribute themselves within an area so as to achieve the greatest efficiency in realizing the values they hold most dear.*[24] Thus man's ecological behavior in a large American city becomes the function of several variables, both socio-cultural and "non-cultural."

One writer has pointed out that the early ecologists "envisaged an abstract ecological man motivated by physiological appetites and governed in his pursuits of life's goals by competition with others who sought the same things he sought because physiologically they were like him."[25] It is quite evident now that this ecological creature was the product of the same intellectual miscegenation which begot the now somewhat extinct "economic man." The men and women observed in this study are not abstract entities; they are very real persons with physical needs. But they are also governed and motivated in the pursuit of culturally determined goals by culturally determined habits and ways of living. They compete for things high in the hierarchy of their value system which may or may not be the same things for which other individuals and groups strive. It hardly seems possible to achieve a systematic theory of ecology that squares with empirical observation and meets the needs of logical consistency without the cultural component as an integral part of such formulations.

NOTES

1. Milla A. Alihan, *Social Ecology*, New York, 1938.

2. The "classical" ecological position is perhaps best expressed by: Robert E. Park, "Succession, an Ecological Concept," *American Sociological Review*, I, April, 1936; "Human Ecology," *The American Journal of Sociology*, XLII, July, 1936; "Reflections on Communication and Culture," *The American Journal of Sociology*, XLIV, Sept., 1938; Robert E. Park, Ernest W. Burgess, Roderick D. McKenzie, *The City*, Chicago, 1925; Ernest W. Burgess, ed., *The Urban Community*, Chicago, 1925; Roderick D. McKenzie, *The Metropolitan Community*, New York, 1933; "The Concept of Dominance and World Organization," *The American Journal of Sociology*, XXXIII, July, 1926. Following the general orientation but differing somewhat from the "classical" position we have: James A. Quinn, "The Nature of Human Ecology—Re-examination and Redefinition," *Social Forces*, 18: 161–168, 1939; "Ecological Versus Social Interaction," *Sociology and Social Research*, 18: 565–570, 1934; "Culture and Ecological Phenomena," *Sociology and Social Research*, XXV: 313–320, March, 1941; Amos H. Hawley, "Ecology and Human Ecology," *Social Forces*, 22: 398–405, May, 1944.

3. Perhaps the most forceful expression of the "socio-cultural" position is in the writings of: Walter Firey, *Land Use in Central Boston*, Cambridge, Massachusetts, 1947; "Sentiment and Symbolism as Ecological Variables," *American Sociological Review*, X, 140–204, April, 1945; August B. Hollingshead, "A Re-examination of Ecological Theory," *Sociology and Social Research*, 31: 194–204, January 1947; Warner E. Gettys, "Human Ecology and Social Theory," *Social Forces*, 18: 469–476, 1939.

4. See C. T. Jonassen, *The Norwegians in Bay Ridge: A Sociological Study of an Ethnic Group*, University Microfilms, Ann Arbor, Michigan, 1947.

5. A. B. Hollingshead, *op. cit.*

6. See A. N. Rygg, *The Norwegians in New York 1825–1925*, Brooklyn, New York, 1941.

7. Smaller settlements have also been formed in suburban sections of Staten Island, Queens, and the Bronx, but the main group is located in Bay Ridge. See Figure 13–1.

8. As of 1938.

9. See Figure 13–1.

10. *Brooklyn Daily Eagle*, April 17, 1910.

11. Edward Hungerford, "Across the East River," *Brooklyn Life*, 1890–1915, p. 81.

12. See Figure 13–2.

13. *Brooklyn Daily Eagle*, December 5, 1926.

14. Cf. R. D. McKenzie, *The Metropolitan Community*, p. 241; Ernest W. Burgess, "The Growth of the City: An Introduction to a Research Project," in Robert E. Park,

et al., The City, pp. 55, 56; Harvey W. Zorbaugh, *The Gold Coast and the Slum*, Chicago, Illinois: University of Chicago Press, 1929, pp. 11, 128.

15. Cf. Leonard Covello, *The Social Background of the Italo-American School Child: A Study of the Southern Italian Family Mores and Their Effect on the School Situation in Italy and America*, New York: New York University School of Education, (Ph.D. thesis) 1944.

16. Cf. Louis Wirth, *The Ghetto*, Chicago, Illinois, 1929.

17. Cf. Paul F. Cressey, "Population Succession in Chicago: 1898–1930," *American Sociological Review*, August 1938, pp. 59–69.

18. *Nordisk Tidende*, March 3, 1947.

19. *Loc. cit.*

20. *Ibid.*, September 5, 1946.

21. *Loc. cit.*

22. *Ibid.*, March 3, 1947.

23. James A. Quinn, "Hypothesis of Median Location," *American Sociological Review*, April, 1943.

24. This conclusion is essentially in agreement with the "theory of proportionality" as proposed by Walter Firey, *Land Use in Central Boston*, p. 328.

25. A. B. Hollingshead, *op. cit.*, p. 204.

14
PAUL HATT

THE RELATION OF ECOLOGICAL
LOCATION TO STATUS POSITION
AND HOUSING OF
ETHNIC MINORITIES

There is abundant evidence in the literature of human ecology of a definite relationship between spatial location and status position. It is obvious that the segregated and gradient distribution of good and bad housing is one evidence of this. It is also a common sense observation that ghettos may be placed on the housing quality gradient and in general, are areas of medium or low housing quality. In fact the ideal type ghetto is a spatial pattern within which economic level, ethnic character, and other social phenomena coincide to produce a homogenous area which has a prestige level consistent with the low social status of its occupants.[1] It should be noted that "status" here refers to the general status value within the entire community attaching to a person by reason of his race, creed, or nationality. It is recognized that within the ghetto there are wide status differences, but it is also recognized for the purpose of this paper that generally speaking, certain minority types as a whole, have lower status than the majority population. It is ecological expression of this fact which is dealt with here.

The relatively complete spatial segregation characteristic of homogeneous ghettos may operate to interfere with the use of such a factor as rental value as a status index by disturbing the balance of supply and demand normally basic to ecological distribution. For example, members of minorities must frequently pay relatively high rents for inferior housing. This seems most likely to occur in very homogeneous areas where the supply of potential residents exceeds the available dwelling units in the

Reprinted with permission from *American Sociological Review* 10 (1945): 481–485.

ghetto, or in the vanguard of invasion where the pioneer representatives of the minority are the first of a new ethnic type to occupy a given residential area. Under such circumstances, one of the resistances to invasion is the appearance of discriminatory rentals or property values. A study of the relation between ecological location and status and housing of minorities then should avoid patterns of the pure ghetto type.

An area of mixed population type has been described by the writer in another paper.[2] In such a polyethnic area the difficulties mentioned above are at least lessened. Differential rentals for similar properties among the several ethnic types do not seem to exist here. Analysis shows no significant difference between the various minorities in amount of rent paid for similar units in size and condition. Nor is there any difference on this score between the minority types and the Gentile White population. This may be due to the fact that this is an area thoroughly invaded by several minorities even though the majority of the units are occupied by Gentile Whites. Certainly, as an area, its status value for Gentile Whites is low, and there are still many units available for the minority populations. This, then, allows the use of rental value as a rough socioeconomic index comparable for all groups in the area.[3]

As stated earlier, the distribution of ethnic types in this population is mixed and overlapping. This does not imply, however, that the types are equally distributed throughout the entire area. The pattern may be divided roughly into thirds. The western extremity contains large populations of all the colored ethnic classes. The concentrations continue but with decreasing frequency, into the central portion of the area where an increasing incidence of Jewish whites is encountered.[4] The eastern third is characterized by decreasing frequency of Jews, an almost total absence of colored racial types, and thus has an almost exclusively Gentile White population. It should be noted again, however, that this majority population is clearly dominant throughout the entire area, even in the western third.

The degree of concentration of each of the minority types varies throughout the area and no category is limited by the special rental values which may be associated with a true ghetto. It thus seems possible that with these greater limits to mobility, the relationship between rental value and ethnic type should be closely related to the economic status of the ethnic minorities. Certainly the relationship would be clearer here than in the case of using a series of homogeneous ghettos.

Table 14–1 presents a series of coefficients of correlation by the rank method between selected housing indexes and concentration of ethnic type. These correlations were secured by Spearman's method of Rank

TABLE 14-1

Coefficients of Correlation Between Ethnic Type Concentration and Selected Housing Indexes

	HOUSING INDEXES			
ETHNIC TYPE	RENTAL VALUE	PERCENTAGE IN GOOD CONDITION	PERCENTAGE UNFIT	AGE OF STRUCTURE
Ashkenazim	− .65	− .65	− .34	− .20
Gentile White	− .55	− .67	− .62	− .38
Sephardim	− .37	− .41	− .16	− .28
Chinese	− .55	− .54	− .53	− .19
Negro	− .62	− .62	− .68	− .42
Filipino	− .68	− .69	− .54	− .20
Japanese	− .81	− .77	− .87	− .58

Association from the rankings of twenty-two sub-areas.[5] These coefficients clearly indicate that those areas which show the highest indexes of good housing tend also to show the highest proportion of population in the white ethnic categories, and those with the lowest housing indexes, the highest proportions of the non-white ethnic types.

To the extent that these ethnic types approach a pattern of segregation it is possible to rank them in "goodness" of area in the order in which they are listed in Table 14–1. It can be observed that there is a close relationship among the indexes presented with the exception of "Age of Structure" which shows the lowest relationship to the general pattern. The remaining consistent pattern of relationship shows only one discrepancy in the reversal of the rank order between Ashkenazim and Gentile Whites from rental value to percentage of units in good condition. It is apparent that the Ashkenazim are more concentrated in areas of higher rental value then are the Gentile Whites who are spread throughout the entire area. However, since there is a gradient pattern of Ashkenazim, there is a certain amount of segregation which for them limits the range of rental values. Also the area most heavily settled by this type is an older area than is that earlier characterized as almost totally Gentile White. Thus the larger proportion of unfit units associated with the Ashkenazim reflect the process of deterioration which has not yet reached the areas most heavily populated by Gentile Whites.

The validity of such a ranking as descriptive of the status of ethnic types is certainly open to question since the correlations in Table 14–1 are based on spatial units and in view of the fact that the segregation of ethnic types is not clearly marked in this population. The validity of the ranking must be checked by comparing the relative position of the ethnic types in the housing factors without reference to spatial units. Table 14–2 presents the housing indexes for all households in each ethnic category regardless of spatial location.

These distributions of housing characteristics for the several ethnic types are in close agreement with the implications of Table 14–1. Approximately the same order is shown except that the Negro drops slightly below the Japanese, and the Gentile White below the Sephardim. In the latter case this is easily understood since the Gentile White population is the only one scattered throughout the entire area thus having its mean rental value affected by considerable numbers of low values in the western portion of the area. The exchange of position by the Japanese and Negroes could be explained by chance since in both cases the differences are slight.

It has been observed in the preceding tables that the ethnic minorities can be placed on a continuum of desirability of housing, and that their positions on that continuum are reflected by appropriate spatial relationships between ethnic type and indexes of housing as in Table 14–1. However, it remains to be seen whether or not the actual housing conditions of these minorities are more or less desirable than the averages within the areas of concentration for each type. To this end, Table 14–3 is a series of indexes showing the relationship of each minority in rental value and condition of structure to the average for the area within which each is concentrated. Thus, the Japanese are compared to the figure for the total population within the area of concentration of Japanese.[6] The same procedure is followed for each category. The index is the mean rental value and the percentage of units unfit for use for each of these areas divided by the mean rental value and the percentage of units unfit for use for the appropriate ethnic type. When rental value of proportion of units unfit for

TABLE 14-2

Indexes of Condition of Structure and
Rental Value Characterizing Each Ethnic Type

ETHNIC TYPE	MEAN MONTHLY RENTAL VALUE IN DOLLARS	PERCENTAGE OF UNITS IN GOOD CONDITION	PERCENTAGE OF UNITS UNFIT FOR USE
Ashkenazim	27	47	4
Sephardim	24	36	3
Gentile White	18	29	11
Chinese	17	20	22
Japanese	16	13	24
Negro	16	10	30
Filipino	15	2	20

TABLE 14-3

Housing Indexes Comparing Six Ethnic
Types to the Total Population of the Areas
in Which Each is Concentrated

ETHNIC TYPE	RENTAL VALUE	PERCENTAGE OF UNITS UNFIT FOR USE
Ashkenazim	1.1	.8
Sephardim	1.1	.5
Chinese	1.2	.9
Japanese	1.1	1.1
Negro	1.0	1.3
Filipino	1.2	.9

use is greater for the ethnic minority than for the area, the index is more than one, and when it is less, the index is below one.

It is clear from Table 14–3 that all minorities pay higher rents than does the average occupant in the area in which they live. Four of the six types also occupy fewer unfit dwellings than is typical of their area. The Negroes and Japanese are the only exception to this with Unfit for Use indexes slightly in excess of 1.0.

There is ample evidence in the United States today to assume that lower status, in general, is assigned to Jews than to Gentiles, and to colored persons than to whites. Since Ashkenazim, Sephardim, Chinese and Filipinos are of relatively low ascribed status, other factors being equal, but still pay higher rents and occupy fewer unfit dwelling units than is typical of the areas in which they live, it may be concluded that the purely economic status of these types is greater than that of the Gentile White populations with which they live. Such an area, then, is an area with a *Gentile White* status level lower than the economic or occupational status of the minority types found in that area. The seeming variance of the Negroes and Japanese from this pattern does not necessarily indicate that they occupy locations within a Gentile White population of higher status. It may rather be explained by the fact that these types are consistently at the bottom of any housing scale and presumably also the general status scale. Thus even the poorest of Gentile White housing is apt to be superior to that of these two minorities. Family size and structure also plays a role in these cases. Filipinos, for example, are largely single men. Filipinos being in the youthful age categories and employed show slightly better housing than the single men of the Gentile White population who are, to a considerable extent, aged and receiving public assistance. The Negro and Japanese, on the other hand, are to a large degree family groups, although they live in the same area which is heavily populated by aged, single, Gentile White men receiving public aid. Thus, although the two minorities seem to be paying greater rents, they are paying them for larger units. It seems safe to say that actually the rental level for the Negroes and Japanese is lower than for the Gentile Whites in the same area. This would square with the fact that the units of the minorities are more likely to be unfit for use than is true of the Gentile White dwelling units. We thus see that the assumption of the status level of these groups must be to assign them the lowest position on the continuum judged by the level of the areas in which they live, by their housing characteristics, and by the fact that they alone of all the minorities, are not superior in quality of housing to the Gentile White population which lives with them.

It is well known that ascribed, or socio-economic status, and actual economic status of social classes are frequently divergent. It has been seen in this study that insofar as these statuses are reflected in housing characteristics and in spatial location, both have an ecological expression. If similar relations were found to be characteristic of American cities, and if the validity of these relations were demonstrated by the use of such an objective measure as a Social Status Scale,[7] it would be possible to secure accurate status ratings of minority ethnic types through ecological study of their space relations with other ethnic types. Without being able to show this one may suggest the hypothesis that status relations between minority and majority ethnic categories are such that invasion by a minority can take place in a majority area only when the minority population has achieved a definitely higher economic status than is characteristic of the resident majority type.

NOTES

1. Andrew Lind, "The Ghetto and the Slum," *Social Forces*, vol. IX, no. 2, December, 1930; Harold A. Gibbard, "The Status Factor in Residential Succession," *The American Journal of Sociology*, vol. XLVI, no. 6, May, 1941; Clifford Shaw and Henry McKay, *Juvenile Delinquency and Urban Areas*, University of Chicago Press, 1940, p. 37.

2. "Spatial Patterns in a Polyethnic Area," *The American Sociological Review*, June, 1945, pp. 352–356. Briefly, this area is the central residential district of Seattle, Wash., lying between the central business district and the city boundary of Lake Washington. In this area representatives of all the large minority populations in the city are found to co-exist in markedly overlapping patterns. It was also noted that the patterns were highly irregular in segregation and that the dominant type was everywhere the majority, Gentile White population.

3. These data are from the Real Property Survey conducted by W.P.A. in 1939, and

thus are unaffected by the war. As a result they show the presence of the Japanese, later to be removed, and the presence of vacancies which have disappeared with the war boom.

4. Strictly speaking Ashkenazic and Sephardic Jews are not true ethnic types. However, since they display the major characteristics of ethnic minorities they are treated as such in this study.

5. These twenty-two sub-areas were delineated on the basis of homogeneity of rental value and presence or absence of colored races.

6. These areas are free hand constructions, each of which however, includes a minimum of eighty-five per cent of the ethnic type concerned.

7. F. Stuart Chapin, *Contemporary American Institutions*, Harpers, 1935, Chap. 19.

15

HARVEY MOLOTCH

RACIAL INTEGRATION
IN A TRANSITION COMMUNITY

Although the in-migration of blacks into previously white areas generally leads to eventual all-black occupancy, thus continuing the pattern of residential racial segregation in U.S. cities (cf. Taeuber and Taeuber, 1965), it is possible that at least during the transition period, geographical propinquity may lead to some degree of racial integration. Three possible forms of integration may conceivably realize themselves during the transition process: (1) *Demographic* integration, whereby a given setting contains both blacks and whites in some specified proportions; (2) *Biracial interaction*, whereby non-antagonistic social interaction is occurring between blacks and whites to some specifiable extent; (3) *Transracial solidarity*, defined as conditions in which whites and blacks interact freely and without constraint, and in a manner such that race ceases to function as an important source of social cleavage or as a criteria for friendship and primary group selection. This report describes the extent, form, and most common contexts of these various sorts of integration in one changing area on the South Side of Chicago—the community of South Shore. Utilizing the data gathered, an attempt will be made to explicate the more general processes at work which, in the context of black-white propinquity, inhibit or promote the cross-racial sharing of social life. (In another publication, the author has described the speed and ecological patterns of South Shore's transition. cf. Molotch, 1969.)

Reprinted with permission from *American Sociological Review* 34 (1969): 878–93.

General Strategy

There have been many descriptions of communities striving for integration, yet seldom do data on the subject of actual interracial contact go beyond the anecdotal level. Many community studies (cf. Johnson, 1965; Biddle and Biddle, 1965) cheerfully recount instances when whites and blacks serve on the same committee or come together in a constructive joint enterprise. Precise information is lacking which would indicate the frequency of such contacts, the contexts in which they most often appear, or the dynamics of their development. The absence of such information inhibits the development of a sound theory of cross-racial interaction and, at a more practical level, precludes rigorous comparative analysis or evaluation of various forms of intervention which have integration as their goal.

An attempt is thus made in the present study to depict objectively the extent and forms of integration in South Shore. Basic to the more mechanical means utilized to carry out this task was a two-year (July 1965–July 1967) participant observation study in the community—particularly of the area's major community organization and its subsidiary committees and groups (cf. Molotch, 1967, 1968, 1969). Data of a more precise sort were gathered by taking simple head counts of the racial composition of various local settings—including schools, churches, recreation facilities, retail shops and voluntary organizations. In some instances, reports of organizational officers were utilized; in others, organizational group-photographs appearing in the local community newspaper or on bulletin boards were inspected. In most instances, however, actual visits were made to the setting and the numbers of whites and blacks present were recorded. The racial mix of such settings is taken as an important clue to the possible existence of other forms of integration as well.

The Study Area

"South Shore" commonly denotes not only a specific aerial unit of the city of Chicago, but also a certain "community." That is, the phrase brings to the mind of Chicagoans, and especially those living in the South Side, an image of certain geographical boundaries, certain landscapes and landmarks and a certain life style. Both residents and non-residents utilize the concept "South Shore" as a means of identifying those living within its boundaries. The imagery has traditionally been one of middle-class living, lakeside recreation and well-kept lawns, homes and buildings. South Shore has long been administratively utilized by local politicians, religious denominations, public and private civic agencies and businesses in distributing services and in naming stores and branch offices. Persons indigenous to the area have used the term "South Shore" to name their own shops and organizations and to adopt as constituencies for such institutions those persons living within its boundaries.

That South Shore is an entity which continues to have an existence in the minds of local residents was documented by a series of informal interviews carried out by the writer on the major business arteries of the area (cf. Molotch, 1966, 1968, Chap. 2). Passersby were stopped and asked such questions as: "What area is this?" "What part of town is this?" The answer would almost always be South Shore, although additional probing would often reveal additional place names corresponding to the smaller-scale elementary school districts which serve the region. Community boundaries were established by utilizing the answers to such questions as "How far does South Shore go?" or "Where does this area end?" Under varying conditions of context and an individual's purposes in reporting such information, the relevant unit of "community" might be smaller than South Shore (e.g., an elementary school district) or considerably larger (e.g., the South Side, or Chicago). For present purposes it is asserted that South Shore is one important source of community identification utilized by both local and non-local residents and that, in this sense, it is a meaningful unit of analysis. Further, the common recognition of the area and widespread tendency to self-identify oneself as a resident of "South Shore" is indicative of a common stake in the area, and thus a basis for the commonalty of interests and the "we feeling" which McKenzie (1923:344) held to be the defining attribute of community.

Approximately 80% of South Shore's 70,000 residents have come to live in basically sound apartment structures—generally of the walk-up variety, mostly constructed in the early 1930's.[2] In terms of the characteristics of its population, housing and geographic location, it is generally prototypical of racially changing communities in the United States (cf. Taeuber and Taeuber, 1965; Fishbein, 1962). Its residents were, at least when racial change began in 1960, Protestant, Catholic and Jew in approximately equal proportions.[3] By the time the data for this study was gathered, South Shore's population was approximately one-third black, with blacks preponderant in the Northwestern portion of the area (contiguous to the previously existing ghetto), whites predominant in the southeastern region (adjoining the Chicago lake shore) and mixed occupancy in more central areas.

A strong community organization, the South Shore Commission was formed in anticipation of racial change and eventually came to subscribe explicitly to the goal of "stable racial integration" for the area. By the close of the study period, the Commission was widely cited for its success —success at organizational growth (a $90,000 annual budget and a paid staff of six), and success in the near-achievement of "stable racial integration" in the area. The city government, school authorities, and private welfare groups were all enthusiastic Commission supporters; both local and national media touted it for its "grass roots success" at "preserving" racial integration in the community.[4]

Ordered Segmentation in South Shore

It needs to be noted that the inhibitions to integration in an area such as South Shore can not be properly understood by reliance upon such concepts as "prejudiced attitudes," "bigotry," or white "status anxiety," as these terms are ordinarily employed to "explain" interracial avoidance behavior. It is reasonable to anticipate that what Suttles (1968) refers to as "ordered segmentation" is natural to any community; thus, the fact that South Shore blacks differed from South Shore whites in terms of religion (few black Catholics, no Jews), ethnicity, economic status (blacks lower),[5] stage of life cycle (blacks younger with more children), and length of residency in the area would all act to deter many sorts of biracial contact. That is, racial distinctions coincided with other commonly utilized bases for social differentiation.

Urban settings have as their critical social characteristic the fact that intimate relationships between all parties are precluded by the sheer vastness of the numbers involved (cf. Wirth, 1938). Selection is thus necessary. In South Shore, as everywhere else in American society, people are "up tight" in the presence of persons who are unknown, unproven, and thus, to them, undependable. The genuine psychic (and occasionally, physical) risks, which accompany encounters with strangers, lead local residents to develop certain techniques for "gaining associates, avoiding enemies and establishing each other's intentions" (Suttles, 1968:234). These techniques evolve in the search for cues which bespeak similarity, or existence of some other form of personal tie (e.g., mutual friendship, blood relationship) which would imply dependability and trustworthiness. Where such cues are not forthcoming, mutual avoidance behavior (or outright hostility) results.

In the case at hand not only authentic social and demographic differences exist between the black and white populations, taken as a whole, but there are also differences of a more subtle sort in virtually all black-white confrontations. A few examples may be cited. Whites and blacks in South Shore *sound* different; among whites, speech varies with length of residence in Chicago, family status background, and ethnicity. Blacks have an analogous internal pattern of speech differentiation—in addition to a common touch of Southern Negro dialect, not quite absent even among the most "middle-class" of Chicago born blacks. Young blacks *walk* differently from young whites; many of the boys, especially, utilize a swagger which sets them apart from their white school mates (cf. Suttles, 1968; Finestone, 1957). Without carrying out a complete inventory of black and white habits and folkways, we know these differences exist, and that, whether they speak of them or not, both blacks and whites in South Shore were sensitive to them.

Public Places and Private Behavior

All of these distinctions, some obvious and some subtle, are more or less problematic for the persons involved, depending upon the public place in which whites and blacks happen to come together. "Public" places are defined, for the present discussion, as settings in which no *explicit* criteria exist for the exclusion of any person or group. Yet public places vary in the degree to which they tend to actually exclude certain types of persons or social groups. Given the inhibitions to random intimacy which exist in urban settings, public places can be viewed as exclusive in the degree to which they serve as arenas for the kinds of informal, intimate, and uninhibited sorts of behaviors ordinarily associated with informal peer group activity. In contrast, public places are inclusive in so far as they act as settings in which formalized roles are routinely attended to carefully by participants—places in which participants expect that they, as well as others, will guardedly attend to the performance of prescribed activity and behavior. Thus, public places may be differentiated according to the degree to which they serve as arenas for public as opposed to more "private" behavior.

Retail Stores

An example of a relatively *public* place for *public* behavior is the local retail store. Such settings in South Shore are rather formal in that patrons arrive to purchase merchandise and then exit. Although various forms of informal activity occur, including chats between owners and customers, the usual undirected patter and diffuse banter evident in lower-class business settings (cf. Suttles, 1968) tend to be absent.

Yet despite the relatively formal nature of shopping in South Shore (relative both to shopping in other kinds of areas and to other South Shore public settings), it is indeed a social activity as well as a utilitarian one. Shopping is the social activity which most frequently takes adult residents out of their homes and into the community. An examination of racial compositions of shopping settings may, in addition to providing benchmark data on the status of "demographic" integration in this important social setting, also indicate something of the extent to which a significant "opportunity context" exists for the promotion of other kinds of integration.

South Shore has two major internal shopping strips (71st and 79th Streets) both of which run east-west traversing black, mixed, and white residential areas. These streets are depicted in Figure 15–1 along with a

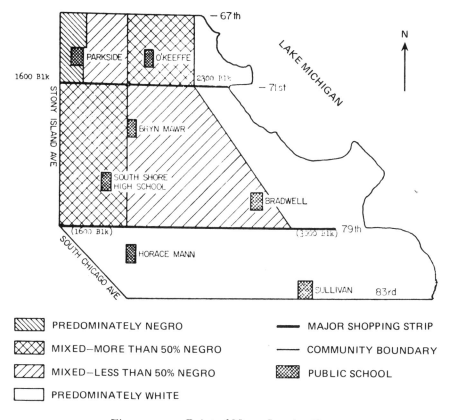

Figure 15–1   Point of Negro In-migration

portrayal of the approximate racial composition of the surrounding neighborhoods. Each of the shopping strips was visited during business hours of shopping days, and racial headcounts were made for all street-level retail establishments (including restaurants and taverns) on both streets.[6]

Racial retail shopping patterns were found to generally coincide with racial residential patterns. That is, individual stores and business blocks surrounded by predominately black residents were patronized almost exclusively by blacks; those in white areas by whites, those in mixed areas by members of both races. Table 15–1 presents the results of headcounts taken of shopping blocks; Table 15–2 presents results of the same operation in terms of composition of individual stores.

If a setting is arbitrarily considered to be demographically integrated if at least 10% of its population consists of members of each race, then it can be said that the 71st Street area is integrated for its entire length and that 70% of its shops are integrated. However, 79th Street is generally segregated in its entire length with only 22% of its shops integrated. The congruence of this pattern with the nature of the surrounding residential areas would indicate that the factor of distance outweighs other possible considerations (e.g., the desire for psychically "safe" shopping territory) in determining shopping patterns.

Certain interesting exceptions to this pattern are provided by those

TABLE 15-1

Racial Composition of South Shore Shopping Areas[a]

STREET AND HUNDRED BLOCK[b]	NUMBER OF BLACK PATRONS IN SHOPS	NUMBER OF WHITE PATRONS IN SHOPS	TOTAL BOTH RACES	PERCENT OF ALL PATRONS WHITE
71st Street				
1600, 1700	35	6	41	15
1800, 1900	67	36	103	35
2000, 2100	74	142	216	66
2200, 2300	19	148	167	89
69th Street				
1600, 1700	49	3	52	6
1800, 1900	33	40	73	55
2000, 2100	2	29	31	94
2200, 2300	5	36	41	88
2400, 2500	0	41	41	100
2600, 2700	8	211	219	96
2800, 2900	5	92	97	95
3000	1	93	94	99

[a] Based on a single visit, daytime weekday count, April, 1967.
[b] Each row represents two sides of two shopping blocks.

TABLE 15-2

Racial Composition of Individual Stores on Two Shopping Strips, Daytime South Shore[a]

Shopping Street	Number of "White" Stores[b]	Number of Persons in "White" Stores	Number of "Black" Stores[b]	Number of Persons in "Black" Stores	Number of Integrated Stores[b]	Number of Persons in Integrated Stores	Percent of All Stores Integrated	Percent of All Persons Integrated
71st Street	4	85	2	16	14	235	70	70
79th Street	12	212	2	21	4	67	22	22

[a] Consideration was given only to shops serving 8 or more persons.
[b] Stores classified as "White" or "Black" were those in which at least 90% of persons on the premises were of the same race. "Integrated" stores were those in which fewer than 90% of persons on the premises were of the same race.

establishments which by their nature or traditional neighborhood usage render personal services and/or which serve as settings for informal, more intimate interaction. All barber and beauty shops, regardless of location, were segregated. Establishments catering to recreational and social needs were often segregated; three of seven restaurants on otherwise integrated 71st Street were serving only whites, whereas all six super markets on the same street were integrated. Perhaps consistent not only with its attraction for customers of a particular ethnicity, but also with its function as a social setting, the kosher butcher shop was the only food store which was not serving a biracial clientele.

Saturday Night Racial Patterns

This tendency toward greater segregation of social and recreational settings is confirmed by analogous data collected on a Saturday night during the same time period. Not only is it the case that Americans typically reserve Saturday night as a social, festive occasion, but that almost all activities which occur during those hours partake of a heightened air of sociability.[7] With many of the retail stores closed, but with bars and restaurants open and catering to large numbers of persons, both 71st and 79th Streets were more segregated at night than during the day.[8] Table 15–3 presents the results of a "head-count" made of business establishments open on a Saturday night.

The integrated types of settings on Saturday night included motion picture theaters (a leisure setting, ordinarily with minimal interaction), several restaurants, and those grocery stores and supermarkets keeping late

211

TABLE 15-3

Racial Composition of South Shore Shopping Areas, Saturday Night[a]

Shopping Street	Number of "White" Stores[b]	Number of Persons in "White" Stores	Number of "Black" Stores[b]	Number of Persons in "Black" Stores	Number of Integrated Stores[b]	Number of Persons in Integrated Stores	Percent of All Stores Integrated	Percent of All Persons Integrated
71st Street	4	120	10	300	10	141	42	34
79th Street	14	359	7	272	2	19	9	3

[a] Consideration was given only to establishments observed to be serving 8 or more persons.

[b] Stores classified as "White" or "Black" were those in which at least 90% of persons on the premises were of the same race. "Integrated" stores were those in which fewer than 90% of persons on the premises were of the same race.

hours. Yet even in the case of restaurants and groceries, there was a tendency toward increased segregation on Saturday night, compared to weekdays. South Shore's two bowling alleys, integrated by day, become all-black at night.

This tendency toward Saturday night segregation (including a significant increase in the numbers of blacks relative to whites on the streets) may be explained in various ways. It may be due to a white fear of being in a black setting at night when "crime in the streets" is a more salient concern. Or, whites may be simply experiencing different forms of recreation than blacks—forms which are only available outside of South Shore (e.g., in the Loop area). The increased segregation of non-recreation settings may simply reflect that these are the hours in which black housewives, more likely to be working during the day, are shopping for household goods. Such factors notwithstanding, the fact that South Shore's business district, integrated by day but segregated (and heavily black) at night, is consistent with the observation that intimate contexts tend to inhibit integration. It is reasonable to find that during the hours reserved for intimacy, segregation increases.

Special scrutiny of one sort of segregated leisure setting, the neighborhood tavern, can provide some insight into explaining the metamorphosis of places from white to black status. There was almost total racial segregation in taverns with, in certain places, *alternating* black and white establishments along a given block.[9] Tavern owners can themselves influence racial patterns by, in the words of one bartender-owner, "give them (blacks) the big hello." But the several tavern owners who were interviewed felt that although the owner can influence the racial process, he cannot determine it. A bar "just becomes colored" as blacks patronize it with increasing frequency. For white tavern patrons, it is simply a matter of "the colored took the place over" or "the colored forced everybody out." Such were the phrases used to explain again and again "what happened" to a particular establishment which once was frequented by whites but eventually became a black setting.

To make sense of this "explanation" of tavern change, it must be noted that of all public settings in South Shore, probably none was more private than the neighborhood tavern. That is, although the tavern is officially open to the public, it is in fact (at least in South Shore) an intimate setting frequented by a small and stable group of "regulars" who use the establishment as the very focal point of their social lives.[10] For the few middleclass taverns in South Shore (which also were segregated) this characterization is likely less accurate than for working class establishments. But even here, the tavern is a place where people "let their hair down," where back-stage and on-stage behavioral routines (cf. Goffman, 1959) tend to merge and thus where increased social vulnerability makes for anxiety in the presence of persons who fail to emit satisfactory signals of trustworthiness and forgiving acceptance of what may be transgressions of various normative codes. Thus blacks, who share mannerisms, clothing tastes, musical preferences and other tavern-specific behavior habits at variance with white cultural counterparts are "outsiders" in the white environment. Their very presence can thus serve to inhibit the very kind of interactions for which the tavern is sought out by neighborhood whites; they can thus "take over" an establishment by simply being in it.[11]

Outdoor Recreation

Parks are a day-time setting in which informal social activity is routine.[12] A headcount was made at South Shore's largest park ("Rainbow Beach"), which provides facilities (e.g., tennis, beach bathing, formal gardens, field houses) available nowhere else in South Shore. On a sunny Sunday in May 1967, only two of the several thousand persons at the park were black, and these were small children in the company of white adults. It should be noted that Rainbow Beach Park in 1962 was the scene of a nonviolent civil rights "wade-in," protesting the racial segregation of some of the city's beaches (including Rainbow). Ironically, this much publicized event and the accompanying acrimonious remarks by whites, may have served to dramatize Rainbow Beach's *de facto* status as a white public place, thus deterring blacks from risking the cost of a subsequent spontaneous visit. That Rainbow Beach was also a place where individuals routinely appear in abbreviated costume (bathing suits, tennis clothes, etc.), and thus routinely expose body areas ordinarily considered private, would act to increase anxieties stemming from interpersonal vulnerability.

Yet the special circumstances of Rainbow Beach was actually not significant since almost all of South Shore's parks were racially segregated—including those completely internal to the community and without any known history of "incidents." Seven smaller parks and playlots were inspected on the same warm Sunday; almost all were catering exclusively to small children with a few parents supervising. The only park catering to adult "passive recreation" (located on South Shore Drive at 68th Street) was occupied by 13 white adults and three white children, all of whom sat on benches, and one black child who sat with his dog on the grass at an opposite end of the small greensward.

South Shore's six remaining parks were all scenes of active recreation. In those parks located in segregated areas (either all black or all white), participation was limited to persons of the same race as the surrounding area. Thus at a soccer field at Phillips and 82nd, all game participants and spectators (approximately 200) were white; only black children were present at two playlots (one at Parkside School, 69th at East End, and one at O'Keeffe School, 69th at Merrill) located in predominately (although not exclusively) black areas.

One park located in a racially mixed residential area (69th at Oglesby) served only black children. The playlot at Bryn Mawr School (74th at Chappel), also located in a biracial residential area, was being utilized by approximately 50 black children and 40 white children. One ball game was in progress; all players were white. Of the various playgroups, only one—a dyad—was racially mixed, although the two playlots were serving equal numbers of white and black children.

Rosenblum Park, at 76th Street and Bennett, stands contiguous to both black and white residential areas. Seven ball games were in simultaneous progress at the time observations were made, all consisting of adolescent boys. Four games were all-black; two were all white; one was racially mixed. The two tot lots in the park are situated in diagonally opposite corners of the recreation area, with clear visibility from one to the other. The tot lot in the northwest corner was being utilized by approximately 35 black children, one white child, and seven supervising black adult women. The tot lot in the southwest corner of the park showed an opposite racial pattern; it was being utilized by 20 white children, one black child and four white supervisors. It is noteworthy that two such playlots in the same park situated at a distance of no more than 200 feet from one another should be almost completely racially segregated.

The lack of evidence of demographic integration leads to the suspicion that South Shore residents, when taking outdoor recreation as well as public indoor recreation, do not lead integrated social lives. Members of different races do not accompany one another to parks and do not mingle once they arrive in parks. For children, some limited cross-racial contact seems to occur; for adults, there seems to be none whatsoever.

Schools

Schools in a community are a crucial determinant of the social lives of children; they provide settings for intimate interaction and their attendance boundaries tend to circumscribe a child's opportunities for friendship formation (Roper, 1934). For some parents, schools are also a social setting (e.g., PTA, volunteer work), but because of parents' more numerous alternative sources of social interaction, and because of the relatively small proportion of their time spent in school contexts, the school is of much less social significance.

The racial composition of South Shore's public schools for 1963 through 1966 are presented in Table 15-4. As is common in transition areas in

TABLE 15-4

Racial Composition of South Shore Public Schools
1963, 1964, 1965, 1966

SCHOOL	PROPORTION OF STUDENT BODY BLACK			
	1963	1964	1965	1966
Parkside	90.3	96.6	97.8	99.1
O'Keeffe	39.8	67.3	85.4	93.9
Bryn Mawr	16.3	37.2	55.2	66.1
Mann	7.0	26.6	43.0	55.1
Bradwell	0.1	0.2	0.7	3.7
Sullivan	0.0	0.0	0.0	2.3
South Shore High[a]	1.5	7.0	24.8	41.8

Sources: 1963 data: *Chicago Sun-Times*, October 24, 1963; 1964, 1965 data: *Southeast Economist* (Chicago) October 17, 1965; 1966 data: *Southeast Economist* (Chicago) October 23, 1966.

[a] High school boundary zone was modified between 1964 and 1965 with the inclusion of Parkside and O'Keeffe and the exclusion of a larger all-black elementary school as "feeder" schools in the fall, 1965. The net effect of this change on the high school's racial composition was negligible.

which attendance is based on the "neighborhood" principle, schools closest to the original point of Negro in-migration (the area's northwest corner) are most heavily black, with an increasing number of schools becoming predominately black over time. In 1966, two of the community's six elementary schools were demographically integrated (again, using the 10% convention). The South Shore High School and one of the three Catholic schools were also demographically integrated.[13]

PTA meetings held in 1966 at the three integrated public schools (Mann, Bryn Mawr, and the high school) were attended by members of both races—as were PTA meetings at the predominately black O'Keeffe school which drew an approximately equal number of whites and blacks to its meetings, although its student body was 74% black. In general, whites participated most in South Shore's school affairs, including its biracial schools. In all schools in which any appreciable number of white children were enrolled, whites dominated the adult organizations. Thus all newly elected officers of the high school PTA were white despite the fact that over 42% of the school's student body were black at the time of the 1967 PTA Spring elections. In other biracial schools, as in almost all of South Shore's biracial settings, blacks were always underrepresented in top leadership positions.

Religious Institutions

South Shore's religious organizations provide settings which are a mix of formality and informality. During worship services individuals find themselves in a situation whereby virtually every move of every participant, including gestures and signs of affect, is determined either by explicit ritual, tradition or local habit. In other types of church activity, such as funerals, weddings, bowling games, club meetings, etc., social interaction is more spontaneous, intense, and intimate.

It is thus not surprising to find that whatever integration existed in church organizations, existed primarily in terms of worship activity and not in terms of church parareligious social life. Four of South Shore's 16 Protestant churches hold integrated (again, by the 10% criterion) church services; one had an integrated *membership* list. Table 15–5 presents a detailed summary of the racial composition of South Shore's churches and church-related schools.[14]

Church life, outside of worship services, was virtually completely segregated and completely white. Two church membership screening commit-

TABLE 15-5

Racial Composition of South Shore's Christian Churches and Church-Related Schools

Denomination of Church	Number of Church Members (Parishoners)	Number of Blacks in Membership	Percent of Membership Black	Number Sunday Attenders	Number Black Sunday Attenders	Percent Sunday Attenders Black	Number Enrolled in Sunday School	Number of Blacks in Sunday School	Percent of Sunday School Black
Protestant:									
Community	1,775	14	0.8%	625	27	4.3%	350	160	45.0%
Episcopal	450	30	6.6%	250	25	10.0%	87	20	23.0%
Lutheran	305	25	8.0%	113	10	8.8%	45	25	55.0%
Methodist	650	25	3.8%	200	30	15.0%	390	250	64.0%
Methodist	210	21	10.0%	90	9	10.0%	159	157	99.0%
Christian Science	250	1	0.4%	250	7	2.8%	160	12	7.5%
Bible Church	75	5	6.6%	65	35	53.0%	150	100	66.0%
Sub-Totals	3,715	121	3.3%	1,593	143	8.9%	1,360	724	53.0%
Nine Other Prot. Churches	2,285	0	–	994	0	–	140	0	–
Prot. Totals	6,000	121	2.0%	2,587	143	5.5%	1,500	724	48.0%
Catholic:[a]									
1) Catholic	1,200[b]	70[b]	5.0%	4,000	100	2.5%	485	110	23.0%
2) Catholic	1,900[b]	1[b]	0.5%	3,000	0	–	200	10	5.0%
3) Catholic	2,700[b]	325[b]	12.0%	9,000	477	53.0%	732	40	5.5%
Catholic Totals	5,800[b]	396[b]	6.8%	16,000	577	3.6%	1,417	160	11.0%

[a] Catholic school data refer to day school enrollments, not Sunday school. Except for Church No. 3, attendance data based on actual head counts on a Sunday, Spring, 1966.

[b] Refers to number of families, rather than individuals.

Other sources: Reports of clergymen to the writer and to E. Maynard Moore, III. (cf. Moore, 1966).

tees had a black member (to help find the "good element," according to the white chairman); several churches had black Sunday school teachers and one church had two black women helping to establish a youth program. Of these "active" blacks (as was true of most black church members in South Shore), all were women.

In part, the near-total absence of blacks from church social life was a result of deliberate white exclusion. In one case, revealed with dismay by the pastor of the church involved (and subsequently confirmed by an interview with the "victim"), a black woman, upon invitation of the pastor's wife, joined a church bowling team which previously had only white members. The other bowlers' resultant demand that the woman be excluded were resisted by the clergyman. In consequence, the bowling team severed formal ties with the church. Rather than force such issues, thereby risking damage to church programs, most South Shore clergymen seemed to handle the inevitable role strain by insisting upon "welcoming" blacks to church services (thus fulfilling official denominational dictates as well as their own stated positions of "conscience") while permitting social activities to continue in a segregated fashion. This "compromise" can be said to have "worked," given the formality and constrained behavior characteristic of the church service, in contrast to the very different nature of other church-related activity.

Another important variation in church racial patterns, one strikingly revealed in Table 15–5, was the difference in the degree to which black children, compared to black adults, were being served by South Shore churches. Eight church Sunday schools were at least 10% black; in one case a church with only 10% black membership had a Sunday school which was 98% black. Fully 48% of Protestant Sunday school attenders were black; 11% of those enrolled in Catholic day schools were black.

This contrast between adult and child integration in church settings is again suggestive of the significance of interpersonal vulnerability as a determinant of racial patterns. Parents (of both races) were willing to place their children in racially mixed settings because such settings provided no psychic difficulties for *them* (the parents). Children, perhaps having different criteria for mutual identification and for establishing boundaries of community (e.g., sex, age, territory, athletic standing), were possibly less likely to find such settings painful, although the segregation patterns at play, as well as evidence presented by Suttles (1968, Chapters 9, 10), would suggest otherwise. In any event, children are not as free as their parents to pick and choose their social settings, regardless of the inconvenience or personal discomfort they might experience.

An Exception: The Baptist Church. A fundamentalist Baptist church, located in a predominately Negro area, stood apart from all other religious institutions in South Shore in that equal numbers of whites and blacks attended services; it was, in other respects as well, the most completely integrated of all South Shore religious institutions.[15] It was also distinct in that worship services were a more basic part of the life of the church than in other denominations. Worship was a time of spontaneity and much animated social interaction. Church members were working class and lower-middle class; it was the poorest church in South Shore—poor in terms of the income of its worshippers, and almost the poorest in terms of annual church budget. Among South Shore clergy, its minister had the least familiarity with the "liberal" conventional wisdom concerning the role of the urban ministry, the "crisis in the city," etc.—utterances which permeated interview responses from most other area clergy. This fundamentalist minister was the only South Shore clergyman to ever indicate a past history of "prejudice" toward blacks.

That such conditions gave rise to the only case of trans-racial solidarity in a church context is perhaps surprising; for this reason the Baptist church and several other such "deviant" cases will be discussed at length in a later discussion. For the present, however, it should be noted that the conditions of spontaneity and intimacy characteristic of fundamentalist religion could lead *only* to one of two states: either complete racial exclusion *or* complete racial integration with concomitant total acceptance. If blacks were to be present at all, their presence would have to be unreservedly accepted; otherwise, the resultant inhibitions would have destroyed the nature of the religious experience and thus the very reason for the coming together.

Voluntary Associations

Many national charity and service organizations (e.g. Lions, American Legion, Veterans of Foreign Wars, B'nai B'rith) had chapters serving the South Shore area and all were exclusively white.[16] Of over 50 organizational group photographs published in the *Southeast Economist*[17] (the community newspaper serving the area), none which involved South Shore residents included blacks. The South Shore Country Club, the boards and officer corps of two local hospitals and of the Chamber of Commerce were also without black participants.

That charity and service groups, organizations which are generally based in friendship cliques, were not integrated is not surprising. That the governing bodies of major local institutions were also exclusively white can be taken to simply reflect a combination of similar social patterning of organizational participation linked with the positions of the two races in the American stratification system.

The South Shore Commission

The most prominent exception to the general pattern of black exclusion (or omission) from the ranks of important community groups was the South Shore Commission which, at least after 1964, was biracial in its leadership as well as in membership. Although blacks remained greatly underrepresented in Commission leadership positions during the study period, several on the Board of Directors and one of six officers were black. Many of the Commission's subgroups were also biracial, including several committees and various block club organizations. But it is quite safe to say that since only a small proportion of South Shore's residents involved themselves in any block club or other Commission activity,[18] its effectiveness in creating biracial contacts was probably limited to a small leadership group in the community.

From its very inception, the Commission was not an informal social organization; as an association of Protestants, Catholics and Jews, it had from the beginning brought together persons who were less than at complete ease in each other's presence. It continued to function primarily as an instrumental organization, and not as a setting for intimate socializing as blacks were brought into membership. Thus, the Commission provided a series of public meetings, outings, and fund-raising entertainments wherein public behavior was the accepted norm.

In the context of Commission activity, as in the case of other biracial voluntary organizations in South Shore, cross-racial interaction was more formal and guarded than were interactions (also quite formal) between members of the same race. Because of the uniqueness of biracial interaction in American society, blacks and whites were in the difficult situation of having to create *de novo* a formal mode for social interaction, given the obvious and subtle differences between blacks and whites and the lack of mutual knowledge of what the other party might consider "appropriate" talking behavior. Thus there was a need to avoid the unknown transgressions which might occur if spontaneous behavior were to run its course. This was accomplished by both blacks and whites by resort to a zealous interpersonal courtesy (to ward off any conceivable slight or "misunderstanding"), unrelenting pleasantness, and a well-understood, tacit, mutual agreement to limit the subject of all conversation to small talk. Behavior was carefully guarded; words and expressions were selected with extraordinary care.

For blacks, this heightened self-consciousness generally resulted in deferential postures toward their white colleagues, and an ongoing monitoring of behavior to avoid any possible controversy which might set them in opposition to policies favored by any significant number of whites. Several substantive examples may be cited. The Commission was known by black members to be cooperating through its tenant referral service with landlords who refused to rent housing to non-whites. The actions entailed in such cooperation were probably illegal under the Chicago Fair Housing Ordinance and were a source of distress to black Commission members. Yet they preferred, in the words of one, not to "make a fuss" against a policy which they indicated (to the writer) they found obnoxious. Similarly, black Commission members assented to quota systems for maintaining whites in buildings and blocks which otherwise would have become predominately black. Again, there was public acquiescence in spite of privately held feelings that such policies were improper and also in violation of the Housing Ordinance.

That this effect of biracial interaction was most pronounced in the case of blacks, and not whites, is perhaps explicable in terms of another important feature or biracial interaction in South Shore: blacks and whites seldom come together as equals. This fact thus adds an additional dimension to the vulnerability of the "alien" persons who were not only in a numerical minority but, because of such status differences, were especially vulnerable to the sanctions of those who possessed so disproportionate an amount of wealth, power and expertise.

These status differences were pervasive. In general, blacks moving into South Shore were of lower socioeconomic status than the whites they replaced.[19] The same status differentiation was reflected within organizational contexts such as the Commission. Thus, white males of the Commission's governing board were almost all proprietors, lawyers, physicians, and stock brokers, and black members were salesmen, school teachers, and low-level supervisors.

Furthermore, unlike white leaders, blacks did not find their way to the Board because of their state of personal wealth, power, or expertise, but instead because of their race and an acceptance of Commission goals. The Commission originally "took in" blacks in order to be more "representative" and to avoid being labeled "racist" or "bigoted," and blacks were thus largely interchangeable with any number of other blacks, with the consequence that their status vis-à-vis their white "colleagues" could only suffer. Several black members were viewed approvingly by whites as "real work horses" who make a "fine contribution," but none had the contacts with the political, religious, and business leaders of Chicago which were seen to be the really important determinants of South Shore's future. A good "work horse" may be hard to find, but a member of the Chicago School Board or the editor of a Chicago daily newspaper is impossible to replace. Such differences in the degree to which people are important to an organization's goals do not bode well for parity in interpersonal relationships.

The case of biracial interaction in the Commission would seem to provide an explanation for the findings generated by tests of the "contact hypothesis." A large body of literature suggests that more "favorable" white attitudes toward blacks results from biracial interaction in which whites and blacks share the same status, are in mutually dependent roles, and where contact is "intimate" rather than superficial.[20] These are precisely the conditions in which social vulnerability to alien and unknown individuals is minimized for members of both races. Where such conditions are not present, the contact hypothesis suggests that biracial interaction is expected to yield either no effects or an increased amount of "negative" white evaluation of blacks.

Indeed, these latter results were the consequences in such groups as the Commission. For whites, participation with blacks led to the observation that they (blacks) "aren't real leaders," or, in the words of one of the area's most liberal clergymen, they aren't "take charge people." The middle-class analogue of the "lazy colored boy" remained the dominant white stereotype. For blacks, interaction in such settings would seem to debilitate energies as whites come to be seen as the real makers of decisions and holders of power (cf. Piven and Cloward, 1967). The really crucial organizational skills which blacks observed were those involving the utilization of contacts (e.g. friends in high places) and resources (e.g. personal fortunes) which they neither possessed nor stood a very good chance of ever possessing.

"Marginal Groups": Instances of Transracial Solidarity

In addition to the case of the Baptist church, of which mention has been previously made, there were three other contexts in South Shore which seemed to have provided settings in which transracial solidarity could be said to have been extant. These were "marginal" organizations—marginal in that meetings were held only on an irregular basis and in that they were organizations founded on premises of dissent and protest which limited their appeal to only a small number of participants. One such group was a local branch of Veterans for Peace in Vietnam, an organization with leftist political orientations (including several persons of militant Marxist ideology) which held occasional meetings above a South Shore store during the study period. Another group was the O'Keeffe Area Council—technically a part of the South Shore Commission but with an active leadership which, because of its rather "pro-Negro," anti-"establishment" orientation, was often independent of the Commission in spirit and in action.

Finally, there was the South Shore Organization for Human Rights, a group active in fostering open occupancy and other civil rights goals in South Shore and metropolitan Chicago. This group was indigenous to South Shore, having been stimulated by a young clergyman during his rather brief association with a South Shore Protestant church. Like Veterans for Peace and the O'Keeffe Area Council, its active membership consisted of only a handful of persons, but, unlike the other groups, it carried out independent programs such as "testing" the racial practices of local real estate firms, as well as the racial politices of a tenant referral service managed by the South Shore Commission.

These three organizations differed from other South Shore institutions not only in terms of their militancy and marginality, but also in terms of the "tone" of biracial interactions shared by members. In all of these contexts, as in the case of the Baptist church, interaction across racial lines seemed to come easily; interaction was unstilted, informal and direct. Except possibly for the Veterans for Peace, these were all informal social organizations, with blacks and whites living out shared social as well as shared institutional lives. Race ceased to operate as a source of cleavage or determinant of institutional roles.

In other respects, these groups were quite diverse. The Baptist church was largely working-class with many recent migrants from the South and Appalachia. The O'Keeffe Council consisted of young well-educated professionals; to a lesser extent, the same was true of the Organization for Human Rights. Veterans for Peace was an extremely diverse group of blue collar workers, small businessmen, and a few professionals. Congregators of the Bible Church were apolitical, religious fundamentalists; members of the other groups were identified with secular, left-leaning ideologies.[21]

Yet there were certain important similarities. Within each of these groups, race and status differences were not correlated; businessmen or professionals within each were as likely to be black as white.[22] In addition, these groups were alike in that members were in an alien environment. The church was surrounded by more stolid, richer congregations; Veterans for Peace, the Organization for Human Rights, and the O'Keeffe Council existed in the shadow of the powerful South Shore Commission and other "moderate" or conservative institutions which supported Chicago's and the nation's on-going political arrangements. The various deviant traits of these groups' members thus created a situation in which organizational alternatives within the South Shore area were lacking. The result may have been an organizational commitment of sufficient strength to overcome any inhibitions which racial differences might have created. Finally, members of these groups were similar in that most were either new to the South Shore area, or, because of their youth, new to South Shore organizational life. A lack of previous ties to existing structures may thus similarly facilitate commitments to organizations which, in that they are biracial, operate with new kinds of *modus vivendi*.

Summary

Although South Shore's total racial composition provided initial evidence of some forms of racial integration in the area, social life is essentially segregated. The nature of the contexts in which varying forms of integration are found suggests that fear of exposure and mutual suspiciousness between members of the two races inhibit biracial sharing of public places which serve as loci of private behavior. Thus some degree of demographic integration and a slight amount of biracial interaction can occur in public places in which public behavior traditionally ensues. That is, extensive integration (primarily by demographic indices) occurs in places such as retail shops, church chapels and formal organizations oriented toward the accomplishment of instrumental goals. In such settings, social interaction across racial lines is not reflective of transracial solidarity. Nor can the results of such interaction be assumed to promote eventual solidarity, given the problematic power disparities which are general concomitants of such black-white interaction. Presumably because of the greater psychic and practical dilemmas it would create, integration of any sort is absent from informal settings such as church socials, service clubs, taverns, Saturday night bowling and parks.

Women, because they are more local in their activity and interests, are more likely than men to find themselves in biracial circumstances. Protestants are more likely than are Catholics or Jews, and children—perhaps because they are less free to vary their milieu according to preference—to have the most experience of biracial contact.

Although there are some communalities in the problems which both blacks and whites face under conditions of biracial propinquity and contact, the consequences on the two groups are not identical. In South Shore, as in the rest of the society, the integration "experiment" opens with the most important and useful institutions, organizations and settings as white, and the "challengers" or "invaders" as black. *The circumstances are thus not parallel.* The widely shared community conceptions so generated of "intruders" versus "preservers," applied to blacks and whites respectively, provide still another distinction consistent with the status and power disparities widely observed to exist between blacks and whites. Not only is the development of transracial solidarity made more difficult as a result, but, in addition, the psychic difficulties which blacks must face when entering the alien white context is further intensified.[23] That is, biracial interaction challenges members of both races to overcome certain fears of the dissimilar, the unproven, and the threatening. But for blacks, there is the added problem of knowing that in presenting oneself in a biracial setting, one is challenging and "pushing" to gain something otherwise unavailable. The modal black response would seem to be either a show of hostility (as in some manifestations of the current phase of the civil rights movement) or, as was common in South Shore, a show of deference and total capitulation to white preferences.

Integration of a thoroughgoing type, what has been termed "transracial solidarity," occurred in South Shore in only a few settings. These were instances in which there were cross-racial communalities of a shared and deviant ideology (mutual recognition of which provided bases for the development of needed social alternatives); an equality in occupational status and organizational usefulness (thus providing cross-racial parity in interpersonal vulnerability); and, among both blacks and whites, a lack of previously constituted local organizational ties (thus precluding habit and/or social pressures from inhibiting affiliation with groups which have integration as one of their innovative features).

All settings observed in South Shore (an attempt was made to be exhaustive) which shared these characteristics were found to approximate the circumstance of transracial solidarity; no other instances of this form of integration were found. If other possible contingencies to racial integration are to be uncovered, or if those observed in South Shore are to be confirmed as determinant (either singly, or in some "value-added" combination), additional case studies and eventual comparative analysis will be necessary. But for the present, it is well to note that the conditions cited as concomitants of transracial solidarity in South Shore are precisely those which are likely to provide the overarching cues of similarity, reliability, and trust which would seem requisite for the building and maintenance of racially integrated associations, institutions, and community.

NOTES

1. The author wishes to thank Tamotsu Shibutani and J. Michael Ross for helpful comments on an earlier draft of this manuscript and John Dyckman for his assistance in carrying out observations. Financial support was provided by a grant from the Bowman C. Lingle Foundation to the Center for Urban Studies, University of Chicago, and by a Faculty Research Fellowship, University of California, Santa Barbara.

2. Data are based on 1960 census reports as contained in Kitagawa and Taeuber (1963). (South Shore is taken to constitute census tracts 635 through 644 and the northerly portion [above 83rd Street] of tracts 662 through 665).

3. Impressionistic estimates based on reports of local clergymen.

4. See, for example: "Self-Help Pays Off in South Chicago," *Christian Science Monitor*, (Boston), July 21, 1967; "The South Shore Plan," *Chicago Sun Times*, April 14, 1967.

5. Changes in South Shore's welfare case loads, crimes rates, etc. provide some evidence documenting this point (see Molotch, 1968). Although differences in net income between black and white family units is generally small (or nonexistent) in changing areas, the fact that black-households are more likely to have multiple breadwinners and that black males are more likely to hold blue-collar jobs, are differences indicative of real status differences. (See Taeuber and Taeuber, 1965, Chaps. 7, 8).

6. For some types of establishments, such as beauty shops, there was no way to make a complete count unobtrusively; in such instances, only those patrons visible through plate glass windows were counted. Employees, detectable by uniforms, positions behind counters, or general demeanor, were excluded from the counts.

7. It is for this reason that for persons excluded from social activity on Saturday night, these hours are, as the lyrics of the popular song imply, "the loneliest night of the week."

8. For example, the 71st Street daytime count included only one segregated bar whereas the night count included six segregated bars. Given the fact that many retail shops are closed at night, the prevalence of open bars has the consequence of dramatically increasing the *proportion* of establishments which are segregated as well as the absolute number of segregated establishments.

9. Except for one bar which was observed as having one black patron and nine white patrons, all 21 South Shore taverns were completely segregated on Saturday night.

10. Gans (1962) has confirmed that this pattern is also the case for Italian-American working class males.

11. The same phenomenon can be observed in the case of houseguests' "taking over" a home by simply being in it for a period longer than that desired by the hosts. Guests, who often can not "understand" if confronted with such an accusation, can avoid the problem by either "becoming just like a member of the family" (i.e. host accepts guest as an intimate) or by devising schemes whereby extensive absences from the scene can be gracefully arranged.

12. The situation is not strictly comparable to taverns, however, in that the relative expansiveness of space may permit a greater degree of insularity to an intimate gathering.

13. Unfortunately, no intensive observations were made of student life within schools.

14. Interviews with local clergy were carried out during the Summer of 1965 and Spring of 1966. The author personally interviewed 12 clergymen; additional interview material was provided by E. Maynard Moore III, who based part of his interview schedule upon that of the author's, thus generating a total of 23 comparable cases. Respondents interviewed by both investigators generally gave identical responses to the two researchers. (Cf. Moore, 1966).

15. The divergence in this church between the number of Negro *attenders* and number of black *members* (as indicated by data in Table 15–5) was due to the fact that a "personal revelation" was a requisite for formal membership; many blacks were thus in the situation of having formal induction pending such a revelation.

16. The author has been advised that a tutoring center at the South Shore YMCA was being operated during the study period on a racially integrated basis. Pressures of time did not permit a first-hand investigation of this program.

17. *The Southeast Economist* serves South Shore as well as a much larger region of the South Side as a "community newspaper." An organization was considered to be located in South Shore if at least half of all addresses of those photographed were within the study area.

18. The Commission's "grass roots" were actually rather shallow. It is likely that there were no more than 12 block clubs operating during the study period, although statements printed about South Shore in national and local media implied there were many more. (Cf. Molotch, 1968: 71).

19. See note 5.

20. Various studies have yielded somewhat conflicting evidence on the validity of the "contact hypothesis." Three classic studies which indicate a positive relationship between "improvement" in white attitudes toward blacks with increasing contact are Deutsch and Collins (1951); Starr, *et al.* (1949); and Merton, *et al.* (1949). Three reports providing evidence for the opposite conclusion are Allport and Kramer (1946); Kramer (1950); and Winder (1952). A synthesis of these mixed findings, one which is consistent with the criteria for effective positive attitude change as specified in the above text, appears in Wilner, *et al.* (1955).

21. These findings are consistent with other studies which have uncovered the extremely diverse conditions under which racial integration occurs and the seeming irrelevance of "prejudice" or racial "attitude" in determining when and where integration exists. Grier and Grier (1960) found integrated housing developments to be heterogeneous in terms of the income, education, ethnicity, stage of life cycle, and geographical origin of residents. Supporting findings are also reported in Rapkin and Grigsby, 1960, and Mayer, 1960.

22. Membership status of the Baptist church was relatively homogenous. Veterans for Peace was led by a well-to-do black funeral director and several of his black business colleagues, whereas whites included in their ranks (along with a few professionals) a TV repairman and a sign painter. The O'Keeffe Council included in its top leadership cadre a black businessman and a black lawyer along with a white businessman and a white engineer. The Organization for Human Rights was dominated by a white clergyman and a group of black and white women who were either white collar workers or had lower middleclass husbands.

23. Levy (1968) provides a description of an instance (whites in the southern civil rights movement) in which the tables are turned, that is, where biracial interaction occurs in a black dominated context (with analogous intensification of difficulties for *whites*).

227

REFERENCES

Allport, Gordon and Bernard Kramer.
1946   "Some roots of prejudice." Journal of Psychology 21 (Fall): 9–39.
Biddle, William and Loureide Biddle.
1965   The Community Development Process: The Rediscovery of Local Initiative. New York: Holt, Rinehart and Winston.
Deutsch, Morton and Mary Collins.
1951   Interracial Housing: A Psychological Evaluation of a Social Experiment. Minneapolis: University of Minnesota Press.
Finestone, Harold.
1957   "Cats, kicks and color." Social Problems 5 (July): 3–13.
Fishbein, Annette.
1962   The Expansion of Negro Residential Areas in Chicago. Unpublished Master's dissertation, Department of Sociology, University of Chicago.
Gans, Herbert.
1962   The Urban Villagers. New York: The Free Press.
Goffman, Erving.
1959   The Presentation of Self in Everyday Life. New York: Doubleday.
Grier, George and Eunice Grier.
1960   Privately Developed Interracial Housing: An Analysis of Experience. Berkeley: University of California Press.
Johnson, Philip A.
1965   Call Me Neighbor, Call Me Friend. New York: Doubleday.
Kitagawa, Evelyn and Karl Taeuber. (eds.)
1963   Local Community Fact Book: Chicago Metropolitan Area, 1960. Chicago: Chicago Community Inventory, University of Chicago.
Kramer, Bernard M.
1950   Residential Contact as a Determinant of Attitudes Toward Negroes. Unpublished Ph.D. dissertation, Department of Social Relations, Harvard University.
Levy, Charles J.
1968   Voluntary Servitude: Whites in the Negro Movement. New York: Appleton-Century-Crofts.
McKenzie, Roderick O.
1923   The Neighborhood: A Study of Local Life in the City of Columbus, Ohio. Chicago: University of Chicago Press.
Mayer, Albert J.
1960   "Russel Woods: Change without conflict: A case study of neighborhood racial transition in Detroit." In Nathan Glazer and Davis McEntire (eds.), Studies in Housing and Minority Groups. Berkeley: University of California Press.
Merton, Robert, et al.
1949   "Social facts and social fictions: The dynamics of race relations in Milltown" New York: Columbia University Bureau of Applied Social Research.
Molotch, Harvey.
1966   "Urban community boundaries: A case study" Working Paper No. 60, Center for Social Organization Studies, University of Chicago, multilith.
1969   "Toward a more human human ecology: An urban research strategy" *Land Economics* 43:3 (August): 336–341.
1968   Community Action to Control Racial Change. Unpublished Ph.D. dissertation, Department of Sociology, University of Chicago.

1969 "Racial change in a stable community." American Journal of Sociology 75 (forthcoming).

Moore, E. Maynard, III.

1966 The Church and Racial Change in South Shore. Unpublished paper, The Divinity School, University of Chicago.

Piven, Francis Fox and Richard Cloward.

1967 "The case against racial integration." Social Work 12 (January): 12–21.

Rapkin, Chester and William Grigsby.

1960 The Demand for Housing in Racially Mixed Areas. Berkeley: University of California Press.

Roper, Marion.

1934 The City and the Primary Group. Unpublished Ph.D. dissertation, Department of Sociology, University of Chicago.

Star, Shirley, Robin M. Williams, Jr. and Samuel A. Stouffer.

1949 "Negro Soldiers" in Samuel Stouffer, et. al. The American Soldier: Adjustment During Army Life. Vol. I. Princeton: Princeton University Press.

Suttles, Gerald.

1968 The Social Order of the Slum. Chicago: University of Chicago Press.

Taeuber, Karl and Alma Taeuber.

1965 Negroes in Cities. Chicago: Aldine.

Wilner, Daniel, Rosabelle Walkley and Stuart Cook.

1955 Human Relations in Interracial Housing: A Study of the Contact Hypothesis. Minneapolis: University of Minnesota Press.

Winder, Alvin.

1952 White Attitudes Towards Negro-White Interaction in an Area of Changing Racial Composition. Unpublished Ph.D. dissertation, Committee on Human Development, University of Chicago.

Wirth, Louis.

1938 "Urbanism as a way of life" American Journal of Sociology 44 (July).

16
HARRY V. BALL AND DOUGLAS S. YAMAMURA

ETHNIC DISCRIMINATION AND THE MARKETPLACE: A STUDY OF LANDLORDS' PREFERENCES IN A POLYETHNIC COMMUNITY

During the past decade, empirical studies dealing with "intergroup behavior occurring as part of various economic activities" have found it "difficult to demonstrate any relationship whatsoever between ethnic attitudes and intergroup behavior."[1] As a result, investigations of intergroup relations in economic settings have given increased attention to the characteristics of cultural and social structures.[2]

This paper reports a study of the tenant-ethnicity preferences of the landlords of private rental housing in Honolulu in 1952. The goal of the study was to ascertain, on the one hand, the extent to which these preferences were manifestations of non-economic ideologies of intergroup relations, and, on the other, the degree to which they were shaped by the opportunities or limitations of the market situation.

Under the so-called "normal law of landlord and tenant," the selection of tenants takes place within the institution of the market. The landlord seeks a tenant who can pay the rental he desires; he may accept or reject any potential tenant for any or no reason.[3] Although there are usually no specific situational norms to this effect, it is frequently presumed that landlords tend toward affective detachment or neutrality in their selections due to the primacy of the profit motive.

With respect to non-economic factors, considerable evidence[4] indicates that the cultural structure of Honolulu contains at least two major competing ideologies of intergroup relations: assimilationism and separatism.

Reprinted with permission from *American Sociological Review* 25 (1960): 687–694.

Assimilationism centers upon the belief that discrimination on the basis of race or nationality is "wrong." For many years this ideology has been referred to as Hawaii's "unorthodox race doctrine."[5] It is unorthodox, however, mainly in that it is publicly proclaimed and not because of the absence of an alternative ideology, especially in the more private spheres of interaction. The core of *separatism* includes the ideas that ethnicity is a legitimate basis for the classification of individuals, that "groups get along best if they remain separated," and that people have a "natural" preference for their "own group." These beliefs led to the first general hypothesis, namely, that two major competing policies of tenant-ethnicity preference would be manifested by the landlords: first, a denial of any preference or restrictive policy on the basis of ethnicity; and second, a stated preference for the landlord's "own group" and a non-preferential or restrictive policy toward all others.

However, it was assumed that these alternatives in the cultural structure should be viewed in the light of the opportunities or limitations presented by the market situation. The most obvious consideration here was the fact that landlords who practiced exclusive-own group preference would find that its implementation depends upon an adequate supply of tenants of their own ethnicity. On the other hand, it could be presumed that landlords who favored assimilationism would be *subject* to social pressures to give exclusive preference to their own group to the extent that they could do so without facing a tenant shortage. This reasoning supports the second general hypothesis: that the frequencies of exclusive-own group preferences would be directly related to the availability of potential "own group" tenants.

Also to be considered were the possible cases of landlords who favor assimilationism generally, but who either fear trouble with existing tenants if *certain* ethnics are admitted or are themselves intensely hostile to *certain* ethnicities. It was expected that in both instances the policies of preference would deviate from complete non-discrimination by a process of *progressive exclusion*. This is to say that decisions would be made with the intention to eliminate the most "objectionable" ethnics without at the same time destroying the potential market or completely negating non-discrimination as the "ideal."

There remained the cases of landlords with separatist-own group orientations who are frustrated by a shortage of potential tenants. Their ideology offers two alternatives according to which of the ideas, separation or own-group preference, is given more weight. Those who gave dominant consideration to preferences for their own group were expected to favor one or more other ethnic groups with a preferred status. This is a process of *progressive inclusion.* On the other hand, those landlords leaning toward separation, when frustrated, might select some ethnic group other than their own the members of whom are in "adequate supply," giving them exclusive preference. This possibility is the third general hypothesis of the study.

Finally, it was expected that the processes of progressive exclusion and progressive inclusion would tend to be consistent with the general rank order of the several ethnic groups in the city's stratification complex. Exclusion was expected to begin with the "lowest" ethnicity and move upward; inclusion to begin with the ethnicity viewed by the landlord as "most like" his own and to move downward through the ethnic ranks. No adequate independent index of the system of ethnic stratification was available. If these expectations are correct, however, the preferences should show an orderly pattern. Thus, the final general hypothesis is that the operation of progressive exclusion and inclusion would produce a scalability similar to Guttman's in the landlords' preferences, provided that landlord ethnicity is controlled.

The State of the Market

The state of the private rental housing market was ascertained by the study of a five per cent sample of the accommodations registered with the Rent Control Commission. This sample contains 1,522 dwelling units.[6] In keeping with current practices of housing market analysis,[7] the total market was divided into four submarkets according to monthly rent: (a) 30 dollars and less, (b) 31 to 50 dollars, (c) 51 to 75 dollars, and (d) over 75 dollars. To relate these submarkets to the hypotheses presented above, the ethnicities of the landlords and their tenants were analyzed in each case.

Landlords and the Markets. Caucasian, Chinese, and Japanese landlords together controlled 87 per cent of the total market, of which each of these groups controlled between one-quarter and one-third.[8] But these three major groups of ethnic landlords had quite different types of rental units. The Caucasian landlords dominated the submarket of highest rental units, controlled fewer units as the rents declined, and operated only a very small portion of the cheapest housing. The properties of the Japanese landlords represented a pattern just about the opposite of that of the Caucasians, while the Chinese landlords controlled between one-fifth and one-third of *each* submarket.

Tenants and the Markets. Most rental units were occupied by families or other groups. Therefore, the tenants were classified according to the ethnicity of each group, or tenant-unit, rather than the ethnic status of each individual. The categories employed are: Caucasian, Caucasian-plus, Chinese, Filipino, Hawaiian, Japanese, and Others and Unknown.[9] Each tenant-unit was also placed within one of the submarkets according to the "most rent" they could pay if for any reason they had to move, as reported in an interview by an adult member of the unit.[10]

On the "demand" side, the breakdown of submarkets according to ethnicity also produced a rather clear pattern. Although Caucasians constituted 31 per cent of all potential tenants, they dominated the most expensive locations and were a highly significant component of the 51–75 dollar submarket, but they sought few of the two less expensive types of dwellings. The Caucasian-plus tenants were similarly distributed. Japanese made up 34 per cent of the tenants, again showing an opposite pattern to that of the Caucasians. They constituted about one-half of the potential tenants in the two less expensive submarkets, but only about one-twelfth in the two higher categories. Chinese tenants constituted only six per cent of all homeseekers, and most of them were unattached males or elderly couples looking for housing in the cheaper submarkets. The vast majority of the Chinese residents of Honolulu were home-owners. Most of the other ethnicities were concentrated in the two lower submarkets. The Japanese, followed by the Filipinos and the Chinese, represented the most important element in the demand for "rooming house" quarters.

Landlords, Tenants, and the Markets. Table 16–1 presents the results

TABLE 16-1

An Index of the "Demand" by "Own Group" Tenants to the "Supply" of Rental Units by Landlord Ethnicity and Rental Submarket: Honolulu, 1952*

		SUBMARKET					
		HOUSES AND APARTMENTS					
LANDLORD ETHNICITY	ROOMS	$30 AND BELOW	$50 AND BELOW	$31–$50	$51–$75	ABOVE $75	TOTAL
Caucasian	0	−18	(−4)	−2	0	+.5	+.2
Chinese	−3	−9	(−5)	−3	−3	−12	−4
Japanese	0	−2	(+.2)	+2	−.2	−.5	+.1

*Interpret this table as follows: A minus sign (−) indicates a surplus of units over tenants, that is, a shortage of tenants of "own group" ethnicity. A plus sign (+) indicates a surplus of tenants over units. A figure indicates the number of times the surplus item is greater than the item in short supply. A zero indicates an approximate match of tenants to units.

of the correlation of these two aspects of the market, the first according to landlord ethnicity, the second according to tenant ethnicity. The most striking findings are, first, that the Chinese landlords faced a shortage of potential Chinese tenants in each submarket; second, that the Caucasian landlords enjoyed a surplus of own group tenants in the most expensive submarket, a match of tenants and units in the next dearest submarket, and thereafter a progressive shortage of such tenants; and, finally, that for the Japanese the relationship between units and own group tenants was, once more, the converse of that for the Caucasians.[11]

Specific Predictions

This market information made it possible to convert the general hypothesis presented above into the following specific predictions:

(a) With respect to tenant-ethnicity, the policies of the landlords of Honolulu would be oriented primarily toward either complete non-discrimination or exclusive preference for one ethnicity, generally that of the landlord's own group.

(b1) In comparison with Japanese and Caucasian landlords, Chinese landlords would show low exclusive-own group preferences.

(b2) Caucasian landlords would be least exclusively-own group oriented in the lowest rental category, but this orientation would be increasingly manifest with higher rent levels.

(b3) Japanese landlords would be most exclusively-own group oriented in the lower rental categories, but would be less and less so through the higher submarkets.

(c1) Japanese tenants would be increasingly preferred by Chinese and Caucasian landlords as the rent levels decreased.

(c2) Caucasian tenants would be increasingly preferred by Chinese and Japanese landlords as the rent levels increased.

(d) The landlords' tenant-ethnicity preferences would form a scale similar to Guttman's scales.

Expressed Preferences

To ascertain the tenant-ethnicity preferences of the landlords, a questionnaire was mailed to the landlord of each of the 1,522 rental units in the sample. Altogether, 1,068 completed questionnaires, about 70 per cent of those mailed, were employed in this analysis.[12]

The questionnaire item concerning these preferences was in the form of a double list of seven alphabetically ordered ethnicities: Chinese, Filipino, *haole* (Caucasian), Hawaiian, Japanese, Negro, and Puerto Rican. Each landlord was asked to check any groups in the first listing whom he "preferred," and to check any in the second listing whom he "restricted."[13]

Table 16–2 presents the percentage distributions of the expressed tenant-ethnicity preferences and restrictions of the 1,068 completed questionnaires and schedules.[14] The rank order correlation between preferences and restrictions is — 1.0. However, a number of different kinds of responses were obtained. Some landlords checked one or more categories as "restricted" and checked none as "preferred." Others checked one or more "preferred" and indicated no "restrictions." Still others checked one or more "preferred" and one or more "restricted."[15]

The responses of the landlords were dichotomized to test these data for scale-like properties. The category of "preferred" was selected because it provides a wider range of responses than the others and is more pertinent to the hypotheses previously presented. Accordingly, each response of each landlord was reclassified as "preferred" or "not preferred," and the Guttman scaling technique was applied.[16] Scales were sought for (a) the total sample of landlord responses, (b) each ethnic category among the landlords, and (c) each housing submarket within each landlord ethnicity.

TABLE 16-2

Percentage Distributions of the Preferred and Restricted Statuses of Seven Selected Tenant Ethnicities for 1,068 Rental Units, Honolulu, 1952

ETHNICITY	PREFERRED	NEITHER PREFERRED NOR RESTRICTED*	RESTRICTED
Japanese	45.0%	49.0%	6.0%
Caucasian	37.3	56.1	6.6
Chinese	27.0	62.0	11.0
Hawaiian	15.2	64.5	20.0
Filipino	12.0	62.2	26.8
Puerto Rican	4.8	60.5	34.7
Negro	1.4	59.8	38.8

*Over 39 per cent of the respondents indicated a policy of no differential treatment on the basis of ethnicity. In this table all such responses are included in the "neither preferred nor restricted" column.

Findings

Prediction (a). Of the total reports, 39.3 per cent indicate a policy of non-discrimination, and 29.4 per cent a preference for a single ethnicity. With respect to landlord ethnicity, 39.5 per cent of the Caucasian, 34.4 per cent of the Japanese, and 36.8 per cent of the Chinese landlords' reports signify non-discrimination,[17] while 38.3 per cent of the Caucasian, 37.5 per cent of the Japanese, and 16.4 per cent of the Chinese reports indicate an exclusive preference for some one ethnicity.[18] For the total, 76.5 per cent of all those showing a preference for only a single ethnicity noted that the preference was for their own group. Thus, substantial evidence suggests that the preferential policies split between non-discrimination and a preference for a single ethnicity, generally own group.

Prediction (b1). When only own group preferences are considered, the percentages are 34.7 for the Japanese, 32.0 for the Caucasian, and only 1.8 for the Chinese reports.[19] The specific hypothesis is thus supported by the data.

Prediction (b2). Moving from the most to the least expensive submarket, the percentages of exclusive-own group preferences for the Caucasian landlords are 63.1, 33.7, 3.8, and 7.0 per cent, respectively. Moreover, in the two most expensive submarkets Caucasian tenants were the most preferred ethnic group, while in the two least costly the Japanese were the most preferred, being so designated on 24.1 per cent of the reports in the cheapest submarket. Again, the prediction is supported by the data.

Prediction (b3). Moving from the least to the most expensive submarket, the percentages of exclusive-own group preferences for the Japanese landlords are 40.7, 40.7, 22.9, and 4.2 per cent, respectively. With these landlords, Japanese tenants were the most preferred ethnic group in the three lowest submarkets, but in the top submarket Caucasian tenants were the exclusive choice of 12.5 per cent of the Japanese landlords. These findings also support the prediction.

Prediction (c1). From the top to the bottom submarket, the percentages of Chinese landlords who *included* Japanese tenants in their preferred status groupings were 80.9, 88.9, 95.9, and 88.3 per cent, respectively,[20] and the percentages of such landlords who indicated an *exclusive* preference for Japanese tenants were 2.4, 6.3, 16.3, and 8.8 per cent, respectively. The unexpected drop in the least costly submarket is due to the fact that more separatist landlords made use of an exclusive preference for the similarly numerous Hawaiians and Filipinos in this submarket than in the submarket above. However, the combined percentages of those separatist Chinese landlords who indicated either "Japanese only" or "Chinese and Japanese only" (progressive inclusion) are, from the top to the bottom submarket, 9.5, 14.3, 30.6, and 39.3 per cent, respectively.[21]

The percentages indicating that Japanese tenants were *included* within the Caucasian landlords' preferred status groupings are 32.6, 62.9, 91.2, and 89.6 per cent, from the top to the bottom submarket, and the percentages showing an *exclusive* preference for Japanese tenants are 0.0, 0.0, 11.2, and 24.1 per cent, respectively. The percentages indicating a preference for either "Japanese only" or "only Caucasian and Japanese" are 3.1, 6.7, 15.0, and 34.5 per cent, respectively.[22] Once more, the data support the hypothesis.

Prediction (c2). With respect to the Chinese landlords' choices, the percentages indicating that Caucasians were included among the preferred tenants are, from the bottom to the top submarket, 45.6, 72.1, 80.9, and 88.1 per cent,[23] respectively, and the percentages denoting Caucasians as the only preferred ethnic group are 0.0, 0.0, 6.4, and 16.7 per cent, respectively. No Chinese landlord declared a preference for "Chinese and Caucasians only." For the Japanese landlords, the percentages which include Caucasians among the preferred ethnic groups are 48.8, 55.8, 70.5, and 83.3 per cent,[24] respectively, from the bottom to the top submarket. The percentages favoring Caucasians as the only preferred tenants of Japanese landlords are 0.0, 0.0, 6.6, and 12.5 per cent, and the combined percentages of the reports indicating a preference for "Caucasians only" or for "Japanese and Caucasians only" are 0.0, 8.1, 13.1, and 12.5 per cent, respectively. In this case too, the data support the prediction.

Prediction (d). The 7,476 dichotomized responses produced a scale on the order of Guttman's with a coefficient of reproducibility of .949. The rank order is: (1) Japanese, (2) Caucasian, (3) Chinese, (4) Hawaiian, (5) Filipino, (6) Puerto Rican, and (7) Negro. Of all the errors, 60.9 per cent were due to landlords indicating a single choice other than "Japanese," and 15.7 per cent resulted from the choice of "Japanese and Chinese only."

Only the scale for the Japanese landlords retains the original ranking of the ethnicities, raising the coefficient of reproducibility to .978. In this case, only 36.5 per cent of the errors were brought about by a single choice other than "Japanese," but 32.7 were credited to the choice of "Japanese and Chinese only." The Caucasian landlords' scale moves "Caucasian" to first rank and "Japanese" to the second, yields a coefficient of .972, and 57.8 per cent of its errors are attributable to a single preference other than "Caucasian." The scale for the Chinese preferences shifts "Chinese" to the second rank and "Caucasian" to the third, produces a coefficient of .950, and 64.5 per cent of its errors were due to a single choice other than "Japanese." Each of these rank changes is consistent with the hypotheses presented above: the landlords' tenant-ethnicity preferences, with landlord ethnicity controlled, are scalable, as required by the processes of progressive inclusion and progressive exclusion.

Consequences

The manner in which the cultural and social structures shaped the preferential policies raises the important questions of whether or not the policies were effectuated and of the nature of their consequences for the locations of tenants in the rental market structure. With respect to the first question, two checks were made. One indicates that in only three instances in which a landlord respondent made use of the "restricted" list in answering the questionnaire was a tenant found in that accommodation whose ethnicity was among those restricted, and in each instance the tenant had resided there prior to the landlord's acquisition of the property. The second check shows that in 82 per cent of the cases in which a landlord utilized the "preferred" list, the ethnicity of the tenant-unit was included among those given a preferred status. The evidence strongly suggests that the declared policies were enforced to a very large degree.

Two analyses were also undertaken with respect to the question concerning the consequences of these policies. In the first, which centers upon the overall effects of the tendency toward own group preferences, the numbers of actual "own group tenants" were converted into percentages of the expected numbers of such tenants for each house-apartment submarket of each major landlord ethnic group.[25] From the least to the most expensive submarket, the percentages for the Caucasians were 180, 263, 156, and 110; for the Chinese, 357, 293, 339, and 100; for the Japanese, 169, 149, 222, and 115. For each ethnic group, own group tendencies had little direct consequence in the most expensive submarket, but they had considerable effect on the particular accommodations occupied by the tenants of each ethnicity in each of the other submarkets.

The numbers of actual tenants of each ethnicity also were computed as percentages of the expected numbers in each submarket without regard to landlord ethnicity. The results are presented in Table 16–3. Twenty-three of the 35 percentages are between 80 and 120 per cent, and the Chinese,

TABLE 16-3

Numbers of Tenants by Ethnicity as Percentages of the Expected Numbers for Each Submarket: Honolulu, 1952

| ETHNICITY | ROOMS | SUBMARKET | | | | LEVEL OF SIGNIFICANCE |
| | | HOUSES AND APARTMENTS | | | | |
		$30 AND BELOW	$31–$50	$51–$75	ABOVE $75	
Caucasian	206	42	109	101	101	.001
Caucasian-plus	367	69	115	87	75	.001
Chinese	64	132	105	100	130	.30
Filipino	100	111	89	84	111	.95
Hawaiian	219	66	94	82	98	.001
Japanese	96	114	92	105	43	.02
Other	98	80	94	134	111	.50

Filipino, and "Other" tenants are distributed as expected. The Caucasian, Caucasian-plus, and Hawaiian tenants are under-represented in the cheapest house submarket and over-represented in the room submarket. The number of Japanese and Caucasian-plus tenants is also fewer than expected in the most expensive house submarket. The reports of the interviews with the tenants revealed that very large percentages of the Caucasian, Caucasian-plus, and Hawaiian tenants living in rooms were seeking to move, but were experiencing difficulty in finding low-cost housing. The vacancy ratio for houses and apartments renting for 50 dollars or less per month was about 1.2 per cent. These interviews also indicated that virtually all of the Japanese and Caucasian-plus tenants who believed that they could pay more than 75 dollars a month, but who were not doing so, were planning to move into their "own home" in the near future.

Discussion

In spite of the fact that a large proportion of the landlords did consider ethnicity in developing their policies of tenant selection and did effectuate these policies, such considerations had relatively little effect upon the general locations of tenants in the structure of the housing market. This was due primarily to two factors. The first is the way in which the holdings of the landlords of the different ethnicities were distributed relative to the distribution of the tenants among the submarkets. The second factor is the manner in which the preferential policies of the landlords were themselves influenced by the market situation. The presence of a variety of ethnic groups in fairly large numbers seems to have provided considerable fluidity for landlords with a separatist orientation, although the particular "solutions" adopted tended to be limited sharply in many instances by the market situation. The main impact, then, of these preferential policies upon the tenants concerned the particular accommodations and not the general type of housing in which they resided. Thus, although 60 per cent of the rental units were operated under some kind of preferential ethnicity policy, the market, viewed as a structure of alternatives and multiple individual decisions, tended to be non-discriminatory.

With respect to the practice of non-discrimination by individuals, it is frequently implied that market situations are likely to be non-discriminatory in practice because they tend toward functional specificity and affective detachment generally.[26] This study, however, reveals no clear pattern of general affective detachment due to instrumental considerations. Rather, it suggests that in the housing market of polyethnic Honolulu the practice of systematic non-discrimination was in large measure the result of a positive orientation toward the moral creed of assimilationism. As Parsons has pointed out, affective neutrality or detachment may mean the primacy of moral as well as instrumental considerations.[27] These findings suggest as well that the same market conditions which "permit" individuals so inclined to practice discrimination also determine the extent to which persons of non-discriminatory inclinations are exposed to social pressures to discriminate.

NOTES

The authors wish to thank the following for their assistance, professional or financial, in the collection of the data here presented: Linton Freeman, Kiyoshi Ikeda, Norman Meller, the Citizens Rent Committee of Honolulu (1952), the Rent Control Commission of Honolulu, and the several undergraduates of the University of Hawaii who served as interviewers.

1. John Harding, Bernard Kutner, Harold Proshansky, and Isidor Chien, "Prejudice and Ethnic Relations," in Gardner Lindzey, editor, *Handbook of Social Psychology*, Cambridge, Mass.: Addison-Wesley, 1954, Vol. II, pp. 1032–1033.

2. Robin M. Williams, Jr., "Racial and Cultural Relations," in J. B. Gittler, editor, *Review of Sociology*, New York: Wiley, 1957, p. 446; and Arnold M. Rose, "Intergroup Relations vs. Prejudice," *Social Problems*, 4 (October, 1956), p. 174.

3. For a detailed discussion of the processes of rent-setting and the special motivations of landlords, see Harry V. Ball, "Social Structure and Rent Control Violations," *American Journal of Sociology*, 65 (May, 1960), pp. 598–604.

4. See, e.g., Edgar E. Vinacke, "Stereotyping and National-Racial Groups in Hawaii:

A Study in Ethnocentricism," *Journal of Social Psychology,* 30 (November, 1949), pp. 265–291; Doris V. Springer, "Awareness of Racial Differences in Preschool Children in Hawaii," *Genetic Psychology Monographs,* 41 (May, 1950), pp. 215–270; Linton C. Freeman, "Homogamy in Interethnic Mate Selection," *Sociology and Social Research,* 36 (July–August, 1955), pp. 369–377; Leonard Broom, "Intermarriage and Mobility in Hawaii," *Transactions of the Third World Congress of Sociology,* London: International Sociological Association, 1956, pp. 277–282; C. K. Cheng and Douglas S. Yamamura, "Inter-racial Marriage and Divorce in Hawaii," *Social Forces,* 36 (October, 1957), pp. 77–84.

5. Romanzo Adams, "The Unorthodox Race Doctrine of Hawaii," in E. B. Reuter, editor, *Race and Cultural Contacts,* New York: McGraw-Hill, 1934, pp. 143–160.

6. The selection of every twentieth case in the Commission's files yielded an initial sample of 2,090 units. Of these, 1,522 dwelling units were subsequently verified (by visit) to be in fact for rent; the remainder had become owner-occupied.

7. See, e.g., Chester Rapkin, Louis Winnick, and David M. Blank, *Housing Market Analysis,* Washington, D. C.: Housing and Home Finance Agency, Division of Housing, 1953, Chapter 1.

8. The landlord ethnicities employed were "Caucasian," "Chinese," "Japanese," and "Other." "Other" included Hawaiian, Korean, Filipino, and Indian individuals, and such organizations as trust companies and land estates. Classifications were by name. While this procedure resulted in some misclassification, for example, a Korean as "Chinese," a telephone check indicated that such errors were few.

9. A family or other tenant-unit was classified as "Caucasian" only if every member was of only Caucasian ancestry. If only one member was Caucasian, the unit was classified as Caucasian-plus. If both members were Hawaiian or part-Hawaiian, the unit was designated as "Hawaiian." Classification of the remaining groups was based upon the ethnicity of what was believed to be the lower-status ethnicity represented in each case. The resulting descending order of ethnic status was Chinese, Japanese, Korean, Samoan, Filipino, Puerto Rican, and Negro. This procedure maximized the estimation of the number of households expected to encounter discrimination in seeking rental housing.

10. To distribute the tenant-units among the submarkets, a choice was made from three possible bases of classification: (a) the rents the tenants were paying; (b) some percentage of the income of the tenant-unit; or (c) the tenant respondents' own estimates of the most rent they could pay. The third basis (c) was selected because it is subject to less distortion by the main factor under study (ethnicity preference) than is the first (a), and it takes greater account of the different orientations of permanent and non-permanent residents toward rent and housing than does the second (b).

11. The Japanese faced an apparent shortage of tenants in the "$30 and below" submarket, but the large surplus in the "$31–$50" category forced many to reside in less expensive units. For the combined submarket of "$50 and below," only the Japanese enjoyed a surplus of tenants over units.

12. About 66 per cent of the questionnaires were returned by mail. Comparisons of respondents and non-respondents indicated significantly larger proportions of non-response by Caucasian landlords and landlords of units in the top-priced submarket (correlated variables). Ten per cent of the non-respondents were interviewed. Because of the numbers involved, comparisons between the respondents and non-respondents with respect to ethnicity preferences with landlord ethnicity controlled were limited to the Caucasians in the most expensive submarket, the Japanese in the lowest two submarkets combined, and the Chinese generally. The differences in each of these comparisons were not statistically significant by the test of Chi-square with a required level of significance of .05. Thus, the questionnaires and schedules were combined for this analysis, and no attempt was made to reduce further the level of non-response.

13. The questions explicitly referred to the particular rental units identified in the

questionnaire. They did not inquire into the landlord's "general attitude," but in most instances asked specifically about a decision made by the landlord within the recent past.

14. It is believed that the expressed preferences possess adequate validity for the following reasons: First, only 39.3 per cent of the total reports indicate either a policy of non-discrimination *or* a refusal to answer the question. Second, in virtually all of these instances the landlord did indicate preferences or restrictions based upon numbers, age, occupational activity, etc. Third, as discussed below under "Consequences," there was a very high correspondence between the expressed preferences and restrictions and the actual ethnicity of the tenants in the particular accommodations.

15. Caucasian landlords made significantly greater use of the category "restricted" than did the Chinese or Japanese, but this effects the results only slightly since almost all landlords seemed to fill their units from among the "preferred."

16. Margaret J. Hagood and Daniel O. Price, *Statistics for Sociologists*, New York: Holt, 1952, pp. 143–159. It is stressed that there was no intention in this study to produce a "classical," unidimensional Guttman scale, but rather to test whether or not progressive exclusion and progressive inclusion operated in a systematic manner with respect to the rank order of preferences.

17. These differences are not statistically significant (do not attain a .05 level of probability by the test of Chi-square with five degrees of freedom). Over 59 per cent of the landlords in the "other" category which includes several quasi-public trusts and estates, reported non-discrimination; this differed significantly from the other groupings.

18. The differences between the Chinese and the Caucasians and Japanese are significant at the .01 level.

19. These differences are significant at the .001 level (Chi-square with five degrees of freedom).

20. These differences are not statistically significant (Chi-square with seven degrees of freedom).

21. These differences are statistically significant (Chi-square at the .02 level of probability with seven degrees of freedom).

22. These differences are significant at the .001 level (Chi-square with seven degrees of freedom).

23. These differences are significant at the .001 level (Chi-square with seven degrees of freedom).

24. These differences are significant at the .02 level (Chi-square with seven degrees of freedom).

25. The expectancies were calculated upon the basis of a model of the market which takes account of the tenants' own estimates of maximum rent-paying ability and the non-ethnic preferences of the landlords. Because of this latter factor, tenant-units composed of "unattached" or non-related individuals who placed themselves in the 31–50 dollars a month submarket were allocated instead to the 30 dollars and less submarket.

26. See, e.g., Williams, *op. cit.*, p. 446.

27. Talcott Parsons, *The Social System*, Glencoe, Ill.: Free Press, 1951, p. 132.

17

LEONARD BROOM AND ESHREF SHEVKY

THE DIFFERENTIATION
OF AN ETHNIC GROUP

We have initiated this study in the context of a larger interest in the analysis of urban phenomena. In addition to the examination of population growth and concentration, which have gained much attention, we feel the need for more work on the differentiation of urban populations. Some progress has been made in this direction, especially in the field of ethnic studies, and minority groups provide the most promising material with which to delineate the problems of urbanization and devise techniques of analysis. The study of ethnic groups, however, has been directed toward other objectives, and, as a result, the problem of differentiation has been approached only by implication. The attainment of even the apparent objectives of ethnic studies has been hampered either when the groups are not small or are not clearly delimited by community boundaries, that is when gross spatial criteria do not define the group. As the process of acculturation of immigrant groups proceeds, and many enclaves lose their homogeneity, the populations themselves may be lost to analysis if techniques of differentiation are not devised. In this paper we wish to point out an approach which seems to be applicable to this problem, and to present one exploratory study.

The Jewish minority is well constituted for the kind of analysis we propose. The group is set in a complex metropolitan situation, there are varying degrees of isolation of and cultural differences within the group, and we lack direct measures of the numbers and demographic characteristics of the population. These circumstances make the task of differentiation a precondition to intensive analysis. Otherwise the study must be arbitrarily delimited on some *a priori* organizational conception or

Reprinted with permission from *American Sociological Review* 14 (1949): 476–481.

expensive and time-consuming censuses of the population must be undertaken.

We make the following working hypotheses:

1. That Jewish populations may be distributed on a continuum of urbanization.
2. That Jewish populations may be distributed on a continuum of status.
3. That Jews have varying degrees of association and isolation, with Jews and with other populations, each of which has different features of distribution within the criteria of status, urbanization, and association.
4. That Jewish populations are culturally differentiated.
    a) Jews represent a diversity of origins which still affect the cultural attributes of the group.
    b) The Jews may be conceived as distributed along a series of continua converging on acculturated American urban modes.

Granting the foregoing, and given a large population, but one of indeterminate size, the task of the differentiation of meaningful samples is an absolute precondition to economical and orderly research. Our basic instrument of analysis is an urban typology, framed by a tridimensional social space bounded by status, urbanization, and segregation, which is based on census tract data.[1]

Our task is twofold: First, to discover if the typology may be employed as an instrument to differentiate segments of the population selected on ethnic criteria, criteria which were not directly involved in the construction of the typology. Second, if differentiations are discovered, to use them as steps toward the specification of the attributes of the Jewish population and *pari passu* as specifications for sampling an urban Jewish population.

Of the possible samples which might be available we have directed this brief exploration to an analysis of the predominantly Jewish Russian-born population in Los Angeles County. In addition, reference is made to a sample of Jewish petitioners for name-changing and a sample of Jewish fraternities.

I

The Russian-born, who in 1940 numbered 31,430 in Los Angeles County, may be taken as essentially Jewish. A colony of Molokans were concentrated in a single census tract (Tract No. 122) with a Russian-born population of 615, and we have excluded this tract from our analysis. We found it unnecessary to refine out of other tracts a scattering of White Russians which slightly reinforced the statistics for the Jewish Russian-born. A summary of the degree of concentration of the Jewish Russian-born by tracts is presented in Table 17-1. Almost one-third of this population was concentrated in 9 out of the 570 tracts in the southern portion of Los Angeles County.[2] In these they comprised 10 per cent or more of the tract population. There were no Russian-born Jews in 45 tracts. In 489 tracts the Russian-born Jews were thinly distributed, but this group of tracts accounted for nearly one-half the Russian-born Jewish population of the County. The neighborhoods popularly regarded as Jewish included all tracts with a high concentration of Russian-born. These neighborhoods, however, even when most broadly defined, account for only 50 per cent of the Jewish Russian-born, and this fact points up one of the limitations of the conventional "community study." Community studies of ethnic groups tend to be focused on areas of high visibility and it is generally assumed that although many highly acculturated individuals may not be included in such spatially deterministic studies, at least the culturally distinctive population strongly identified with the ethnic group are accounted for. The data from Los Angeles indicate that this assumption is not justified.

The wide distribution of Russian-born Jews is not merely a dispersion through geographical space but also through social space as expressed by the typological grid. This is shown in Figure 17-1 in which Jewish neighborhoods and the tracts containing and lacking the Russian-born are identified. Jewish neighborhoods are found in the upper ranges of urbanization and in the full range of social rank. Tracts lacking Russian-born

TABLE 17-1

Distribution of Russian-Born by Tracts, Los Angeles County, 1940

PERCENT OF TRACT POPULATION RUSSIAN-BORN	NUMBER OF TRACTS	NUMBER OF RUSSIAN-BORN	PER CENT OF RUSSIAN-BORN
0.0	45	0	0.0
.1— .9	396	7,130	23.1
1.0— 2.9	93	7,874	25.5
3.0— 4.9	20	4,432	14.4
4.0— 9.9	6	1,742	5.7
10.0—24.9	9	9,637	31.3
Total	569	30,815	100.0

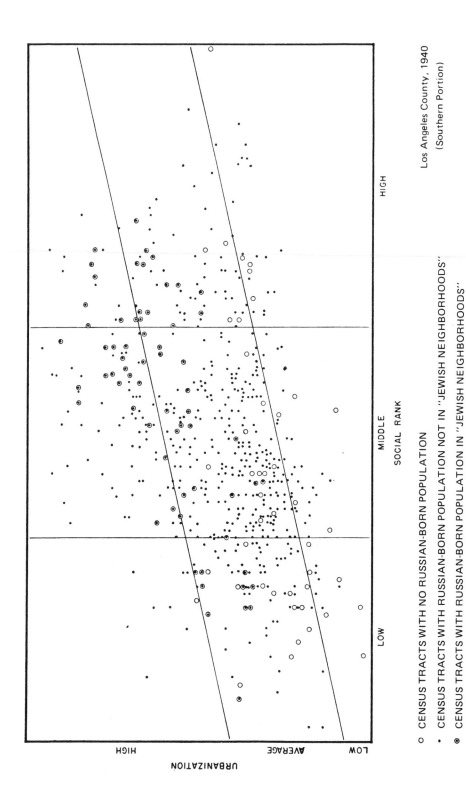

Figure 17-1 Russian-born Population (Predominantly Jewish)

tend to fall in the lower ranges of urbanization with a noticeable cluster at the lowest levels of rank. Underlying this is an associational feature which we may refer to parenthetically. The Jews are negatively associated in the lower ranks with that segment of Mexicans of lowest urbanization, but in the areas of average to high urbanization Jews are positively associated with Mexicans but negatively with Negroes. The contrasting distributions are more graphically set forth in Figure 17–2 in which Jewish neighborhoods and tracts without Russian-born are indicated.

The wide distribution of Jews through the status continuum, even when the sample is restricted to tracts in visible neighborhoods, deserves further comment. In Figure 17–3 we have plotted the tracts comprising three of the chief Jewish neighborhoods indicated by their identifying place names. The decided clustering of the tract attributes occurs at three levels of status which coincide with the three named neighborhoods. This, of course, is a reflection of the fact that there is not a single status system embracing the entire population of Jewish neighborhoods but a number of status groupings of the general population within which the Jews find their place. The simple fact that ethnic status systems should be interpreted in the context of the larger status system deserves to be specified

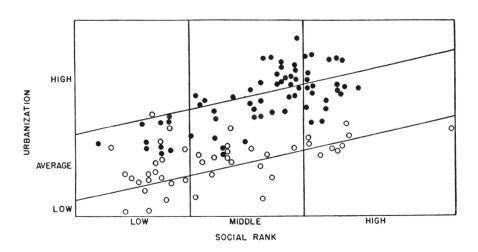

● CENSUS TRACTS WITH RUSSIAN-BORN POPULATION IN "JEWISH NEIGHBORHOODS"

○ CENSUS TRACTS WITH NO RUSSIAN-BORN POPULATION

Los Angeles County, 1940
(Southern Portion)

Figure 17–2   "Jewish Neighborhoods" and Tracts Lacking Russian-born

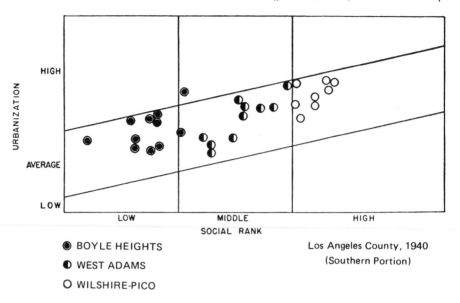

Figure 17-3   Census Tracts in Three "Jewish Neighborhoods"

whenever possible. By operational criteria, of course, the two systems need not be congruent. A topic meriting investigation remains unanswered here: How closely do the Jews approximate the attributes of the populations with which they are associated in social space? If they do approximate the attributes of the rest of the areal populations the nature of their interaction with these populations will be functionally different than if their attributes are highly differentiated.

As would be expected, the ethnic institutional services are located with minor exceptions in the identifiable neighborhoods. The plotting of synagogues according to the social rank of their locations in Los Angeles showed a bi-modal distribution. The Orthodox and Reformed components in the distribution were fairly sharply separated and Orthodoxy was negatively related to status. It should be a point of more than casual interest that it is possible to differentiate institutional services in this fashion.

The analysis of social space raises the question of our acculturation hypothesis but does not solve it. A testable formulation of the acculturation problem might be expressed as follows: That the degree of acculturation of Russian-born Jews is inversely proportional to their degree of concentration. Alternatively, the dispersion of Russian-born Jews varies directly with their association with the more highly acculturated second generation Jews. The differentials in the distribution of Russian-born

Jews and Jews of other national origins, which deserve to be investigated, would throw light on both the acculturation problem and the variable of social status.

II

Our second sample represents as sharp a contrast as possible with the Russian foreign-born. It is composed of 500 Jewish petitioners for name changes in Los Angeles County in 1946–47 and was compiled for another purpose which will be reported on in a separate paper. We compared the tract distribution of Jewish petitioners for name-changing with two populations by projecting them on the two-dimensional grid (see Figure 17–4).

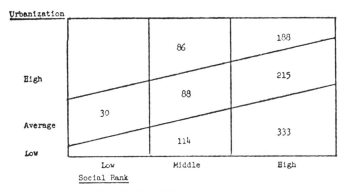

100 = Distribution of Russian-born

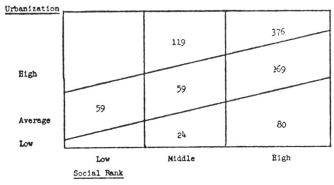

100 = Distribution of total population

Figure 17–4   The Relative Distribution of Jewish Name-Changers
(501 cases in Los Angeles)

We found that the petitioners were sharply differentiated from both the Russian-born Jews and the total population. The name-changers fell in areas of higher social status than the Russian-born but were proportionately less urbanized. The name-changers were also found in tracts of higher social status than the total population, as well as in those more highly urbanized than the total population.

III

Our third sample consists of the membership of four Jewish fraternities on the Los Angeles campus of the University of California. Two of these are by campus consensus rated "high" and two are rated "low." The home addresses of the members from Los Angeles County were plotted on the grid. The samples of Russian-born and petitioners for name-changing were chosen not only because they were sociologically "real" but because we assumed they were sharply differentiated populations. We felt that if the instrument of analysis were to serve any useful purpose it should show discriminatory power in this case. In the fraternity subsample we intended to stack the cards against the instrument on the assumption that the "organized" part of an ethnic group attending a single metropolitan institution would prove to be quite homogeneous. It was found, however, that the status value of tract locations of members of the high status fraternities was significantly above that of members of the low status fraternities.

The sharpness of separation between the fraternity subsamples leads us to conclude that objective criteria such as we have used are sufficient to reveal significant differentials even in presumed homogeneous populations. Through the use of these criteria, the degree of differentiation between highly contrasting populations may be brought into the same frame of reference as apparently similar populations. We therefore claim for the instrument of analysis some discriminatory power. It may be employed in the fashion outlined in selecting meaningful samples for research with a variety of objectives, and dependence on spatial criteria becomes unnecessary. At another level the burdening of analysis with subjective operational data may, for typological purposes, be largely avoided.

As for our second objective, this paper represents some progress toward the specification of the attributes of an ethnic population. By projecting the attributes of these samples and others to be compiled within the typological framework utilized here, we can achieve a successive approximation to a rounded description of the manifold social characteristics of an ethnic group.

NOTES

1. See Eshref Shevky and Marilyn Williams, *The Social Areas of Los Angeles: Analysis and Typology.* Berkeley: University of California Press, 1949.

Status is measured by an index which is an average of the percentile scores of three factors—level of occupation, level of schooling, and income. The index of *urbanization* is the average of the percentile scores of three factors—fertility, women in the labor force, and single-family dwelling units. The third variable, *segregation*, is not referred to in this paper. Tracts are placed in a two-dimensional attribute space with the index of urbanization related to the base, social rank. The base was divided into three intervals of approximate thirds of the range, indicating low, middle, and high social rank. The index of urbanization is divided into three intervals with the middle or average interval determined by the space of two standard errors about the regression line of urbanization related to social rank. Census tracts in each of the resulting nine cells represent populations that are homogeneous in their basic differential characteristics of rank and urbanization, irrespective of their geographic location. (See Figure 17–1.)

2. Twenty tracts in the thinly populated northern area are excluded in the construction of the Shevky-Williams typology.

PART III

The Neighborhood in the Larger Setting

18

H. W. GILMORE

THE OLD NEW ORLEANS
AND THE NEW:
A CASE FOR ECOLOGY

New Orleans is sufficiently different from the general run of American cities to make it an interesting laboratory for studying ecological principles evolved on the basis of data from other cities. Its topography, on casual observation, appears to be rather similar to that of Chicago or of any number of plains cities. Yet in certain respects its topography is very different, and uniquely, it has been changed fundamentally during the history of the city. In its population history it has shown evidence of the processes of accommodation and assimilation of minority groups characteristic of other cities plus long standing patterns of accommodation of racial groups which assimilated very slowly or not at all. As a result of these complex factors, ecological maps of New Orleans look like a crazy-quilt to sociologists acquainted with the ecology of conventional American cities. Actually, however, the city is not without an ecological pattern and this pattern is not difficult to see once the city's topography and history of ethnic groups are understood.

As was said above, the topography of the city is in some respects typical but in other respects it is unique. The city is located on a strip of land roughly five to seven miles wide between Lake Ponchartrain on the north and the Mississippi River on the south. Though eighty miles from the gulf, this land, like all land in the area, was built up by a long process of sedimentation. Therefore, in contrast to inland areas, the higher land is found along streams or where streams once existed while the lowest land is found farther away from streams. Thus, while the land may appear to be

Reprinted with permission from *American Sociological Review* 9 (1944): 385–394.

perfectly flat, a contour map shows that the land ranges from fifteen feet above to two feet below mean gulf-level. (See Figure 18–1.)

The highest land in the city is found along the river and ranges from five to fifteen feet above mean gulf-level. Passing north from the river, the altitude declines to two feet below gulf-level. The low area, however, is transversed by "ridges" where bayous are or have been. Thus there is Metairie Ridge, two feet above sea-level running east and west almost parallel with the river and about half way between the river and the lake. There is also a ridge about two feet above gulf-level, running north-south from the end of Bayou St. John to the river, passing the lower end of the French Quarter. We will call this Esplanade Ridge. This ridge divides the city into what may be conceived as two saucers sitting edge to edge, the other edges being formed by Metairie Ridge and the high land along the river. Each saucer is two feet below sea-level at its center and is from two to fifteen feet above sea-level at its periphery. Until relatively modern

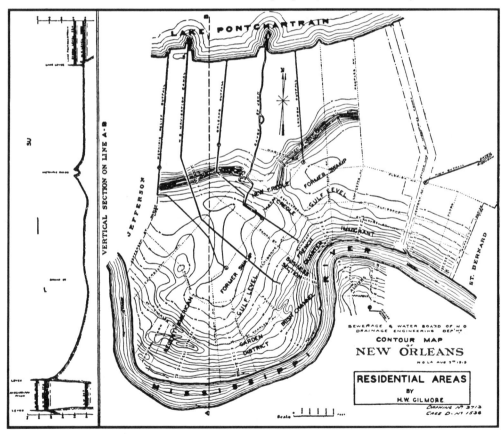

Figure 18–1   Contour Map of New Orleans Residential Areas

times the centers of these saucers were swamps and habitation was feasible only along the rims of the saucers. It is in terms, therefore, of the struggle of the nationality groups for residential space around the edges of the saucers that the ecology of the city is to be understood.

Creole New Orleans

New Orleans, of course, was settled by the French. Presumably the particular site was selected because they wanted an inland water route to the gulf coast of the present state of Mississippi where they already had a settlement at Biloxi. Such a route was available through Bayou St. John, Lake Ponchartrain and a series of lakes and bayous which link this lake to the gulf. A short and easy portage between the river and Bayou St. John was provided by Esplanade Ridge which was already in use for this purpose by the Indians when the French explorations and settlement were made. The settlement originated at the junction of Esplanade Ridge and the River and as it expanded it did so mostly to the west where the land was higher than it was to the east. This is the area that is now known as the French Quarter.

Like the settlers in most colonies, the early French settlers of New Orleans were a rather motley lot. They came from various walks of life and various stations in France and probably are not to be considered as coming primarily from any particular social element of the homeland. After a period of frontier hardship, however, they began to be moulded into a quite distinctive and homogeneous group. The French government followed a very liberal policy of land grants to individuals with the result that most of the early settlers became big land holders. This policy was continued by the Spanish government when this territory passed into the hands of that nation. Thus under both France and Spain, there was a tendency for government officials and military personnel sent out to the colony to acquire sizeable land holdings usually without having to purchase them. On these holdings the French established plantations worked with slave labor and rapidly attained prosperity on this basis. Most of them, however, continued to live in the city particularly during the winter and if they lived on their plantations at all they did so in the summer. Their city life was based almost as much on slave labor and the labor of free Negroes as was their plantation life. Thus at the time of the Louisiana Purchase there were twice as many Negroes as whites in the city. As time went on these French plantation owners came to refer to themselves as Creoles and they will be so referred to in the remainder of this paper. The term itself does not refer to land ownership but merely to unmixed descendants of French or Spanish settlers.

This prosperous, land-endowed group, plentifully supplied with colored labor, and gathering in the city for a winter of leisure, made a very favorable situation for an elegant social life. The city being also the colonial capital made this almost inevitable. Such a development seems to have taken place in a large way from 1743 when the great marquis, Pierre Francois de Riguod, Marquis de Vaudreuil, came as governor of Louisiana. He and his wife were accustomed to life in the royal courts of Europe and apparently sought with considerable success to set up a similarly pretentious society in New Orleans. Once established, this pattern was continued by succeeding governors, French and Spanish, with the exception of a brief period under General ("Bloody") O'Reilly who was sent by Spain to suppress a revolt against Spanish rule.

Spanish rule does not seem to have altered the situation in any significant way. The Spanish made no attempt to colonize New Orleans or Louisiana. They did make a half-hearted attempt to teach Spanish in the colony but it attained very indifferent success. For the most part, Spanish officials and military men seem to have found the Creole social life much to their taste and to have been accepted by the Creoles into that social life. Thus they came nearer being assimilated by the Creoles than the reverse. In reality many of them did marry Creoles and others received land grants, established plantations and became part of the Creole aristocracy.

Thus, prior to the Louisiana Purchase, the city was dominated by this Creole landed aristocracy centered around the colonial capital. It was a typical Estate pattern. The emphasis was on inherited wealth in the form of land. There was a law of primogeniture with the surplus sons placed in professions or the government service and stress was laid on social life or leisure time pursuits instead of occupational attainment.

The following description by a French traveler, C. C. Robin, of a reception given in 1803 may give a glimpse of the life of these Creoles prior to the Louisiana Purchase:

> The Louisiana Ladies appeared there with a magnificence that was astonishing in such a colony, and that magnificence could be compared with what is most brilliant in our principal towns in France. The stature of the ladies, generally tall, and their fair complexion, which was set off to advantage by their light dresses adorned with flowers and rich embroideries, gave a fairy-like appearance to these festivities. The last one, especially, astonished me by its

magnificence. After the tea, the concert, the dances, the guests descended at midnight into a hall where, on a table of sixty to eighty covers, rose from the midst of rocks the temple of Good Faith, surrounded with columns and surmounted by a dove; underneath was the statue of the allegorical goddess. But further, outside of that hall, the brilliance of the lights attracted the guests under an immense gallery closed by awnings. Forty to fifty dishes, served in different styles, were offered to the choice of four or five hundred guests who were assembled in little groups.[1]

In addition to the Creoles and the Negroes, there were other nationality groups in the city prior to the nineteenth century. A number of Germans had come to the Louisiana territory during the John Law boom in the 1720's and after unsuccessful attempts at settlement on the Arkansas River had settled in the vicinity of New Orleans. Also French immigrants came from Santo Domingo as a result of slave uprisings and from France as a result of the French Revolution during the latter part of the eighteenth and early part of the nineteenth century. Most of these groups were unable to get large land grants and hence did not become plantation owners. In large part they seem to have become dairymen and truck gardeners though many of them also became artisans. There were also, of course, some representatives of numerous other nationalities but they can be ignored in an ecological study.

With this information before us, let us try to get a picture of the city at the time of the Louisiana Purchase in 1803. It contained only 8,475 population (census of 1805) and covered a correspondingly small area. The heart of the city was what is now known as the French Quarter, bounded by Canal Street, Rampart Street, Esplanade Avenue and the River. In this area were the government buildings, what business there was and the homes of the Creoles. The slaves were housed on the premises of their owners so far as possible. Since most of the Negroes, whether free or slave, were employed in service around the homes of the Creoles, and hours were long and travel was by foot, the Creoles desired them to live close to their homes. Thus those who could not be quartered on the premises formed a residential fringe around the Creole section. Outside this Negro zone was the immigrant truck gardening and dairying zone, the latter using land which was too swampy for residence or cultivation but usable as pasture. On the high land adjacent to the river and east of the city this trucking zone expanded into a considerable area. Outside of this area were plantations wherever the land was high enough to permit cultivation. Thus there were plantations along Bayou St. John and along the river on both sides of the city.

259

Creole-American Conflict

Up to the Louisiana Purchase the infiltration of Americans into New Orleans had been small. They came in and out with the shipping and there were some permanent residents but in some degree immigration of Americans had been held back by unfavorable Spanish laws. With the Louisiana Purchase, however, the dam was breached and the tide began to flow. Thus within the five year period from 1805-1810 there was a 125 per cent increase in the white population of the city, and a large part of this increase undoubtedly was American.

These incoming Americans were a sharp contrast to the polished, wealthy Creoles with their elegant social life. While as a group the Americans who came to New Orleans were perhaps not as crude as the American frontiersman in the open country, certainly they had among them many who were just that crude. In fact the river men who floated down the Mississippi on barges and were known locally as the Kentucks were just as crude and rough and ready as the frontiersmen in any part of the country. Thus in New Orleans, the spreading American frontier ran into a culture which, on a basis of manners and fine appearance at least, was superior to its own; the only case of its kind in American history.

The difference in degree of cultural refinement, however, was not the only difference between the Creoles and the Americans. The Creoles, it will be remembered, laid stress on family tradition, hereditary wealth, leisure and social position. The American, on the other hand, had as his sun god the self-made man. The individual who had been born free and equal, had through his own initiative, industry and thrift gained wealth or success, was the man to be worshiped whether he was the son of a prince, a millionaire, a beggar, a criminal or a simple frontier woodchopper. Thus the two had basically different social philosophies as well as social systems; neither understood the philosophy of the other and neither was much impressed if he did understand. Also the fact that the Creoles were Catholic whereas most of the Americans were Protestant did little to foster mutual affection. Language differences of course increased these tensions, and furthermore, the question which language would be the official language, was an issue of serious moment.

On the basis of their culture, their wealth and their numbers in a more normal situation, the Americans might have been expected to have assumed the role of a minority group but, as usual, New Orleans was not a normal situation. The Americans were representatives of the nation which had just purchased Louisiana and now controlled the government and they were in no psychological mood to be a minority group. Nor was the government in any mood to insist on their playing a minority role. Thus from the beginning, to the tune of much conflict, overt and covert, with the Creoles, they were forced by the factors of the situation into a position somewhat better than that of a minority group.

The course of events brought a rapid improvement in their situation. The passage of the Louisiana Territory into the hands of the United States ended all barriers to commerce on the Mississippi River and brought a rapid commercial development in New Orleans. The Creoles with their philosophy of hereditary wealth and leisurely social life, had never had much taste for the make or break drive for efficiency characteristic of the commercial world and they did not take to it now. Since most of the tillable land was already held by the Creoles, most of the Americans had little chance of establishing themselves as landlords. In any event, the uncertainties, the big stakes and the competition of the business world, had a natural appeal to the worshipers of the self-made man, and they rapidly took over the competitive area as their special domain.

Thus the port figures for the first six months of 1803 show that the shipping was already largely in American hands even before the Louisiana Purchase. Of the 153 cargo ships entering the Mississippi during that period 93 were American, 58 were Spanish and only 2 were French.[2] Similarly, Vincent Nolte who visited New Orleans in 1806, three years after the Purchase, informs us that the mercantile system was made up of four or five French establishments founded during the French rule, three Scotch counting-houses, one German concern and eight or ten commission houses lately opened by young American merchants from New York, Philadelphia and Baltimore.[3]

This near-monopoly on the thriving commerce of the port city rapidly brought prosperity to the Americans and along with it brought a rapid increase in their numbers. With their nationality status thus backed by wealth and numbers, the Americans increasingly challenged the Creoles for the leadership role, culture or no culture, and the struggle between the two groups grew in severity and bitterness.

Ecology of the Old New Orleans

This struggle made inevitable an ecological separation of the two groups. The first Americans did live and have their business in the French Quarter but the crowded conditions plus the Creole-American struggle brought growing pressure for them to go elsewhere. Being so heavily engaged in commerce, it was imperative that they stay on the high land along the river but the fact that they moved west instead of east of the French Quarter was perhaps the result of the Marigny affair.

About 1822 two Americans, James H. Caldwell and Samuel J. Peters, planning to develop a succession of warehouses and cotton presses and other important enterprises (hotel, gas works and water works, etc.), approached Bernard de Marigny with a proposition to buy the whole of his extensive property along the Elysian Field Section. The Creole was extremely unwilling to deal with the Americans, whom he disliked intensely, but was finally persuaded to do so, for a stipulated sum. When the necessary legal documents had been drawn up to conclude the sale, Mrs. Marigny failed to appear at the notary's office. Her signature was necessary to ratify the sale and Marigny used her absence as an excuse to prevent the sale. Infuriated, Mr. Peters is said to have cried out to the Creole: "I shall live, by God, to see the day when rank grass shall choke up the streets of your old faubourg."
. . . Outraged but not discouraged, the two pioneers transferred their interests above Canal Street. They felt that the Americans would be glad to congregate there since they would be separate from those whom they regarded as their oppressors. With the assistance of other local American capitalists a considerable part of the holdings of Jean Gravier was purchased.[4]

Whether or not this event is a full explanation, at any rate from about this time on an American section did grow rapidly to the west of the French Quarter. Into this section moved both American residents and American business. This movement was particularly rapid in the early 30's and a survey made by a local newspaper in 1834 showed that about three fifths of the "merchants," two fifths of the "retailers" and four fifths of the "brokers" were by that time in the American section.[5] Thus the city quickly evolved a pattern with the business section around Canal Street as the center, the Creole section to the east and the American residential section to the west of this. Each of these residential areas had Negro slaves living on the premises and a horseshoe shaped fringe of Negro residences around it with the open side of the horseshoe being towards the business section. Outside of this was the trucking-dairying zone.

The strife which produced this residential segregation was manifest in a severe degree in political circles. The Creoles, considering themselves the settlers of Louisiana, felt the government belonged to them, and the Americans, considering that they had purchased Louisiana, felt the government was theirs. The Creoles had been accustomed to use government positions to support their sons who could not inherit land under primogeniture, and the Americans had no inclination to use tax funds to support

Creole families. In contrast the Americans wanted the government to build all sorts of facilities which would be of aid to commerce, and the Creoles were not interested in being taxed to bring prosperity to the Americans. These differences were so great that as the two factions attained near equality numerically and financially one government could no longer contain them. Thus in 1836 New Orleans was divided into three municipalities, having one mayor but for all practical purposes having separate governments. In the center was the Creole city bounded on the east by Esplanade Avenue and on the west by Canal Street. To the east of it was the immigrant truckgardening city and to the west of the Creole section was the American municipality. In all three cases the river was the southern boundary and the lake was the northern boundary.

This separation of the city into three municipalities practically established Canal Street and Esplanade Avenue as national boundary lines. It became a matter of honor and of loyalty to one's cause to live on the proper side of these streets; those who moved into enemy territory were viewed askance if not actually as deserters. And after more than a century these definitions have by no means disappeared.

With this division the American municipality launched an almost extravagant program of public improvements. Old wharves were improved and new ones were built, streets were paved, public schools were developed and public buildings were constructed. Accompanying this was a growing prosperity and a rapid inflow of white population. Thus the white population in the whole city (three municipalities combined) increased from 21,281 in 1830, to 59,519 in 1840, and 91,431 in 1850. Meanwhile there were no more Negroes in the city at the end of this period than at the beginning.

A significant part of this influx of white population was Irish workmen. The growth in commerce and shipping brought laboring jobs and the public works program of the American municipality meant the need for many workmen. To meet these needs there was virtually no local labor supply. There were not enough free Negroes, slaves were too expensive, and the immigrants were happily employed in their crafts and agricultural pursuits. As a result, outside laborers were brought in and these for the most part were Irish immigrants.

This growth in population with the influx of a new immigrant element brought an expansion and reshuffling of the residential areas in the American section. With their mounting wealth the American elements were in a position to move farther out and build themselves new homes. South was the river, north were the swamps, and to the east were the business section and Creole land. Their logical move, therefore, was toward the strip of higher land adjacent to the river, and this move they made, developing a pretentious residential section with large homes and spacious grounds. This section has since been known as the Garden District. At the time it was built, it equaled or surpassed anything the Creoles possessed either in the city or on their plantations, and doubtless served to give the Americans a psychological compensation for their lack of "culture" and family background as compared with the Creoles.

This move of the Americans meant that the Negro residential fringe and the truck gardening zone had to be invaded and pushed out farther. It was the beginning of a process which continued up to relatively recent times both in the Creole and American sections. While in both cases the invasion did take place, the succession was not completed, particularly with reference to the Negro residences, for in all of the older sections of the city today there are scattered small groups of Negro residences which are remnants of a once solid Negro residential zone. Also in moving out the Americans deserted their old residences. Since the Irish were working for the Americans, they were not welcomed in other sections of the city, and being laborers, they needed no land to cultivate. Thus they were glad enough to get the discarded residences and New Orleans gave birth to what has since been known as the Irish Channel.

As the city grew, the Creole area, being adjacent to the central business section, tended to deteriorate and this, with a natural increase in Creole population, created pressure for that group to move out also. If the Americans had their fate sealed as to where they might move, so also did the Creoles. To move east meant crossing the national boundary line of Esplanade Avenue and invading the immigrant truck gardening section and this would violate their pride and honor. To the west was Canal Street, the central business section and the unthinkable American section. Their only recourse was to move out Esplanade Ridge to Bayou St. John, and here today New Orleans has lovely old homes which are a product of this period. The migration process in this area was similar to that in the American section with some significant differences. The invasion process was about the same but the tendency of the Creoles to stay in the French Quarter in spite of deterioration was much greater. Thus there resulted an extraordinarily large number of what in other cities would be called marooned families, and there are in that area today many homes which are still owned and occupied by descendants of the families who originally built them.

Due to administrative and financial difficulties, the three municipalities were recombined into one in 1855, but by that time the ecological pattern was firmly fixed. Esplanade Avenue and Canal Street were made and the

Creole section limited to Esplanade Ridge while the American section was confined to its ridge west of the city.

The strips of habitable land on these ridges were rather narrow and any tendency of these residential areas to widen was quickly checked by the swamps or the river. Therefore, expansion could only take place by building farther and farther out along these ridges. Such building, however, meant greater and greater distances from the central business section, and greater distance meant serious inconvenience when travel was by walking, bicycle or horse and buggy. In the American section, where the growth had been the greatest, the distances became so great as practically to reach the toleration point. Thus further expansion was made with a minimum of land and a minimum of added distance. This was done by making the yards inconveniently small and building the houses close together. Economically, of course, this was reflected in very high land values.

The immigrant truck-gardening section to the east of the city seems to have had, by comparison, relatively few growing pains. Being engaged in agriculture, the residents were not densely settled and, as the city developed, the population turned more and more to non-agricultural occupations. There was little accretion to this area by migration, and the rate of natural increase was not enough to take up for residential uses the land which was thrown out of cultivation. Thus while other sections were crying for land, this section had land to spare. As a result, land in this section became a quicksand for real estate speculators who knew land but did not know New Orleans. For the same reason there was a plentiful supply of land on that side of town for military uses during the First and Second World Wars.

Thus up to the early part of this century the basic ecological pattern of the city was T-shaped. The T was formed by the intersection of Esplanade Ridge and the ridge running along the river. The French Quarter (original French settlement) was approximately at the intersection of this T. The immigrant truck-gardening area was at the east end of the cross bar and on the west end were the central business section, the Irish Channel and the Garden District (American section), respectively. The newer Creole area was on the leg of the T, Esplanade Ridge, running vertically to the river. All of these were long narrow rectangular shaped areas, strung out along the top of the ridges, flanked on both sides by the swamps or the river. The American section and the Creole area were fringed by horseshoe shaped residential areas for Negroes and outside of these was a truck-gardening and dairying zone. The latter used land which was dry enough to cultivate or pasture but too low for residential use.

The New Ecology

During the present century several developments have been taking place which have been materially altering this ecological pattern. About 1910 the city began to attain success in a long effort at artificial drainage of surface water. The city had early used canals and drainage ditches to hasten the flow of water from the ridges to the swamps. Then in the latter part of the last century it tried canals with windmill powered pumps to drain lower sections. These pumps were found inadequate and in 1903 they were replaced by electric-powered centrifugal pumps. These were an improvement but still did not have the capacity necessary for a city with the heavy rainfall which New Orleans has. Finally in 1917 a large screw type of electric pump, something like a ship's propeller installed in a large pipe, was developed and this proved adequate to the task. With these pump developments went a gradual improvement in surface and underground drainage facilities. From small beginnings this system was thus expanded until today it has a pumping capacity of 16½ billion gallons per day (24 hours), enough water to cover eighty square miles of land one foot deep. As a result, the water level was gradually lowered until by the 1930's all of the former swamp areas were as effectively drained as the higher areas.

The development of this drainage system ecologically had the effect of changing the topography of the city. In virtually no place in the city is the change of altitude sudden enough that there is any visible difference between high land and low land. With drainage, therefore, the land, for ecological purposes, is perfectly flat and as far as topography is concerned it is all equally desirable for building purposes. Hence the barrier which the swamps had formerly been to residential expansion was now removed and the residential areas began to respond accordingly. The American section most strikingly turned squarely north away from the river and directly toward the center of a former swamp. Thus during the past two decades, census tracts which are in this former swamp area, show population increases of from 700 to 1400 per cent. The Creole section correspondingly spread out in both directions from the Bayou St. John area, though the population pressure here was not nearly so great as in the American section.

About the time these drainage developments were taking place transportation developments were in process which also had marked effects on the ecological pattern. So far as this city is concerned probably the most important transportation development was the street car. Like other social developments, this one cannot be very specifically dated. Horse-drawn cars and steam "dummies," of course, date well back into the past century. The successful electric car was not developed until about 1885 and its effect on the ecology of the city was not very evident until well into the present century. While the street car aided greatly in relieving pressures in the American and Creole sections, probably its most pronounced effect was on the Negro residential fringe. With the street car available it was no longer necessary for the Negroes to live so close to where they worked. In other words, the electric street car made the Negro residential fringe obsolete. As a result, this fringe began to disappear. In its stead, large Negro residential areas began to develop back towards the central business section in the formerly swampy areas between the white residential sections. This concentration has in turn attracted to these areas schools and other facilities for Negroes which are an incentive for more Negroes to move there.

The automobile which had such profound effects on most American cities had a relatively small effect on New Orleans. It augmented the effect of the street car in a number of ways but since it was not commonly used by Negroes and other poor elements in the population, it created no new trends related to these residential areas. The only part of the city where there was sufficient residential pressure to make a demand for residential suburbs was the American side of the city, and here the outlying areas were so swampy that this was impractical. There did develop on the west end of Metairie Ridge over in an adjoining parish a suburb known as Metairie. However, the 1940 census still showed New Orleans as ranking among the lowest cities in the country in the proportion of its population living in the metropolitan area outside the official city.

In general, the drainage system, the street car and the automobile combined, have created a tendency for New Orleans to shift from its former ecological pattern to a zone system similar to that recognized in other cities. However, this pattern is by no means yet completed and it seems likely it will not soon be completed. Vast areas of the city are still socially taboo to large elements of the population and these do not conform to a symmetrical zone pattern. In addition, on the American side of the city, the drainage did not provide enough land to bring the price of building lots down to what would be considered elsewhere as "reasonable." Therefore, building new homes is still expensive and as a result old ones are not recklessly discarded. Consequently the "nice" old residential areas do not deteriorate except under the greatest of duress. And by the time the natural pressures for deterioration have become sufficiently great these areas have accumulated enough tradition to make them antiques. Thus the French Quarter is now protected by special legislation designed to prevent invasion and deterioration. Under this protection it has actually been undergoing a restoration with middle and upper class Americans moving in. Correspondingly the Garden District has tenaciously remained respectable. The 1940 rent map shows that this district is still one of the high rent areas of the city. Very high order rooming houses are about the only degradation it has yet suffered and to date it has not needed special legislation to protect it. However, should that necessity come, its antiquity is such that it will doubtless be museumized in the legislative halls.

In summary, the ecological pattern of New Orleans up to the present century was primarily the result of its topography. This pattern was set by the ridges and limited by the swamps and the river. In the historical process, sections of these ridges were occupied by the different nationality groups and came to be considered their special domain. Due to the ethnic conflicts and status differences between these nationality groups the social definitions of these areas became very strong and highly emotionalized. As a result of the division of the city into three municipalities in 1836 Canal Street became the accepted boundary line between the American section and the Creole section.

NOTES

1. Fortier, Alcie, *History of Louisiana*, New York, 1904, II, pp. 240–241. Nellie Warner Price, "Le Spectacle de la Rue St. Pierre," *Louisiana Historical Quarterly* I, p. 218.

2. *Annals of Congress, Seventh Congress—Second Session*, Washington, 1851, p. 1525.

3. *Biographical and Historical Memories of Louisiana*, Chicago, 1892, I, p. 30.

4. Klein, Selma L., Social Interaction of the Creoles and Anglo-Americans in New Orleans, 1803–1860, M.A. Thesis, Department of Sociology, Tulane University, 1940, pp. 35–36.

5. *The Bee*, May 29, 1935.

19

WALTER FIREY

SENTIMENT AND SYMBOLISM
AS ECOLOGICAL VARIABLES

Systematization of ecological theory has thus far proceeded on two main premises regarding the character of space and the nature of locational activities. The first premise postulates that the sole relation of space to locational activities is an impeditive and cost-imposing one. The second premise assumes that locational activities are primarily economizing, "fiscal" agents.[1] On the basis of these two premises the only possible relationship that locational activities may bear to space is an economic one. In such a relationship each activity will seek to so locate as to minimize the obstruction put upon its functions by spatial distance. Since the supply of the desired locations is limited it follows that not all activities can be favored with choice sites. Consequently a competitive process ensues in which the scarce desirable locations are preempted by those locational activities which can so exploit advantageous location as to produce the greatest surplus of income over expenditure. Less desirable locations devolve to correspondingly less economizing land uses. The result is a pattern of land use that is presumed to be most efficient for both the individual locational activity and for the community.[2]

Given the contractualistic milieu within which the modern city has arisen and acquires its functions, such an "economic ecology" has had a certain explanatory adequacy in describing urban spatial structure and dynamics. However, as any theory matures and approaches a logical closure of its generalizations it inevitably encounters facts which remain unassimilable to the theoretical scheme. In this paper it will be our purpose to describe certain ecological processes which apparently cannot be embraced in a strictly economic analysis. Our hypothesis is that the data to

Reprinted with permission from *American Sociological Review* 10 (1945): 140–148.

be presented, while in no way startling or unfamiliar to the research ecologist, do suggest an alteration of the basic premises of ecology. This alteration would consist, first, of ascribing to space not only an impeditive quality but also an additional property, *viz.*, that of being at times a symbol for certain cultural values that have become associated with a certain spatial area. Second, it would involve a recognition that locational activities are not only economizing agents but may also bear sentiments which can significantly influence the locational process.[3]

A test case for this twofold hypothesis is afforded by certain features of land use in central Boston. In common with many of the older American cities Boston has inherited from the past certain spatial patterns and landmarks which have had a remarkable persistence and even recuperative power despite challenges from other more economic land uses. The persistence of these spatial patterns can only be understood in terms of the group values that they have come to symbolize. We shall describe three types of such patterns: first, an in-town upper class residential neighborhood known as Beacon Hill; second, certain "sacred sites," notably the Boston Common and the colonial burying-grounds; and third, a lower class Italian neighborhood known as the North End. In each of these land uses we shall find certain locational processes which seem to defy a strictly economic analysis.

The first of the areas, Beacon Hill, is located some five minutes' walking distance from the retail center of Boston. This neighborhood has for fully a century and a half maintained its character as a preferred upper class residential district, despite its contiguity to a low rent tenement area, the West End. During its long history Beacon Hill has become the symbol for a number of sentimental associations which constitute a genuine attractive force to certain old families of Boston. Some idea of the nature of these sentiments may be had from statements in the innumerable pamphlets and articles written by residents of the Hill. References to "this sacred eminence,"[4] "stately old-time appearance,"[5] and "age-old quaintness and charm,"[6] give an insight into the attitudes attaching to the area. One resident reveals rather clearly the spatial referability of these sentiments when she writes of the Hill:

It has a tradition all its own, that begins in the hospitality of a book-lover, and has never lost that flavor. Yes, our streets are inconvenient, steep, and slippery. The corners are abrupt, the contours perverse. . . . It may well be that the gibes of our envious neighbors have a foundation and that these dear crooked lanes of ours were indeed traced in ancestral mud by absent-minded kine.[7]

Behind such expressions of sentiment are a number of historical associations connected with the area. Literary traditions are among the strongest of these; indeed, the whole literary legend of Boston has its focus at Beacon Hill. Many of America's most distinguished literati have occupied homes on the Hill. Present day occupants of these houses derive a genuine satisfaction from the individual histories of their dwellings.[8] One lady whose home had had a distinguished pedigree remarked:

I like living here for I like to think that a great deal of historic interest has happened here in this room.

Not a few families are able to trace a continuity of residence on the Hill for several generations, some as far back as 1800 when the Hill was first developed as an upper class neighborhood. It is a point of pride to a Beacon Hill resident if he can say that he was born on the Hill or was at least raised there; a second best boast is to point out that his forebears once lived on the Hill.

Thus a wide range of sentiments—aesthetic, historical, and familial— have acquired a spatial articulation in Beacon Hill. The bearing of these sentiments upon locational processes is a tangible one and assumes three forms: retentive, attractive, and resistive. Let us consider each of these in order. To measure the retentive influence that spatially-referred sentiments may exert upon locational activities we have tabulated by place of residence all the families listed in the Boston *Social Register* for the years 1894, 1905, 1914, 1929, and 1943. This should afford a reasonably accurate picture of the distribution of upper class families by neighborhoods within Boston and in suburban towns. In Table 19-1 we have presented the tabulations for the three in-town concentrations of upper class families (Beacon Hill, Back Bay, and Jamaica Plain) and for the five main suburban concentrations (Brookline, Newton, Cambridge, Milton, and Dedham). Figure 19-1 portrays these trends in graphic form. The most apparent feature of these data is, of course, the consistent increase of upper class families in the suburban towns and the marked decrease (since 1905) in two of the in-town upper class areas, Back Bay and Jamaica Plain. Although both of these neighborhoods remain fashionable residential districts their prestige is waning rapidly. Back Bay in particular, though still surpassing in numbers any other single neighborhood, has undergone a steady invasion of apartment buildings, rooming houses, and business establishments which are destroying its prestige value. The trend of Beacon Hill has been different. Today it has a larger number of upper

TABLE 19-1

Number of Upper-Class Families in Boston,
by Districts of Concentration, and in
Main Suburban Towns, for Certain Years

	1894	1905	1914	1929	1943
Within Boston					
Beacon Hill	280	242	279	362	335
Back Bay	867	1166	1102	880	556
Jamaica Plain	56	66	64	36	30
Other districts	316	161	114	86	41
Suburban Towns					
Brookline	137	300	348	355	372
Newton	38	89	90	164	247
Cambridge	77	142	147	223	257
Milton	37	71	106	131	202
Dedham	8	29	48	69	99
Other towns	106	176	310	403	816
Total in Boston	1519	1635	1559	1364	962
Total in Suburbs	403	807	1049	1345	1993
Totals	1922	2442	2608	2709	2955

Tabulated from: *Social Register, Boston*.

class families than it had in 1894. Where it ranked second among fashionable neighborhoods in 1894 it ranks third today, being but slightly outranked in numbers by the suburban city of Brookline and by the Back Bay. Beacon Hill is the only in-town district that has consistently retained its preferred character and has held to itself a considerable proportion of Boston's old families.

There is, however, another aspect to the spatial dynamics of Beacon Hill, one that pertains to the "attractive" locational role of spatially referred sentiments. From 1894 to 1905 the district underwent a slight drop, subsequently experiencing a steady rise for 24 years, and most recently undergoing another slight decline. These variations are significant, and they bring out rather clearly the dynamic ecological role of spatial symbolism. The initial drop is attributable to the development of the then new Back Bay. Hundreds of acres there had been reclaimed from marshland and had been built up with palatial dwellings. Fashion now pointed to this as the select area of the city and in response to its dictates a number of families abandoned Beacon Hill to take up more pretentious Back Bay quarters. Property values on the Hill began to depreciate, old dwellings became rooming houses and businesses began to invade some of the streets. But many of the old families remained on the Hill and a few of them made efforts to halt the gradual deterioration of the district. Under the aegis of a realtor, an architect, and a few close friends there was

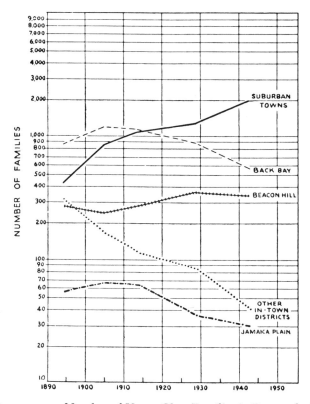

Figure 19–1 Number of Upper Class Families in Boston, by Districts
of Concentration, and in Suburbs, for Certain Years

launched a program of purchasing old houses, modernizing the interiors
and leaving the colonial exteriors intact, and then selling the dwellings to
individual families for occupancy. Frequently adjoining neighbors would
collaborate in planning their improvements so as to achieve an architectural consonance. The results of this program may be seen in the drift of
upper class families back to the Hill. From 1905 to 1929 the number of
Social Register families in the district increased by 120. Assessed valuations showed a corresponding increase: from 1919 to 1924 there was a rise
of 24 percent; from 1924 to 1929 the rise was 25 percent.[9] The nature of
the Hill's appeal, and the kind of persons attracted, may be gathered
from the following popular write-up:

To salvage the quaint charm of Colonial Architecture on Beacon Hill,
Boston, is the object of a well-defined movement among writers and professional folk that promises the most delightful opportunities for the home
seeker of moderate means and conservative tastes. Because men of discernment
were able to visualize the possibilities presented by these architectural land-

marks, and have undertaken the gracious task of restoring them to their former glory, this historic quarter of old Boston, once the centre of literary culture, is coming into its own.[10]

The independent variable in this "attractive" locational process seems to have been the symbolic quality of the Hill, by which it constituted a referent for certain strong sentiments of upper class Bostonians.

While this revival was progressing there remained a constant menace to the character of Beacon Hill, in the form of business encroachments and apartment-hotel developments. Recurrent threats from this source finally prompted residents of the Hill to organize themselves into the Beacon Hill Association. Formed in 1922, the declared object of this organization was "to keep undesirable business and living conditions from affecting the hill district."[11] At the time the city was engaged in preparing a comprehensive zoning program and the occasion was propitious to secure for Beacon Hill suitable protective measures. A systematic set of recommendations was drawn up by the Association regarding a uniform 65-foot height limit for the entire Hill, the exclusion of business from all but two streets, and the restriction of apartment house bulk.[12] It succeeded in gaining only a partial recognition of this program in the 1924 zoning ordinance. But the Association continued its fight against inimical land uses year after year. In 1927 it successfully fought a petition brought before the Board of Zoning Adjustment to alter the height limits in one area so as to permit the construction of a four million dollar apartment-hotel 155 feet high. Residents of the Hill went to the hearing en masse. In spite of the prospect of an additional twenty million dollars worth of exclusive apartment-hotels that were promised if the zoning restrictions were withheld the petition was rejected, having been opposed by 214 of the 220 persons present at the hearing.[13] In 1930 the Association gained an actual reduction in height limits on most of Beacon Street and certain adjoining streets, though its leader was denounced by opponents as "a rank sentimentalist who desired to keep Boston a village."[14] One year later the Association defeated a petition to rezone Beacon Street for business purposes.[15] In other campaigns the Association successfully pressed for the rezoning of a business street back to purely residential purposes, for the lowering of height limits on the remainder of Beacon Street, and for several lesser matters of local interest. Since 1929, owing partly to excess assessed valuations of Boston real estate and partly to the effects of the depression upon families living on securities, Beacon Hill has lost some of its older families, though its decline is nowhere near so precipitous as that of the Back Bay.

Thus for a span of one and a half centuries there have existed on Beacon Hill certain locational processes that largely escape economic analysis. It is the symbolic quality of the Hill, not its impeditive or cost-imposing character, that most tangibly correlates with the retentive, attractive, and resistive trends that we have observed. And it is the dynamic force of spatially referred sentiments, rather than considerations of rent, which explains why certain families have chosen to live on Beacon Hill in preference to other in-town districts having equally accessible location and even superior housing conditions. There is thus a non-economic aspect to land use on Beacon Hill, one which is in some respects actually dis-economic in its consequences. Certainly the large apartment-hotels and specialty shops that have sought in vain to locate on the Hill would have represented a fuller capitalization on potential property values than do residences. In all likelihood the attending increase in real estate prices would not only have benefited individual property holders but would have so enhanced the value of adjoining properties as to compensate for what-ever depreciation other portions of the Hill might have experienced.

If we turn to another type of land use pattern in Boston, that comprised by the Boston Common and the old burying grounds, we encounter another instance of spatial symbolism which has exerted a marked influence upon the ecological organization of the rest of the city. The Boston Common is a survival from colonial days when every New England town allotted a portion of its land to common use as a cow pasture and militia field. Over the course of three centuries Boston has grown entirely around the Common so that today we find a 48-acre tract of land wedged directly into the heart of the business district. On three of its five sides are women's apparel shops, department stores, theaters and other high-rent locational activities. On the fourth side is Beacon Street, extending along-side Beacon Hill. Only the activities of Hill residents have prevented business from invading this side. The fifth side is occupied by the Public Garden. A land value map portrays a strip of highest values pressing upon two sides of the Common, on Tremont and Boylston streets, taking the form of a long, narrow band.

Before considering the ecological consequences of this configuration let us see what attitudes have come to be associated with the Common. There is an extensive local literature about the Common and in it we find interesting sentiments expressed. One citizen speaks of:

. . . the great principle exemplified in the preservation of the Common. Thank Heaven, the tide of money making must break and go around that.[16]

Elsewhere we read:

> Here, in short, are all our accumulated memories, intimate, public, private.[17]

> Boston Common was, is, and ever will be a source of tradition and inspiration from which the New Englanders may renew their faith, recover their moral force, and strengthen their ability to grow and achieve.[18]

The Common has thus become a "sacred" object, articulating and symbolizing genuine historical sentiments of a certain portion of the community. Like all such objects its sacredness derives, not from any intrinsic spatial attributes, but rather from its representation in peoples' minds as a symbol for collective sentiments.[19]

Such has been the force of these sentiments that the Common has become buttressed up by a number of legal guarantees. The city charter forbids Boston in perpetuity to dispose of the Common or any portion of it. The city is further prohibited by state legislation from building upon the Common, except within rigid limits, or from laying out roads or tracks across it.[20] By accepting the bequest of one George F. Parkman, in 1908, amounting to over five million dollars, the city is further bound to maintain the Common, and certain other parks, "for the benefit and enjoyment of its citizens."[21]

What all this has meant for the spatial development of Boston's retail center is clear from the present character of that district. Few cities of comparable size have so small a retail district in point of area. Unlike the spacious department stores of most cities, those in Boston are frequently compressed within narrow confines and have had to extend in devious patterns through rear and adjoining buildings. Traffic in downtown Boston has literally reached the saturation point, owing partly to the narrow one-way streets but mainly to the lack of adequate arterials leading into and out of the Hub. The American Road Builders Association has estimated that there is a loss of $81,000 per day in Boston as a result of traffic delay. Trucking in Boston is extremely expensive. These losses ramify out to merchants, manufacturers, commuters, and many other interests.[22] Many proposals have been made to extend a through arterial across the Common, thus relieving the extreme congestion of Tremont and Beacon streets, the two arterials bordering the park.[23] Earlier suggestions, prior to the construction of the subway, called for street car tracks across the Common. But "the controlling sentiment of the citizens of Boston, and of large numbers throughout the State, is distinctly opposed to allowing any such use of the Common."[24] Boston has long suffered from land shortage and unusually high real estate values as a result both of the narrow confines of the peninsula comprising the city center and as a result of the exclusion from income-yielding uses of so large a tract as the Common.[25] A further difficulty has arisen from the rapid southwesterly extension of the business district in the past two decades. With the Common lying directly in the path of this extension the business district has had to stretch around it in an elongated fashion, with obvious inconvenience to shoppers and consequent loss to businesses.

The Common is not the only obstacle to the city's business expansion. No less than three colonial burying-grounds, two of them adjoined by ancient church buildings, occupy downtown Boston. The contrast that is presented by 9-story office buildings reared up beside quiet cemeteries affords visible evidence of the conflict between "sacred" and "profane" that operates in Boston's ecological pattern. The dis-economic consequences of commercially valuable land being thus devoted to non-utilitarian purposes goes even further than the removal from business uses of a given amount of space. For it is a standard principle of real estate that business property derives added value if adjoining properties are occupied by other businesses.[26] Just as a single vacancy will depreciate the value of a whole block of business frontage, so a break in the continuity of stores by a cemetery damages the commercial value of surrounding properties. But, even more than the Common, the colonial burying-grounds of Boston have become invested with a moral significance with renders them almost inviolable. Not only is there the usual sanctity which attaches to all cemeteries, but in those of Boston there is an added sacredness growing out of the age of the grounds and the fact that the forebears of many of New England's most distinguished families as well as a number of colonial and Revolutionary leaders lie buried in these cemeteries. There is thus a manifold symbolism to these old burying-grounds, pertaining to family lineage, early nationhood, civic origins, and the like, all of which have strong sentimental associations. What has been said of the old burying-grounds applies with equal force to a number of other venerable landmarks in central Boston. Such buildings as the Old South Meeting-House, the Park Street Church, King's Chapel, and the Old State House—all foci of historical associations—occupy commercially valuable land and interrupt the continuity of business frontage on their streets. Nearly all of these landmarks have been challenged at various times by real estate and commercial interests which sought to have them replaced by more profitable uses. In every case community sentiments have resisted such threats.

In all these examples we find a symbol-sentiment relationship which has exerted a significant influence upon land use. Nor should it be thought that such phenomena are mere ecological "sports." Many other older American cities present similar locational characteristics. Delancey Street in Philadelphia represents a striking parallel to Beacon Hill, and certain in-town districts of Chicago, New York, and Detroit, recently revived as fashionable apartment areas, bear resemblances to the Beacon Hill revival. The role of traditionalism in rigidifying the ecological patterns of New Orleans has been demonstrated in a recent study.[27] Further studies of this sort should clarify even further the true scope of sentiment and symbolism in urban spatial structure and dynamics.

As a third line of evidence for our hypothesis we have chosen a rather different type of area from those so far considered. It is a well-known fact that immigrant ghettoes, along with other slum districts, have become areas of declining population in most American cities. A point not so well established is that this decline tends to be selective in its incidence upon residents and that this selectivity may manifest varying degrees of identification with immigrant values. For residence within a ghetto is more than a matter of spatial placement; it generally signifies acceptance of immigrant values and participation in immigrant institutions. Some light on this process is afforded by data from the North End of Boston. This neighborhood, almost wholly Italian in population, has long been known as "Boston's classic land of poverty."[28] Eighteen percent of the dwellings are eighty or more years old, and sixty percent are forty or more years old.[29] Indicative of the dilapidated character of many buildings is the recent sale of a 20-room apartment building for only $500. It is not surprising then to learn that the area has declined in population from 21,111 in 1930 to 17,598 in 1940.[30] To look for spatially referable sentiments here would seem futile. And yet, examination of certain emigration differentials in the North End reveals a congruence between Italian social structure and locational processes. To get at these differentials recourse was had to the estimation of emigration, by age groups and by nativity, through the use of life tables. The procedure consists of comparing the actual 1940 population with the residue of the 1930 population which probably survived to 1940 according to survival rates for Massachusetts. Whatever deficit the actual 1940 population may show from the estimated 1940 population is a measure of "effective emigration." It is not a measure of the actual volume of emigration, since no calculation is made of immigration *into* the district between 1930 and 1940.[31] Effective emigration simply indicates the extent of population decline which is attributable to emigration rather than to death. Computations thus made for emigration differentials by nativity show the following:

TABLE 19-2

Effective Emigration from the North End, Boston, 1930 to 1940, by Nativity

NATIVITY	1930 POPULATION	PER CENT OF 1930 POP. IN EACH NATIVITY GROUP	EFFECTIVE EMIGRATION 1930—1940	PER CENT OF EMIGRATION ACCOUNTED FOR BY EACH NATIVITY GROUP
American-born (second generation)	12553	59.46	3399	76.42
Italian-born (first generation)	8557	40.54	1049	23.58
Totals	21110	100.00	4448	100.00

Calculated from: census tract data and survival rates.

Thus the second generation, comprising but 59.46 percent of the 1930 population, contributed 76.42 percent of the effective emigration from the North End, whereas the first generation accounted for much less than its "due" share of the emigration. Another calculation shows that where the effective emigration of second generation Italians represents 27.08 percent of their number in 1930, that of the first generation represents only 12.26 percent of their number in 1930.

Equally clear differentials appear in effective emigration by age groups. If we compare the difference between the percentage which each age group as of 1930 contributes to the effective emigration, and the percentage which each age group comprised of the 1930 population, we find that the age groups 15-24 account for much more than their share of effective emigration; the age groups 35-64 account for much less than their share.[32] In Table 19–3 the figures preceded by a plus sign indicate "excess" emigration, those preceded by a minus sign indicate "deficit" emigration.

In brief, the North End is losing its young people to a much greater extent than its older people.

These differentials are in no way startling; what is interesting, however, is their congruence with basic Italian values, which find their fullest institutionalized expression in the North End. Emigration from the district may be viewed as both a cause and a symbol of alienation from these values. At the core of the Italian value system are those sentiments which pertain to the family and the *paesani*. Both of these put a high premium upon maintenance of residence in the North End.

279

TABLE 19-3

*Difference Between Percentage Contributed by
Each Age Group to Effective Emigration and
Percentage It Comprised of 1930 Population*

AGE GROUPS AS OF 1930	Differences between Percentages	
	MALE	FEMALE
under 5	−1.70	−0.33
5−9	+0.38	+0.04
10−14	+0.21	+2.66
15−19	+4.18	+3.01
20−24	+2.04	+2.35
25−34	−0.97	−0.07
35−44	−2.31	−1.09
45−54	−1.43	−1.17
55−64	−2.29	−1.19
65−74	−1.13	−0.59
75 and over	uncalculable	

Calculated from: census tract data and survival rates.

Paesani, or people from the same village of origin, show considerable
tendency to live near one another, sometimes occupying much of a single
street or court.[33] Such proximity, or at least common residence in the
North End, greatly facilitates participation in the *paesani* functions which
are so important to the first generation Italian. Moreover, it is in the
North End that the *festas,* anniversaries, and other old world occasions
are held, and such is their frequency that residence in the district is almost
indispensable to regular participation. The social relationships comprised
by these groupings, as well as the benefit orders, secret societies, and religious organizations, are thus strongly localistic in character. One second
generation Italian, when asked if his immigrant parents ever contem-
plated leaving their North End tenement replied:

No, because all their friends are there, their relatives. They know everyone
around there.

It is for this reason that the first generation Italian is so much less inclined
to leave the North End than the American-born Italian.

Equally significant is the localistic character of the Italian family. So
great is its solidarity that it is not uncommon to find a tenement entirely
occupied by a single extended family: grandparents, matured children

with their mates, and grandchildren. There are instances where such a family has overflowed one tenement and has expanded into an adjoining one, breaking out the partitions for doorways. These are ecological expressions, in part, of the expected concern which an Italian mother has for the welfare of her newly married daughter. The ideal pattern is for the daughter to continue living in her mother's house, with she and her husband being assigned certain rooms which they are supposed to furnish themselves. Over the course of time the young couple is expected to accumulate savings and buy their own home, preferably not far away. Preferential renting, by which an Italian who owns a tenement will let apartments to his relatives at a lower rental, is another manifestation of the localizing effects of Italian kinship values.

Departure from the North End generally signifies some degree of repudiation of the community's values. One Italian writes of an emigrant from the North End:

I still remember with regret the vain smile of superiority that appeared on his face when I told him that I lived at the North End of Boston. "*Io non vado fra quella plebaglia.*" (I do not go among those plebeians.)[34]

As a rule the older Italian is unwilling to make this break, if indeed he could. It is the younger adults, American-born and educated, who are capable of making the transition to another value system with radically different values and goals.

Residence in the North End seems therefore to be a spatial corollary to integration with Italian values. Likewise emigration from the district signifies assimilation into American values, and is so construed by the people themselves. Thus, while the area is not the conscious object of sentimental attachment, as are Beacon Hill and the Common, it has nonetheless become a symbol for Italian ethnic solidarity. By virtue of this symbolic quality the area has a certain retentive power over those residents who most fully share the values which prevail there.

It is reasonable to suggest, then, that the slum is much more than "an area of minimum choice."[35] Beneath the surface phenomenon of declining population there may be differential rates of decline which require positive formulation in a systematic ecological theory. Such processes are apparently refractory to analysis in terms of competition for least impeditive location. A different order of concepts, corresponding to the valuative, meaningful aspect of spatial adaptation, must supplement the prevailing economic concepts of ecology.

NOTES

1. See Everett C. Hughes, "The Ecological Aspect of Institutions," *American Sociological Review*. 1: 180–189, April 1936.

2. This assumption of a correspondence between the maximum utility of a private association and that of the community may be questioned within the very framework of marginal utility analysis. See particularly A. C. Pigou, *The Economics of Welfare*. Second Edition, London: 1924, Part II, ch. 8. For a clear presentation of the typical position see Robert Murray Haig, "Towards an Understanding of the Metropolis— the Assignment of Activities to Areas in Urban Regions," *Quarterly Journal of Economics*. 40: 402–434, May 1926.

3. Georg Simmel, "Der Raum und die räumlichen Ordnungen der Gesellschaft," *Soziologie*. Munich: 1923, pp. 518–522; *cf*. Hughes, *op. cit*.

4. John R. Shultz, *Beacon Hill and the Carol Singers*. Boston: 1923, p. 11.

5. *Bulletin of the Society for the Preservation of New England Antiquities*. 4:3, August, 1913.

6. Josephine Samson, *Celebrities of Louisburg Square*. Greenfield, Mass.: 1924.

7. Abbie Farwell Brown, *The Lights of Beacon Hill*. Boston, 1922, p. 4.

8. *Cf*. W. Lloyd Warner and Paul S. Lunt, *The Social Life of a Modern Community*. New Haven, 1941, p. 107, on this pattern.

9. *The Boston Transcript*. April 12, 1930.

10. Harriet Sisson Gillespie, "Reclaiming Colonial Landmarks," *The House Beautiful*. 58: 239–241, September, 1925.

11. *The Boston Transcript*. December 6, 1922.

12. *The Boston Transcript*. March 18, 1933.

13. *The Boston Transcript*. January 29, 1927.

14. *The Boston Transcript*. April 12, 1930.

15. *The Boston Transcript*. January 10, January 29, 1931.

16. Speech of William Everett, quoted in *The Boston Transcript*. March 7, 1903.

17. T. R. Sullivan, *Boston New and Old*. Boston: 1912, pp. 45–46.

18. Joshua H. Jones, Jr., "Happenings on Boston Common," *Our Boston*. 2: 9–15, January, 1927.

19. *Cf*. Emile Durkheim, *The Elementary Forms of the Religious Life*. London: 1915, p. 345.

20. St. 1859, c. 210, paragraph 3; Pub sts. c 54, paragraph 13.

21. M. A. De Wolfe Howe, *Boston Common*. Cambridge: 1910, p. 79.

22. Elisabeth M. Herlihy, Ed., *Fifty Years of Boston*. Boston: 1932, pp. 53–54.

23. See, for example, letter to editor, *The Boston Herald*. November 16, 1930.

24. *First Annual Report of the Boston Transit Commission*. Boston: 1895, p. 9.

25. John C. Kiley, "Changes in Realty Values in the Nineteenth and Twentieth Centuries," *Bulletin of the Business Historical Society*. 15, June, 1941, p. 36; Frank Chouteau Brown, "Boston: More Growing Pains," *Our Boston*. 3, February, 1927, p. 8.

26. Richard M. Hurd, *Principles of City Land Values*. New York: 1903, pp. 93–94.

27. H. W. Gilmore, "The Old New Orleans and the New: A Case for Ecology," *American Sociological Review*. 9: 385–394, August, 1944.

28. Robert A. Woods, Ed., *Americans in Process*. Boston, 1903, p. 5.

29. Finance Commission of the City of Boston, *A Study of Certain of the Effects of Decentralization on Boston and Some Neighboring Cities and Towns*. Boston: 1941, p. 11.

30. Aggregate population of census tracts F1, F2, F4, F5: *Census Tract Data, 1930 Census*, unpublished material from 15th Census of the United States, 1930, compiled

by Boston Health Department, table 1; *Population and Housing—Statistics for Census Tracts, Boston.* 16th Census of the United States, 1940, table 2.

31. By use of *Police Lists* for two different years a count was made of immigration into a sample precinct of the North End. The figure (61) reveals so small a volume of immigration that any use of it to compute actual emigration by age groups would have introduced statistical unreliability into the estimates. Survival rates for Massachusetts were computed from state life tables in: National Resources Committee, *Population Statistics, 2. State Data.* Washington: 1937, Part C, p. 38. The technique is outlined in C. Warren Thornthwaite, *Internal Migration in the United States.* Philadelphia: 1934, pp. 19–21.

32. Obviously most of the emigrants in the 15–24 age group in 1930 migrated while in the age group 20–29; likewise the emigrants in the 35–64 age group migrated while in the 40–69 age group.

33. William Foote Whyte, *Street Corner Society.* Chicago: 1943, p. xix.

34. Enrico C. Sartorio, *Social and Religious Life of Italians in America.* Boston: 1918, pp. 43–44.

35. R. D. McKenzie, "The Scope of Human Ecology," in Ernest W. Burgess, Ed., *The Urban Community.* Chicago: 1926, p. 180.

20

LEO F. SCHNORE

THE GROWTH OF
METROPOLITAN SUBURBS

Decentralization is clearly one of the most significant movements in the long history of urban communities. In the United States the shift to the suburbs began around a few large cities toward the close of the nineteenth century,[1] but it is no longer confined to a mere handful of super-cities. As time has passed, the outward thrust of urban population has become characteristic of smaller and smaller places, and there is no indication that the movement is abating.

Fortunately, social scientists have charted the major trends involved in this suburban revolution during recent decades. The careful historical studies by Thompson, Bogue, and Hawley have described the outstanding population shifts from the turn of the century to the most recent census.[2] They show the principal patterns of growth in the major geographic components of the metropolitan area as a whole, and though they concentrate on comparisons *between* the central city and its surrounding ring, they also show patterns of re-distribution *within* these broad areas.

Within the framework provided by these extensive studies of decentralization, two major tasks remain: (1) intensive research filling in the *descriptive* details of the suburban movement, and (2) refinement of a general theory making greater *analytical* sense out of the facts assembled. This report is part of a larger study undertaken in accordance with these broad objectives.

On the descriptive side, this report has a narrow focus. Growth rates for a single decade (1940–1950) are shown for only the larger incorporated places (10,000 and over) lying within the rings of the Standard Metropolitan Areas of the United States.[3] On the conceptual side, the paper has

Reprinted with permission from *American Sociological Review* 22 (1957): 165–173.

broader scope, exploring the relationship between the growth and the functions of these larger suburbs.

The Functions of Urban Areas. Theoretically, urban areas are usually conceived as large and dense concentrations of people engaged in non-agricultural functions. Since they cannot be self-sufficient, they must produce some goods and/or services for exchange, i.e. for consumption by another population. Urban areas differ widely in the major functions that they discharge, and the literature contains a large number of urban typologies in which places are classified according to their "basic" functions.[4] Internally, however, every urban place must maintain a substantial complement of persons employed in the ancillary activities that provide for the requirements of the inhabitants directly engaged in its major industries. Thus no matter what the principal export it produces, every urban area must allocate a certain portion of its activities to "non-basic" maintenance functions.[5]

Urban Population Growth. Existing urban theory holds that population growth and the major functions of a given area are definitely related. Urban population is assumed to have a functional base, for the very support of the population of a particular place is thought to depend upon its participation in an extensive set of exchange relationships. Population growth requires an increase in this participation, with a corresponding expansion of economic opportunities. Relative differences in the spatial distribution of these opportunities are thought to be the major influences operating to bring about changes in population distribution by determining the size and the direction of migrant streams.[6]

In this theoretical context, a number of writers have recently spoken of a so-called "multiplier principle" to describe the dynamics of urban population growth. Stated in simplified form, the principle is that (1) increasing economic opportunities in "basic" industries cause population growth; (2) population growth, in turn, causes further increases in employment opportunities—this time in the "non-basic" industries—so that (3) still further increments are added to the total population of the area.[7]

On the whole, available theory offers a coherent set of hypotheses regarding urban population growth. Urban growth is related to urban functions in a remarkably clear-cut fashion. Moreover, empirical studies of large areal units have indicated a high degree of predictive power for this conceptual approach.[8]

Suburbs, however, pose a different population-growth problem. The relationships between growth and function, as stated for urban areas in general, are not immediately evident when suburbs are examined.

The Functions of Suburbs. Suburbs obviously differ widely in the functions that they discharge. In the traditional popular image, the suburb is little more than the dwelling place of people who work in the central city. While it is correct to characterize many suburbs as literally "dormitory towns" and "bedroom cities," a true picture of metropolitan suburbs must not ignore the fact that many of them are far from exclusively residential areas. Some are primarily devoted to the fabrication of manufactured goods. At the present time, for example, both light and heavy industries are the dominant elements in the functioning of some suburbs in every part of the country. Industrial suburbs, in fact, have a long history.[9] Still other suburbs are basically given over to the provision of specialized services of one kind or another—notably education and recreation—and it is even possible to find suburbs primarily dependent upon extractive industries, such as mining and oil production. In an economic sense, then, the range of specialties found among suburbs approaches that discoverable in other cities.

Despite this wide variation in specific functions, however, a strong case has been made in the literature for the recognition of only two major types of suburb—*industrial* and *residential*. Douglass, an observer of an earlier phase of suburban development, saw these as the two types most apparent in the 'twenties.[10] Moreover, this view was also adopted by Harris, despite the fact that he developed a detailed six-part suburban typology. "The commonest types of suburb," he wrote in 1943, "are housing or dormitory suburbs and manufacturing or industrial suburbs."[11]

More generally, suburbs can be identified as *residential* and *employing*. Centers of employment mainly devoted to education, mining, recreation, etc. may be combined with those concentrating in manufacturing. Such places may be called *employing suburbs*, no matter what their specific products may be. They can be contrasted with *residential suburbs*, which employ relatively few people within their own boundaries. The basis for this distinction is whether or not the suburb draws more workers to its confines every day than the number of working people who sleep there every night. These two types of suburb are "attracting" and "dispersing" areas, reflecting the shift between day-time and night-time population.[12]

Suburban Population Growth. Existing theory tends to assume that both types of suburb, like other urban areas, grow primarily in response to an expansion of employment opportunities, particularly in the so-called "basic" industries. On theoretical grounds, however, they would not be expected to grow equally. Since the employing suburb has a net excess of jobs, it offers more economic opportunities, and it should logically exhibit higher rates of growth than the residential suburb. The only immediately relevant findings from prior research are to be found in a study by Harris, in which growth rates between 1930 and 1940 were reported for the suburbs in eleven large Metropolitan Districts. "Among individual suburbs of more than 10,000 population," according to Harris, "those classified as residential averaged 11.7 per cent increase in population, compared to 1.7 per cent for those classified as industrial."[13]

In the present study, a similar differential was found for the 1940–1950 decade. The rate for all residential suburbs (31.9 per cent) was almost twice that for all employing suburbs (17.0 per cent). Although this differential is not so large as that reported by Harris, it is in the same direction, i.e., in favor of the residential suburbs.

Moreover, this differential tends to persist when other relevant factors are held constant. The limited number of cases prohibits simultaneous control in a cross-tabular format, but successive controls can be applied.[14]

Horizontal examination of Table 20–1 shows that residential suburbs tended to grow faster than employing suburbs in all regions (Panel A), in all central city size classes (Panel B), in all suburban size classes (Panel C), in all concentric distance zones (Panel D), and in metropolitan areas of every major type of economic activity (Panel E).

Only one exception appears in Panel F, where the prevailing differential is reversed in one of the three rental classes, i.e., among high-rent suburbs. The only major reversal is found in Panel G, where suburbs are classified according to their dates of incorporation. The differential in favor of residential suburbs is seen to characterize only the older suburbs, i.e., those incorporated before 1900.[15]

These data are difficult to interpret in terms of economic opportunities. On first examination, the growth rates of *employing* suburbs in the past two decades might appear to support the theory. The very low average rate of growth between 1930 and 1940 can be viewed as nothing more than the result of the severe limitations on manufacturing activity that occurred during this depression decade. In turn, the resumption of substantial industrial activity between 1940 and 1950 might seem to account for the ten-fold increase in growth rates in this type of suburb.

By definition, the employing suburb does offer economic opportunities, since it provides jobs for more than the number of local residents who are employed. Still, the subordinate status of many employing suburbs prevents them from enjoying full autonomy with respect to growth. For example, employing suburbs that provide goods and services primarily for the central city are necessarily sensitive to events occurring there, such as changes in the number of inhabitants of the metropolis, or changes in its income level. At best, then, the theory offers an incomplete explanation of growth in employing suburbs.

TABLE 20-1

Growth Rates in Metropolitan Suburbs of 10,000 or More Inhabitants, by Functional Type and Other Characteristics

Selected Characteristics of Metropolitan Suburbs	Per Cent Increase in Population, 1940–50			Number of Suburbs		
	Residental	Employing	All Suburbs	Residential	Employing	All Suburbs
A. Region location						
Northeast	13.3	6.1	8.1	65	110	175
North Central	30.0	17.1	22.8	65	57	122
West	63.6	47.1	53.1	37	43	80
South	77.4	47.4	60.4	20	19	39
B. Central city size						
500,000 or more	27.8	12.4	18.2	136	142	278
100,000–500,000	36.1	13.8	21.6	32	40	72
Less than 100,000	79.5	36.9	42.9	19	47	66
C. Suburban size						
50,000 or more	15.1	10.0	11.5	17	31	48
25,000–50,000	18.8	14.9	15.8	18	55	73
10,000–25,000	30.9	19.1	24.4	90	102	192
Less than 10,000	104.1	92.6	99.3	62	41	103
D. Distance from central city						
0–10 miles	27.2	16.4	20.8	112	92	204
10–20 miles	40.8	18.2	25.3	61	84	145
20 miles or more	29.4	15.9	18.1	14	53	145
E. Metropolitan area economic base						
Manufacturing	23.6	12.2	16.1	79	105	184
Diversified	33.0	19.3	23.9	89	98	187
Retail	68.9	23.4	39.2	17	23	40
Other	412.7	64.8	103.4	2	3	5
F. Suburban rent level						
Low	31.7	12.8	15.9	7	26	33
Average	29.0	15.1	18.8	91	173	264
High	36.3	44.1	38.4	89	30	119
G. Age of suburb						
More than 50 years	21.8	12.2	15.0	102	178	280
40–50 years	33.1	36.2	34.6	35	31	66
30–40 years	51.8	66.2	57.5	25	12	37
Less than 30 years	116.6	168.5	126.6	25	8	33
All suburbs	31.9	17.0	22.1	187	229	416

However, if the existing theory of urban growth meets resistance in the case of employing suburbs, *residential* suburbs are even less amenable to it. The higher average rates of growth in these suburbs during both of the last two decades can hardly be attributed to an expansion of economic opportunities within their own boundaries. It must be remembered that the residential suburb itself employs relatively few people within its own confines, and these chiefly in such "non-basic" activities as retail trade and services. As indicated above, increases in these "non-basic" employment opportunities are commonly treated, within the very framework of the theory, as themselves dependent upon local population growth.

More important, residential suburbs are intrinsically dependent upon other areas. With respect to population growth, almost nothing than can occur within the boundaries of such a suburb is potentially as significant as changes that may occur in the other areas that employ its residents. In the light of these considerations, existing theory falls far short of explaining over-all suburban growth, and it fails entirely to account for growth differentials between types of suburb.

Limitations of Existing Theory. Why should the available theory offer so much in explaining growth differentials between large areas (e.g., regions) and fail to explain growth differentials between suburbs? The first major difficulty encountered by the theory in the case of suburbs stems from the fact that these places are only parts of a larger functional entity, the metropolitan community. The theory of economic opportunities contains a hidden assumption with respect to functional self-containment. As a result, the theory can be valid only for areal units that possess a rather high degree of self-sufficiency. This is apparently the reason for the theory's great explanatory utility in the studies of whole regions and even nations.

Moreover, the theory does not take full account of the increasing flexibility of local transportation in recent decades. Innovations in transportation and communication have permitted community functions to be diffused over a wider territory within loss of contact, and this spatial spread involves an increasing flow of persons between the sites of their various activities. The significance of commuting for population growth is that it may supplant migration as an adjustment on the part of the local labor force to shifting or declining opportunities for employment.[16] As a consequence, residential areas may continue to grow as long as employment opportunities continue to expand anywhere within an extremely broad commuting radius.

It can hardly be said that transportation improvements have been ignored in urban theory. They have received some attention in most discussions of decentralization to be found in the literature. These innovations, however, have been conceived as little more than permissive factors. They are generally said to have set the conditions under which suburban growth could occur. Other factors are undoubtedly at work, but these other factors are increasingly sought in a rather narrow sphere.

Most analysts who have devoted attention to the subject of suburbanization have apparently assumed that the causes of the centrifugal shift are ultimately to be found in the motives of the individuals involved in the movement. Even the human ecologists, who are often thought to be "anti-psychological," are prone to shift to motivational explanations when it comes to suburbanization. In keeping with a general tendency within our discipline, social psychology is coming to supplant the sociological approach in this problem area.

Thus while stressing the key role of economic opportunities for larger units, such as regions, most writers turn to an analysis of the motives of individual migrants in dealing with decentralization within local areas. Such a procedure rests upon the tacit assumption that explanations of growth in areas of different size must somehow require entirely different approaches, involving different units of analysis and a different range of variables.

It might appear that the evidence presented here offers additional support for such a procedure. After all, the theory—as it has been stated for urban areas in general—clearly fails to account for the observed growth differential in favor of residential suburbs. These results might seem to call for an immediate shift to a social-psychological approach. Indeed, the ultimate explanation may very well lie in the attitudes, motives, values, etc. of the individuals involved in this movement. However, there is a theoretical alternative at least worthy of exploration. The admitted weaknesses of the existing theory might better be resolved not by its abandonment but by modification of certain basic concepts.

A Proposed Modification of the Theory

The first step in this direction is to state the conditions under which factors other than narrowly defined economic opportunities might be important in the determination of growth differentials. Rather than to abandon the concept of opportunities, a logical alternative is to expand it to subsume more than employment.

One consideration so fundamental that it is easily overlooked is that the population of any area must have housing and the related amenities of life. Our attention is drawn to the housing factor for a very simple reason: dwelling units must exist in a given area before people can be enumerated there on a *de jure* basis, and before population growth can be registered in U. S. census statistics.

If the concept of opportunities is broadened to include opportunities for housing, we can propose the following general hypothesis. Within local areas of the metropolitan community, differential population growth is primarily determined by the distribution of differential housing opportunities, and especially by the different patterns of building activity evidenced in various sub-areas.[17] Within this theoretical context, in which emphasis is placed upon *housing opportunities,* it is possible to develop specific sub-hypotheses regarding growth differentials between types of suburb. (1) Residential suburbs are growing rapidly because they are becoming even more residential in character, by means of large increments in housing construction. (2) At the same time, employing suburbs are growing less rapidly because they are becoming more exclusively devoted to industry and other employment-providing activities. In these employing places, the net effect of this increased specialization in production and employment is (a) to drive out pre-existent residential uses of land, and (b) to discourage new construction of housing.

Indirect evidence in support of these hypotheses can be adduced by considering central cities themselves. The typical central city is obviously undergoing a conversion to a different range of land uses. Formerly the principal place of residence of its own labor force, it is now being turned over to other urban uses—commerce, industry, and transportation. The concomitant of this trend in land-use conversion is the outward shift of population that is reflected in the growth differentials in favor of the metropolitan ring.[18]

The established employing suburbs appear to be undergoing the very same process of land-use conversion. Thus the oldest employing suburbs themselves are evidently decentralizing at a fairly rapid pace, with only their rates of natural increase preventing most of them from suffering absolute losses in population. In fact, the older employing suburbs are probably losing large numbers directly to the residential suburbs via migration.[19]

The Role of Housing. The hypotheses stated above assert that differential housing opportunities are the major determinants of growth differentials between sub-areas of the metropolitan community. In the interest of complete analysis, we must go on to ask *why* new housing construction is occurring *where* it is, since we are dealing with growth in different types of area.

Here again a social-psychological approach might seem to be in order, since it is obviously individuals who occupy dwellings and who change residences. But it should be pointed out that relatively few people in a metropolitan area choose a site and then have a house "built to order." On the contrary, the typical purchase is "ready-made" in a large development. Very few urbanite home owners have a hand in the selection of sites where residential construction will take place, and control over location is even more limited in the case of renters.

In a complex economy, the choices of building sites are made by contractors, real estate operators, and others, notably those involved in the initial capitalization of new developments. Families and individuals are not decisive agents in the process of land-use conversion.[20] When asked about their residential movements, the "reasons" they offer to an interviewer may be misleading in the extreme.

Like other "choices" the housing decisions of individuals are strictly limited by objective conditions. Among these conditions, which include the timing and placing of available housing facilities, the *location* of dwelling units will continue to receive emphasis here, since we are dealing with growth differentials between types of area. Once again it will be instructive to consider the case of the metropolis itself.[21]

The existing literature contains a number of hypotheses that attempt to account for the rapid expansion of residential construction in the metropolitan ring as a whole, and the limited building activity within the central city. First, high rates of construction at the periphery may simply be a consequence of the *exhaustion of space for residential development* in the central city. There is undoubtedly some merit to this view, but sheer space alone is hardly decisive, since the percentage of vacant land in most large cities is strikingly high.[22] However, a large proportion of this area is unsuitable for residential development for reasons of cost, location, or prohibitive zoning laws. Among these limitations, it seems probable that *the high cost of land* in the central city is particularly significant, acting as a deterrent to residential use.

Less frequently mentioned, but a matter of increasing importance, is the fact that great economies are made possible by *the mass production of housing*. While vacant land within the city itself is considerable in the aggregate, it tends to be split into a multitude of small parcels. The increasing use of mass production methods in constructing dozens or even hundreds of dwelling units at the same time and in the same contiguous area permits large savings to be made by the builders, with mass buying of materials adding still further savings.[23]

However, purely "spatial" or "economic" considerations are not the only factors operating to determine the sites of housing construction. There is also an important sociological factor. It appears that the locations of the *dominant units in the community* set the broad pattern of land use for smaller and less powerful units, such as households. In one sense, this is nothing more than another expression of the relationships already observed between (1) "basic" industries, (2) residential population, and (3) "non-basic" industries.[24] The re-distribution of residential population must be viewed in a context that recognizes the vital influence of these other factors.

Conclusions and Implications

If the hypotheses set forth here have any validity, one important theoretical conclusion is in order. The metropolitan community must be undergoing a process of increasingly specialized land use, in which sub-areas of the community are devoted more and more exclusively to a limited range of functions. The result of this mounting "territorial differentiation" is increasing segregation, with similar units and similar functions clustering together.[25] At the very least, there is a bifurcation between the broad functions of consumption and production, i.e., between residence and employment,[26] and the real significance of transportation improvements for the local re-distribution of population is in creating a new scale of distance. In this context, the growth differentials discussed here may be interpreted as mere reflections of a fundamental alteration of community organization in the direction of greater functional and territorial complexity.

Technological and organizational changes are apparently crucial in determining both numerical and distributional changes in population. The outward shift of residential population measured in recent studies can be viewed as one aspect of an important modification in the internal organization of the modern urban community. Under the impetus of technological advances in transportation and communication, the compact city is a thing of the past. Increasing territorial differentiation has been made possible by the increasing flexibility of movement within the total community. Urban functions and urban populations are now spread over a greatly expanded area. Such a radical change in the spatial distribution of urban functions and of urban people apparently represents an adaptive response to the changing conditions of modern urban life. In long-range terms, decentralization can be conceived as a shift toward a new equilibrium that was initiated by the development of new facilities for the movement of persons, commodities, and information.

NOTES

Revised version of paper read at the annual meeting of the American Sociological Society, September, 1956. The data presented in this report were initially assembled while the writer held a Research Training Fellowship from the Social Science Research Council.

1. Adna F. Weber, *The Growth of Cities in the Nineteenth Century*, New York: Columbia University Press, 1899.

2. Warren S. Thompson, *The Growth of Metropolitan Districts in the United States, 1900–1940*, Washington: Government Printing Office, 1947; Donald J. Bogue, *Population Growth in Standard Metropolitan Areas, 1900–1950*, Washington: Government Printing Office, 1953; Amos H. Hawley, *The Changing Shape of Metropolitan America*, Glencoe: Free Press, 1956.

3. Among the 168 Standard Metropolitan Areas defined in the 1950 Census only 66 contain incorporated suburbs of 10,000 or more inhabitants. Among those with more than one officially-designated central city, only the largest is treated as the central city in this study, with all other places classified as suburbs. Exceptions to this procedure were made in three areas (Allentown-Bethlehem, Pa., Minneapolis-St. Paul, Minn., and Springfield-Holyoke, Mass.) where twin central cities were recognized.

4. See the references cited in Leo F. Schnore, "The Functions of Metropolitan Suburbs," *American Journal of Sociology*, 61 (March, 1956), p. 453.

5. See Otis Dudley Duncan and Albert J. Reiss, Jr., Part IV, "Functional Specialization of Communities," in their *Social Characteristics of Urban and Rural Communities, 1950*, New York: John Wiley, 1956; and John W. Alexander, "The Basic-Nonbasic Concept of Urban Economic Functions," *Economic Geography*, 30 (July, 1954), pp. 246–261.

6. See Amos H. Hawley, *Human Ecology*, New York: Ronald Press, 1950. Population can grow by either natural increase or net migration, but the latter component has served as the major source of over-all urban growth in the past. As a result, the literature on urban growth has understandably stressed migration.

7. For a detailed discussion and further references see John R. P. Friedmann, *The Spatial Structure of Economic Development in the Tennessee Valley*, Chicago: University of Chicago Program of Education and Research in Planning, Research Paper No. 1, 1955.

8. See Harry Jerome, *Migration and Business Cycles*, New York: National Bureau of Economic Research, 1926; and Dorothy S. Thomas, *Social and Economic Aspects of Swedish Population Movements, 1750–1933*, New York: Macmillan Company, 1941.

9. Graham R. Taylor, *Satellite Cities*, New York and London: D. Appleton and Company, 1950.

10. Harlan Paul Douglass, *The Suburban Trend*, New York and London: Century Company, 1925, and "Suburbs," in *The Encyclopedia of the Social Sciences*, New York: Macmillan Company, 1934, 14, pp. 433–435.

11. Chauncy D. Harris, "Suburbs," *American Journal of Sociology*, 49 (July, 1943), p. 6.

12. This dichotomy is based upon the "employment–residence ratio" computed by Jones for all places of 10,000 or more inhabitants in 1950. It is simply the ratio of (1) *the number of people employed in the suburb* in (a) manufacturing, (b) retail trade, (c) wholesale trade, and (d) personal, business, and repair services to (2) *the number of employed residents of the suburb,* and it is computed by the formula: (1) $\div$ (2) $\times$ 100. The suburbs identified as *employing* centers in this study have a ratio of 85 or above, with all suburbs having a lower ratio classified as *residential* centers. Source: Victor Jones, "Economic Classification of Cities and Metropolitan Areas," in *The Municipal Year Book,* 1953, Chicago: International City Managers' Association, 1953, pp. 49–57. These and the other data from the same source are used here with the kind permission of the publisher.

13. Harris, *op. cit.,* pp. 10–11.

14. The definitions of the control variables are as follows: (A) The *regional* delineation used here is the one developed by the U. S. Bureau of the Census. (B–C) *size* classifications are according to the number of inhabitants in 1940, the beginning of the decade under study. (D) Each suburb's *distance* classification is based upon radial measurement between its approximate geographic center and the site of the city hall in the central city. (E) Each suburb is classified according to the *economic base* of the metropolitan area as a whole in 1950. The areas Jones has designated as "Mm" (manufacturing centers) are treated as *manufacturing* areas in this study. Areas classified by Jones as "M" (industrial centers) and "Mr" (diversified centers with manufacturing predominant) are here combined under the heading of *diversified* areas. Jones' types "Rm" (diversified centers with retail trade predominant) and "Rr" (retail trade centers) are here labelled *retail* areas. All of the other types identified by Jones (mining, education, wholesale trade, government, transportation, and resort or retirement centers) are here combined in the residual *other* category. Space limitations preclude a listing of the detailed definitions of each type, which may be found in Jones, *op. cit.* (F) Median *rent* levels for the suburbs in 1950 are classified as follows: *low*—five dollars or more below the median for the entire metropolitan area in which the suburb is located; *average*—within a range of five dollars below to ten dollars above the median for the entire area; *high*—more than ten dollars above the median for the entire area. (Source: Jones, *ibid.*) (G) the *age* of the suburb is approximated by its date of incorporation.

15. A vertical examination of Table 20–1 suggests that growth rates are related to six of the seven variables taken separately, for both types of suburb. These relationships merely serve here as *prima facie* evidence of the need for controlling these variables in the examination of growth differentials according to functional type.

16. See Hawley, *Human Ecology, op. cit.*; and Kate K. Liepmann, *The Journey to Work,* New York: Oxford University Press, 1944.

17. Housing opportunities, of course, represented the operational definition used in Samuel Stouffer's well-known study, "Intervening Opportunities: A Theory Relating Mobility and Distance," *American Sociological Review,* 5 (December, 1940), pp. 845–857.

18. These statements are documented in Dorothy K. Newman, "Metropolitan Area Structure and Growth as Shown by Building-Permit Statistics," *Business Topics,* 4 (November, 1956), pp. 1–7.

19. Space limitations preclude the discussion of fertility and mortality differentials between types of suburb that may contribute to the observed growth differentials.

20. See William H. Form, "The Place of Social Structure in the Determination of Land Use," *Social Forces,* 32 (May, 1954), pp. 317–323. In addition, the historical context must be kept in mind. Available housing data indicate that the typical metropolitan area comprised a seller's market between 1940 and 1950. In other words, aggregate demand was usually well in excess of the supply of housing available.

21. It may be objected that this presentation ignores the decision-making process

among contractors and others who actually initiate housing construction. It is true that discussion of the social-psychological aspect of residential mobility and population redistribution is deliberately avoided in this paper. Those who are interested in motivational aspects of decentralization might do well to explore the motives of contractors, real estate operators, and financiers, rather than concern themselves exclusively with those of individual householders.

22. Harland Bartholomew, *Land Uses in American Cities*, Cambridge: Harvard University Press, 1955.

23. The importance of large tracts of vacant and cheap land is itself suggested by the fact that the very highest rates of growth in the metropolitan area between 1940 and 1950 were registered in unincorporated rural territory.

24. Hawley, *Human Ecology, op. cit.*, pp. 276–286. "Basic" industries locate at particular sites with the residential population taking up positions with reference to these centers of production and employment. The distribution of residential population, in turn, is the prime determinant of the location of such "non-basic" activities as retail trade and services.

25. The clearest statement of this development is to be found in R. D. McKenzie, *The Metropolitan Community*, New York: McGraw-Hill Book Company, 1933. For more recent empirical evidence, see Leslie Kish, "Differentiation in Metropolitan Areas," *American Sociological Review*, 19 (August, 1954), pp. 388–398.

26. See Leo F. Schnore, "The Separation of Home and Work: A Problem for Human Ecology," *Social Forces*, 32 (May, 1954), pp. 336–343.

21

WILLIAM H. FORM, JOEL SMITH, GREGORY P. STONE,
AND JAMES COWHIG

THE COMPATIBILITY OF
ALTERNATIVE APPROACHES
TO THE DELIMITATION
OF URBAN SUB-AREAS

Locating the boundaries of urban sub-areas has been an emerging contro-versial issue among sociologists over the past decade. Before that time, traditional ecologists dominated the scene by presenting rather simple and direct means of isolating sub-areas or census tracts. More recently some urban sociologists have contended that the distribution of social phenomena may not be directly dependent on variations in land use, natural barriers, and other ecological factors. They contend that the social integration of areas should be considered as important in this regard as ecological criteria. Demographers have also suggested that population indices are very sensitive to differences among the social sub-areas of cities. Other interested students have adopted a synthetic approach— suggesting that ecological, demographic, and social criteria are equally important in deriving a set of urban sub-areas useful for sociological inves-tigations.[1] Yet, almost no research has attempted to show the relations among these criteria.[2]

During the past two years a research team at Michigan State College has attempted to attack this problem as part of a long range study in Lansing, Michigan.[3] In the process of setting up a census tract plan, ecological, demographic, and social indices were used to derive separate sub-areas for the city. The question this study posed is, "What are the various implications for sociological research of subdividing a city accord-ing to one or the other of the sets of indices used?" The resolution of this

Reprinted with permission from *American Sociological Review* 19 (1954): 434–440.

question has consequences both theoretical and methodological for urban sociology, ecology, and deriving census tracts in urban areas.

Answering this question involved the amassing of a great amount of data, most of which had to be obtained from unpublished sources and extensive interviewing. Ecological data were made available from the Lansing City Plan Commission, demographic data from the U. S. Bureau of the Census, social data from about 550 interviews with residents of the city and 200 interviews with local businessmen. These data were supplemented by continuous field study. Because the analysis is still in its preliminary stage, the observations made here are restricted to selected methodological problems in deriving a sub-area plan.

Ecological Sub-Areas

The preparation of an ecologically drawn map of sub-areas[4] was achieved on the basis of traditional criteria. Specifically, they were:

(1) Natural boundaries or barriers, such as rivers, parks, playgrounds, topographic features, railroads, main streets, factories, and highways.
(2) Prevailing land use and zoning plans.
(3) Value of dwelling units.
(4) Racial segregation.

Data for determining boundaries according to the last three criteria were available by blocks. Other data, such as monthly rental and number of dwelling units, were also available but were not useful. The clearcut distribution of rivers, railroads, industry, public property, and main streets facilitated the task of locating sub-areas in Lansing by the ecological approach. The resultant 35 natural ecological areas appear in Figure 21–1.

Demographic Sub-Areas

The task here was to see whether Lansing could be subdivided by the criterion of homogeneity applied to demographic data.[5] These were made available by the U. S. Census Bureau for all of the 139 enumeration districts of Lansing. These data were computed to establish for each district the percentages of population non-white, foreign-born, male, under

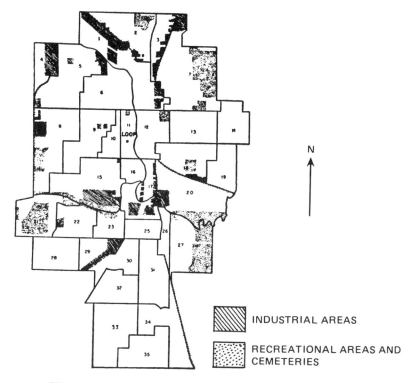

N

INDUSTRIAL AREAS

RECREATIONAL AREAS AND
CEMETERIES

Figure 21–1   Areas of Lansing Based on Ecological Criteria

21 years, over 55 years, and the ratio of population under 21 to population 55 and over, and the fertility ratio.

Two operations were involved—(1) the development of a technique to
describe the demographic characteristics of each district that would make
its position *on each of the seven sets of data comparable,* and (2) the
development of a technique to group districts with similar profiles.

(1) It was decided to shift from a classification of districts based on
raw data to a classification *based on deviations from city ratios.* Thus a
chi-square test of goodness of fit was computed for each enumeration
district on all seven demographic indices, making it possible to describe
the probability that each enumeration district departed from the city distribution for each demographic characteristic. Then districts were grouped
in classes according to a prearranged set of seven probability limits[6] and
were mapped.

(2) In order to develop a technique to group districts with similar
profiles, it was decided to subject the enumeration district probability
data in (1) above to a Guttman scale analysis. The steps in this process
are reported elsewhere.[7] Only the results need to be reviewed here. The

66 enumeration districts with a surplus of foreign-born formed a scale with 90 per cent reproducibility on the items of "under 21 years," "race," and "sex." This yielded five scale types. The 63 districts with surpluses of native-born residents were found to form a scale with 85.2 per cent reproducibility on the items of "age ratio," "fertility ratio," and "sex." This yielded five scale types.

These areas of demographic homogeneity were then mapped as in Figure 21–2 by combining contiguous enumeration districts of like scale types. About sixty per cent of the area and population of the city were included in these contiguous areas. It would have been possible to include another twenty per cent of the districts and population in the demographic map by admitting a wider range of scale types. The substantive interpretation of Figure 21–2, which cannot be done here, involves an analysis of the composition, relative size, and distribution of each scale type. Suffice it to say that the size and shape of these demographic areas vary considerably. Some areas stretch across almost half of the city, while others are smaller and more compact. The boundaries of these demographic areas do not follow ecological barriers in any consistent way. Confusion in interpreting Figure 21–2 is heightened by the arbitrary

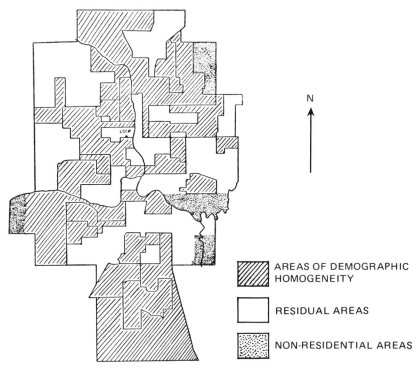

Figure 21–2   Demographic Areas of Lansing

character of the boundaries of the enumeration districts. However this method of spatial demographic analysis is useful and will be explored further when population data are made available for more meaningfully drawn sub-areas of the city.

Social Sub-Areas

Deriving the pattern of social areas for Lansing proved to be the most difficult step. Initially, the research committee decided to give the social criterion primacy in determining the final sub-area plan. The central hypothesis was that the city may be divided into areas which may vary in a range from high integration to either disintegration or non-integration. The criteria selected to determine the state of integration of a sub-area were: (1) consensus on local boundaries, (2) consensus on community solidarity, (3) identification with the local area, (4) locality consciousness, (5) use of local facilities, and (6) development of local formal and informal organization. Information on all of these factors was available from over 500 interviews with Lansing residents. These interviews represented at least one family in slightly more than one-half of the blocks in the city. Thus a relatively large spatial sample was available. However, using each of these factors separately or together to locate the social areas presented an almost insurmountable problem.

To orient ourselves, overlay spot maps were made of many of the above social items in the hope that clusterings of traits in different sections of the city would be apparent. Extreme responses which reflected differences in neighborhood intimacy, estimates of types of neighborhood change, shopping patterns inside the neighborhood, and social activities (such as visiting friends and relatives, and playing cards with neighbors) were plotted on separate overlays. This disclosed that different indices of social integration and intimacy had different territorial distributions. Some of them pointed to integration on the neighborhood level, some to the sub-community, and others to the city as a whole. Some indices of economic and social integration, such as grocery shopping and visiting friends, had only a slight locality concentration, and were discarded for the purposes at hand. Other activity indices of social integration were eliminated because only a minority of the population engaged in these activities. These included bowling, watching TV at a neighbor's home, and going to movies, parks, taverns, and restaurants.

Six social attributes which clustered consistently on spot maps pointed to some aspects of neighborhood intimacy and identification. These questions were:

(1) How well do you think the people in the neighborhood know each other?

(2) About how many of them would you say you know by name?

(3) About how many do you spend a whole afternoon or evening with every now and then?

(4) If you had your choice would you continue living in this neighborhood?

(5) How many families in your neighborhood do you come in contact with for a few minutes every day or so?

(6) Do you think this neighborhood is getting better or getting worse?

The responses to these six items were then trichotomized and subjected to a Guttman scale analysis. Ultimately, the first four of them (one trichotomous and three dichotomous) were found to scale, with a coefficient of reproducibility of .894. The resulting six scale types for degree of social intimacy[8] in the neighborhood appear in Table 21–1.

TABLE 21-1

Neighborhood Social Intimacy Scale

QUESTION	INTIMATE (+)	INTERMEDIATE (0)	NON-INTIMATE (−)
1	quite well, very well	fairly well	not at all, not so well
2	one or more		none
3	about half or more		none, a few
4	yes		no, don't know

IDEAL SCALE TYPES	PATTERN OF RESPONSES TO ITEMS				NUMBER OF CASES*
	1	2	3	4	
I	+	+	+	+	34
II	0	+	+	+	19
III	0	−	+	+	12
IV	0	−	−	+	16
V	−	−	−	+	14
VI	−	−	−	−	21

$$\text{Coefficient of Reproductibility} = 1 - \frac{49}{4 \times 116} = .894*$$

*This scale was developed on the basis of a randomly selected 20 per cent sample of the block interviews. Previous experience of the authors with scales based upon samples of this magnitude shows that coefficients of reproducibility can be expected to vary only within a small range of one per cent. The coefficient is computed after the formula presented in Samuel A. Stouffer, Louis Guttman, *et al.*, *Studies in Social Psychology in World War II: Volume IV, Measurement and Prediction,* Princeton: Princeton University Press, 1950, p. 117.

The 566 blocks in which interviews were secured were then designated as exhibiting either high or low social intimacy according to whether they fell into the upper or lower three scale types. These intimacy extremes were plotted on a map of the city, and areas having adjacent blocks falling into the same categories were demarcated. Perhaps the most impressive characteristic of Figure 21–3 is the very small area in which there are wide variations in social intimacy from block to block ("mixed" in Figure 21–3). In general, Lansing is characterized by broad areal bands in which social intimacy is consistently high or low.

It must be emphasized that the areas which were homogeneous in intimacy were not necessarily neighborhoods, but contiguous areas with similar intimacy scores. The high and low intimacy areas of Lansing were about equally distributed, each accounting for almost one-half of the city as a whole, with a very small residual area of mixed social intimacy. High and low intimacy areas were found in sections with both high and low property values. However, high intimacy areas seemed to be more frequently associated with areas exhibiting a high degree of home ownership. The area of highest intimacy was an ecologically segregated middle

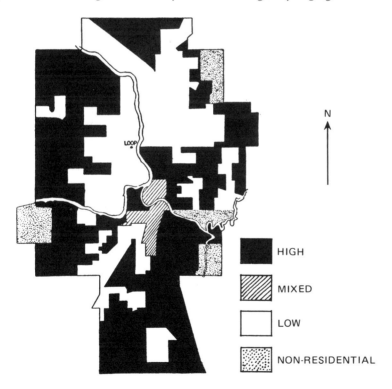

Figure 21–3   Areas of Lansing Based on a Scale of Social Intimacy

income area of high home ownership containing families with children of grammar school age and below. There appeared to be no consistent association between social intimacy and the presence of local shopping and other facilities. A more detailed evaluation of the spatial distribution of these scale types awaits further analysis.

Comparison of Sub-Area Plans

A systematic and detailed comparison of the maps based on the ecological, demographic, and social criteria cannot be made here. Some of the outstanding convergences and dissimilarities among them may be noted, as well as some of the problems involved in such a comparative analysis.

(1) There is no direct, simple, or unilinear relationship among areas drawn according to ecological, demographic, or social indices. Indeed, it is possible, using each approach, to derive separate plans roughly alike in the number of sub-areas and the size of population contained in them.

(2) Every type of ecological barrier, including rivers, railroads, main streets, and factory districts was violated when demographic and social indices were used to locate boundaries.

(3) The problem of finding to what degree ecological boundaries also constitute boundaries for demographic areas is complicated by the areal basis of collecting demographic data. Boundaries used by the Census Bureau for enumeration districts are apparently not determined by any systematic procedure. In addition, the districts are generally so large that they hide considerable internal demographic variation. Ideally, data for residential units are needed to test the question of demographic sensitivity to ecological boundaries.

(4) Only in a very general sense, with some important exceptions, areas in the periphery of the city tend to exhibit high social intimacy, while internal areas tend to exhibit low or mixed social intimacy. Lowest intimacy sections were found in the oldest section of the city and along some thoroughfares.

(5) Very generally speaking, internal areas of the city which fell into demographic scale types tended to be in areas characterized by low social intimacy. Extensive analysis of the *composition* of the scale types is needed to make the above generalization more meaningful. Probably these areas are demographically homogeneous in the sense that they contain inhabitants whose characteristics deviate from those of middle size, middle status group, native-born families in similar directions.

(6) Exceptions to the generalizations in (4) and (5) above are found in the southern and east south central sections of the city. Apart from isolating areas for intensive sociological field work, these non-convergences suggest a variant relationship between social intimacy and some types of demographic characteristics such as particular nationality concentrations, age-groupings, and family structures.

(7) All three maps in one manner or another isolate areas which are populated mostly by Negroes. However, this convergence is only of the grossest type. The area is by no means internally homogeneous either in its demographic composition or in the degree of social intimacy. This internal heterogeneity reflects internal social stratification, as well as the dynamics of the ecological process of invasion outward from a central core.

(8) The ecological approach yielded areas of rather equal size because some kinds of barriers were generally available for purposes of delimitation. The odd-shaped areas provided in the demographic and social plans are useful to locate territorial divisions which demand intensive sociological study.

(9) Several boundary agreements were found by all three approaches. All of them isolated certain heavy industry areas, a few residential neighborhoods, and some large outlying sectors.

(10) The social and demographic techniques also singled out small, highly homogeneous, and distinctive areas of the city which were concealed by the ecological approach. For example, Figure 21–4 shows a segment of the city which is completely enclosed by rivers, railroads, factories, and main thoroughfares. The boundaries indicated by the demographic and social indices do not correspond to the ecological ones. Further, this area is not internally homogeneous from other points of view. Two types of demographic areas have boundaries which at places coincide, fall within, and extend beyond the ecological boundaries. The same applies for two types of social intimacy which lie across the area in question.

Obviously compromises among the boundaries were necessary to arrive at a satisfactory general sub-area plan for the city. Since no one of the three plans was satisfactory in every way to meet census tract requirements, they were all used in making the eventual plan. How the compromises were made will be reported elsewhere.

NOTES

Adapted from a paper read at the annual meeting of the American Sociological Society, August, 1953. The materials reported here derive from a project of the Social Research Service of the Department of Sociology and Anthropology at Michigan State College. The research is partially financed by grants from the Lansing City Plan Commission and the East Lansing City Council. Members of the Research Committee include: J. A. Beegle, J. Cowhig (Research Assistant), J. R. DeLora (Research Assistant), W. H. Form (Chairman), C. P. Loomis, J. Smith, G. P. Stone, D. G. Steinice, and J. F. Thaden—all of the Department of Sociology and Anthropology—and G. Belknap of the Department of Political Science and Public Administration. The authors wish to thank Professor D. L. Gibson for his helpful criticism.

1. Calvin F. Schmid, "The Theory and Practice of Planning Census Tracts," *Sociology and Social Research*, 22 (1938), pp. 228–238; *Census Tract Manual*, U.S. Department of Commerce, Bureau of the Census, January, 1947.

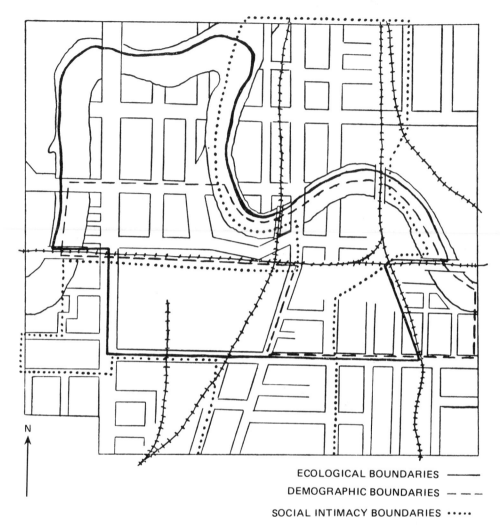

ECOLOGICAL BOUNDARIES ———

DEMOGRAPHIC BOUNDARIES — — —

SOCIAL INTIMACY BOUNDARIES •••••

Figure 21–4   Boundary Divergences in a Small Area of Lansing

2. Some exceptions are: Trenton W. Wann, "Objective Determination of Urban Sub-Culture Areas," unpublished Ph.D. dissertation, Department of Psychology, University of California (Berkeley), 1949; Eshref Shevky and Marilyn Williams, *The Social Areas of Los Angeles, Analysis and Typology, Berkeley and Los Angeles*, Berkeley: University of California Press, 1949.

3. Lansing, Michigan, contains roughly 100,000 people. It is the capital of the state and its main industries are automobile and metal manufacturing.

4. The authors are indebted to Jack DeLora for preparing the ecological map.

5. See Joel Smith, "A Method for the Classification of Areas on the Basis of Demographically Homogeneous Populations," *American Sociological Review*, 19 (April, 1954), pp. 201–207. Most of the material in this section is taken from the above paper.

6. These limits are presented in the following table:

CLASS INTERVALS USED FOR COMPARABLE DESCRIPTIONS OF
ENUMERATION DISTRICTS ON DIFFERENT TYPES OF DATA

Probability Limits	Sign	Meaning Based on Assumption that Sub-Area Not Different from City
.01 and below	—	Very significantly less than expected
0.1–.20	—	Significantly less than expected
.20–.70	—	Less than expected
.70–.70	±	As expected
.70–.20	+	More than expected
.20–.01	+	Significantly more than expected
.01 and below	+	Very significantly more than expected

7. Joel Smith, *op. cit., passim*.

8. It is recognized that the scale items used connote both intimacy and identification. For purposes of simplicity, however, we refer to the items as a scale of social intimacy.

22

SCOTT GREER AND PETER ORLEANS

~~~~~~

THE MASS SOCIETY AND
THE PARAPOLITICAL STRUCTURE

Observers of the social and political worlds of urban man have frequently presented a gloomy argument.[1] In the growth of modern large-scale society they have emphasized the rise of megalopolis, the mass city. In such a community no structured force is interposed between massive power and the isolated (and therefore vulnerable) person. Our urban communities, in this interpretation, show a weakness fatal to the preservation of democratic values and individual freedom, leading toward the totalitarian society and administrative state. The widespread anxiety concerning the effects of rapid (and perhaps, eventually, near-total) urbanization upon the inherited norms of democratic government leads us to ask: how does democracy fare in a society dominated by giant formal organizations, the metropolis, and the nation-state?

The general theory of urban sociology does nothing to quiet such fears. Indeed, the work of Simmel, Tönnies, Park, Wirth, and others is remarkably congruent with such an interpretation.[2] The sociological picture of the city as culturally heterogeneous, dominated by bureaucratic structures and mass media, and destructive of smaller social units, is simply mass society viewed from a slightly different perspective.

However, sociologists have been busy for the past decade or so with the task of documenting the social structure of the city. The work of Janowitz, Axelrod, Bell and Boat, Wright and Hyman, and others, points toward a widespread and relatively stable associational structure in the contemporary American metropolis.[3] The network of kinship, friendship, and neighboring seems to be widely cast, involving a very large proportion of the population. Formal voluntary organizations exist in luxuriance among some populations of the city, and even the extended family system has

Reprinted with permission from *American Sociological Review* 27 (1962): 634–646.

persisted in the urban milieu beyond our expectations. In short, the hypothesis that the city leads inescapably towards the state of the masses requires some re-thinking. The problem may be posed as follows: how does the associational structure disclosed by this research relate to the polity of the metropolis, and what implications does this have for the argument sketched in above?

A Theory of the Parapolitical and Some General Hypotheses

Durkheim, at the turn of the century (and, more recently, Lederer and Nisbet) emphasized the importance of "mediating organizations," groups which stand between the isolated individual and massive power.[4] All three see the plural organization of society as a precondition for individual choice and thus freedom. They consider such mediating organizations —the structural expression of a plural society—as effective because they can mobilize the population in such a way as to limit the administrative state. The groups they refer to range from B'nai Brith or the C.Y.O. to the garden and 4-H clubs, from the industrial association and labor union to the philatelist or madrigal society.[5] They are on-going organizations, based on the routine of everyday life, which represent an area of autonomous social value, and *can* represent that value in political items if necessary. Therefore, we shall call such voluntary formal organizations "parapolitical." Though not specifically oriented to politics in their major activities, they may become overtly political (as, for example, the Little Rock P.T.A. when it became a political machine committed to keeping the public schools open).

The parapolitical structure of a society allows the translation of norms, commitments, and interests, into political behavior. For the individual citizen, political information, influence, and identification require such a sub-set of organizations in which he may participate. His participation, in turn, allows him to be represented at the crux of decision-making. Thus parapolitical organizations are a precondition for the translation of individual "attitude" into social action. Though these organizational structures of everyday life may derive from a wide range of activities, important sources are the role in the world of work, the necessities of the household, and the consequences of ascribed ethnic identity. Each has salience for specific sub-populations, and each is the basis for strong social groups, since out of the interdependence entailed in such associations grow communication, norms, and constraint. They in turn allow a dependable structure for mobilizing political opinion and action.

Such organizations do not make a pluralistic polity inevitable. They may be dominated by the state or they may not be related to the polity in any meaningful sense. Yet, though they are not a sufficient condition for the development of a pluralistic polity, they are a necessary one. Thus it is possible to clarify, in some degree, the mass society hypothesis by ascertaining the patterns of membership in the parapolitical structure, and the relationship between parapolitical organizations and the political process.

Availability of and Access to Social Opportunities

The contemporary metropolis consists of a variety of sub-areas which represent variations in the social concerns and commitments of resident populations, and, therefore, variations in opportunities for social interaction. In this sense the various sub-areas of the metropolis represent differentiated opportunity structures.[6] The social characteristics of individual residents are indicative of their potential for interaction (their access to the structure of social opportunities), whereas the aggregated social characteristics of spatially district sub-area populations denote the prevailing conditions for social interaction (the structure of available social opportunities).

It is our general hypothesis that variation in the structures of available social opportunities, as indicated by variation in the aggregated characteristics of sub-area populations, will be related to the parapolitical order and, through it, to the political process of the metropolis. Knowledge of the type of population residing in a given sub-area, then, should provide cues to the characteristics of the developing or extant parapolitical structure. Our research is therefore designed to analyze the interrelationship of sub-area population type and parapolitical structure with an eye to the way in which the co-variation of these two factors affects the political process.

Sub-Area Population Type. The contiguity and relative homogeneity of sub-populations in the metropolis enable and justify the use of indices which aggregate persons by their residence in small sub-areas.[7] To this end the Shevky-Bell typology has been employed. The typology consists of a set of indices which allows one to differentiate sub-area populations according to their level of (1) urbanism (or familism), (2) social rank, and (3) ethnicity.[8] Each of these indices summarizes a set of attributes which have been hypothesized to indicate preconditions affecting the scale of spatially-based interaction[9] or, as suggested above, the developing or extant structure of social opportunities.[10]

The average "life style" of a sub-area population is reflected in the urbanism index which is based on measures of fertility, house type, and women in the labor force. The use of this index involves the assumption that the less urban a given sub-area population, the more important are the dwelling unit, the neighborhood, and the local community for everyday family-oriented life. With an increase in the urbanism of a sub-area population, the structure of available social opportunities should broaden out from its local base.

The social rank index, based on measures of education and occupation, operates as an indicator of the prevailing level of "cultural equipment" in a sub-area population, a level which limits the structure of available social opportunities.[11] The assumption involved in the use of this index is that with an increase in the social rank of a sub-area population there will be a wider structure of more varied social opportunities. Thus, for example, membership in voluntary organizations outside the local area should increase with increased social rank.

Parapolitical Structure. Although the indices of the Shevky-Bell typology may denote differentials in the structure of social opportunities available to differentiated sub-area populations, they cannot fully explicate the kind and rate of associated interaction. To indicate differentials in sub-area populations' access to available social opportunities, or in other words, to translate such interaction into social structure and political process, *it is necessary to relate gross variations in sub-area population type to a theory of spatially-based social organization.*[12] This has been done elsewhere.[13]

Briefly, it is asserted that geographical contiguity becomes the basis for sociologically meaningful interdependence only when it constitutes a field for social action. Three such fields—the neighborhood, the local community, and the municipality—delimit successively inclusive conditions for interaction. Variations in informal participation, access to the operative communication networks and affiliation with *local* voluntary organizations characterize participation in these fields of social interaction. Access to the structure of available social opportunities differs in the neighborhood and the local community. Therefore, these two fields of social interaction have been used to generate three types of social participators:

(1) *Community Actors*, who are members of voluntary organizations based in the local community, and who are informed with respect to the affairs of the area;

(2) *Neighbors*, who participate in the small world of the neighborhood, but who are not involved in the larger worlds of the local community; and

(3) *Isolates*, who are involved at neither level. (Parenthetically, there is a non-type: *Deviants*, who are members of local organizations but are not a part of the local communication flow, via the local press or neighboring.)

Our analysis is based on the use of constructed types which, as empirically defined, roughly approximate the types of social participators described above. These types simultaneously indicate (1) the ways in which people are involved in the parapolitical structure, and (2) the parapolitical structure as evidenced in the behavior of a sample of people. Objective indicators, logically related to organizational involvement and information flow at various levels, were used to construct the types.[14] The types of social participators should be important predictors of political activity and competence, for they summarize involvement in and access to the communication flow of the parapolitical structure, and through it, we hypothesize, to the local polity.

Available social opportunities are assumed to vary with sub-area population type, whereas differential access to the structure of social opportunities is indicated by the various types of social participators. The relative incidence of one or another type of social participator is, in turn, assumed to depend upon sub-area population type; thus, given types of social participators will be disproportionately concentrated in different types of sub-area populations.

It is to be expected that the less urban (and therefore the more familistic) the sub-area population, the more extensive will be the involvement of the residents in the network of neighboring relations and local voluntary organizations. Therefore, with a decline in urbanism we expect an increase in the incidence of Community Actors and a decrease in the proportion of Isolates.

We expect these variations by urbanism at all levels of social rank, for we see variations in the social organization of the local areas of the metropolis as largely a result of variations in commitment to a familistic life style at whatever level of social rank. However, at each level of urbanism we expect variations in social rank to make an important difference. As social rank declines, we expect a larger proportion of the residents to be Neighbors, who participate only in the neighborhood, while a smaller proportion are expected to be involved in the larger residential community as Community Actors.

In summary, we conceive of urbanism and social rank as independently varying dimensions which delimit the available social opportunities characteristic of sub-area populations and, therefore, their existing social relations. Variation in the nature of the specific social relations of the residents, as indicated by the types of social participators, reflects differential access to the parapolitical structure. The parapolitical structure, in turn, is hypothesized to have important effects upon the polity.

Political Process. The metropolitan complex is both a mosaic of social worlds and a mosaic of political units. There is a dramatic dichotomy between the city districts and the suburban residential settlements. Disregarding for the moment the great variety within each of these, we may note a plausible assumption of the city-suburban dichotomy: the polity of the city, with its enormous budget and widespread news value, presents a very different arena for political action from the dwarf polities of the suburbs. In the latter, the government is small and personal; in the former, it is large and impersonal. The politics of the city have a broad significance, while those of the suburbs may very well appear trivial. In short, the city polity is of wider scale than are those of the suburbs. Its politics are mirrored in the metropolitan press, available "across the board" to all sub-populations in the metropolis.

We have suggested that the parapolitical structure will have a significant effect on political involvement. We have also suggested that available social opportunities will vary with the type of sub-area population. If the configuration of sub-area population types in the city differs from that in the suburbs, then the parapolitical structure will also vary and, with it, the incidence of the various types of social participators. Further, the difference in political involvement among types of participators in the parapolitical structure will change, as between the politics of central city and suburban municipality.

Involvement in the parapolitical structure is more diffuse (in the sense of being less tied to the specific local area) in the city. Municipal politics are also larger scale, encompassing a host of local residential communities. Therefore, we expect more of the local Isolates in the city than in the suburbs to be at least minimally involved (as opposed to being completely disinterested) in citywide politics. The structure of political and parapolitical opportunities available to the local Isolate in the city is not as restricted to the local area as is the case for his counterpart in the suburbs. In the city, to put it somewhat differently, political opportunities are available beyond the boundaries of the local area, whereas in the suburbs they tend to be coterminous with the village limits. Therefore the political and parapolitical structures are likely to be more disjunctive in the city and this would suggest a qualitative difference in the effects of the parapolitical structure on the polity.

By virtue of the same line of reasoning, we would expect Community

Actors in the city districts to be less intensely involved in the local political process than those in the suburban municipalities. The major issues in the city are usually settled at the level of a centralized government, in whose decisions no single local area weighs very heavily. (The exception would be the case in which the policy of the centralized government is directed at a particular local area as, for example, in the case of land clearance for urban renewal.)

Basically, however, we expect continued involvement in local political affairs to be closely related to involvement in the parapolitical structure in both the central city and the suburbs. The role of the parapolitical structure might be altered in the larger scale polity, but its function is not likely to be obliterated. Controlling for parapolitical structure, then, we are able to see more clearly the effects of the *political unit* on involvement in politics. Controlling for political unit, we are able to estimate the constant effects of given population types on the parapolitical structure, and through it, the political process.

The Research Design

The data on which this research report is based were collected in an extensive sample survey carried out in the St. Louis Metropolitan Area during the spring of 1957. One randomly selected adult in every one hundredth household in the suburbs was interviewed. In the city, a ¼% sample was employed. Interviewing was halted at the 87% response level in the suburbs, and the final sample consisted of 1,285 interviews. Comparable figures for the city are 515 interviews or an 81% response level.[15]

We turn now to summary measures used to test the hypotheses. As noted earlier, sub-area population types are described by means of the Shevky-Bell indices. The parapolitical structure is identified through the typology of local social participators. Our final effect variables, local political involvement and competence were estimated as follows.

Political Participation. We have summarized four aspects of political involvement through a scale of participation in local government. The four indicators employed were: (1) voting in any (one or more) of six local government elections, (2) taking a position on local government issues, (3) trying to persuade others regarding local government issues, and (4) attending public meetings dealing with local government issues. These items, with responses dichotomized, follow the hypothesized Guttman pattern. Of 1,604 respondents, only 346 respondents had any error in scale score. A score of 0 indicates that the respondent did not participate at all in any of the four areas of local government, a score of 1 indicates that he voted, but was not sufficiently involved to take a position, persuade others, or attend local meetings. Scores of 2, 3, and 4, indicate that the respondent not only voted but was increasingly involved in the local political scene.

Political Competence. Ability of the respondent to name leaders in the local community was taken as an independent measure of the respondent's political competence. Scored as competent were those who named one or more local community leaders when asked: "In your opinion, who are the people who are leaders in (local community) and can get things done around here?"

Hypotheses and Findings

On the basis of the preceding theoretical discussion, hypotheses were formulated and tested. These refer to relations between (1) sub-area population type and the parapolitical structure, (2) the parapolitical structure and political process, and (3) sub-area population type and political process. The hypotheses, together with the findings, are discussed below.

Sub-Area Population Type and the Parapolitical Structure

H:1 The proportion of Isolates in a given sub-area will increase with an increase in urbanism.

H:2 The proportion of Neighbors in a given sub-area will decrease with an increase in urbanism.

H:3 The proportion of Community Actors in a given sub-area will decrease with an increase in urbanism.

H:4 The proportion of Isolates in a given sub-area will decrease with an increase in social rank.

H:5 The proportion of Neighbors in a given sub-area will decrease with an increase in social rank.

H:6 The proportion of Community Actors in a given sub-area will increase with an increase in social rank.

These hypotheses were tested through aggregating the sample by the social rank and urbanism scores of the neighborhoods of residence (see Tables 22–1, 22–2, and 22–3). The sampled population of the St. Louis metropolitan area did not include enough households for certain sub-area population types to be represented. Therefore, the bivariate distribution in Table 22–3 includes no cells of the most highly urban sub-

TABLE 22-1

**Percentage Distribution of Four Types
of Social Participators for Four Categories
of Social Rank with Urbanism Held Constant
(N=629)**

	SOCIAL RANK			
	LOW 1	2	3	HIGH 4
Isolates	39	40	33	25
Neighbors	22	20	18	15
Community Actors	23	30	35	50
Deviants	16	10	14	10
Totals	100	100	100	100
Number	74	322	173	60

area populations, and only one cell of the sub-area populations lowest in social rank. Nine of the sixteen logically possible sub-area population types are represented. Our discussion can only apply to these types.

The first six hypotheses can be tested by examining the proportions found in Tables 22–1 and 22–2. These tables record the shifting proportions of the various social participation types, as urbanism or social rank is increased. Comparing adjacent percentages in Table 22–1 (and excluding from consideration the Deviants), nine predictions were made with respect to the effects of social rank; all but one are borne out. (The proportions of Isolates are virtually identical for the two lowest quartiles, 39 and 40 per cent.) In Table 22–2, comparing adjacent percentages (and excluding from consideration the Deviants), six predictions were made

TABLE 22-2

**Percentage Distribution of Four Types
of Social Participators for Three Categories
of Urbanism with Social Rank Held Constant
(N=629)**

	URBANISM			
	LOW A	B	C	HIGH D
Isolates	31	33	44	0
Neighbors	20	23	15	0
Community Actors	42	31	26	0
Deviants	7	13	15	0
Totals	100	100	100	0
Number	192	202	235	0

TABLE 22-3

Percentage Distribution of Four Types of Social Participators by Social Area
for the Metropolitan St. Louis Combined Sample (N = 629) *

high Urbanism / low

1D	2D	3D	4D
1C	2C	3C	4C
1B	2B	3B	4B
1A	2A	3A	4A

low   high

Social Rank

Number of Respondents

74	107	54	
	116	56	30
	99	63	30

Isolates

39	50	40	
	34	28	36
	36	31	14

Neighbors

22	12	14	
	26	20	16
	20	23	13

Community Actors

23	26	28	
	30	37	39
	38	40	61

Deviants

16	12	18	
	10	15	9
	6	6	12

*City and suburban respondents residing in segregated areas (as defined according to the Shevky-Bell Social Area index) have been deleted from the sample. In addition, 47 city respondents and 16 (weighted) suburban respondents in social areas 1A, 1B, 3D, 4C, and 4D have been deleted as the total n's for these social areas were too small to allow for computation of meaningful percentages. Of the sample arrayed above, all residents of the highest quartile on urbanism are in the city; all in the lowest quartile are in the suburbs. Combined marginals are given in Table 22-1 and Table 22-2.

with respect to the effects of urbanism; again, all but one are sustained. (The proportion of Neighbors is slightly higher for the second quartile of urbanism than for the first, 23 as compared to 20 per cent.)

H:7 The relations stated in hypotheses 1–6 between social rank and social participation type should hold at each level of urbanism.

H:8 The relations stated in hypotheses 1–6 between urbanism and social participation type should hold at each level of social rank.

Here the findings are generally consistent with the hypotheses but, as Table 22–3 indicates, there are more exceptions. When social rank is controlled by means of sub-group comparison, the proportion of Community Actors decreases consistently with increasing urbanism. However, counter to hypothesis 7, the proportion of Isolates at the second level of

317

urbanism is slightly lower in two cases than at the lowest level of urbanism, and the proportion of Neighbors at the second level of urbanism is slightly higher in two cases than at the lowest level of urbanism. When urbanism is similarly controlled, the effects of social rank are more erratic. The proportion of Community Actors increases consistently with increasing social rank, but the proportion of Neighbors also increases slightly with increasing social rank at both the highest and lowest levels of urbanism.

Comparing adjacent percentages in Table 22–3 (and excluding from consideration the Deviants), thirty-three predictions were made; twenty-five were borne out, eight were not. Five of these errors occurred at the second level of urbanism, where city and suburban neighborhoods are both represented. From other analyses one can infer a greater heterogeneity in these cells, which may account for the disruption in the predicted patterns. Five of the eight errors occurred in predicting relations between social rank and social participation type; three occurred with respect to urbanism and social participation type. Thus, with respect to hypotheses 7 and 8, Table 22–3 suggests that urbanism is a more consistent and powerful differentiator with respect to social participation types than is social rank.

Parapolitical Structure and Political Process. These hypotheses were tested through comparing types of social participators by scores on the scale described above, and by their political competence as indicated by their ability to name local community leaders.

H:9 Of those individuals classifiable as Isolates, Neighbors, or Community Actors, political involvement will be directly related to social participation type with Isolates being least involved and Community Actors being most involved. (This reflects involvement in the organization of the parapolitical system.)

From Table 22–4 it is clear that different types of social participators vary greatly in their political involvement. The proportion totally unpolitical ranges from a quarter of the Isolates to 11 per cent of the Community Actors in the City, and 29 per cent of the Isolates to 10 per cent of the Community Actors in the suburbs. At the other end of the scale, the proportion of social participation types with scale scores of 3 or 4 ranges from 14 per cent of the Isolates to 24 per cent of the Community Actors in the city, and from 14 per cent of the Isolates to 41 per cent of the Community Actors in the suburbs. Thus the hypothesized order holds in each part of the metropolis, but there is a stronger relationship between political involvement and the parapolitical system in the suburbs.

318

TABLE 22-4

*Percentage Distribution of Political Involvement Scale Scores
for Three Types of Social Participators in City and Suburban
Samples in the Non-Segregated Social Areas of Metropolitan
St. Louis*

| CITY SAMPLE | TYPE OF SOCIAL PARTICIPATOR | | | | | |
| POLITICAL INVOLVEMENT | ISOLATES | | NEIGHBORS | | COMMUNITY ACTORS | |
	N	%	N	%	N	%
None (0)	40	25	17	25	11	11
Low (1–2)	96	61	42	61	62	65
High (3–4)	22	14	20	14	23	24
Total	158	100	69	100	96	100
x^2=11.2 p<.05						

| Suburban Sample | TYPE OF SOCIAL PARTICIPATOR | | | | | |
| POLITICAL INVOLVEMENT | ISOLATES | | NEIGHBORS | | COMMUNITY ACTORS | |
	N	%	N	%	N	%
None (0)	29	29	14	23	11	10
Low (1–2)	57	57	36	58	59	49
High (3–4)	14	14	12	20	49	41
Total	100	100	62	101	119	100
x^2=27.8 p<.001						

H:10 Among those individuals classifiable as Isolates, Neighbors, or Community Actors, political competence will be directly related to social participation type with Isolates being least competent and Community Actors being most competent. (This reflects access to communications flow in the parapolitical system.)

The data relating to this hypothesis indicate that the predicted order holds in the city. There, 43 per cent of the Community Actors, 36 per cent of the Neighbors, and only 27 per cent of the Isolates are competent. In the suburbs, however, while Community Actors are more competent than suburban Isolates—59 per cent compared with 28 per cent—the proportion of competent suburban Neighbors exceeds that of the Community Actors by 6 per cent. (The size of the proportion of Neighbors who are informed is rather surprising when compared with Community Actors. The relationship between neighboring and competence is not. In constructing the types, neighboring was viewed as relevant to *communication*, not to organizational involvement.)

The percentage differences between Isolates and Community Actors are, for the city, 16 per cent, and for the suburbs, 51 per cent. The larger percentage difference in the suburbs, indicated in Table 22–5, is chiefly due to the difference in competence between Community Actors in the city and the suburbs.

Sub-Area Population Type and Political Process. It has been postulated that variations in the extent of political involvement of different types of sub-area populations might be expected. Since the city districts tend to be higher in urbanism and lower in social rank than the suburban settlements, it is to be expected that the level of involvement in local political affairs will vary with city-suburban residence. The extent to which each of the various types of social participators is politically involved may also be expected to vary from city to suburb inasmuch as the structure of available political opportunities, and access to that structure, is likely to vary with sub-area population type and governmental unit. In line with this reasoning, the three hypotheses stated below were formulated and tested.

> H:11 A larger proportion of the city residents than suburban residents will
> have a low level of political involvement in the local area; and a larger
> proportion of suburban residents than city residents will have a high
> level of political involvement in the local area.

The percentages of city and suburban residents completely uninvolved politically in the local area are roughly comparable; 21 per cent for the city and 19 per cent for the suburbs. Of the remaining city residents, 62 per cent have a low level of involvement with local area politics and 17 per cent have a high level of involvement with local area politics. The comparable percentages for the suburbs are 27 per cent highly involved and 54 per cent with low involvement. Of those city residents who are involved in the local polity, 48 per cent vote only, while the comparable percentage for the suburbs is 39. It is interesting to note that, of those

TABLE 22-5
Political Competence and Social Participational Type

TYPE OF SOCIAL PARTICIPATOR	PER CENT WHO NAMED LOCAL LEADERS IN:			
	CITY		SUBURBS	
	N/BASE N	%	N/BASE N	%
Isolates	43/158	27	28/100	28
Neighbors	25/ 69	36	40/ 62	65
Community Actors	41/ 96	43	70/119	59
	$x^2=6.93$ p<.05		$x^2=21.35$ p<.001	

citizens who are involved at all in the local polity, a majority do more than just vote (although the percentage is greater in the suburbs, 61 per cent, than in the city, 52 per cent).

> H:12 A larger proportion of the city Isolates will be at least minimally involved in the local polity than will suburban Isolates. (The polity is more meaningful "across the board" but less clearly related to the parapolitical system.)

On the average, in the city 25 per cent of the Isolates are not involved at all with the local polity, while 41 per cent of all city Isolates do no more than vote. In the suburbs 29 per cent of the Isolates are not politically involved, but 36 per cent vote only.

> H:13 A smaller proportion of Community Actors in the city will be highly involved in the local polity than will suburban Community Actors. (The disjunction in scale of parapolitical and political weakens the interrelation of the two.)

On the average, 50 per cent of the city Community Actors do more than just vote, whereas 64 per cent of the suburban Community Actors do more than just vote.

The evidence offered in support of these three hypotheses, while suggestive, is not statistically significant (by Chi-square tests). This may indicate that the constructed types, being derived from structural characteristics of local political *sub-divisions* within the city, do not adequately account for some results of the large scale polity. Two kinds of evidence support this interpretation.

First, further analysis indicates that the politically involved city Isolates are significantly more apt to belong to *non-local* parapolitical organizations than the uninvolved city Isolates (44 compared to 27 per cent).[16] We take this as one indication of the existence of a larger scale parapolitical structure in the city, one which is relatively independent of the local political sub-divisions but which operates as an effective stimulus to political involvement in the polity.[17]

Second, city residents, regardless of participational type, prefer the mass media to specific people as sources of politically relevant information. Respondents were asked: "Which helps you most in making up your mind about local elections—talking with people, or things like radio, television, and the newspapers?" It was expected that, in the familistic neighborhoods and small scale polities of the suburbs, specific persons would be more influential than mass media, whereas in the city, with its large scale polity and coverage by the mass media, the reverse would be the case. As Table 22–6 shows, this is dramatically supported by the findings. In contrast to the city residents, suburbanites prefer specific people to the mass media. Thus, it appears that for the city resident the metropolitan daily, the radio and TV, with their city-wide orientations, serve as alternate sources of political information.

It is possible, then, that a spatially inclusive and diffuse parapolitical system in the city is effective in mediating local political participation for some of the electorate.

Political and Parapolitical Systems in City and Suburb

We have found that, regardless of city-suburban residence, a majority of the citizens involved in the local polity do more than just vote. We have offered evidence to support our contention that there is a differential in the structure of available political and parapolitical opportunities between the two parts of metropolitics which affects local area based political activity. It seems appropriate at this juncture, therefore, to consider the consequences of the resultant socio-political organization for the competence of the affected citizenry, both as political actors and as social actors located in overlapping but non-congruent fields of action.

Of the city *Isolates* who are involved with political affairs in the local area, 54 per cent prefer the mass media to specific people as sources of relevant political information, but only 30 per cent are politically compe-

TABLE 22-6

Preferred Source for Political Information Designated by Politically Involved Social Participators

PARTICIPATIONAL TYPES	RESPONDENT PREFERS:					
	MASS MEDIA		PERSONAL INFORMANT		NO PREFERENCE	
	N	%	N	%	N	%
Isolates						
City	64	54	33	28	21	18
Suburbs	25	35	40	56	6	8
x^2=15.368 p<.001						
Community Actors						
City	51	60	30	35	4	5
Suburbs	28	26	74	69	5	5
x^2=23.221 p<.001						

tent in the sense of being able to name leaders in the local political unit. For the suburbs, however, the comparable percentages are 35 per cent preferring the mass media with 35 per cent being politically competent. This is in contrast to *Community Actors* involved in local political concerns, of whom 60 per cent in the city prefer the mass media and 44 per cent are politically competent. In the suburbs, 26 per cent prefer the media but 62 per cent are competent.

It appears from these results that residents of suburban areas are (1) more apt to rely on other people for political information, and (2) are not only involved in political affairs, but are also involved at a higher level of competence. The reason for this, we suggest, is that the political and social (parapolitical) worlds of suburbia are roughly comparable, largely overlapping, and therefore mutually reinforcing. By contrast, in the city (where the mass media are in large part external to and more extensive than the wards), reliance on the media and non-local parapolitical organizations, although related to political involvement, does not appear to result in political competence with respect to the local area. The city dweller is likely to be more aware of leaders in the metropolitan government than at the precinct level. Nonetheless, the Community Actor in the city is involved in the local political area; perhaps as a reaction to the larger scale polity. In other words, he is something of a "displaced person," whose political involvement in the local area is weaker because there is no meaningful political structure which corresponds to the boundaries of the local parapolitical structure.

Summary and Conclusions

The theory of the mass society postulates an administrative state, a massified citizenry, and no mediating organizations between. We have discovered, in metropolitan St. Louis, that a widespread network of parapolitical organizations has consequences for the involvement and the competence of the citizenry with respect to local government.

However, the strength of the parapolitical varies widely among the sub-areas of the metropolis. This we have explained by the concept of variations in available social opportunities derived from sub-area population types. These, in turn, are based on differences in style of life and level of living.

This variation in sub-area population types is closely related to the city-suburban dichotomy. The city populations, on the average, are higher in urbanism and lower in social rank than those in the suburbs. Both variables work in the same direction: a higher degree of local isolation, a lower density of locally based parapolitical organization. However, differences in population type between city and suburbs are not dichotomous; many city neighborhoods are familistic and middle-class, while suburban enclaves may be working class and urbane. At the same time, the scale of the polity is much greater in the city, and it has therefore been necessary to partial by *both* population type and governmental dichotomy, in order to see the effects of each.

Involvement in central city politics takes three quite different forms: there are (1) those whose political actions are mediated by the local parapolitical structure, (2) those who are isolates from the local community but involved in a larger scale parapolitical structure, and (3) those who are not involved in any parapolitical structure but interact with the polity chiefly through the mass media. The last fit the image of the massified citizenry. They are far from a majority.

In the suburbs the first type of engagement is the predominant one. The small scale polity fits the localized parapolitical structure like a glove. Such suburban populations we may well identify with the "localities" studied by Merton and Gouldner.[18] Their relationship to the polity of their suburban municipality is organizationally similar to the relationship Lipset, Trow, and Coleman discovered in the International Typographical Union, where politics was mediated by the "occupational community."[19]

The "cosmopolites" (or, more accurately, "metropolitanites"), on the other hand, are unengaged in the local area as a community. They may be involved in the non-local parapolitical structure, however, through organizations based upon occupational, class, and ethnic interests. Or they may be, in some cases, individuals who do not participate in either a local community or a geographically wider structure. The latter are casualties of increasing scale in metropolitan society.

In conclusion, we must caution against the over-interpretation of these findings. First, a study limited to a given metropolis is a case study, be the case ever so well documented. We believe the general trends of increasing scale make them generalizable, but that remains to be determined by further research. Second, we have underlined the rather rough and somewhat erratic distribution of social participational type when both urbanism and social rank are controlled. This may indicate some weakness in the sub-samples. It may reflect disrupting influences not included in the theory but perhaps necessary for increased empirical power; or it may simply indicate the crudity of the measures adopted.

It must also be borne in mind that the study says little about the content of political interest and information. The population types employed here have been shown to have considerable predictive power with respect to turnout and direction of vote in both Presidential and local elections. Several more recent studies indicate that the gap between the Community Actor and the Isolate is wide, with respect to knowledge and concern about metropolitan government, voting in a referendum election, and knowing the details of governmental machinery and the personnel of government in a suburban municipality.[20] Thus we have reason to believe that the generalizations tested here, in a rather formal manner, will be useful in studying specific public issues.

Finally, we wish to re-emphasize the limited degree to which these analyses test the theory of the mass society. We have shown that, for certain types of metropolitan sub-area populations, a parapolitical structure does exist; when this is true, it increases the likelihood that those involved in it will also be political actors, who are more politically informed than the average. We have not shown the consequences of their action for the local governors, nor the way in which this feeds back as change and adaptation in policy. These matters, at least, demand investigation before we can answer fully our earlier question: "how does democracy fare in a society dominated by giant formal organizations, the metropolis, and the nation-state?" We believe we have made a beginning.

NOTES

This paper is a revised and extended version of one presented at the section on Urban Communities at the meetings of the Midwest Sociological Society, April 28, 1961. The writers wish to express their appreciation to the Graduate School of Northwestern University and to the Eagleton Institute of Politics which furnished funds enabling the execution of this analysis. The data were collected by the Metropolitan St. Louis Survey, a project supported by the Ford Foundation's Public Affairs Program, and the McDonnell Aircraft Charitable Trust.

1. Lewis Mumford, *The City in History: Its Origins, Its Transformations and Its Prospects*, New York: Harcourt Brace & World, 1961; Robert A. Nisbet, *The Quest for Community*, New York: Oxford University Press, 1953; and Emil Lederer, *State of the Masses*, New York: W. W. Norton & Company, 1940.

2. Georg Simmel, "The Metropolis and Mental Life," in Paul K. Hatt and Albert J. Reiss, Jr., editors, *Cities and Society*, Glencoe Ill.: The Free Press, 1951; Frederick Tönnies, *Fundamental Concepts of Sociology*, trans. by C. P. Loomis, New York: American Book Company, 1940; Robert E. Park, *Human Communities*, Glencoe, Ill.: The Free Press, 1952; and Louis Wirth, "Urbanism as a Way of Life," in Paul K. Hatt and Albert J. Reiss, Jr., editors, *Cities and Society*, Glencoe, Ill.: The Free Press, 1951.

3. Morris Janowitz, *The Community Press in an Urban Setting*, Glencoe, Ill.: The Free Press, 1952; Morris Axelrod, "Urban Structure and Social Participation," *American Sociological Review*, 21 (February, 1956), pp. 13–18; Wendell Bell and Marion D. Boat, "Urban Neighborhoods and Informal Social Relations," *American Journal of Sociology*, 62 (January, 1957), pp. 391–398; Charles R. Wright and Herbert H. Hyman, "Voluntary Association Memberships," *American Sociological Review*, 23 (June, 1958),

pp. 284–294. Most of these studies and some others are summarized and discussed in Scott Greer, "Individual Participation in Mass Society," in Roland Young, editor, *Approaches to the Study of Politics*, Northwestern University Press, 1957.

4. Lederer, *op. cit.*, and Nisbet, *op. cit.* Durkheim discusses the relation of the individual to the state and the role of mediating organizations in *Professional Ethics and Civic Morals*. He suggests that the state, extending its influence over groups which mediate between itself and the individual, operates to secure the rights of individuals against the coercive repression of such groups. Durkheim visualizes a situation in which the forces of the state and the mediating groups are counter-balanced, thereby assuring the maximization of individual liberty. He states, for example, ". . . if that collective force, the State, is to be the liberator of the individual, it has itself need of some counter-balance; it must be restrained by other collective forces, that is, by . . . secondary groups. . . . It is not a good thing for the (secondary) groups to stand alone, nevertheless they have to exist. . . . Their usefulness is not merely to regulate and govern the interests they are meant to serve. They have a wider purpose; they form one of the conditions essential to the emancipation of the individual." p. 63. See Emile Durkheim, *Professional Ethics and Civic Morals*, Glencoe, Ill.: The Free Press, 1960, pp. 1–31.

5. Durkheim, however, emphasized the importance of work-related secondary organizations (or occupational groups). See particularly "Some Notes on Occupational Groups," the preface to the second edition of *The Division of Labor*, Glencoe, Ill.: The Free Press, 1960, pp. 1–31.

6. The term "opportunity structure" as used here has the same denotation as when it is employed by Cloward in his discussion of deviant behavior (although it is not restricted to deviant behavior). Richard A. Cloward, "Illegitimate Means, Anomie, and Deviant Behavior," *American Sociological Review*, 24 (April, 1959), see particularly pp. 168–173.

7. By relative homogeneity we mean no more than the probability that differences by a chosen criterion are greater between areas than within each area.

8. Eshref Shevky and Wendell Bell, *Social Area Analysis*, Stanford, California: Stanford University Press, 1955. While we shall not in this paper be able to discuss the effects of ethnicity, we can indicate that its chief consequence, segregation, seems logically to define one kind of limitation on the scale of interaction in various sub-populations in the metropolis.

9. Eshref Shevky and Wendell Bell, *ibid.*, pp. 3–19.

10. Richard A. Cloward, *loc. cit.*

11. Axelrod among others has found, for instance, that formal group membership and participation, rather than being randomly distributed, are directly related to education, occupation and income. See Morris Axelrod, *op. cit.*

12. The differentiation of sub-populations, aggregated and categorized according to sub-area characteristics, enables the *description* of empirical regularities which may be viewed as structural or compositional effects as discussed by Blau and Davis in two recent articles. See Peter Blau, "Structural Effects," *American Sociological Review*, 25 (April, 1960), pp. 178–193, and James A. Davis, Joe L. Spaeth, and Carolyn Huson, "A Technique for Analyzing the Effects of Group Composition," *American Sociological Review*, 26 (April, 1961), pp. 215–225. However, it is to be noted that whereas behavioral variations from one to another differentiated sub-population may be a function of the location of each in conceptually distinct and distinctive social areas (or social contexts), an *explanation* of how and why these variations occur will depend upon an adequate theory of social organization. The discussion which follows, based on an earlier formulation (*vide infra*, note 13), is an attempt to set forth such a theory for residential areas. In it the consequences of compositional variation are taken as given and are conceptualized as differentials in available social opportunities. It is the specifi-

cation of variations in the structure of access to these differentially available social opportunities which constitutes the elaboration.

13. Scott Greer, "The Social Structure and Political Process of Suburbia," *American Sociological Review*, 25 (August, 1960), pp. 514–526.

14. The indicators selected were these: (1) for neighborhood interaction, those were defined as interactors who answered the question, "How often do you visit with any of your neighbors? Is it once a week or more, a few times a month, once a month, a few times a year or less, or never?" by saying either "once a week or more" or "a few times a month"; (2) for local community role, those were defined as role players who answered the question, "Which organizations or clubs do you belong to?" by naming one or more voluntary organizations, and, further, in answer to the question "And does that organization meet in (local community)?" indicated that one or more met locally; (3) for access to communication flow, those were defined as having access who, in answer to the question, "Do you get any local community newspaper or shopping news?" said "yes" and, to the further question, "What do you like best in it?" said "local community news." For an extended discussion of the paradigm on the basis of which the social participational types were constructed, see Scott Greer, *ibid*. For a detailed discussion of the formulation and partial testing of the measures, see Scott Greer, "The Social Structure and Political Process of Suburbia: An Empirical Test," in *Rural Sociology* (forthcoming).

15. Because of the difference in the intensity of the city and suburban samples, where percentages are based on combined samples the number of respondents in the suburban sample has been divided by four to obtain comparability.

16. This is consistent with the evidence reported by Wright and Hyman to the effect that, in their Denver sample, membership in voluntary organizations is related to political involvement. See Charles R. Wright and Herbert H. Hyman, *op. cit.*

17. Gusfield, in an article which explores how isolation from mass culture may actually accentuate local sources of extremist political response, notes that the lack of *local* attachments may result in attachments to *supra-local* institutions. See Joseph R. Gusfield, "Mass Society and Extremist Politics," *American Sociological Review*, 27 (February, 1962), p. 28.

18. Robert K. Merton, "Patterns of Influence: Local and Cosmopolitan Influentials," in Robert K. Merton, *Social Theory and Social Structure*, revised edition, Glencoe, Ill.: The Free Press, 1957, pp. 387–420; Alvin W. Gouldner, "Cosmopolitans and Locals: Toward an Analysis of Latent Social Roles—I," *Administrative Science Quarterly*, 2 (December, 1957), pp. 281–306; and Alvin W. Gouldner, "Cosmopolitans and Locals: Toward an Analysis of Latent Social Roles—II," *Administrative Science Quarterly*, 2 (March, 1958), pp. 444–480.

19. Seymour M. Lipset, Martin A. Trow, and James S. Coleman, *Union Democracy*, Glencoe, Ill.: The Free Press, 1956. More recently, Maccoby has corroborated the Lipset, *et al.*, findings in a community setting. He reports that members of a voluntary organization studied are more likely than non-members to be voters, to remain voters, and to become voters if they had been non-voters. See Herbert Maccoby, "The Differential Political Activity of Participants in a Voluntary Association," *American Sociological Review*, 23 (October, 1958), pp. 524–532.

20. The voting study is reported in Walter C. Kaufman and Scott Greer, "Voting in a Metropolitan Community: An Application of Social Area Analysis," *Social Forces*, 38 (March, 1960), pp. 196–204. The evidence for the utility of the types of social participators in the referendum election will be published in *Metropolitics: A Study of Political Culture*, by Scott Greer with the advice and assistance of Norton E. Long (forthcoming). The suburban study is reported in "Social and Political Participation in Winnetka," Northwestern University Center for Metropolitan Studies, 1960 (mimeographed).

Index

Acculturation: of Russian-born Jews, 248–249; of Southwestern Spanish, 134–135. *See also* Assimilation

Adjustment, in Wisconsin Norwegian settlements, 151–153

Administrative state, and cities, 308

Age: and emigration from North End, 279; and formal association participation, 84–86

Aggression, as subcultural pattern, 128

Agriculture, in San Luis Jilotepeque, 168

Alihan, Milla A., 182

American Sociological Association, 17

American Sociological Review, 3, 4

Americans, and residence in New Orleans, 260, 261–262, 263–264

Analgesic subculture: in Appalachia, 124–129; autostability of, 129–131; components of, 125–129; definition of, 118

Anglo social structure: discrimination in, 144; Spanish in, 137–138; and Spanish leadership deficiency, 140–146

Appalachia: analgesic subculture in, 124–129; problems of, 122–124

Area names: appropriateness of, 52–54; functions of, 52; use in social interaction, 54–55. *See also* Named areas

Articles, selection of, 3–4, 5

Ashkenazim, and housing, 199, 201

Assimilation: definition of, 231; and ethnic identity, 12. *See also* Acculturation

Association(s): formal organization of, 109–110; informal organization of, 110; majority in, 108–111. *See also* Formal associations

Authority: of majority, 109; in Spanish culture, 140

Automobile, effect on New Orleans, 267

Autonomy, local. *See* Decentralization

Back Bay, 271, 272

Baptist Church, in South Shore, 219

Bay Ridge: living conditions in, 193; Norwegian settlement in, 186–187

Beacon Hill, spatial patterns in, 270–275

Beacon Hill Association, 274

Behavior: in biracial voluntary association, 220–221; frustration-instigated, 118–121; motivation-instigated, 119–120; public and private, 208

Bible Church, 223

Bicultural community, leadership in, 134–146. *See also* Biracial interaction; Triracial community

Bilingualism, in Mountain Town, 137

Biracial interaction: and marginal organizations, 223–224; in South Shore Commission, 220–224. *See also* Bicultural community; Triracial community

Biloxi, 257

Blacks: and definition of Indian, 161–162; and housing, 200, 201–202; migration of, 204; in New Orleans, 254; and outdoor recreation, 213–215; in PTA, 216; and religion, 216, 218–219; and self segregation, 16; shopping patterns of, 209–211; social activities of, 211–213; in South Shore Commission, 220–224; in voluntary organizations, 219

Booth, Charles, 37, 43–44

Boston, land use in, 270

Boston Common, and spatial symbolism, 275–277

Boston Social Register, 271, 273

Bowling alleys, segregation in, 212

Brookline, 271

Brooklyn, growth of port in, 184–185

Brooklyn Heights, Norwegian settlement of, 185